BITTER KNOWLEDGE

BITTER KNOWLEDGE

Learning Socratic Lessons of Disillusion and Renewal

THOMAS D. EISELE

University of Notre Dame Press
Notre Dame, Indiana

Notre Dame, Indiana 46556
www.undpress.nd.edu

Published in the United States of America

Library of Congress Cataloging-in-Publication Data

Eisele, Thomas D., 1948–
Bitter knowledge : learning Socratic lessons of disillusion and renewal / Thomas D. Eisele.
p. cm.
Includes bibliographical references and index.
ISBN-13: 978-0-268-02774-2 (pbk. : alk. paper)
ISBN-10: 0-268-02774-9 (pbk. : alk. paper)
1. Socrates. 2. Questioning. I. Title.
B318.M48E37 2009
183'.2—dc22

2009034996

∞ *The paper in this book meets the guidelines for permanence and durability of the Committee on Production Guidelines for Book Longevity of the Council on Library Resources.*

To my wife, Sandra,

and to our children, Adam, Carolyn, and Spencer—

wonderful people,

wonderful moments,

wonderful memories,

wonderful lives

As [Maitland] says himself, "the new truth generally turns out to be but a quarter truth, and yet one which must modify the whole tale": and in a world so perplexingly contrived as this is, a frank and joyous acknowledgement of ignorance is the only way of wisdom. "We must go into the twilight, not haphazard, but of set purpose, and knowing well what we are doing"; and, when all the other classes have been abolished, there will remain the distinction between those who know that all hypotheses, interpretations, creeds, programmes, and what not, are questions, and those who suppose them to be answers.

—G. M. Young, "Maitland," in
Daylight and Champaign

CONTENTS

ACKNOWLEDGMENTS

These readings of several of Plato's dialogues have put me in debt to others who have worked on these same materials. Among them are Gregory Vlastos, who set a high mark in accuracy and acuity in his scholarship; Myles Burnyeat, who continues to offer us creative and careful readings of Plato (especially, but not solely, with respect to his career-long effort to understand the *Theaetetus*); Alexander Nehamas, whose work is both rigorous and rich with suggestive detail and implication; Roslyn Weiss, whose work on the *Meno* challenges what seem to be settled opinions on that dialogue; Martha Nussbaum, whose erudition illuminates so much of Greek philosophy and tragedy; Eva Brann and Joe Sachs and other members of that remarkable faculty at St. John's College (including the late Jacob Klein), who manage to sustain the Socratic tradition in the twenty-first century; Seth Benardete's valuable meditations collected in his book, *The Argument of the Action;* J. Peter Euben's nimble work on Greek philosophy, political theory, and tragedy; Robin Waterfield's helpful series of translations (including the *Republic,* the *Theaetetus,* the *Gorgias,* and the *Meno*); John M. Cooper's yeoman service in gathering all of the materials and revising a number of translations in the Hackett volume of Plato's complete works; the new translations being issued by Focus Publishing Company; the newly revised translations currently coming out in the Penguin line of translations; and the older Clarendon series of translations. My work here does not match any of these scholarly achievements. I hope, though, that there remains room in the general discussion for the voice of a teacher who comes to Plato's dialogues from the disciplines of law and philosophy, who has a sense of the reality of the classroom, and who wishes to say something responsive to the challenge that Socrates poses to any teacher.

This occasion also gives me an opportunity to recall (and to thank) some of my own teachers. As an undergraduate at Wisconsin, I was introduced to the study of philosophy by Fred Dretske, Dennis Stampe, and Jon Moline, all of whom examined my fledgling work rigorously. Stanley Paulson was a teacher and a friend, both at Wisconsin and, later, at Harvard Law School. In law school, I had the chance to work with Laurence Tribe, and this effort benefitted me over the years. It was while studying at Harvard that I cross-enrolled in Stanley Cavell's course on the later Wittgenstein, which was for me a transformative experience. Later, in graduate school at Michigan, I benefitted from working on the history of philosophy with Nicholas White and Louis Loeb. At Chicago, as a Bigelow Teaching Fellow, I learned about law and philosophy from Tony Kronman, about law teaching from Geoffrey Stone, and about all of these things and more from James Boyd White. I have been fortunate in my teachers, who have befriended me, and counseled me, and tested me.

It remains to be said that James Boyd White and Thomas L. Shaffer read every word of an earlier draft of my typescript and offered many helpful suggestions. I have tried to go to school on the basis of their good offices and good advice. My research assistant at the College of Law, University of Cincinnati, has been Vasilios Spyridakis. He did what he could to improve my readings as well as to inform me of a number of variations and other issues that arose in the several translations that I used of the dialogues. His help with the original Greek texts and terms was invaluable. Dean Louis Bilionis at the College furnished financial and collegial support for my work, as did former deans Joseph Tomain and Donna Nagy. Many of my colleagues at the College have encouraged me in my efforts, but I wish to thank in particular Gordon Christenson and Joseph Biancalana. This book has been long in preparation, and all of these folks have been its long-suffering supporters. The Harold C. Schott Foundation provided financial backing for my efforts over the years.

My indebtedness to Stanley Cavell and to James Boyd White shows in my writing, but I do not wish to forgo thanking both of them for the inspiration of their lives as writers and teachers. Can anyone confront their works and come away without some gain in understanding and self-knowledge? This book is one immeasurable benefit that I trace to their evocative and inexhaustible examples.

My wife, Sandra, and our children, Adam, Carolyn, and Spencer, well know the effort that has gone into this project, even as we all try to assess its cost. In my dedicatory note, I have tried to express, however inadequately, some sense of my gratitude in our having shared our lives together. I also take this moment to acknowledge the long-term support of my mother and my father, and to greet my brothers, a clan of five. A family is an extended affair, something the Greeks knew as well as we do.

Chapter 3 appeared in a slightly different form in the *University of Cincinnati Law Review* 63 (1994): 221–67; and portions of the Epilogue appeared in "Bitter Knowledge: Socrates and Teaching by Disillusionment," *Mercer Law Review* 45 (1994): 587–620. I thank the editorial boards of both journals for permission to reprint here.

Excerpts from the following are reprinted by permission of Hackett Publishing Company, Inc., Indianapolis, all rights reserved: *Plato's Meno,* trans. G. M. A. Grube, © 1980; *Protagoras,* trans. Stanley Lombardo and Karen Bell, © 1992; and *Theaetetus,* ed. with an introduction by Bernard Williams and trans. M. J. Levett, rev. translation by Myles Burnyeat, © 1992.

Excerpts from the following Bobbs-Merrill editions are reprinted by permission of Pearson Education, Inc., Upper Saddle River, New Jersey: *Apology,* in *Euthyphro, Apology, Crito,* trans. F. J. Church, rev. translation and with an introduction by Robert D. Cumming, © 1956; *Meno,* trans. Benjamin Jowett and with an introduction by Fulton H. Anderson, © 1949; *Protagoras,* ed. with an introduction by Gregory Vlastos, trans. Benjamin Jowett, rev. translation by Martin Ostwald, © 1956.

PREFACE

Every teacher knows the trepidation felt prior to entering the classroom; not simply the knot in one's stomach, but also the gnawing doubts about the lesson plan for the day, or anxieties about how one will connect—or fail to connect—with that particular group of students. Similarly, students know the fears and concerns that an approaching class can evoke. And authors offering their work to the public are not immune from such doubts and concerns.

One way to quiet such anxieties is to succumb to the thought that one might offer prospective readers a kind of map to what awaits them. But, try as one might, it is not possible in a few prefatory pages to give any reader the lay of the land ahead, certainly not when what awaits is an extended reading of three Platonic dialogues (with a fourth glanced at in the closing chapter), along with an attempt to set out the details involved in drawing twin lessons of disillusion and renewal from Socrates' activities within those several dialogues. Still, it may afford the reader some initial orientation toward the text ahead if I offer a brief account of this book—always realizing that any such account must be truncated and, in some sense, partial.

Here, I explore what we might learn from participating in Socratic conversational inquiry. Two claims are commonly made about Socrates' performances in Plato's dialogues. The first is that Socrates' method of inquiry teaches only negative lessons, that is, it shows what we do not know, but not what we do know. The second is that (especially in the earlier dialogues) Socrates' inquiries fail to reach any conclusions. These two claims, if not false, are importantly incomplete in the following respects: first, while Socrates' elenctic refutations may be negative in the sense that they are meant to disillusion us, they are not intended to end there. Rather, through a process of recollection made in response to our disillusion, Socratic refutation is meant to lead us to renewal, such that a positive lesson about our resources (as philosophical investigators) becomes available to anyone who engages in Socrates' robust conversational inquiry. And, second, while the frequent inconclusiveness of Plato's dialogues does teach us that human knowledge is always provisional and subject to revision (and revisiting), these dialogues repeatedly reach conclusiveness in the sense that they carry their readers through a complete cycle. They take us, again and again, through the process of disillusion and renewal. The continuity and the repetition of this rhythm—from disillusion to renewal, and back again, all while we examine our thoughts and our ideas as expressed during the continually evolving (sometimes digressive) conversation—bring the argument around to conclusion. We reach conclusion in periodically and repeatedly (if unpredictably) reaching renewal by way of disillusion and its aftermath. This is all the conclusiveness that the poverty of Socrates' method promises us.

In my account of Socrates' way of proceeding with his inquiries and investigations, I have not tried to digest and catalogue the various portrayals of Socrates that appear throughout the two dozen or so dialogues written by Plato. Even if this were possible, I am not sure that it would be productive. Instead, my approach is to consider in depth the portrayals of Socrates that we find in Plato's *Protagoras, Meno,* and *Theaetetus.* I take these three dialogues to be representative. They are among the five or ten best dialogues written by Plato, whether graded along dimensions of literary flair and finesse, or philosophical drama and imagery, or logical rigor and argumentative fireworks. Then, too, they span the traditional division of Plato's writing into early, middle, and later periods (as these matters are debated in the literature, although only limited consensus exists with respect to the specific dialogues assigned to each period). Or, in more contemporary terms, these three dialogues cover the three divisions known as the early Socratic or "search" dialogues, the so-called "transitional" dialogues, and the middle dialogues (from which point, in the remaining ones, Socrates substantially recedes from view). Thus, my consideration of the figure of Socrates in Plato's dialogues attempts to sketch some Socratic continuities (and to point out some of his discontinuities) ranging across the Platonic canon.

What are some of these continuities and discontinuities? Consider what goes on in these three dialogues. The *Protagoras* involves the attempt by Hippocrates, a friend of Socrates, to be accepted as a student of the great sophist, Protagoras. The dialogue explores Hippocrates' ignorance in failing to know what Protagoras can teach him, but it also portrays Socrates confronting Protagoras with the latter's own ignorance of what it is to teach virtue or excellence to any person. What ensues is a bitter exchange on the questions, "Who can teach us? And what can they teach us?" The *Meno* also is concerned with educational themes, but more from the student's side of that complicated relationship. Three different types of student (Meno, Meno's slave, and Anytus) undergo examination at the hands of Socrates, and they all are found lacking. In addition, the experience or process of learning itself comes under Socratic investigation in the *Meno,* through the discussion of Socrates' idea that recollection is the basis of knowledge. In the *Theaetetus,* both the student Theaetetus and the geometry teacher Theodorus are subjected to the fire of Socratic testing, with surprising results. Disillusion of a sort certainly ensues; but with that disillusion also comes Theaetetus' increased ability to pursue the search for an adequate account of human knowledge. The lesson of renewal comes in response to disillusion.

While my book attempts to achieve sufficient breadth by covering dialogues from three different periods in Plato's work, it also treats each dialogue in such depth that my readers can gain a sense of the tensions involved in the way in which Socrates engages with Protagoras, and vies with Anytus, and refutes Theaetetus, and chagrins Meno, and goads Theodorus, and leads Meno's slave through some geometrical puzzles. Despite the attention that I pay to the interactions of Socrates with his interlocutors, however, I do not spend significant time examining or assessing the substantive arguments in which Socrates and his companions engage throughout these dialogues. Rather, I stay focused on the activities by means of which Socrates and these others inquire into the vexed issues that concern them. This is where we can locate and identify the teaching and the learning that transpire.

My brief sketches are, of course, severely selective. They may suggest, however, the extent to which I study the conversational details in a

Platonic dialogue as a means of evoking specific educational interactions that take place among its participants. As I try to show in this book, it is possible to envision Socrates' educational activities *as* his philosophy. To name only one instance, I propose a reading of Socrates' signature gesture—his disavowal of knowledge, or his claim of ignorance, while others freely assert or assume that they know—which takes his gesture as having both epistemological and pedagogical implications. And the one because of the other. By my lights, the educational activities *are* the pertinent philosophy of the particular dialogue under consideration.

In one respect, then, this book is about entering the classroom and what we do in this defined space. The activities that we undertake there are among the conditions that define a classroom. Not that Socrates had classrooms to enter or to leave; he dealt with the people of ancient Athens as he found them, or, more often, as they found him. (In Plato's dialogues, the people of Athens most often impose upon Socrates for an answer to some question or problem that *they* happen to be facing at the moment when sociable Socrates turns the corner and presents himself to them.) Even though, so far as we know, Socrates never taught in a classroom, we contemporary students and teachers can still learn much from a careful observation and review of his activities; and, similarly, we can learn by observing and reflecting upon the various paces through which Socrates puts his interlocutors in these dialogues.

In a closing chapter devoted to Socrates' denial that he is a teacher (which denial he expresses during his defense statement in the *Apology*), I consider both the sense in which Socrates does not fill the role of being a teacher, and the further sense in which he proves to be a teacher *extraordinaire*. It can fairly be asked whether I suppose Socrates to be an apt model for any and every teacher. No, I do not. For Socrates to be pertinent to one's teaching, a teacher must be concerned with a certain kind of intellectual curiosity, one that expresses itself in terms of a person being willing to investigate things on the surmise that we do not already know about them. For Socrates, this is fundamental. Before we can learn, before we can teach, we must inquire. And yet, as it turns out, in Socrates' case, inquiry becomes a form of learning as well as a style of teaching. Inquiry in this instance becomes learning that is based upon ignorance, and thus (despite Meno's Paradox) it is based upon inquiring into the unknown. Similarly, such an inquiry becomes a form of teaching, both instruction of ourselves and of others, when two people converse together.

Anyone who can speak can investigate matters of philosophical interest, but also, anyone who can speak will inevitably be captive to a number of illusions (in particular, the illusion that he or she knows something when in fact he or she does not). Both of these matters—our capacity for philosophical inquiry and investigation as well as our initial captivity in a life of illusion—are apt to be discovered, or revealed, when a person submits to the trials of a conversation in which any participant may claim to speak, or enter a question, or make an assertion, or propose a definition, or offer an account, at any point. Socrates' method of inquiry is built upon the notion that our minds work best when we gather together to circulate our words and thoughts in serious, engaged conversation (even though, for both Socrates and Plato, an element of playfulness enters into such talk). When two people inquire together, each helps the other to see and to understand better than if either had been alone.

Why this should be so, may remain a mystery; but it appears to be a permanent condition of education. The circles we form in storytelling, in conversation, and in school are conducive to the circulation of thoughts and words among people. And what many of us as teachers (and as students) seek in our classes is the sharing of ideas based upon a circulation or exchange of voices in the classroom. I do not conceive of this exchange as though it were a marketplace of ideas, or even as a laboratory, but rather as a crucible of experience and examination, beginning with the task of self-scrutiny. And, whatever Socratic lessons can be learned in reading Plato's dialogues, the process of such Socratic learning requires that each of us must submit his or her self to the specific examination undertaken. To learn, we must participate in the search, subjecting ourselves alongside Socrates to examination. After all, Socrates means his refutations of his interlocutors (and of himself) to be humbling, even humiliating. This is the bitterness of the lessons to which my title refers.

Subjecting oneself to the rigors of such conversational give-and-take is Socrates' version of leading an examined life; it mimics or models how any serious concern with life, be it philosophical or otherwise, is to be pursued. An examined life is available to anyone—anyone who wishes to participate in the inquiry, anyone who wishes to speak (up) or to ask a question or to entertain a doubt or to explore a hypothesis or to express a qualification or to give an account or to propose a definition. In Socrates' conversational inquiry, there is a radical equality among participants.

When we read a Platonic dialogue, we are being offered not a discrete doctrine to be learned or committed to memory, but rather a way in which to approach any problem or issue that arises for us in our experience of ordinary life. And we are invited to participate in the inquiry on equal terms with Socrates. He has his way of approaching life and inquiring into its problematic moments and events. Whether we inheritors of his manner of proceeding wish to accept the invitation from Socrates and Plato is left to us. Their invitation stands.

BITTER KNOWLEDGE

ONE

Introduction

Participating in Disillusion and Renewal

> *The question of philosophy's audience is born with philosophy itself. When Socrates learned that the Oracle had said no man is wiser than Socrates, he interpreted this to mean, we are told, that he knew that he did not know. And we are likely to take this as a bit of faded irony or as a stuffy humility. What I take Socrates to have seen is that, about the questions which were causing him wonder and hope and confusion and pain, he knew that he did not know what no man can know, and that any man could learn what he wanted to learn. No man is in any better position for knowing it than any other man—unless* wanting *to know is a special position. And this discovery about himself is the same as the discovery of philosophy, when it is the effort to find answers, and permit questions, which nobody knows the way to nor the answer to any better than you yourself.*
>
> —STANLEY CAVELL[1]

When, as an undergraduate philosophy major, I first read some of Plato's dialogues, I did not find them fascinating, nor was I captivated by the figure of Socrates. The dialogues were assigned texts; I was a diligent student, so I did the assigned reading. At the time, my main concern was to try to understand the dialogues as vehicles for Plato's thoughts about what my teachers had told me were some of Plato's central doctrines (the immortality of the human soul, for example, and his theory of knowledge as recollection, and certainly the mysterious notion called the Platonic "Forms" or "Ideas"). My engagement with Plato's texts was dutiful but uninspired. This may have been due to the fact that I went to those texts not because various questions were (in Stanley Cavell's words) "causing [me] wonder and hope and confusion and pain," but rather because the texts were assigned.

After I graduated, I went on to law school, where I encountered firsthand one version of the Socratic method at work. It was a daunting experience. Then, after some years of practicing law, I found my way back to graduate studies in philosophy, at a point in my development where I generally studied philosophical texts for my own reasons as much as for institutional or professional ones. Even so, however, I still found myself—whether as a teaching assistant, or in taking my share of graduate classes, or in preparing for the doctoral preliminary examinations—approaching the Platonic canon with the expectation that Socrates would serve as Plato's mouthpiece.[2] Given that I approached Plato's texts with this expectation, it is no surprise that, in my further readings of those dialogues, my expectation was fulfilled.

Reading in this way, what I gained from each text was an impression of Socrates as someone who espoused thoughts and ideas that could be ascribed to Plato's philosophical commitments. Dramatically speaking, the words in the dialogues may have been uttered by Socrates; but, philosophically speaking, they seemed motivated by Plato's agenda. These terms seemed pertinent philosophically only insofar as they enabled me to better understand Plato's system of thought. But then I began to teach in law school. And teaching in law school changed the way that I read these dialogues. It was through my struggles with teaching that the figure of Socrates came to the foreground, while matters of Platonic doctrine receded.

Learning How to Read by Teaching

I had come late to teaching, after a five-year stint as a lawyer in Chicago and another five-year span of graduate studies at the University of Michigan (sandwiched around one year at the University of Chicago as a Bigelow Teaching Fellow). Going into the classroom was a discomfiting experience, especially when I thought about how the law school model of "Socratic teaching" seemed to be far out of my reach. Did I regard myself truly as an inheritor of the Socratic method? Well, no, I did not. I could not ask questions of students with Socrates' perspicuity, and I could not create at a moment's notice hypothetical cases for the class to consider and analyze. Nor could I harangue or harass students into humiliation (something that Socrates seemed to do regularly with his interlocutors). And I know that I did not have Socrates' facility for putting probing queries that promised a full afternoon of interesting investigation and discussion. In all these respects, while conscientious, I was a plodder. I had my own way of working through the materials, and I took very seriously the questions that either I or my students raised. As well, I was committed to engaging my students' attention in the cases and rules and statutes that we were studying.

But how could this way of teaching compare with Socratic teaching? Was it even clear that my style was inspired by Socrates or that my method related to the way in which Socrates taught? Staring me in the face were the obvious discrepancies between what I did in the classroom and what Socrates managed to achieve in his long-ago Athenian streets and courtyards. Given that the locales were quite different, what really did I share with Socrates in terms of how I went about the task of teaching? And what was Socrates, in his own inimitable way, trying to do back then? These questions bothered me.

I now realize that it was the bothersome aspect of this experience that held value for me. Although I failed to realize it at the time, these questions about teaching and learning and inquiring were alive for me in a way that questions concerning Plato's doctrine of the Forms, or his belief in the immortality of the soul, were not. I had finally stumbled across "questions which were causing [me] wonder and hope and confusion and pain," and these questions mattered to me. And I had not gone looking for them, nor were they assigned to me by my teachers; rather, my life and its direction or development had posed these problems to me. *They* found *me*, not I, them. Or perhaps it would be better to say that I had reached a juncture in my life's work and found myself at a stand-still. Not knowing whether to go forward or to go back, I set out to find a path on which I could tread. In all events, I was committed to working out the problems on terms that I could unearth for myself, and on the basis of which I could proceed. This commitment placed me in a profitable relation with a medium or field of work in which I might fruitfully participate and to which I might helpfully contribute. However it came about, I had discovered something that was of philosophical interest to me, even compellingly so.

Giving myself permission to inquire further, I set out trying to answer the questions that were bothering me. I began by rereading some of the dialogues that, either as an undergraduate or as a graduate student, I had read before. I needed a new start with these same texts; after all, given my prior focus when absorbed with these dialogues, how much did I even know or understand about Socrates?

As I worked my way through these dialogues and then began exploring others that I had never read, I came to realize that the lessons made available to us by means of Socrates' method of inquiry were provisional.[3] A conversation begins between Socrates and someone else; it gathers momentum and gradually finds a rhythm or a course of its own, perhaps it is joined by others, perhaps it goes through an entire series of interlocutors, exhausting them in turn. Eventually, the conversation reaches some mild clarification or apparent conclusion. But rarely (if ever) does the course of the discussion yield certainty; seldom (if ever) does it end in stout-hearted confidence. Rather, some careful formulation of a position or of an opinion, some tentative belief, is offered (usually by Socrates), and this tentative remark gains provisional assent from those participating in the discussion, and perhaps even from those gathered around the conversing parties. But usually this assent is accompanied by an expression of hesitation or doubt about the position reached. There remains, then, the distinct possibility that some factor or some consideration has been overlooked or misstated or forgotten or otherwise neglected. In this respect, Plato's dialogues are openended. They seem to require (or to call for) completion.

I discovered, as I read, that I was no longer clear about what Socrates was attempting to do in his conversations (or, for that matter, what Plato was trying to do in his dialogues). My earlier certainties vanished, and they were replaced by questions with very few answers. And then it dawned on me that this loss of assurance was the point that Socrates and Plato were making to any member of the audience who might want to open his eyes and trust his ears.

Openness is not an especially viable position to take in an American law school, either for the teacher or for the student. That was the position, however, in which my rereading of Plato (and my reconsideration of Socrates) left me. I began to ask myself, "What did American law schools (or law professors) know about Socrates? What, specifically, was the image of Socratic activity that found its way into the law school model of teaching?" For all of the talk that one heard in these schools concerning "the Socratic method," it struck me that most references to Socrates and his method of teaching were long on generalities and short on specifics.[4] Law teachers within my hearing mostly thought that the Socratic method was a way of teaching by questioning one's students, without oneself ever answering the questions put to the class (or, heaven forbid, answering the occasional questions tossed back by an intrepid student). "The Socratic method" was, in this regard, a title given to some generic nondirective method of teaching, one that did not take away from the law student the fun of intellectual adventure, the thrill of discovering the law for himself or herself. While there is something valuable in this traditional way of teaching law, as a model of teaching it places a heavy emphasis on a particular image of who Socrates was and what he did. Who was Socrates? And how did he conduct himself and his inquiries?

The Figure of Socrates

Plato's dialogues are our chief source of information about Socrates. Other accounts and portraits of Socrates exist in the ancient literature, of course, but Plato's dialogues have a special authority. Scholars have debated the extent to which Plato's dialogues give an accurate account of the historical Socrates who lived in Athens and who ended his life by drinking hemlock in 399 B.C. Gregory Vlastos, some time ago, lent his authority to the idea that "the Socrates of Plato's early dialogues . . . is a faithful and imaginative recreation of the historical Socrates."[5] Others have demurred. I have nothing useful to contribute to this debate. I think that we are left in a Socratic position such that we simply cannot claim to know one way or the other. From my perspective, Alexander Nehamas expresses our dilemma very well: "The Socrates who first practiced living as an art is the figure we find in Plato's Socratic dialogues. And though . . . we now find it difficult to believe that Plato's Socrates is not the Socrates of history, the fact is that to all effects and purposes Plato's literary figure is a fictional character. Even if we could isolate those elements in Plato's representation that correspond to his historical original, it is the whole character who confronts us in those works, not some smaller cluster of his features, that fired the imagination of the tradition he created."[6] My interest here is in trying to understand the figure of Socrates as portrayed in several of Plato's dialogues. It is, I think, only through an engagement with these texts (and whatever consistencies or inconsistencies they may possess) that we can have anything akin to a "figure" with whom to work. I have, accordingly, tried to read these dialogues as though they were tracing the image of one person, historical or fictional, engaged in a series of conversations with various interlocutors.

Considering Socrates on this basis, the value that I find in what the law school tradition takes from his way of conducting himself as a man of inquiry, is the idea that Socratic inquiries are meant to be undertaken by each individual investing himself or herself in the process of conversation. Each participant is exposed to the excitement that comes from pursuing answers to questions and problems and concerns that are alive and real for that participant. To the extent, then, that the law school tradition of teaching Socratically makes a conscious commitment to active inquiry conducted by both students and teachers within the law school community, this tradition seems to me to remain true to the figure of Socrates in Plato's dialogues.

Still, our law school tradition may slight other aspects of Socrates' practice. Earlier, I spoke of a general tendency in law teaching to engage in a generic nondirective method of teaching. The danger here is that this tendency can lead a teacher to overemphasize the need to be nondirective. In my experience, such an emphasis can translate into a failure of the law teacher fully to participate in the search or the inquiry being enacted in the classroom. Nondirective teachers do not themselves risk refutation; they do not risk Socratic humiliation because their nondirective teaching style entails that they not supply answers to the questions and problems posed in class. When this occurs, such teachers avoid committing themselves to a position or to an answer that can be criticized and refuted by the students or even, on second thought, by the teachers themselves. In such instances, the educational exercise in the classroom is just that—an exercise, not an inquiry.

Socrates in Plato's dialogues often exposes himself to the risk of refutation. He does so, for example, when he offers some definition or some argument during the process of discussion. He also frequently criticizes himself when he comes to bethink himself of what he has been saying; or, for that matter, when he reminds himself of something that he had neglected or forgotten during the course of the conversation. In addition, as humiliating as Socrates can be toward others (and sometimes I find him painfully so), he can be equally curt and dismissive toward himself. In Plato's dialogues, we often find Socrates expressing his dissatisfaction or disgust with his own feeble try at making an argument or giving an explanation or formulating a definition.

If Socrates acts this way, why does he do so? Behaving in this manner enables him to acknowledge that he has no greater assurance than anyone else involved in the conversation of knowing what he claims to know, no better position from which he can claim to be correct. Socrates has many thoughts and ideas to offer, and during the course of the discussion, he is not fainthearted about offering them; often he leads the discussion. But he remains adamant in his claim of ignorance (his disavowal of knowledge). He does this, in part, so that he can enact the equality of the seekers. Socrates is only one person among equals—an important member of the group, granted, but still only one person, one source of data among many. In this regard, he is as willing to expose himself to humiliation, refutation, or censure as he is willing to subject any other person in the conversation to the same withering criticism.

Gregory Vlastos characterizes Socrates' way of proceeding as "his method of moral inquiry."[7] Moral inquiry is, in this regard, one person confronting another person and arguing with her or examining him. These two people confront one another on the same level; they have access to the same knowledge or ignorance, to the same claims or excuses. Thus, Vlastos says, Socrates' method "makes moral inquiry a common human enterprise, open to every man. Its practice calls for no adherence to a philosophical system, or mastery of a specialized technique, or acquisition of a technical vocabulary. It calls for common sense and common speech. And this is as it should be, for how man should live is every man's business . . . . But while the Socratic method makes moral inquiry open to everyone, it makes it easy for no one."[8] Not even for Socrates himself. Or, perhaps, especially not for Socrates, for he is at least as demanding of himself as he is of others. And his demands are daunting. Vlastos enumerates the challenge of Socrates' method of moral inquiry in these terms: "It calls not only for the highest degree of mental alertness of which anyone is capable, but also for moral qualities of a high order: sincerity, humility, courage."[9]

Here I want to develop Vlastos's observation that what is wanted during the course of Socrates' engagement with others is a sample of "common sense and common speech," not some specialized knowledge or technical expertise. In a Socratic inquiry, we seek to investigate those aspects of the world and of our experience that we share in common. For example, Socrates frequently declares that he does not know. In such situations, do we? Do we know any better (or any more) than Socrates? I doubt it, and yet we may think or claim that we do. Here it may help to recall how Cavell (in the epigraph to this chapter) formulates the lesson of this particular Socratic declaration: "What I take Socrates to have seen is that . . . he knew that he did not know what no man can know, and that any man could learn what he wanted to learn. No man is in any better position for knowing it than any other man." Some kinds of claimed knowledge are beyond our ken, no matter who we are or in what position we may find ourselves. Socrates, at least, realizes that he does not know "what no man can know." And his recognition of the limits of human knowledge helps him not to overstep those bounds. Socrates' declaration also suggests, on the other hand, that he appreciates the fact that "any man [can] learn what he want[s] to learn." Learning what we want or need to know is in part a matter of our seeking to learn, and then too of our persevering in the search.

Granting oneself the right to pursue these questions further in one's own way is not an escape into solipsism or egotism, because one must simultaneously grant to others engaged in the inquiry an equal right. As it stands, our positions are the same. This ancient aspect of Socrates' practice shares with the modern practice known as "ordinary language philosophy" a concern for philosophical inquiry that is based upon (and guided by) remarks and revelations that generate self-knowledge.[10] Cavell states the relevant connection this way:

> But in the philosophy which proceeds from ordinary language, . . . the way you must rely upon yourself as a source of what is said when, demands that you grant full title to others as sources of that data—not out of politeness, but because the nature of the claim you make for yourself is repudiated without that acknowledgment: it is a claim that no one knows better than you whether and when a thing is said, and if this is not to be taken as a claim to expertise (a way of taking it which repudiates it) then it must be understood to mean that you know no better than others what you claim to know. With respect to the data of philosophy our positions are the same. This is scarcely a discovery of ordinary language philosophy; it is the latest confirmation of what the oracle said to Socrates.[11]

As Cavell says, the commitment of ordinary language philosophy to using ourselves as the sources of data (as sources, for example, of "what we say when") is simply a late instance of Socratic investigation. We still are proceeding on the basis of inquiries directed toward what Vlastos calls "common sense and common speech." These are matters that we all share, both in terms of our possessing them jointly and in terms of our passing them on to others, sharing them with others, distributing them through the act of expressing our varied samples of "common sense and common speech," and discoursing with one another about them. We are seeking to find answers and to permit questions, "which nobody knows the way to nor the answer to any better than" we ourselves. And the way to these questions and answers is not known a priori; rather, its discovery or establishment is itself a part of the search.

Socrates proceeds conversationally. Anyone who can speak can join the discussion and can contribute to it.[12] No one is ruled out (or ruled in) a priori; instead, we must wait and see, we must test and examine and scrutinize and criticize, and then we must think again. As Cavell has reminded us, for any person (including Socrates), "[Y]ou know no better than others what you claim to know. With respect to the data of philosophy our positions are the same." We all are sources of the data of philosophy, because we all can think and speak—and that is what it takes to generate the data from which to produce any satisfying answers or solutions to our philosophical problems and questions.

There is no time like the present; and there is no one more qualified to respond to this challenge than you and I are—we who speak together, we who speak the same language. Cavell describes this particular aspect of ordinary language philosophy as it is exemplified in the practice of J. L. Austin: "The matter of ordinary language philosophy—its content, so to speak—is trivial, is nothing, without its method(s). . . . The questions raised here are to be decided by us, here and now. No one knows more about what mistakes and accidents are, or heedlessness or lack of thought, than we do, whatever we think we do or do not know. It is a frightening, exhilarating prospect."[13] When Socrates proceeds to examine himself and his companions in Plato's dialogues, he is putting himself and others to the test. The scrutiny being undergone is both real and threatening. This is why Vlastos reminds us that, "while the Socratic method makes moral inquiry open to everyone, it makes it easy for no one." This also is why, I take it, Vlastos lists for us not only the mental requirement of alertness but also the moral qualities of "sincerity, humility, courage" as traits that Socrates' method demands of its participants.

I should note that in all of this there is an element that is apt to make us feel uncomfortable. We were, for example, just speaking of qualities and character traits demanded of people who are involved in a Socratic inquiry. What we may find off-putting is the aspect of Socrates' method of inquiry that involves us in examining and criticizing other people or ourselves. This suggests that Socrates is as interested in gaining knowledge of people as he is in getting to know something about propositions or doctrines or rules or laws, matters that may strike us as being more objective than is the search for and acquisition of knowledge of persons. Even if distasteful, this aspect of Socrates' practice seems to me to be unavoidable and undeniable. Vlastos confronts it, I believe, when he identifies Socrates' manner of proceeding as being a "method of moral inquiry." To my way of thinking, this label suggests that the Socratic method of inquiry directs our attention toward trying to understand people and their lives—rather than its being, for instance, a way for a teacher to present the results of his or her inquiries, didacted for the students. In his book, *The Art of Living,* Nehamas also locates a similar aspect of Socrates' practice. He there names Socrates as the progenitor of the practice of philosophy as an art. On this reading, Socrates' method is one means by which we not only learn but also learn to live. "Philosophy as the art of living began with Socrates."[14]

It is true that traditionally Western philosophy has concentrated its attention on the study of issues such as what we can or cannot know; and what we mean by what we say as well as the truth or falsity of any particular claim that we make about the world; and what rules or laws we may or must live by; and other such matters. But I take Nehamas to be staking the claim that, equally important with these considerations, is the matter of who we are as people, as individuals. In Nehamas's view, following Socrates, the philosopher of the art of living is concerned with creating a self by means of what Nehamas calls "caring for the self." In this respect, the Socratic project includes becoming a critical, self-examining individual who leads a life unafraid of examination and testing. For Nehamas, to proceed Socratically is to engage in discovering who we may become if we master the art of philosophy: "the truth of one's views is still an issue, but what also matters is the kind of person, the sort of self, one manages to construct as a result of accepting them."[15] Or, as Nehamas later puts it, "The [Platonic] dialogues ask their readers . . . to make their life harmonize with their views."[16]

Vlastos emphasizes Socrates' method as a matter of "moral inquiry." Combine this emphasis with Nehamas's notion that a Socratic commitment to the art of living depends upon the possibility of philosophically caring for the self. Both of these conceptions lead me to think that we should conceive of Socrates' project in a way that sufficiently accounts for the Socratic aim of gaining personal knowledge, or a knowledge of persons. If we consider a Socratic inquiry to be a matter of investigating the fitness or condition of the self, then it is possible for Socratic activity (beheld in this light) to become an example of what Cavell calls "moral perfectionism." This is an approach to moral inquiry that in some respects refuses the approach to moral issues made respectable by the two traditional schools of moral thought in Western philosophy, namely, teleology and deontology.[17] So how are we to understand Cavell's conception of moral perfectionism?

"Perfectionism," says Cavell, "proposes confrontation and conversation as the means of determining whether we can live together, accept one another into the aspirations of our lives."[18] Such a philosophy, he goes on to say, makes upon us "the moral demand for intelligibility."[19] What this comes to is summarized by Cavell as follows: "The claim of this field of concern to the status of morality is that the conversation required to assess my life . . . is one designed to make myself intelligible (to others, by way of making myself intelligible to myself). One could say that in the more academically established dispensations of morality I must justify myself (offer or refuse reasons on which I am acting) whereas in perfectionism I must reveal myself, . . . What links the exchanges in these domains is the sense of moral confrontation as one soul's examination of another."[20] For Socrates, we make ourselves intelligible, either to others or to ourselves, by examining what we say and do.

We confront ourselves with our words, actions, and thoughts or beliefs. In such a confrontation, we examine what is said, what is claimed, what is believed. And we do so in part so that we can assess the consistency of these propositions and assertions and beliefs, which may involve investigating and testing both the meaning and the truth of what we say and believe. But we also and equally examine these matters for the light that they shed upon who we are, and on the kind of a life that we are leading and where it may be taking us. What we say expresses the person who says such things; what we do reveals the person who does such things. These expressions and actions are ways of making the self intelligible, of revealing the self, because they are commitments of the self. Our words and our deeds are our representations and our representatives. Their examination becomes an examination of a person, of a self: "one soul's examination of another."

Lessons in Disillusion and Renewal

I have been describing the progress of my rereading of some of Plato's dialogues, and how this reengagement with those texts left me placed. I found myself learning to appreciate that Socrates' method was a way to pursue inquiries that concern our persons and our lives—inquiries into what we think and believe, and who we are and how we behave. By their very nature, such inquiries are apt to result in clarifications and conclusions too provisional and openended to lead any of the participants in such a process to accept any fixed opinions or beliefs about ourselves or about the place of human beings in this world of ours. This suggests that Socrates' method of proceeding is not meant to be a means of conveying didactic lessons. In a sense, according to Cavell, the uncertain or provisional status of these results of Socratic conversational inquiry is what marks them as truly philosophical endeavors, "[f]or when philosophy is called for one cannot know beforehand where it will end."[21] In whatever way that we find a route into philosophy, and however the journey of philosophical inquiry unfolds for us, it remains unforeseeable where, and unpredictable how, we shall end our philosophical travels.

Our situation may be even more precarious than I have just stated, because it is not only the end or conclusion of our labors that is unpredictable. The route taken also is largely undefined. Characterizing the Socratic means of examining ourselves is not, then, an easy task. At a minimum, we should acknowledge that, whatever his method of inquiry, it cannot be rigidly prescribed or described. On the other hand, I am not sure that I would call Socrates' method of inquiry an "improvised" means for responding to the demand to examine ourselves, to make ourselves and our lives intelligible. The concept of improvisation makes Socrates' method seem more amorphous and more indefinite than I personally find it to be. Yet his method of inquiry is flexible; it does seem to be designed to be responsive to the variety of human beings and to the variety of situations in which we find or reveal the human animal. As Eva Brann has recounted for us, Socrates offers us a way, a path, with all the ambivalence and ambiguity that inhere in any activity devoted to making sense of a lived existence.[22]

Granting that little about the Socratic path can be stipulated, I nonetheless want to offer a sketch of how Socratic conversational inquiry normally proceeds. Despite the aspects of uncertainty and unpredictability involved here, it appears to me that some steps along the Socratic path may be normal. In this respect, these various stages of Socratic inquiry can be anticipated or expected. Perhaps this sketch only goes to show that my readings of Plato's dialogues led me to a position where I found it impossible to ignore or to deny that there *are* lessons to be learned from Socrates' practice.

A few years into exploring my concerns with Socrates and his method of inquiry, a happy coincidence occurred. Dick Wirtz, a colleague of mine at the University of Tennessee, asked me to share my tentative thoughts about Socrates with the incoming class of law students for that year. Rough and untutored as my thoughts were at that time, I managed to formulate two competing (yet complementary) lessons from my studies of Socrates.

First, I thought that Socrates, when he examined and tested his conversational companions, meant his incessant questioning to disillusion them. "Disillusion," I took literally to mean that Socrates aimed to help his companions to recognize their illusions as illusions. The chief illusion in this regard is that we know something when, in fact, we are ignorant of it. And, since Socrates' questions are meant to be put to himself as well as to his companions, his own illusions—including those of possessing knowledge—also are intended to be exposed or illuminated during these conversations. Socrates frequently is led to admit his own ignorance or confusion, when, prior to such an admission, he had been saying that he knew something, or had been acting as though he thought that he knew something. Thus, Socrates does not exempt himself from the responsibility of responding to his own questions or from the rigors of testing and examination. What Socrates calls "caring for the soul" includes self-examination of the soul just as much as it includes the examination of the souls of others.

I thought that recognizing one's illusions was a valuable lesson to learn, yet disillusion does not exhaust the lessons that Socrates has to teach. It is a mistake, then, to read the figure of Socrates as though it presents us only with a negative example.[23] Yes, we *are* ignorant of many things about which we think we know. Nevertheless, Socrates does show us that we all have the means by which to inquire into the matters puzzling us. The disquieting realization that we do not know what we claim to know, does not stop the Socratic search for answers. In fact, this self-recognition seems instead to goad Socrates and his companions to investigate further the matter at hand.

Rather than being a disappointing discovery, the process of disillusion seems in these dialogues to act as an instigation for further study.

Or, perhaps it could be put this way: Socrates takes the disappointment in this realization (that one does not know what one has claimed to know), allows it to deflate any arrogance in the person (who thereby gains some insight into himself or herself), and then accepts this deflation as a basis for going on with the investigation already under way. This is the second lesson that I found being taught in the Platonic dialogues featuring Socrates and his conversational method of inquiry.

In making my presentation to the incoming students at Tennessee, I formulated the twin lessons of Socrates as follows:

- You don't know what you think you know.
- You know more (or other) than what you think (you know).

The first lesson is negative in the sense that its result is disillusion. One loses something, and in this respect it is a chastising, even humiliating lesson to learn. In Socrates' practice, this lesson or realization arises most often in those scenes where he is examining and testing the claims to know made by his conversational companions. Socrates tries to get these companions to acknowledge that they do not know the things that they claim to know. This is demonstrated in a number of ways. Sometimes Socrates makes this point by showing his companions that they cannot articulate a coherent definition of some term under discussion, a term that they have claimed to understand very well. Sometimes these people espouse conflicting beliefs that lead (as Socrates shows) to logical contradictions or other inconsistencies. And sometimes Socrates' companions fail to give an adequate account of what they say they know or believe, whereupon he shows them that they are not satisfied (nor is he) with their attempted account or explanation.

All of these are routes toward gaining self-understanding. They are ways that these people can come to realize that they do not know what they claim to know. Most commonly, these scenes of self-recognition feature a moment of insight (perhaps no more than a flash or an inkling), where the companion realizes that he cannot go further, cannot say more; his words stop here. Words fail him. (Or do they save him, since they reveal his inconsistency, his being conflicted?) The moment reached is aporetic.[24]

Socrates' companions are not, however, the only ones who are stopped by someone's questions. Socrates, too, often finds himself at a loss as to how to go on. Here I am thinking specifically of his declarations of his own ignorance, termed his "disavowal of knowledge" by Vlastos.[25] However else they are to be understood, I take these declarations to be a prime way that Socrates has of stopping himself, or of signifying that he is stopped. This gesture prevents him from saying something that he is not yet clear about. His professions of his own ignorance are a way for him to avoid trying to say or claim something that he cannot then and there fully mean. This is a philosophical discovery that Socrates has made, or a philosophical device that he has crafted, to keep himself intelligible.

These declarations of Socrates' own ignorance also are meant to point the way toward a positive lesson. They do not simply prevent Socrates (or us) from saying something that he (or we) cannot then and there mean. Instead, disavowing any claim to knowledge throws us back on our own resources for getting ourselves out of the aporetic fix in which we find ourselves. Rather than taking our *aporia* to signify the appropriate moment to abandon our search for answers, Socrates normally proceeds to renew the search, redoubling his efforts to learn. His declarations of his own ignorance can be taken, then, as a signal to stop and begin again—*if* we are willing to bethink ourselves of where we are and what we possess with which to begin again.[26] In this regard, moments of *aporia* are preparatory steps toward the second lesson mentioned above, namely, that we know more (or other) than what we think we know.[27]

Socrates' faith that we know more (or other) than what we think we know, finds its expression in several features found in Plato's dialogues. One consistent theme throughout these works is Socrates' insistence that he and his companion in conversation must persist in their searches, no matter how often they reach a dead end. Socrates does not simply exhort others in regard to this second, more positive lesson; rather, he persistently enacts this lesson in his continued attempts to dig out the truth of whatever question or dispute happens to be at hand. Whatever the matter under investigation, Socrates' idea is that we already possess what we need in order to inquire into it.

Perhaps the most famous instance of this theme comes in the *Meno* (80d–e), when Meno voices the dispiriting thought that it may not be possible to inquire into something that we do not know. This remark is pounced upon by Socrates and developed into a quandary known in the literature as Meno's paradox. Meno's unhappy suggestion is worked out this way: We cannot inquire into something that we do not know, because we do not yet know our way around in this matter. Yet we also cannot inquire into something that we do know, because no one needs to inquire into something that he or she already knows. Thus, in either case, inquiry seems to be logically impossible. It is Socrates' second lesson—that we know more (or other) than what we think we know—that constitutes his response to the paradox posed.

In the *Meno* itself, Socrates' immediate response to this challenge includes his working out the implications of his view that everything in nature is "akin," such that we are able to inquire into life's mysteries by taking as our starting point that which we do know. Socrates further responds to Meno's paradox by tracing the relational connections within nature, which is a matter of sketching the relations between things (or among our concepts) that literally constitute or establish the "kinship" between or among these related things. In so doing, Socrates demonstrates that we can thereby fasten our conjectures and beliefs about that which we do not know, anchoring them to the secure things which we do know. In this way we fashion a chain of understanding one link at a time.

Socrates' vision of the affinity of nature, of its interconnectedness—along with his vision of the companion affinity of our linguistic or conceptual system—is one expression of his idea that we have more resources and more inherent knowledge than we may currently realize. If we are willing to work at activating these resources, then we can call upon this dormant knowledge when we need it, that is, when we fall into perplexity or *aporia*. This is one form in which Socrates' lesson of "renewal" is taught.

Another instance or expression of this second lesson comes in Socrates' frequent appeals to "recollection" as the source of our knowledge of things as they are.[28] Recollection is an activity central to Socrates' search for knowledge. I have already cited Vlastos's extended description of Socrates' willingness to "re-examine" some previously considered argument or previously established conclusion (see note 3). Socrates' willingness to go over, yet again, the same conceptual territory, to test the steps in the argument once more, is fundamental to his method of conversational inquiry. And, of course, we may learn now that what we had decided or thought we learned earlier is wrong. By unsettling the matter and reconsidering it once more, Socrates is forcing us to remind ourselves of something that we think we now know. And reminding ourselves is meant by Socrates specifically to "put us in mind" of those pieces of information or argument, those previously settled or verified items of knowledge, on which our present position as knowers relies. In this way, the process of recollection refreshes our memory, and, consequently, we realize these thoughts or bits of information anew.

It is by exercising such means of renewal that, according to Socrates, our thoughts or opinions or beliefs can be transformed into knowledge; becoming knowledge, they stay with us, they "abide" with us.[29] Socrates appeals to this image of "knowledge acquired," or "knowledge renewed," at the end of the *Meno:* "this fastening of them, friend Meno, is recollection, as you and I have agreed to call it. But when they are bound, in the first place, they have the nature of knowledge; and, in the second place, they are abiding. And this is why knowledge is more honorable and excellent than true opinion, because fastened by a chain."[30] Recollection as practiced by Socrates proceeds explicitly on the understanding that we already know or possess something more than we currently realize, so we must work to renew our consciousness of it. The work of fastening these opinions or bits of information, of tying them down to what we know, one link at a time, is the way we renew ourselves and come to realize that we know more than we think we know.[31]

Finally, there is yet another feature of the dialogues that expresses Socrates' positive lesson. This feature is the request (which Socrates frequently makes to his interlocutors) that the person talking say what he or she truly believes. Socrates wishes to investigate only that which someone is willing to assert or claim as his or her knowledge, his or her belief. Vlastos calls this Socrates' "say what you believe" requirement.[32]

This Socratic request is consistent with what I said earlier concerning the similarity between the procedure of ordinary language philosophy and Socrates' way of proceeding. If we grant that we are the source of the data with which we work in philosophy, then it is imperative that these data not be skewed or falsified. Socrates' exhortation that we "say what we believe" attempts to ensure that the thoughts and ideas and claims with which we are dealing in our conversational inquiries are genuine. His injunction attempts to limit the data to authentic responses truly expressed. To say what we truly believe is to utter our own thoughts and commitments. This act of fidelity enables us to own our words, to own up to what those words mean and reveal. (In this regard, another characterization by Cavell comes to mind: "In Wittgenstein's work, 'ordinary' or 'every-day' contexts and examples are, I suggest, meant to carry the force of 'authentic' examples authentically responded to in language."[33]) Building upon what we already believe, and upon what we are truly willing to assert in public conversation, Socratic conversational inquiry works in part because we know more, or other, than what we think we know. So, from this perspective, we already have that which we need in order to learn that which we want to know. Or so I believe.

By means of asking questions and attempting to find answers to those questions, Socrates manages to draw out from us what we know and what we do not know, and, in so doing, he activates our otherwise dormant resources and abilities. This aspect of Socrates' practice is depicted most clearly in the exchange in the *Meno* between Socrates and Meno's slave. There, Socrates claims that the responses from Meno's slave show that the slave is remembering or recollecting knowledge gained earlier by his immortal soul. Whether or not we find this image gripping, the tableau between Socrates and the slave illustrates the dual lessons that I have identified in Socrates' way of proceeding. True, the initial result of Socrates' questioning is meant to stun the slave, to stop him from asserting that which he does not know. But the eventual result is not to stop the slave, but rather to start him again. This time he can proceed on a better path, to the extent that he has acquired Socrates' method for inquiring into matters and, thus, for learning what he wants to learn. Socrates' questioning activates whatever knowledge or resources the slave may have, and thereby renews him for the search ahead—*if* the slave wishes to join Socrates in the investigation.

Is Socrates a Teacher?

What I am calling Socrates' twin lessons seldom are the subject of comment by the characters involved in the ongoing conversations. Instead, Plato allows these lessons to work themselves out during the course of the actions and events portrayed in each dialogue. It will not surprise me, then, if other readers of these same dialogues do not find these lessons to be as clearly made out as I find them to be. But this is as it should be, because in the context created by this series of dialogues, the very topics under discussion are the contested ones of who can teach us, and what education consists in, and whether or not virtue may be teachable, and whether there are any teachers or any students of human excellence, and so forth. So the idea that Socrates teaches us—or makes available to us—certain "lessons" is as contentious a claim as are the otherwise contested concerns of "virtue" and "knowing" and "learning" and "education" and "teaching" and "instruction," namely, many of the most central topics under discussion and scrutiny throughout the *Apology*, the *Protagoras*, the *Meno*, and the *Theaetetus*.

The claim that Socrates teaches us anything in these conversations is itself open to question. Socrates, in his defense statement at his trial, told his jurors that he was not a teacher and that he did not teach anything to the people who gathered to hear him converse. As Gary Alan Scott has put it, "Any investigation into Socratic education is immediately faced with the question of whether, or in what sense, Socrates can properly be called a teacher."[34] While I take up this matter more consecutively in chapter 5, it seems worth saying here that I share this anxiety over the appropriateness of fastening the label of "teacher" on Socrates. Whatever learning he makes available to us, rarely comes in a didactic form. Closer to the truth would be for us to say that any lesson that Socrates has to offer is either there in his performances, or it is nowhere.[35]

Richard Kraut has been careful to parse Socrates' denial of teaching, arguing that there are certain respects in which Socrates indeed is engaged in teaching (for example, in the *Meno*), and other respects in which Socrates is not so engaged.[36] Nehamas makes the point that, in general, "Socrates steadfastly refuses the teacher's role in Plato's early dialogues."[37] And we also have the benefit of Vlastos's careful delineation of Socrates' various roles: the fighter, the investigator, the preacher, the teacher, the critic, the professed agnostic, and, first and always, the searcher.[38] Socrates presents many sides of himself to many readers. In considering further the issue of his status as a teacher, my suggestion is this: since it is fundamental to Socrates' method of inquiry that we proceed together (that is, that any critical investigation is to be undertaken jointly), perhaps it will avail us if we identify the people with whom Socrates converses. Whose company does Socrates keep?

In response to this question, the most obvious group are those people of Athens who accost Socrates on the street and ask him questions with the hope that he can answer them and teach them something worthwhile. It seems reasonable to treat these accostive people as potential students. But, if we do call them by that name, then we must add the cautionary note that Socrates regularly disappoints them by disavowing any knowledge of the topics they raise. Normally, then, in response to such people, all that we can say initially is that he disdains the traditional role of a teacher.

With what other groups does Socrates regularly spend his time? The people with whom Socrates argues throughout many of the dialogues can be classified into three camps: the sophists; the poets (or, generally, experts and artisans); and the aristocrats or gentlemen of Athens (possibly including the politicians of Athens). Each group has a colorable claim to being teachers in Greek culture or Athenian society. The poets were the traditional sages or teachers, just as the sophists were their newer competitors and rivals. And Athenian aristocrats or gentlemen were generally seen as the fount of received or conventional wisdom, which becomes the legacy passed on to the younger generation.

There is no love lost between Socrates and the sophists.[39] It is reasonably clear from the outset that Socrates joins in discussion with various sophists in order to dispute with them. Then, too, I take it that Socrates engages the Athenian poets in discussion because they represent "people in the know." The poets and artisans, and experts in general, are presumed to be learned people respected in Athenian society and held in good esteem. And, finally, Socrates converses with the aristocrats or the gentry mostly because they presume to know. If these, then, are the three main groups of people with whom Socrates congregates, can it be said that he uses them as foils, defining himself in opposition to them?[40]

Understood in this way, Socrates chooses to converse with these people not because he is eager to associate with them, but rather because he wishes to vie with them—to contest their claim to be teachers and to oppose their social roles as teachers. Henry Teloh says that "Socrates rejects three educational authorities: poets, sophists, and typical Athenian gentlemen."[41] If this assertion is correct, then it would seem that Socrates is concerned with contesting *their* claim to know, *their* claim to be in a position to teach anyone anything.

This understanding of Socrates and his activities comports with what we are told about the ethos of ancient Athens. As R. L. Nettleship reports in his lectures on the *Republic,* for example, the Greek poets were taken to be purveyors not of aesthetic wisdom, but rather of cultural knowledge and a moral education. Similarly, the new educators in Athenian culture—those who threatened the old order and those who inherited it—were the sophists. Sophistic teaching did not deal simply in rhetoric or the rhetorical arts. Rather, it comprised instruction in profoundly practical advice relating to morals and politics. Nettleship describes these two groups of teachers—the poets and the sophists—as follows:

> It seems strange to us; but nearly all the reflective literature of Greece was then to be found in the poets. The poets were the precursors of Greek philosophy; they first gave expression to the thoughts of man about himself. It was in poetry . . . that the early ideas of the Greeks found expression. The result was that, when people wanted to find their ideas formulated, they went to the poets. . . . In Plato's time the use of the poets in moral discussion had become something more than a sort of instinctive tradition; learning to interpret them formed a recognized branch of culture. . . . The conditions of Greece were different from those of England, and the particular things in which the sophists educated Greece were different from those taught in England by any analogous agency. Nearly all of them taught rhetoric; that is to say, the

> power of using language as an instrument in life. . . . Acquiring the power to express oneself is an indispensable element in education, and in Greece it was absolutely necessary in order to get on with life. The sophists therefore nearly all taught rhetoric. But teaching language is more than teaching the use of words; one learns from it inevitably how to think and speak about subjects of importance. The chief subjects of interest in Greece were subjects bearing on public life or politics, and the sophists practised their pupils in speaking on these. Thus incidentally, and sometimes intentionally, the teaching of the sophists was a moral education, an education in things which have to do with life.[42]

I have already drawn upon Vlastos's characterization of Socrates' method as being one of moral inquiry. Such a characterization helps us to understand why Socrates might see himself as being in conflict with the poets (the traditional teachers of moral instruction) and with the sophists (the purveyors of new or revolutionary moral notions). In contrast to these two groups, Socrates does not wish to accept the mantle of "teacher." He does not imagine himself to be serving the social role performed either by the poets or by the sophists. If Socrates teaches, then he teaches *against* such conceptions of the traditional teacher or the revolutionary teacher. And yet, by the very fact that he measures himself against these others, is he not in some sense competing with them *within* the category of being a genuine or authentic teacher?

Once again, Vlastos's characterization may help us to understand in what respect Socrates might be taken by others to be a kind of teacher or instructor. He teaches not in the sense in which he emulates those other people who are known throughout society as teachers. Rather, Socrates teaches in the sense that he vies with those people. He is not willing to endorse either of the two forms of education generally offered in Athenian society—neither the traditional instruction offered by the poets, nor the modern instruction offered by the sophists. Moreover, Socrates seems to abhor the life led by the typically complacent Athenian aristocrat or gentleman. The status quo regarding teachers and those whom the teachers purport to instruct—the Athenian citizenry—is unacceptable to him. Others (perhaps because they are unthinking and uncritical) may accept the status quo. Not Socrates. For him, such uncritical acceptance of conventional wisdom leads to living an unexamined life of illusion.

Learning and Educational Activities

Socrates does not quite say that the typical Athenian, the average citizen, is a false or failed student, and that the Greek poets and the sophists and the aristocrats (or politicians) are false or failed teachers. But in all of these groups, Socrates finds something deeply repugnant. This is one reason why, I believe, Socrates in the *Apology* becomes belligerent, why he is defiant toward his jurors. He does not treat the jurors as though they were educable, even though his defense statement in one respect is intended exactly to educate them about himself and about themselves.[43] Even given his antipathy toward the people of Athens (and especially toward his jurors), however, Socrates continues to engage them in discussion, controversy, and investigation.

In the three dialogues studied in depth here, we find again and again the theme of Socrates engaging his fellow citizens and their supposed moral authorities or teachers. In the *Protagoras,* Plato places the emphasis on the teaching side of this relationship or engagement, as the main event is Socrates' extended and increasingly bitter discussion with Protagoras, a famous and respected sophist. Other sophists—Prodicus and Hippias—also are briefly yet pointedly included in the discussion that is narrated in the *Protagoras.* In fact, their interjections affect the continuity and direction of the narrative at a critical juncture in the contentious conversation. Also involved is Hippocrates, a friend of Socrates and a much younger man. Hippocrates represents the Athenian citizen as potential student. Yet another young friend and apparent student of Socrates, Alcibiades, makes his appearance in the dialogue too, and he comes to Socrates' defense at a crucial point in the deteriorating conversation. The entire conversation between Socrates and Protagoras takes place within the confines of the home or courtyard of Callias, an important and extravagant member of the Athenian aristocracy. Finally, the poet Critias is present to witness the great debate. As well, the role in Greek education of the poets as traditional moral instructors is aptly represented by the fact that both Protagoras and Socrates take turns in interpreting the moral lessons to be derived from some celebrated lines of the poet Simonides.

All of the representative types of teachers of Greek morality are portrayed, then, in the *Protagoras*. In addition, I note that Socrates' engagement with Protagoras—hinging on the implicit question, "Which of these two men is, as a teacher, more nearly a 'physician of the soul'?"—dominates the scenes in this dialogue. Also involved in the *Protagoras*, however, is Socrates' extensive discussion of oratory, poetry, and conversation as three possible means of educating people. His treatment of these three ways of proceeding fills much of the dialogue with a compendium of their relative pedagogical merits.

In the midst of these educational considerations and concerns, there also are discussions and exchanges that produce the twin lessons (as I have been calling them) of disillusion and renewal. Disillusion becomes an issue in Socrates' conversations with both the student, Hippocrates, and the teacher, Protagoras, although the effect of disillusion is much more telling in the case of Hippocrates than it is in the case of Protagoras. In this, as in other respects, the *Protagoras* is the darkest of these dialogues; it spends more of its time and dramatic energy on the lesson of disillusion than it does on the lesson of renewal. Still, renewal as a theme is certainly there, for otherwise the *Protagoras* would end at the initial breaking point in the discussion between Socrates and Protagoras, rather than picking back up and proceeding another twenty to thirty pages.

Socrates' two main interactions in the *Meno* are his discussions with Meno and his engagements with Meno's slave. In both cases, we witness a conversational companion's disillusion and his subsequent renewal. These twin lessons of disillusion and renewal also come into play in Socrates' terse conversation with Anytus, which ends abruptly. This only goes to show that sometimes the lessons do not take. Instances of disillusion and renewal (or recollection) abound in the *Meno*, but the dialogue also takes time to examine the educational relationship. We see this relationship depicted from the student's side, when in succession Socrates tests Meno, the slave, and Anytus, all of whom reveal their relative capacity for being a student or inquirer. The relationship also is depicted from the teacher's side, when Socrates investigates whether or not virtue is teachable; and when he asks (similar to the concern he expresses in the *Protagoras*) whether there are people who can be said to be teachers of virtue.

While there is less emphasis in the *Meno* on the role of the teacher, the dominating question of the *Protagoras* (namely, "Who can teach what to whom?") still receives some consideration in the *Meno*. To begin, there is the involved discussion of who, if anyone, can teach virtue or *areté*. Socrates, Meno, and Anytus all reach the conclusion that, from among the three groups of most likely candidates, none is adequate to serve as a teacher of virtue or excellence. (Nehamas also mentions this discussion in his essay cited in notes 37 and 41.) In addition, at the opening of the dialogue, Meno mentions the sophist Gorgias as a kind of ideal teacher, and Gorgias' manner of confidently answering questions is invoked as a model for how we should answer the initiating question put to Socrates by Meno. And, of course, we also have Socrates. In his extended discussions with Meno, his less extensive but still forceful conversations with Meno's slave, and his abortive attempts to engage Anytus in conversation, Socrates himself demonstrates many of the attributes of a teacher of human virtue.

Still, the *Meno* pays less attention to the teaching that takes place in the dialogue, and much more attention to the learning that is taking place there. Also under scrutiny in the *Meno* is the nature of learning itself. Here I am thinking of how this dialogue extensively displays the variety of students to be found in educational venues. Learning in action is brought to life by the different reactions to Socrates' teaching as illustrated by Meno, Meno's slave, and Anytus. These three respondents not only exemplify three different types of student, but they also represent three different social strata. Meno is a young aristocrat from Thessaly, Anytus is an important Athenian politician, and Meno's slave would seem to represent the lowest level of Greek society. In addition, the varied responses of these three figures to the multiple educational opportunities offered them by Socrates complicate our sense of the forms in which learning (or refusing to learn, refusing to inquire) can appear. These three conversational companions, accordingly, serve to develop and test Socrates' claim that recollection is the basis of knowledge and, hence, of learning.

The *Theaetetus* grants still more attention to both the student and the teacher sides of the educational relationship. This dialogue contrasts the struggles to learn of a brilliant young student, Theaetetus, with the much less energetic efforts of the older and more settled teacher, Theodorus. While lessons of disillusion are still to be found in this dialogue (for example, the dominant theme of knowledge-as-perception invites us to inquire whether a person's claimed perception is only an illusion), the more positive lesson of renewal comes to the fore. The role of being an attentive and responsive teacher falls to Socrates, who is eager to test the young Theaetetus' ability to look within himself and to give birth to his thoughts or opinions. Theaetetus is assisted in this effort by Socrates in his metaphoric role as midwife, a role that suggests something about what skills it takes in order for a person to successfully teach another person. Once Theaetetus' ideas are elicited, there still remains the task of explaining or defending his thoughts and expressions. This further task engages us in the activity of learning how to give an account of our words and deeds.

Coming to learn, coming to know, is portrayed in the *Theaetetus* as a function of our ability to give an account of what we have said or done (especially, what we have claimed to know). This vision of knowledge is illustrated in the repeated attempts of Theaetetus to say what he means or to define what knowledge is. The first step for Socrates is to encourage Theaetetus to offer us a definition of knowledge, yet he always forces Theaetetus to elaborate his initial formulation of any definition by requiring him to provide us with an acceptable or satisfying account of his proffered definition. This last goal is constantly sought after within the dialogue, but never achieved. If we concentrate on Theaetetus' efforts here, we can gain a deeper grasp of what it is for a student to struggle to find his bearings on a sea of questions and doubts. Even with this emphasis on the student side of the educational relationship in the *Theaetetus,* however, teachers too are present and accounted for.

For one thing, Socrates displays a teacher's skills in his ability to elicit Theaetetus' ideas and opinions, no matter how hesitantly they may be offered, and in subjecting those newly uttered views to a fair-minded critical assessment. This "teacher as midwife" motif is sustained throughout the discussions and digressions of a lengthy dialogue.

Another aspect of the *Theaetetus* that also relates to teaching is the presence of the sophists there. A substantial role in the dialogue is given to several epistemological or perceptual doctrines attributed to Protagoras (for example, "Man is the measure of all things"). Finally, the tired old teacher Theodorus is unfavorably contrasted both to the student Theaetetus, with his youthful vitality, and to the much older Socrates, with his persistent vigor. Joe Sachs remarks upon the latter comparison in his translation of the dialogue: "The ever-youthful Socrates even manages to nag the intellectually exhausted Theodorus into an effort to know. . . . [But, while] Theodorus wants to be sure that others are wrong, . . . [he] can't rouse himself to the effort of seeing or showing what is right."[44] As always, Socrates is willing to persevere when others are not.

In regard to educational themes, the *Apology* is a special case.[45] More truly a monologue than a dialogue, this text features a number of contentious issues relating to the contested topics of knowledge and education and teaching and learning. In addition, the *Apology* contains two of Socrates' most famous disavowals—his disavowal of knowledge, and his disavowal of being a teacher. In my closing chapter, I give sustained attention to these two disavowals. In the portrait sketched in the *Apology* of Socrates' characteristic activities, however, it remains a limitation that there we find Socrates talking about his performance and analyzing it (even defending it), but not exemplifying it. He makes the point in his defense that everything he has done in his methodical inquiries is done as a service; it is meant to benefit others as well as himself. This claim could be a fitting motto for any dedicated teacher.

Our Invitation to Participate

Socrates' method of conversational inquiry is intended specifically to be pursued by two or more people talking together and discussing the fruits of their labor. How are we to understand the claim that Socrates' method works only when another person chooses to join him in the search? I take this claim to be an implicit invitation for the readers of these dialogues to do so.

The effectiveness of Plato's dialogues as an invitation to pursue philosophy is confirmed by the fact that, often enough, we do join in the search. It is beyond familiar to remember (and for commentators on Plato's dialogues to cite) the notable remark of Alfred North Whitehead's, to the effect that the history of Western philosophy comprises a series of footnotes to Plato.[46] Invoking Whitehead's comment is one way of putting our enterprise in perspective; we are, after all, following in the footsteps of genius. And I can imagine that Whitehead's remark may appear to relegate contemporary commentaries on Plato to the status of epigone. Perhaps this is just. But Whitehead's comment can be taken in another way, with a more positive emphasis. To say that the history of Western philosophy consists in a series of footnotes to Plato, simply marks the fact that, for centuries now, the Platonic corpus has been one continuing source of philosophical inspiration and activity, although *how* we have responded to Plato's genius remains remarkably varied. Myles Burnyeat puts this point very nicely: "In general, and contrary to what is often said, little or nothing about Plato's genius is to be explained by the fact that, like other companions of Socrates, he wrote dialogues. What matters is the way Plato wrote *his* dialogues. That is what inspired such a variety of responses in later centuries."[47]

Why did Plato choose to cast his philosophical texts in dialogue form? Doing so invites his readers to participate in the conversations they set out. Each time we read one of Plato's dialogues and actively engage with it, another Socratic conversation takes place. As J. Peter Euben points out, we are "partners in the creation of a dialogue's meaning[s]."[48] In reading these texts, we make the words present to ourselves. If this is so, then are not the figures of Socrates and his interlocutors also present to us? And cannot we then participate imaginatively in their conversations? In some sense, we are implicated in conversations of which the words we share are a part. We read the texts, even as the texts read us. Are these not among the ingredients of a Socratic conversation?[49]

The idea that we must participate in a Platonic dialogue if that dialogue is to perform its function, is central to the argument in Jacob Klein's commentary on the *Meno:* "[A] (Platonic) dialogue has not taken place if we, the listeners or readers, did not actively participate in it;

lacking such participation, all that is before us is indeed nothing but a book."[50] In this respect, Klein goes on to say that "a Platonic dialogue . . . actually continues Socrates' work."[51] This work includes Socratic examination and testing of others and of ourselves. Accordingly, "we, the readers, are being implicitly questioned and examined, . . . [and therefore] we have to weigh Socrates' irony, . . . we are compelled to admit to ourselves our ignorance, . . . [and] it is up to us to get out of the impasse and to reach a conclusion, if it is reachable at all. We are one of the elements of the dialogue and perhaps the most important one."[52] Klein concludes with this thought: "It is possible, then, and indeed necessary, whatever the difficulties, to 'participate' in a Platonic dialogue which we face as a written text."[53] Given the difficulties of participating, however, will we make the effort required?

If we make such an effort, then, as Cavell says, we are making "an effort to discover philosophy for oneself, as if philosophy exists only in its discovery."[54] Or, as Cavell puts it in another essay, the audience for philosophy comes simultaneously with its performance, with philosophical activity itself.[55] The philosophical actor and the philosophical auditor are one and the same: we participate, and we audit. Plato's dialogues are meant to get us involved, to get us to participate in the discussions and conversations being enacted in our presence. Here, the audience for philosophy is anyone willing to entrust himself or herself to the terrifying prospect of examining his or her own life. This entrustment of the self to philosophical inspection and examination can lead, as Cavell further says, to surprising discoveries. For philosophy, at least of the Socratic type, "is the remaining place where one can take philosophy by surprise, I mean with surprise at the fact that there should be such an enterprise that measures the value of our lives."[56] In a similar vein, this is the enterprise that Nehamas has expounded as having as its aim the activity of "caring for the self."[57] And this project of giving care to one's self (or soul) proceeds by way of participation, our engagement.

Plato's dialogues make such participation or engagement possible. "So the dialogues," Bernard Williams tells us, "do not present us with a statement of what might be most significantly drawn from philosophy, but that is not a peculiarity of them or of us; nothing could present us with that, because it cannot be stated anywhere, but can only, with luck and in favourable surroundings, emerge."[58] It can emerge only if we join the search and open our minds to the implications and possibilities sketched during the course of our conversational exploration. As Williams goes on to say, "Plato probably did think himself that the most favourable surroundings would be a group of people entirely dedicated to philosophy, but clearly he supposed that reading the dialogues, thinking about them, entering into them, were activities that could offer something to people outside such a group. He acknowledged, as Socrates makes clear in the *Phaedrus*, that they could not be the vehicles of one determinate message, and it is just because they are not intended to control the minds of his readers, but to open them, that they go on having so much to offer."[59]

In concert with Bernard Williams's suggestion, Joe Sachs, in his translation of the *Theaetetus*, offers us the thought that "the dialogue does not tell us what knowledge is, but offers us the occasion, invitation, and all necessary means to get hold of it for ourselves."[60] Sachs, in fact, goes further and gives us a characterization of the genre composed by Plato's dialogues:

> A Platonic dialogue is constructed to be an especially favorable place in which to go seeking answers, and an especially frustrating place in which to think one already has them. This is not a reflection of skepticism, nor is it a way of speaking in code to certain favored readers while screening out the rest. It is one of the most spectacularly successful ways ever attempted to deal with the seemingly impossible task of writing philosophically. The beginnings of fruitful lines of thought are strewn in abundance through the dialogues, but none of them goes anywhere unless it is picked up by some positive act on the part of the reader. The suggestions to be found in the dialogues are not prepackaged into a "philosophy" but available to be taken up into philosophy.[61]

Socrates and Plato challenge us. Are we willing to make the effort to pick up the lines of thought, the threads of argument, offered us throughout Plato's dialogues and turn them into philosophy? We proceed philosophically, before anything else for Socrates, by proceeding to talk together. We examine what we say and test it not only for its logical rigor and its coherence or sense but also for its intelligibility. This is how Socrates and we are able to respond to the moral demand that we make ourselves intelligible. It is, in part, a matter of asking ourselves and each other questions, and then trying to come up with acceptable answers. Shall we proceed?

TWO

Who Can Teach Us? And What Can They Teach Us?

Socrates Recounts His Conversations in the *Protagoras*

So the conversation ended, and we went our way.

—PLATO, *PROTAGORAS*[1]

We cannot in any case participate in those conversations which [Plato] regarded as the ideal method of philosophical progress, but through the dialogues we learn how they were conducted and watch them unfold.

—W. K. C. GUTHRIE[2]

We can begin to explore how a typical Socratic conversation is conducted by examining the *Protagoras*, which presents us with a set of such conversations. Most commentators on the *Protagoras* rate the dialogue very high as to its level of dramatic mastery and philosophical accomplishment.[3] Myles Burnyeat, in a "Foreword" to the Hubbard and Karnofsky translation, says, "Of all Plato's dialogues the *Protagoras* is the most vigorous presentation of Socrates at work in philosophical discussion."[4] And C. C. W. Taylor begins his translation (in the Oxford "World's Classics" series) with the remark, "In the *Protagoras* Plato represents, with the highest degree of dramatic artistry, a discussion between Socrates and the leading sophists of his day on a fundamental moral issue, how can one acquire the ability to live the best possible life."[5] Similarly, Michael Frede (in his "Introduction" to the Lombardo and Bell translation) notes, "The *Protagoras* is striking not just for the length, complexity, and richness of the argument, but also for the unusually rich and lively detail of its setting."[6] This praise speaks in dual terms, applauding not only the philosophical deftness of argumentation in the *Protagoras,* but also its dramatic presentation of those arguments and its literary style in general. And, finally, translators B. A. F. Hubbard and E. S. Karnofsky follow their opening thought, namely, that "the *Protagoras* is a literary and dramatic masterpiece," with this amplification: "Th[e] duality in the portrait of Socrates, and Protagoras' interesting and persuasive, if flawed, arguments make this dialogue the most well-rounded display of the dialectical method in action that Plato wrote."[7] Long ago, in his Oxford lectures, R. L. Nettleship offered similar praise: "The *Protagoras* is the most finished philosophical drama" among Plato's dialogues.[8] Let us see, then, what we might learn from the figure of Socrates as portrayed in Plato's *Protagoras.*

Overview: Beginnings and Endings

The *Protagoras* begins calmly, continues in conversation of increasing rancor, and ends paradoxically. Socrates confronts Protagoras, reputed to be among the greatest of the sophists, and asks him to say what it is that he teaches and how he manages to teach it. [See Jowett & Ostwald at 13–16 (316b–318d).] Socrates asks these questions as a help to a friend, Hippocrates, who wishes to associate with Protagoras and to acquire whatever wisdom Protagoras teaches. Protagoras, in response to Socrates, identifies his subject as "the art of politics" and self-importantly proclaims himself a maker of "good citizens" [Jowett & Ostwald at 16 (319a)]. Socrates objects to this claim on the ground that politics is not a special art, and it does not depend on anyone's technical skill. Instead, according to Socrates, politics is a matter of common civic virtue, something that any person can exercise or possess. And politics, as civic virtue,[9] is accessible to all, although no one necessarily possesses it; accordingly, no person requires any special education or training in it, nor can anyone receive such teaching or training. [See Jowett & Ostwald at

16–18 (319b–320c).] Some people simply have the knack of serving their city well, while others do not. But these fortunate people do not come by this virtue because they have been taught it; rather, Socrates seems to say that civic virtue is a gift of the gods.

Socrates argues, then, that virtue of the kind that Protagoras claims to teach, cannot be taught. Protagoras responds to this challenge by making a long speech [see Jowett & Ostwald at 18–27 (320c–328d)], but his speech does not have the desired effect. Rather than satisfying Socrates, it provokes him; and from this point on, he proceeds to subject Protagoras to a withering series of questions, during all of which Socrates avows his own ignorance as to the nature of virtue. By the end of the dialogue, under the pressure of Socrates' dialectical examination, a remarkable transformation has taken place.

Protagoras, broken by Socrates' questions, fails to make out any clear or consistent account of virtue; he is reduced merely to assenting to or dissenting from Socrates' barrage. [See Jowett & Ostwald at 66–68 (359c–360d).] In fact, Protagoras eventually refuses to participate at all in the discussion [see Jowett & Ostwald at 68 (360d–e)], leaving Socrates to finish the drama himself, which Socrates concludes by summarizing its inconclusive and rueful closing. [See Jowett & Ostwald at 68–69 (360e–362a).] By dint of Socrates' questions, the now silent Protagoras has been forced to defend the idea that virtue is not a kind of knowledge, not a thing that we can claim to know, and thus is not teachable. Yet, if Protagoras acquiesces in this position, he effectively refutes his own authority to teach what he had earlier claimed to be able to teach (and had been recognized as teaching). His claim (to be able to teach others civic virtue) collapses.

Socrates moves in the opposite direction. From an initial stance of self-professed ignorance concerning the nature of virtue or excellence, and a skeptical stance concerning its teachability, he finds himself moved to assert that virtue is knowledge, such that virtue *is* teachable. (Virtue can be taught because virtue is based on knowledge, and Socrates seems to assume that all knowledge is didactically transmissible.) Yet, Socrates still finds no one who, under the pressure of his insistent questioning, can satisfactorily define virtue. And this inability to define it Socrates takes to indicate an insufficient knowledge as to what exactly the elements of virtue are. If a person does not know what virtue is, how can that person claim to be able to teach virtue to others? How can anyone transmit knowledge which he or she lacks? [See Jowett & Ostwald at 68–69 (361a–d).] Socrates' understanding of these matters, then, leaves us in a quandary: The knowledge of virtue may indeed be teachable or transmissible. Unfortunately, however, no one seems to know well enough what the nature of virtue is, such that he or she can teach it. So, according to Socrates, no one yet is in a position to be able to teach virtue.

Protagoras, a sophist and reputed teacher of virtue, ends up acquiescing in the thought that virtue is not teachable. Socrates, an irritating gadfly of a philosopher, concludes that virtue may be teachable, but that there is no one who knows enough about it to teach it. This paradox is not a happy conclusion, but this is where this Platonic dialogue means to leave us. I do not think that Plato intended us to be happy or satisfied upon reaching the end of this dialogue. In fact, the *Protagoras* instructs us in one of the burdens of searching for knowledge, namely, the unpredictable nature of such inquiries and the unhappiness often attendant upon inquiring into problems that we discover, or that arise for us, in our lives.[10] Socrates' method of conversational inquiry does not aim to bring us happiness. Its effect is more bitter than that.

Back to the Beginning: Why a Narrative?

The *Protagoras* begins calmly, almost uneventfully, I said. But, as it begins, the dialogue unobtrusively provides us with some clues as to what this text is about. We may miss these clues, since the dialogue's proceedings unfold with seeming effortlessness, with a brief exchange between Socrates and someone identified merely as his "friend" or his "companion."

Typical of many of Plato's dialogues,[11] the text commences with someone asking Socrates a question—here, it is the friend or companion. "Where do you come from, Socrates?" [Jowett & Ostwald at 3 (309a)] An opening of this sort is one way that Plato gets a dialogue started: someone accosts Socrates as he is going about his daily business and asks him a question, to which he responds; and the dialogue is off and running.[12] In the *Euthyphro,* as Alexander Nehamas remarks (see note 11), the dialogue begins with Euthyphro stopping Socrates: "What in the world are you doing here in the king's hall, Socrates?"[13] And, similarly, the *Meno* begins with Meno asking, "Can you tell me, Socrates, whether virtue is acquired by teaching or by practice?"[14]

The surprising thing is, though, that this exchange between Socrates and his friend does not last long; barely two pages of the text consist of dialogue. The rest of this text (approximately seventy pages in length) is narrative. Socrates is the narrator, as he recounts for his friend the events and verbal exchanges of the past day and evening, when Hippocrates came to call on Socrates; and then this initial visit eventuated in the two of them visiting Protagoras in turn, whence a long conversation ensued. So the action of the *Protagoras* consists in a very brief exchange of dialogue, followed by an extended narration of two further conversations. Socrates first narrates his conversation with Hippocrates, and then his conversation with Protagoras.

Michael Frede has commented on the fact that the *Protagoras* has these multiple layers or levels, which he calls "frames":

> To begin with the external form of the dialogue, it has a double frame: Socrates meets a friend who asks him whether he has just come from seeing Alcibiades. The ensuing conversation between Socrates and his friend is the first frame. . . . Asked by his friend for an account of the meeting with the famous sophist [Protagoras], Socrates starts out by explaining how he came to have a discussion with Protagoras (310e8 ff.). Hippocrates, a young acquaintance of his, has heard that Protagoras is in town, and wants Socrates to help him persuade Protagoras to take him on as a student (310e2–3). Socrates' report of his conversation with Hippocrates constitutes the second frame.[15]

Why does Plato have Socrates narrate the bulk of the *Protagoras* rather than simply presenting the two conversations directly (which Plato does in the *Euthyphro,* for example, and in the *Meno*)? What is the point of casting the *Protagoras* in narrative form?

To narrate is to tell something, specifically, to tell a story. Stanley Cavell has suggested that, "if a narrative is something told, and telling is an answer to a claim of knowledge, then perhaps any narrative, however elaborated, may be understood as an answer to some implied question of knowledge, perhaps in the form of some disclaiming of knowledge, or avoidance of it."[16] A few pages later, after noting the connections between the concept of "telling" and the concept of "counting," Cavell elaborates on his earlier remarks about narratives: "In counting by numbers, intransitively or transitively, matters like order and size and pace of events are fixed ahead of time, whereas in telling a tale it is the tale's pleasure to work these things out as part of the telling, or as part of a mode or genre of telling—it is why what the teller of a story does is to recount, count *again*."[17] Two aspects about the *Protagoras* seem to me to become more intelligible when viewed within the context provided by Cavell.

The first aspect is this: If we accept Cavell's suggestion that any narrative can be thought of as a response to some implied question of knowledge, then it seems pertinent to remember that Socrates' inquiries begin from his awareness that he does not know. (His awareness is expressed in what Vlastos calls Socrates' "disavowal of knowledge."[18]) Equally important in this regard is the twin awareness from which Socrates' inquiries originate. At least in those dialogues traditionally numbered among Plato's "early" and "middle" periods of writing, I think it fair to say that the action of each dialogue originates from (1) Socrates' awareness of his own ignorance, his own lack of knowledge; and (2) Socrates' awareness of the unconscious ignorance of his partner in conversation.

These twin Socratic recognitions (namely, that both men are ignorant, but that only one realizes his ignorance) serve as the motivating force of Socrates' ensuing investigations. Given Cavell's suggestions about narratives, it is possible to take Socrates' disavowal of knowledge as a functional equivalent for what Cavell notes as "perhaps . . . some disclaiming of knowledge." It also is possible to take the conversational partner's studied indifference to his own ignorance as a functional equivalent for what Cavell notes as an "avoidance of [knowledge]." In most of the Platonic dialogues featuring Socrates, any of the interlocutors is likely to have claimed to know something specific in response to some question put to him by Socrates. Thus, the interlocutor's self-assured claims to know amount to his avoidance of the knowledge that he is ignorant of that which he claims to know.

It seems possible, then, to take the story told by Socrates in the *Protagoras* as a kind of "answer to some implied question of knowledge," as Cavell suggests any narrative will be. The dialogue may be a demonstration by Socrates of just how difficult it is for anyone to gain knowledge; or it may demonstrate the cost of getting someone (perhaps oneself, perhaps someone else) to recognize his or her ignorance, his or her failure of knowledge; or perhaps the dialogue shows us just how little we know.

There is a second aspect of the *Protagoras* that I would like briefly to consider. In his "Introduction" cited above, Frede reminds us that at the very end of the *Protagoras*, when Socrates wants to continue or to renew the inquiry, Protagoras begs off, weary of the entire discussion. Frede observes: "Socrates would like to continue the discussion with Protagoras, but Protagoras has had enough for now. So Socrates leaves, only to run into a friend, the friend he meets at the beginning of the dialogue, and to whom he then tells the whole story of his encounter first with Hippocrates and then with the great sophist himself. This allows him [Socrates], if not to continue the discussion with Protagoras, at least to go over the argument with him [Protagoras] again by recounting it."[19] It strikes me as instructive that Frede here appeals (as does Cavell) to the idea that a narrated story is something being "recounted." Socrates' act of narration makes the story told a recounting of a past experience or event, something that is being once more experienced or remembered; it is being thought over or thought about again. My thought is that Socrates' going over his experience of the conversations in which he had just engaged with Hippocrates and with Protagoras exemplifies his very mode of inquiry. Let me specify two distinguishing characteristics of Socrates' method.

Socrates' way of inquiring into the matters at hand is to ask people to think about what they know, to articulate it, to examine critically the response, and then to go on from there. Sometimes this critical activity of recounting requires Socrates and his conversational partner to count something as something else, or to see it in a certain way (for example, to count virtue as knowledge, or to see virtue as based on knowledge); sometimes this activity of recounting requires Socrates or his partner to tell a story or myth (as when Socrates talks with Protagoras, and they tell each other stories and myths); sometimes this activity of recounting requires Socrates or his partner to examine or criticize what someone has said or has claimed to know. But all of these ways of defining some term, or explaining some action, or giving an account, or telling a story, are ways and means of "making ourselves intelligible," as Cavell put it in chapter 1. Socrates is, by these means, trying to clarify something about ourselves, about who we are and how we are defined or identified in this world by means of our words and our deeds. Or so I believe.

This activity of recounting also identifies or characterizes the kind of education that Socrates offers his fellow conversationalists. This mode of inquiry is a form of learning in which one is never finished with inspecting and criticizing and pondering and testing one's thoughts and words and actions. To leave one's thoughts and words and actions alone—uninspected and untested—is to leave one's life unexamined. And we know that Socrates considers an unexamined life to be not worth living. It is the opposite of the "caring for one's soul" that he endorses and advocates.

To tell a story or to narrate an experience, as to engage in a discussion or to talk with a friend, is to take the time and to make the effort to put on trial our own experience. It is not Socrates' faith (if I understand him correctly) that we engage in such activities with the illusory hope that, by doing so, we shall somehow reach conclusions that, once achieved, will anchor us for the rest of our days. Socratic conclusiveness, such as it is, comes in the form of periodic clarifications, not in the form of final conclusions. In the process of inquiring Socratically into our experience, the insights that we achieve and the answers that we formulate are, at any given point, corrigible in unpredictable ways. I alluded to this aspect of Socrates' method of inquiry earlier, when I gave the extensive quotation from Vlastos, describing Socrates' habit of return or reexamination (see chapter 1, note 3). Our judgments are provisional, as is our knowledge. What we think is settled today may tomorrow become unsettled when we once again examine it. It is Socrates' habitual willingness to return to a matter or to a topic, and thereby to unsettle it, to render it live once more, that also so unsettles his partners in conversation. They seem unable to live a life so open to fundamental reinspection. But, again, for Socrates, this is a function of his commitment to live an examined life—and examination of one's life does not take place once, but endlessly.

Frede wonderfully sums up this aspect of Socrates' teaching:

> It is an argument worth going over again and again; but not because, by going over it, we might finally uncover the veiled truth, the wisdom, it is ready to reveal to the reader who is willing to listen diligently and to follow its clues for long enough. . . . [T]he power of the *Protagoras* seems to be precisely that, instead of closing off and seeming to settle questions, it always provides us with new questions to pursue, new ways to look at familiar things, which, though certainly illuminating, in turn can be and often are questioned themselves. Surely, if wisdom can be taught, it is not by being told the truth—such a truth one would not know how to make one's own—but by being moved to look at things oneself, to consider and reconsider them in all their complexity, from all angles, until, if ever, one arrives at a view of one's own that seems to remain stable however much one is prepared to reconsider it.[20]

Frede is correct, I think, in suggesting that we seek to arrive, "if ever, . . . at a view of one's own that seems to remain stable however much one is prepared to reconsider it." This certainly states an enviable goal. But any arrival at such a point of view is something that we can gain or achieve only ("if ever") by means of our being prepared to reconsider our views again and again, whenever the occasion calls for such reconsideration or review. We never can be sure that today's stable view will remain stable tomorrow. We humans are capable of achieving, at most, what Robert Frost called "a momentary stay against confusion."[21]

What Motivates This Story?

If we take the *Protagoras*, then, to be a narrated response to some question of knowledge, I find that certain words and phrases and sequences in the opening exchange between Socrates and his friend or companion take on a greater significance. Here are the opening passages of the dialogue:

Companion: Where do you come from, Socrates? And yet I need hardly ask the question, for I know that you have been chasing the prime of youth—the prime of youth of Alcibiades. . . .Well, and how do matters stand now? Have you been visiting him, and what are his feelings toward you?

Socrates: Good, I thought, and especially today, for I have just come from him, and he has been helping me in an argument. But shall I tell you a strange thing? I paid no attention to him and several times I quite forgot that he was present.

Companion: What is the meaning of this? Has anything happened between you and him? For surely you cannot have discovered a fairer love than he is, certainly not in this city of Athens.

Socrates: Yes, much fairer. [Jowett & Ostwald at 3–4 (309a, 309b–c)]

The dialogue begins with Socrates being accosted by his companion, who demands to know, "Where have you been?" But Socrates' companion, something of a know-it-all, answers it himself; he thinks it is obvious where Socrates has just been and what Socrates has been doing ("Where do you come from, Socrates? And yet I need hardly ask the question"). Keeping in mind Cavell's suggestion about narratives being a response to some implied question of knowledge, I read the companion's self-confident assertion to be a claim of knowledge: "I know that you have been chasing the prime of youth."[22] But the companion is wrong in his surmise; he does not know what he thinks he knows, nor is he aware of his ignorance.

This lesson in self-ignorance is what Socrates is about to teach his conversational companion as the *Protagoras* opens. And this initial lesson for Socrates' companion is also, perhaps, Plato's subtle way of showing us—his readers—that, at least sometimes, even *we* do not know beforehand the answers to our questions despite what, in our self-assured state, we may think we know. So, for example, in an increasingly fractious discussion about the nature of virtue, and about whether anyone can teach another person how to be virtuous, perhaps we shall discover that we are empty-handed when it comes to answering such questions. I do not say that Plato harps on either of these lessons; he mainly leaves them implicit and allows his stage-setting for the initial exchange between Socrates and his companion to suggest these lessons or morals or inferences to those who wish to draw them. This Platonic reticence is what I take to be a part of the basis for those earlier remarks that I quoted concerning Plato's dramatic artistry. Plato simply does the stage-setting effectively with a minimum of words, and leaves it to us to tease out the implications of what is said and done between these two people.[23]

The *Protagoras* is a dialogue wrapped inside a narrative.[24] What begins the narration is Socrates' noting that something "strange" has happened to him. It is this quality of his experience, together with his companion's subsequent request to be "told" what all this "means," that motivate Socrates to tell his story. "But shall I tell you a strange thing?" Socrates then recounts the conversations that have just taken place between himself and Hippocrates and between himself and Protagoras as well as among some other people who constitute the audience for the exchange between Socrates and Protagoras. It is only when the companion urges Socrates to tell him about it, that we get the rest of the dialogue, in narrative form. In this way, Plato motivates the words, the actions, and the exchanges that are to follow.[25]

There is a further setpiece between Socrates and his friend, which (again, keeping in mind the remarks by Cavell about a narrative being a specific kind of "telling") emphasizes that in the *Protagoras* we shall witness or overhear a conversation told, or recounted, by Socrates.

> *Companion:* But have you really met, Socrates, with some wise one?
>
> *Socrates:* Say rather, with the wisest of all living men, if you are willing to accord that title to Protagoras.
>
> *Companion:* What! Is Protagoras in Athens?
>
> *Socrates:* Yes, he has been here two days.
>
> *Companion:* And do you just come from an interview with him?
>
> *Socrates:* Yes, and I have said and heard many things.
>
> *Companion:* Then, if you have no engagement, please do sit down right here and tell me about your conversation, and my attendant here will give up his place to you.
>
> *Socrates:* To be sure; and I shall be grateful to you for listening.
>
> *Companion:* Thank you, too, for telling us.

> *Socrates:* That is thank you twice over. Listen then. [Jowett & Ostwald at 4 (309c–310a)]

Socrates has "said and heard many things," and if we wish to gain some insight from his experiences, then we had better pay attention and listen to the story that he is about to tell. To his loud-mouth, know-it-all friend, Socrates has to repeat his request to stop talking.[26] "I shall be grateful to you for listening. . . . Listen then." Taking a cue from Socrates' emphatic insistence on the need for us to listen to his story, we might say that apparently something telling is about to be told here, something worth telling.[27] Let us listen.

Who Can Teach Us? To Whom Should We Entrust Our Soul?

What is the story to which Socrates so insistently wants us to listen? I have been suggesting that the narrative in the *Protagoras* serves as an answer to some implied question or claim or denial of knowledge (as Cavell puts it) and, further, that Socrates' account puts him in a position to recount or reexamine the terms and experience of his heated discussions, first with Hippocrates and then with Protagoras. At the center of the *Protagoras* is the joint attempt by Socrates and Protagoras to investigate and answer the question, "What is the nature of *areté* (virtue, excellence)?" Or, more specifically, Socrates and his interlocutor want to know, "Can *areté* (virtue, excellence) be taught? And, if it can be taught, then how is it taught? Who, if anyone, teaches it? If *areté* cannot be taught, why not? What prevents our being able to teach it?" In a sense, then, Socrates' story tells about Protagoras' claim to teach civic virtue (and, a fortiori, his claim to know what it is that he teaches, and to know that he teaches what he claims to teach). And Socrates' story also tells about his own doubts concerning these Protagorean claims, which involve his denial of knowing anything worth telling about the nature of civic virtue (other than Socrates' persistent sense that civic virtue cannot be taught).

While I am willing to say that this description of the progress of the *Protagoras* gives a faithful rendering of the story, so far as it goes, I also think that this description leaves out something essential. For all of the importance that these topics (regarding the nature of virtue, and our knowledge of it, and whether or not virtue can be taught by one human being to another) hold in terms of the inquiry and the arguments that compose the *Protagoras,* it seems to me that any such description emphasizing those topics alone is apt to omit another essential element: Socrates' caring for the welfare of Hippocrates. The heart of the story narrated in this dialogue lies not in the vagaries and vicissitudes regarding virtue, but elsewhere. This story is driven by Socrates' desire to help his friend, Hippocrates, and by Socrates' attraction to the promise offered by Protagoras—namely, his ability to teach wisdom or virtue—and by Socrates' subsequent revulsion when he discovers that Protagoras cannot deliver on that promise. In this respect, then, we need to triangulate the dialogue, seeing how it relates a story involving three leading figures (Socrates, Protagoras, and Hippocrates), rather than reading the dialogue as though it relates a simple dialectical exchange engaging only Socrates and Protagoras.

Socrates does what he does in this dialogue as a way of helping his young friend, Hippocrates, who foolishly (or so it seems to Socrates) is bent upon a potentially destructive course of action. Hippocrates tells Socrates that he wishes to become a student of Protagoras. Socrates is appalled by this announcement. Hippocrates proposes to study with Protagoras without having even the dimmest notion of who Protagoras really is and what Protagoras really teaches. So, as a true friend will, Socrates tries to save Hippocrates from his own folly.

On this reading of the dialogue, the story that Socrates tells in the *Protagoras* is not a depiction of a philosophical exercise in conceptual analysis concerning our understanding of *areté*. It is, rather, a forceful rendering of Socrates' friendship for Hippocrates, whom he sincerely desires to protect from the consequences of his own foolishness. (Or, perhaps we should say that Socrates wants to redress Hippocrates' lack of experience in such matters, as contrasted to Socrates' more seasoned fund of knowledge about, and experience with, the sophists.) His friendship for Hippocrates leads Socrates to quiz him on what he is proposing to do with himself and his life. When Hippocrates' true ignorance in this regard is revealed, Socrates' fond affection for Hippocrates leads them both to approach Protagoras while he is in Athens.

If this description of the course of this dialogue is correct, then it seems right to note that Socrates spends his time examining, in sequence, Hippocrates the prospective student, and Protagoras the prospective teacher. Thus, the *Protagoras* poses the questions, "Who can teach us? And what can any person manage to teach us?" And these two questions come, in Socrates' hands, to be developed into the following question: "To whom should we entrust our soul (since our soul is what becomes educated)?"[28] Who has the knowledge and ability and experience and judgment to teach us what we need to know in order truly to prosper in this life? Do we know the answer to this question? Socrates wonders. Do we even know what it is to live a productive, honorable, and virtuous human life? Again, Socrates wonders. Can we even say what virtue is, and whether it is teachable or not? We all wonder.

These are what I take to be the major questions of the *Protagoras*. They arise from a situation in which Hippocrates believes that Protagoras is the person who can help him to become wise. Socrates questions Hippocrates' self-assured belief. "'[D]o you know what you are about to do now, or does it escape you? . . . [Y]ou are about to hand over your soul for treatment to a man who is, as you say, a sophist. As to what exactly a sophist is, I would be surprised if you really knew. And yet, if you are ignorant of this, you don't know whether you are entrusting your soul to something good or bad'" [Lombardo & Bell at 5 (312b, c)]. Shortly after this series of remarks, Socrates becomes frustrated with Hippocrates' lack of awareness of the threat to the safety and security of his own soul. "'[W]hen it comes to something you value more than your body, namely your soul, and when everything concerning whether you do well or ill in your life depends on whether it [your soul] becomes worthy or worthless, I don't see you getting together with your father or brother or a single one of your friends to consider whether or not to entrust your soul to this recently arrived stranger [Protagoras]. . . . [Y]ou obviously have no idea what this sophist is to whom you are about to entrust yourself'" [Lombardo & Bell at 6 (313a–b, c)].

For Socrates, the question, "To whom can we safely entrust our soul?", is linked to the question, "Who can teach us?" And the *Protagoras* shows us this connection coming under critical Socratic scrutiny. "'But what is the soul nourished on, Socrates?' 'Teachings, I would say. And watch, or the sophist might deceive us in advertising what he sells, the way merchants who market food for the body do'" [Lombardo & Bell at 6 (313c–d)]. This imperfect analogy between feeding the soul and feeding the body leads Socrates to a dire image:

> In the same way, those who take their teachings from town to town and sell them wholesale or retail to anybody who wants them recommend all their products, but I wouldn't be surprised, my friend, if some of these people did not know which of their products are beneficial and which detrimental to the soul. Likewise those who buy from them [such as Hippocrates], unless one happens to be a physician of the soul. So if you are a knowledgeable consumer, you can buy teachings safely from Protagoras or anyone else. But if you're not, please don't risk what is most dear to you on a roll of the dice, for there is a far greater risk in buying teachings than in buying food. . . . [Y]ou cannot carry teachings away in a separate container. You put down your money and take the teaching away in your soul by having learned it, and off you go, either helped or injured. Anyway, these are the questions we should look into, with the help of our elders. [Lombardo & Bell at 7 (313d–314a, 314b)]

A teacher, according to Socrates, is "a physician of the soul." Is Protagoras such a one? Since Hippocrates proposes to entrust his soul to Protagoras, "these are the questions we should look into." The remainder of the dialogue follows through with this promise by exploring the questions put by Socrates to Hippocrates.

As I mentioned, Socrates looks in sequence at Hippocrates as a prospective student and at Protagoras as a prospective teacher. So, in the *Protagoras,* we watch as Socrates examines both sides of the educational relationship. But, interestingly, he does not wish to examine the two of them together; instead, he wants to take them in order, one at a time. This is why, I suppose, Socrates makes a rather ostentatious point of putting off their going to see Protagoras: "'Let's not go there just yet . . . . It's too early. Why don't we go out here into the courtyard and stroll around until it's light. Then we can go'" [Lombardo & Bell at 3 (311a)]. Then, as an aside, Socrates says, as though for the sake of his audience for whom he is narrating these events, "So we got up and walked around the courtyard. I wanted to see what Hippocrates was made of" [Lombardo & Bell at 3 (311a–b)]. Socrates wants to keep Hippocrates apart from everyone else so that he can examine him on his own.

Let us now look at some of this dialogue's events and details, taking things in the order that Socrates presents them in his narrative, turning first to Hippocrates and then to Protagoras.

The Story Begins to Unfold: Socrates Examines Hippocrates

As Socrates says, this is a "strange" tale. Yet what most surprises Socrates is not his relative attraction to Protagoras, and consequent neglect of the young Alcibiades; rather, what he finds strange is that a person might propose to entrust his soul or self to another person about whom he does not know a thing. The story goes that Hippocrates comes banging on Socrates' door early one morning with the news that Protagoras, the famous sophist and teacher, is in town, and Hippocrates desperately wants to meet him. But Hippocrates also wants to enlist Socrates' assistance in getting Protagoras to take on Hippocrates as his student. And Socrates is stunned by this request. Does Hippocrates know what he is doing? Does Hippocrates know who Protagoras is? And what kind of a person he is? Or what kind of a teacher? Or even what Protagoras professes to teach? And, finally, if Hippocrates does *not* know these things, then how can he possibly entrust his soul or self to Protagoras' care? It is absurd.

As I said, Hippocrates has come to Socrates for help. And help is what Socrates gives him, even if Hippocrates is in no position to recognize it. (To change Hippocrates' position in this regard is one goal of Socrates' method of inquiry and personal testing.) It is, nonetheless, help for a friend that Socrates dispenses, his special kind of dialectical therapy. And, I should add, it is exactly Socrates' ability to dispense such aid that allows us to apply to Socrates the sobriquet made famous in the *Protagoras,* namely, someone's being "a physician of the soul."

How does this therapy work? In what does it consist? My response is this: Socrates' dialectical therapy works by dint of his asking questions that force Hippocrates to produce answers. This process of inquiry is meant to reveal to Hippocrates that he is living or acting in accord with an illusion, that Hippocrates does not know what he thinks he knows. Here, in this context, Socrates enters the specific claim that Hippocrates does not know who Protagoras is or what Protagoras teaches. Hence, Hippocrates' haste to enlist as a student of Protagoras is made under the illusion that he knows what kind of a relationship he is getting himself into (were Hippocrates to become a student of Protagoras). Accordingly, I take it that Socrates' conversational art is meant to disillusion Hippocrates.

But how does the Socratic process of disillusioning Hippocrates take place, step by step? When Hippocrates awakens Socrates with the thump of his staff on Socrates' door, Socrates responds, "What news?" [Jowett & Ostwald at 4 (310b)] Hippocrates claims to have good news,[29] that Protagoras has arrived in town. The joke is on Hippocrates, however, because Socrates already is well aware of Protagoras' presence in Athens. "He drew nearer to me and said: Protagoras has arrived. Yes, I replied. He came two days ago; have you only just heard of his arrival?" [Jowett & Ostwald at 4–5 (310b)] Despite, then, the appearance that it is Hippocrates who awakens Socrates at the beginning of this dialogue, which one of these two men proves to be the more awake, the more aware? Plato shows us without telling us.

Hippocrates implores Socrates to speak with Protagoras on his behalf [Jowett & Ostwald at 5 (310e)]; he wants to become a student of Protagoras, but is not sure whether Protagoras will accept him or not. "I who knew the eagerness and excitement of the man [Hippocrates] said: What is that to you? Has Protagoras robbed you of something?" [Jowett & Ostwald at 5 (310d)] Socrates realizes in an instant that Hippocrates is too impulsive for his own good. Socrates, on the other hand, is careful and cautious, a true physician of the soul who is not given to rash actions. Upon seeing Hippocrates' eagerness and enthusiasm for being introduced to Protagoras' art of sophistry, Socrates decides to "test" Hippocrates: "I thought that I would test the strength of his resolution. So I examined him and put questions to him" [Jowett & Ostwald at 6 (311b)].

This older Jowett translation emphasizes that what Socrates is testing in Hippocrates is his resolution to become a student of Protagoras. But the newer Lombardo and Bell translation gives a slightly different twist to this passage: "I wanted to see what Hippocrates was made of, so I started to examine him with a few questions" [Lombardo & Bell at 3 (311b)]. Here the emphasis is not so much on the strength of Hippocrates' resolution, but rather on the entire person. What is he made of? In particular, what does Hippocrates know about his proposed study with Protagoras? Has Hippocrates thought out this course of action, considered its consequences? These are the implications that I find to be directly relevant to Socrates' reason for examining and testing Hippocrates. The conversation between Socrates and Hippocrates is a kind of test of Hippocrates' mettle, and this test is explicitly characterized by Socrates as proceeding by means of questioning. Socrates' questioning of Hippocrates amounts to an "examination" of him, as though he can get to know Hippocrates only by putting him through some sort of trial by interrogation. And a trial by cross-examination is in effect what transpires.

It does not take long for Socrates to discover—and to reveal to Hippocrates—that he is seriously deficient. Hippocrates is eager to meet Protagoras, and to pay him for his services, but Hippocrates cannot even say why he should do so or explain what service is worth such payment. The specific steps in this process of discovery are as follows: First, Socrates has Hippocrates admit that he would be ashamed to call himself a sophist, at least in front of his friends and family [Jowett & Ostwald at 7 (312a)]. Yet, if Hippocrates is not going to Protagoras for the sake of being turned into a sophist, what is he going for? Socrates offers a possible alternative: To "get an education as befits a layman and a freeman?" [Jowett & Ostwald at 7 (312b)] "Just so," Hippocrates replies. But, when challenged by Socrates to say what kind of education this might be ("I wonder whether you know what you are doing" [Jowett & Ostwald at 7 (312b)]), Hippocrates, for the first and about the only time in this dialogue, asserts, "I certainly think that I do know" [Jowett & Ostwald at 7 (312c)].

This is the Socratic moment for disillusion: An interlocutor of Socrates has claimed that he knows something. At this point in many of the Platonic dialogues, Socrates takes over the conversation and proceeds to show the person making the claim that he does not know what he has claimed to know. In Hippocrates' case, disabusing him of his illusion turns out to be child's play. From the point where Socrates offers the thought that Hippocrates does not know what he is doing, to the point where Hippocrates and his claim to know come crashing down, is the matter of only a few lines.

> And yet I hardly think that you know what a Sophist is; and if not, then you do not even know to whom you are committing your soul and whether the thing to which you commit yourself be good or evil. [Jowett & Ostwald at 7 (312c)]

> And what is that which the Sophist knows and makes his disciple know? . . . Indeed, [Hippocrates] said, I cannot tell. [Jowett & Ostwald at 8 (312e)]

> You have quite made up your mind that you must by hook or by crook be a pupil of Protagoras, and are prepared to expend all the property of yourself and of your friends in carrying out this determination, although, as you admit, you do not know him and have never spoken with him; and you call him a Sophist, but are manifestly ignorant of what a Sophist is; and yet you are going to commit yourself to his keeping. . . . When [Hippocrates] heard me say this, he replied: No other inference, Socrates, can be drawn from your words.[30] [Jowett & Ostwald at 9 (313b–c)]

Consider how this transformation in Hippocrates takes place. When Socrates learns that Hippocrates is hurrying to see Protagoras and is eager to pay him for the value of his teaching, Socrates neither accepts nor rejects Hippocrates' conduct at face value. Instead, to test him, he asks Hippocrates: Who is Protagoras and what will he teach you for your money? In other words, Socrates confronts Hippocrates with his own actions and asks him to explain himself [Jowett & Ostwald at 6 (311b)]. When Hippocrates realizes that he cannot explain his actions, then we have the dawning of self-awareness [Jowett & Ostwald at 8 (312a)]. It is not his inability to define virtue that leads to Hippocrates' enlightenment, because he never claimed to know what virtue is or how to define it. Rather, it is his inability to clarify his own actions, for the benefit of Socrates or himself, that makes Hippocrates realize that he is acting foolishly, unreasonably. This knowledge pulls Hippocrates up short; having been stopped, he begins to think.

This is the aporetic moment.[31] Caught in a mental impasse, Hippocrates bethinks himself of where he is and what he is doing. This pause in the face of confusion, or acknowledged ignorance, is a fitting image of the tension that a human being experiences when poised between critical thought or reflection and impulsive action. The knowledge of his self—the dawning awareness of his obliviousness to the meaning of what he hoped and planned to do, and to its potential consequences—is forced upon Hippocrates by Socrates. Socrates' questions have compelled Hippocrates to think critically about himself, to examine and consider who he is and what he is doing.

This discovery of Hippocrates' own deadness to himself is a kind of self-discovery, a kind of self-knowledge, and it is the beginning of the Socratic wisdom for which Socrates himself is famous. And rightly so. The recognition of ignorance is the beginning of wisdom, which is a traditional virtue. Socrates' response to the challenge by the Delphic oracle, "Know thyself," was to generate a method by which to comply with this divine injunction to gain human self-knowledge.[32] It is in the transmission of these means to self-knowledge that Socrates' own virtue (of questioning himself and others) becomes transmitted to Hippocrates, who himself acts wisely (virtuously) in the act of questioning himself and learning something about himself, to his initial chagrin but ultimate salvation.

It is at this point, when Hippocrates has been disabused of his illusion, that Socrates advises him how to take better care of himself. "If you know which of his wares are good and which are evil, you may safely buy knowledge of Protagoras or of anyone; but if not, then, my friend, watch out, don't take risks, don't gamble, with the most precious thing you have." [See Jowett & Ostwald at 9 (313e–314a).] As we know, Socrates calls this ability to care for oneself, being "a physician of the soul" [Jowett & Ostwald at 9 (313e)].[33] And this is the image that emerges from this dialogue: Socrates is a physician of the soul for all those who associate with him and who engage him in conversation (*if* the particular interlocutor leaves himself open to Socrates' specific kind of therapy). Under Socrates' care and tutelage, his method of conversational inquiry becomes a way of caring for one's self or soul.

Having examined Hippocrates the prospective student, and having done what he could to care for Hippocrates' soul, for his healthy development, Socrates now turns to Protagoras the prospective teacher. Let us now turn with him, and see whether Socrates' dialectical therapy can be used to succor Protagoras. Will Protagoras take the proffered medicine, even when its taste is the bitterness of self-knowledge? We shall see.

The Plot Thickens: Protagoras on Trial

Protagoras' examination starts slowly and calmly, without much hint of the strife to follow. While initially he seems somewhat leery of Socrates ("And what is your purpose?" [Jowett & Ostwald at 13 (316b)]), he quickly warms up ("Thank you, Socrates, for your consideration of me" [Jowett & Ostwald at 13 (316c)]), and cheerily announces his readiness to answer Socrates' questions: "You ask good questions, Socrates, and I like to answer a question which is well put" [Jowett & Ostwald at 16 (318d)]. Even when Socrates (in response to Protagoras' initial efforts to explain to him how virtue can be taught) continues to question, rather than applaud, Protagoras' performance, Protagoras seems confident in his ability to resolve all of Socrates' doubts. In response to Socrates' request for "a little more" clarification, Protagoras says: "That I will, Socrates, and gladly. But what would you like? Shall I, as elder, tell you as younger men a myth, or shall I argue out the question?" [Jowett & Ostwald at 18 (320c)] It is at this point that Protagoras launches into his long speech.

The power of Protagoras as a spellbinding speaker and arguer seems undeniable. Plato does not portray him as a buffoon or as easy prey for Socrates' dialectical questioning, nor does Socrates seem to underestimate Protagoras' virtuosity. In this long speech, I think it is fair to say that Plato shows Protagoras' performance to be arresting. Socrates seems to be transfixed (as are, apparently, the other men who constitute the audience); indeed, in reaction to Protagoras' speech, he is (in various translations) "spellbound," "entranced," and "mesmerized" [at

(328d)]. And the fact that it takes Socrates awhile to shake himself out of the trance that Protagoras puts him in ("not without difficulty I began to collect myself" [Jowett & Ostwald at 27 (328d)]) is another acknowledgment of the power of Protagoras' verbal facility.

As we have seen, however, Socrates thinks he has the conversational therapy needed to counter such entrancement. Rather than capitulate to Protagoras' virtuosity, Socrates tests it. How? Socrates' test consists of voicing his own doubts about what Protagoras has said in his long speech, and he insists upon his right to speak (to question) from the source of his own experience.

> Yet I have still one very small difficulty which I am sure that Protagoras will easily explain, as he has already explained so much. [Jowett & Ostwald at 27–28 (328e)]

> Now I, Protagoras, want to ask of you a little question, which if you will only answer, I shall be quite satisfied. [Jowett & Ostwald at 28 (329b)]

> That is the doubt which still lingers in my mind. [Jowett & Ostwald at 28 (329d)]

This seems so little to ask of Protagoras, who himself expresses his assurance that he can satisfy Socrates' lingering doubt ("There is no difficulty, Socrates, in answering" [Jowett & Ostwald at 28 (329d)]). Yet, from this point to the end of the dialogue, Protagoras is unable to answer satisfactorily Socrates' "small" or "little" concerns.

Protagoras' consternation at his inability to satisfy Socrates increases rapidly, and its course can be briefly sketched. His frustration begins with an invitation from Socrates to join him in conversational inquiry: "Well then, I said, suppose that you and I inquire into the particular nature of each [part or aspect of virtue]" [Jowett & Ostwald at 29 (330b)]. Soon, however, Protagoras has to admit something that surprises him about virtue ("I could not help acknowledging the truth of what he said" [Jowett & Ostwald at 30 (331a)]), and this admission leads Socrates to a formulation of virtue that assimilates its various parts: "I would say in like manner on your behalf also, if you would allow me, that justice is either the same with piety, or very nearly the same; and above all I would assert that justice is like piety and piety is like justice. And I wish that you would tell me whether I may be permitted to give this answer on your behalf, and whether you would agree with me" [Jowett & Ostwald at 30–31 (331b)]. At this point, Protagoras suggests that Socrates' formulation seems oversimplified to him, but he can have it that way: "If you please I please; and let us assume, if you will, that justice is pious and that piety is just" [Jowett & Ostwald at 31 (331c)]. Socrates explodes. He wants the two of them to be "tested"; yet, for the kind of test that Socrates wants, they both must speak unconditionally. "Pardon me, I replied. I do not want this 'if you please' or 'if you like'" [Jowett & Ostwald at 31 (331c)]. They both must speak not hypothetically, but in actuality: Socrates wants each of them to be *committed* to the words that each one says.[34]

But this is exactly what Protagoras will not do. He refuses to commit himself to his words, to the claims and assertions that Socrates gets him to produce, ever more reluctantly, during the course of the rest of the dialogue. So, for Protagoras and for Socrates, the conversation deteriorates. A few pages later, in response to more of Socrates' questioning, Protagoras assents "with great reluctance" [Jowett & Ostwald at 34 (333b)]. Then a few lines later, he offers the thought, "I should be ashamed, Socrates, . . . to acknowledge this which nevertheless many [people] may be found to assert" [Jowett & Ostwald at 34 (333c)]. In response, Socrates says: "It makes no difference to me, if you will only answer me and say whether you are of their opinion or not. My object is to test the validity of the argument, and yet the result may be that I who ask and you who answer will both be tested" [Jowett & Ostwald at 34 (333c)]. But Socrates' plea is to no avail: "Protagoras at first played coy and said that the argument was not encouraging; at length he consented to answer" [Jowett & Ostwald at 34 (333d)].

After this portion of the inquiry, Protagoras soon defers or deflects further participation ("I saw that he was not satisfied with his previous answers, and that he would not play the part of answerer any more if he could help" [Jowett & Ostwald at 36 (335a–b)]); it appears, then, that the conversation is prematurely concluding ("I considered that there was no call upon me to continue the conversation" [Jowett & Ostwald at 36 (335b)]). But the members of the audience intercede and, in a brief interlude, they implore the two men to go on with their discussion. [See Jowett & Ostwald at 36–40 (334c–338e).] Later in this chapter, I shall turn our attention more directly to this critical interlude; but, for the moment, I wish to consider the remaining portion of Socrates' examination of Protagoras.

As I said, the audience members manage to prevail on Socrates and Protagoras to continue their conversation; but as the discussion is renewed, it becomes increasingly clear that Protagoras is an unwilling participant: "This [compact] was generally approved, and Protagoras, though very much against his will, was obliged to agree that he would ask questions; and when he had put a sufficient number of them, that he would answer in his turn those which he was asked in short replies" [Jowett & Ostwald at 40 (338e)]. While the discussion ensues for another thirty pages, it never results either in Protagoras' enlightenment or in his admitting defeat, or in what I am calling his being disillusioned—that is, his being disabused, by dint of Socrates' probing questions, of his illusions as to whether he knows what virtue is, or whether virtue is teachable, or whether he can teach virtue to others. Why is this?

In responding to this query, I want to pursue two lines of thought. I want, first, to indicate the sense in which Protagoras *is* refuted by Socrates' persistent questioning, regardless of whether or not he admits that he has been refuted (that is, Protagoras has been shown to believe something inconsistent or incoherent, or to have said something inconsistent or incoherent). Second, I also want to indicate the sense in which mere refutation of Protagoras will not amount, in this instance, to disillusioning him.

In regard to the first line of thought, while Protagoras does not end up becoming disillusioned, as I read this dialogue, he *is* refuted by Socrates' method of question-and-answer. Socrates' method of refutation is called *elenchus,* the procedure by means of which a person is refuted by his or her own words. In this context, Protagoras is shown to be inconsistent in something he thought or said, in something he claimed to know or believe. A typical instance of such a pass comes toward the end of the initial sustained conversation between Socrates and Protagoras:

> Then, Protagoras, which of the two assertions shall we renounce? One says that everything has but one opposite; the other that wisdom is distinct from self-control, and that both of them are parts of virtue; and that they are not only distinct, but dissimilar, both in themselves and in their functions, like the parts of a face. Which of these two assertions shall we renounce? For both of them together are certainly not in harmony, they do not accord or agree; for how can they be said to agree if everything can have only one opposite and not more than one, and yet folly, which is one, has clearly the two opposites—wisdom and self-control. Is not that true, Protagoras? What else would you say? [Jowett & Ostwald at 33–34 (333a–b)]

Socrates forces Protagoras to see that of two propositions, each of which Protagoras has agreed to during the process of question-and-answer, both cannot be true. So (at least) one must be given up. Which will it be? Protagoras concedes that perhaps he was wrong to assert that wisdom and self-control were distinct or separate parts of virtue. This form of argument works insofar as it shows the self to be at war with itself, inconsistently wishing to assent to two propositions or claims that conflict with one another. In this respect, I think that Socrates has refuted Protagoras, because Socrates has shown him to be inconsistent in what he says.

As for the second line of thought, in another sense, Socrates does not succeed in his exchanges with Protagoras; his questioning and inquiry do not end up disillusioning Protagoras. Specifically, I do not think that Socrates manages to get Protagoras to acknowledge that he is wrong, confused, or suffering under an illusion. Why not?

Unless Protagoras willingly participates in the conversation, and either answers Socrates' questions or, at the very least, sincerely assents to (or dissents from) Socrates' propositions and his developments of the question under scrutiny, the conversation cannot progress to any sort of disillusion. This does not mean that any particular line of argument or inquiry cannot be followed out, that it is too much for Socrates to handle on his own; quite to the contrary. Socrates is fully capable of developing the argument itself on his own. But this is not what he wants; neither he nor Plato is trying to create a theory on some particular philosophical topic (say, the nature of virtue). Socrates is, instead, trying to learn how virtue is constituted in his community, and what he and other Athenians can make of it, or have made of it. For such an investigation (as social as our language is, or as shared as the world is), Socrates requires the commitment of his conversational partner (here, Protagoras). To the extent that Protagoras lacks commitment to the conversation, then the argument goes nowhere. It reveals nothing (and can show nothing) about *them*.

Socrates investigates our words and our actions, and in order for this type of investigation to reveal anything personal, it must be ascertained that these words and actions *are* ours. This is why he implores Protagoras: "Uncover your mind to me, Protagoras, and reveal your attitude toward knowledge, that I may know whether or not you agree with the rest of the world" [Jowett & Ostwald at 57 (352b)]. Socrates wants to know where Protagoras stands on these matters, and he can learn this only by hearing what Protagoras has to say. In this regard, Protagoras cannot be "coy," he cannot be a "reluctant" participant. As Socrates' friend Alcibiades remarks, "[E]very man ought to say what he thinks" [Jowett & Ostwald at 38 (336d)]. Without such a commitment to candor, Protagoras will not learn anything about himself—regardless of the outcome of the argument itself (whatever its logic or its consistency)—because he will not be invested in these words and their exchanges. They will not represent or reflect the self who utters them.

At the same time, words or responses by Protagoras that are not truly his also will fail to provide the very data that Socrates' philosophical investigations are meant to uncover. Earlier, in chapter 1, I mentioned the similarity between Socrates' procedure and the method known as "ordinary language philosophy." Both procedures are intended to reveal the data for philosophy by unearthing the terms and the concepts by means of which our world is constituted. As noted in the same chapter (quoting from Cavell), the position of each one of us is the same in this regard. Each of us is an authority, each of us has the right (and the ability) to author or generate the data from which any philosophical inquiry must then proceed. Later in chapter 1, I related this notion to Socrates' frequently voiced injunction, namely, that his interlocutor say what he truly believes.

The idea there (and here) is that, if the person speaking is not truly committed to his or her words, if the person participating is not telling us what he or she truly believes, then to this extent the data are being falsified. A false response to Socrates' questions falsifies the data; then nothing further can be done to investigate these matters, since we at that point have no genuine or authentic data with which to work. According to Cavell, the point of Socratic inquiry and the point of ordinary language philosophy (including Wittgenstein's later philosophy) are the same in this regard: "In Wittgenstein's work, 'ordinary' or 'everyday' contexts and examples are, I suggest, meant to carry the force of 'authentic' examples authentically responded to in language."[35] As I said in chapter 1, Socrates' method of conversational inquiry, which builds upon what we already believe and what we are truly willing to assert in public conversation, works in part because we know more, or other, than what we think we know. (Yet, it remains true that we do not know what we think we know.)

Protagoras begins the inquiry willingly enough, but this is a matter of pride with him, just as Socrates had counted upon its being: "I suspected that he would like to have a little display and glorification in the presence of Prodicus and Hippias, and would gladly show us to them in the light of admirers" [Jowett & Ostwald at 14 (317c)]. And Socrates also had left it up to Protagoras whether this would be a conversation conducted in private or in front of the gathered friends [see Jowett & Ostwald at 13 (316b)]. But by the time Socrates first refutes Protagoras, some twenty pages later, I think that Protagoras has become weary of this exercise and repents of ever having entered into it. And once Protagoras withdraws his commitment to the discussion, I think that he is no longer susceptible to the revelation that he does not know what he thinks he knows. Protagoras cannot, on this basis, be disillusioned.

What Is Socrates Seeking to Learn?

Socrates is the moving force in this dialogue, and his questions control or direct the course of the conversation. Protagoras acknowledges as much when, in the second half of the dialogue, he urges Socrates to proceed under his own steam: "You ought to take the lead, . . . for you are the author of the discussion" [Jowett & Ostwald at 57 (351e)]. Is it clear, however, what moves Socrates to ask his questions?

One answer would be to say that Socrates seeks to learn about several topics during the course of the discussion. I do not think that such an answer is wrong, but it does seem to me to be a response of limited utility. It is true that Socrates examines at least four topics or objects during the course of the *Protagoras*. First, he examines his friend, Hippocrates, who wishes to give his money (and his soul) to Protagoras so that Protagoras will educate him—even though, as it turns out, Hippocrates does not have the slightest idea what Protagoras teaches. Then, second, Socrates also examines Protagoras, who claims to be able to turn his students into good citizens, practitioners of civic virtue, even though Protagoras cannot make out to his own (or to Socrates') satisfaction just exactly what is entailed by this notion of "civic virtue," or how exactly civic virtue can be taught to anyone. Then, too, third, Socrates also inquires into the nature of civic virtue (*areté*), how we define it, what it comprises, and how we teach or transmit it (if we do at all), especially as a matter of transmitting civic virtue to our young members of the city, the next generation of citizens. And, fourth, I should say that Socrates also examines himself. This is not obtrusively done in this dialogue but, nonetheless, I think that he is recording his own experiences, noting them, comparing them, and testing himself, specifically in terms of his concerns as they arise during the discussions that ensue.

These are the four topics or subjects that I would identify as the main objects of Socrates' attention throughout the dialogue. But, as important as these four topics are to the progression of the *Protagoras,* I also wish to take note of one factor at the macro-level of this dialogue, which drives the narration of Socrates' story; and another factor at the micro-level, which drives the questioning that is the main component of the story told by Socrates.

First, on the macro-level, what drives the telling of this story is Socrates' need to go over his experience and to see whether he can make sense of it. Puzzled by life, troubled by life, he cannot leave alone his experience of life. He must analyze it and must make sense of it. (We are again reminded of the injunction, from the *Apology,* that "an unexamined life is not worth living" [at 38a].) For Socrates, to live is to inquire, to examine, to test, to consider, to think, to criticize, and to speak. What motivates the narration of this story is his need to recount his experience and thereby to consider it again, perhaps to learn something new that he had not realized before. (This habit or trait in Socrates, as noted earlier, is what Gregory Vlastos calls his willingness to reexamine things.) It is the nature of the inquiry made, not the nature of the answer obtained, that most matters to Socrates.

The answer that we reach today, may well not be the answer we discover tomorrow, when we go over our experience once more, together in conversation. The fact that the answer may change from day to day, or from context to context, or from conversation to conversation, does not bother Socrates and does not matter to him. What matters to Socrates is the fact that we are engaging in the inquiry. We are making the effort to examine and to test ourselves; we are trying to make ourselves intelligible.

Thus, in one dialogue, Socrates may seem to be making a hedonistic proposal, as is apparently the case in the *Protagoras*. And yet, in other dialogues, he seems to argue against hedonism as an ethical standard or position. This is not inconsistency on his part; rather, it is a part of his unfailing desire to learn what he wants to know. According to some commentators, the "early" dialogues are said to be inconclusive, in the sense that they reach no conclusions or, at most, reach only "negative" ones—telling us, for example, what virtue is not. But from Socrates' perspective, learning even this is an addition to our knowledge. So, in this sense, such an acquisition is a "positive" gain, and not something merely negative. In terms that come into play in the *Meno* [at 97e–98a], such conclusions from purportedly inconclusive dialogues may forge another link in the chain of knowledge that we build, thereby serving to anchor us or our opinions.

Socrates' gorgeous thirst for knowledge is something that he acknowledges in his disavowals. Because he admits that he does not know, the ensuing need to know, the need to learn, drives him on. I take Socrates' professions of ignorance to constitute an instance of a person realizing the need to care for one's soul. It is the realization of one's own ignorance, of the poverty of one's knowledge (including knowledge of the self), that prepares one to attempt to remedy the situation. It is only upon the appreciation that the soul is starving (for the knowledge or learning that is the soul's sustenance) that one is apt to care for its need to be fed. As Socrates tells Hippocrates,

> Surely, I said, knowledge is the food of the soul; and we must take care, my friend, that the Sophist does not deceive us when he praises what he sells, like the dealers, wholesale or retail, who sell the food of the body, for they praise indiscriminately all their goods without knowing what is really beneficial or hurtful for the body. Neither do their customers know, with the exception of a trainer or physician who may happen to buy of them. In like manner those who carry about the wares of knowledge and make the round of the cities and offer or retail them to any customer who wants them, praise them all alike, though I should not be surprised, my dear fellow, if some of them, too, did not know which of their goods have a good and which a bad effect upon the soul; and their customers are equally ignorant, unless he who buys of them happens to be a physician of the soul. [Jowett & Ostwald at 9 (313c–e)]

If, as Socrates claims, "knowledge is the food of the soul," this claim still does not tell us how to acquire such sustenance.[36] For Socrates, the goal of his inquiries is to become "a physician of the soul." How can anyone become such a person?

Second, let us turn our attention to what I am calling the micro-level of this dialogue. If, at the macro-level, the dialogue is driven in general by Socrates' need to know, then what is the motivating force behind the questions that he asks throughout his conversations and discussions? In the *Protagoras,* Socrates wants to help his friend Hippocrates do what is best for Hippocrates' soul; also, Socrates seeks to learn who Protagoras is and what he teaches; and Socrates also wants to learn what virtue is, and whether it is teachable. Socrates investigates these matters by asking Hippocrates, "Why do you wish to become a student of Protagoras? What can you gain or receive from Protagoras' ministrations?" And he asks Protagoras, "What do you do? What can you offer to teach Hippocrates? How might he benefit from your attention and instruction? How do you know that you teach virtue? How do you define virtue? How can you (or anyone else) recognize something as virtue?"

And toward everyone involved in this dialogue, Socrates seems willing to ask, "What does virtue consist in? How is it transmissible from one person to another?"

Answers to questions such as these are what Socrates seeks in his inquiries with Hippocrates and with Protagoras and with the gathering at large of educated, concerned Athenian citizens. Such answers do not end our inquiry; rather, they only begin it, because these answers lead to larger questions: "Who can teach us? And what can they teach us? How do we learn how to care for our souls? And how do we learn how to examine our lives, so that we do not run the risk of living 'an unexamined life'? And how do we learn how to lead the best life possible for us?" These are the questions that hover behind and motivate the conversations that take place in the *Protagoras*.

This process of questioning is entered into by Socrates out of his sense of friendship with Hippocrates. But, in addition to wanting to help Hippocrates, what specifically is Socrates seeking to learn by means of asking *these* questions of *these* people? If one thing is clear in this dialogue, it is that Socrates insists on Protagoras' adopting this conversational mode of question-and-answer. Why does Socrates insist upon proceeding by means of interrogation?

Socrates is looking to learn something specific. He requires this question-and-answer mode of conversation (rather than proceeding by making speeches, or reciting poetry, or holding lectures) because, by means of his questions, he hopes to gain an understanding of the person whom he confronts. His search for knowledge becomes, then, his attempt to get to know a person. Yet, as well, this inquiry also is Socrates' attempt to get to know a claim—an expression of a belief or an opinion. "[T]hose who know him [Socrates] best understand that the elenchus does have this existential dimension—that what it examines is not just propositions but lives."[37]

If, then, Socrates claims to be investigating both a person *and* the expression of a belief or an opinion, how can he manage to accomplish this? What set of activities does such an investigation comprise? Here are two representative passages that suggest the kind of knowledge that Socrates is trying to elicit by means of his question-and-answer mode of conversation:

> Pardon me, I replied. I do not want this "if you please" or "if you like" sort of proposition to be put to the test, but I want you and me to be tested. I mean to say that the proposition will be best tested, if you take the "if" out of it. [Jowett & Ostwald at 31 (331c–d)]

> It makes no difference to me, if you will only answer me and say whether you are of their opinion or not. My object is to test the validity of the argument, and yet the result may be that I who ask and you who answer will both be tested. [Jowett & Ostwald at 34 (333c)]

Socrates does not offer any explanation as to *why* he believes that the "proposition" (or "the validity of the argument") "will be best tested" by the question-and-answer procedure, nor does he explain why the interrogator and the responder will also be tested by this procedure. Nonetheless, what follows is my understanding of Socrates' reasons for proceeding in this way.

To study what someone says in response to a question proposes a study of the investments we make in our words, namely, investments of meaning and investments of ourselves. We define ourselves through our use of language, our invocation of words. And, of course, the words we use equally serve to define or clarify the meaning of what we previously said. (And what we previously said is, after all, what starts Socrates on his way of asking questions in the first place.) In this context, then, conversation is Socrates' means of getting to know the person with whom he is conversing and what that person meant when he or she did or said the strange or startling thing that provoked Socrates to begin the inquiry. I should add that what typically transpires during Socrates' conversational inquiry is that he learns *what this person knows*—especially, in this regard, what this person knows about himself or herself (what he knows about his actions and their consequences; what she knows about her words and their implications).

The conversation, to be fruitful, must proceed by way of question-and-answer among the participants. Why does Socrates maintain this? I take it that he wants, and expects, at least two things to ensue from such philosophical, conversational inquiries. First, he wants a certain kind of knowledge to derive from the process of questioning and answering that he uses (I call this "bitter knowledge"). This knowledge will be revelatory both of the person being examined and of the proposition (or claim or concept) being examined. Second, Socrates wants the inquiry to be jointly taken and jointly finished. So his conversational inquiry becomes an intellectual quest or journey shared. Yet, what such an inquiry reveals—what we shall discover along the way—is not simply something "intellectual." The question of our character also hangs in the balance.

In the middle of the dialogue, for example, Socrates responds to Protagoras' reluctant participation in the discussion with the following:

> So I said: Do not imagine, Protagoras, that I have any other interest in asking questions of you but that of clearing up my own problems as they arise. For I think that Homer was very right in saying that "When two go together, one sees before the other," for all men who have a companion are readier in deed, word, or thought; but if a man "sees a thing when he is alone," he goes about straightaway seeking until he finds someone to whom he may show his discoveries, and who may confirm him in them. And I would rather hold discourse with you than with anyone, because I think that no man can better investigate most things which a good man may be expected to investigate, and in particular virtue. For who is there but you?—who not only claim to be a good man and a gentleman, for many are this, and yet have not the power of making others good—whereas you are not only good yourself, but also able to make others good. Moreover, such confidence have you in yourself that, although other Sophists conceal their profession, you proclaim openly in the face of all Hellas that you are a Sophist or teacher of virtue and education, and are the first who demanded pay in return. How then can I do otherwise than invite you to the investigation of these subjects, and ask questions and consult with you? I must, indeed. [Jowett & Ostwald at 52–53 (348c–349a)]

Socrates says that he is not interested in anything other than being invested wholly in the problems that arise during the course of this conversation. So, for example, he is not acting in his characteristically confrontational way out of any personal malice toward Protagoras. Beyond this declaration of his acting in good faith, Socrates is suggesting that the problem arose initially because Protagoras *claimed to know* what virtue is *and* also claimed to be able to teach virtue to others. Protagoras put himself in this position, in response to Socrates' initial question. How else does Protagoras suppose the problem that he himself created is to be solved? If he helped to create it, should not he also help to resolve it? If Protagoras claims to know what virtue is, then he should be willing to share this knowledge with Socrates, who claims not to know what virtue is.

But notice that Socrates' point is deeper still, for the claim is that Protagoras is both a good teacher of others and a good person in his own right, so in both respects he should know something about virtue, which he claims to be transmissible. And yet, on the other hand, if Protagoras no longer wishes to claim to know what virtue is (as, under Socrates' withering questioning, he may no longer wish to do), then that too will resolve the problem. For then Socrates would not be faced with the perplexity of someone who claims to know what virtue is but who, upon examination, cannot define it.

Socrates continues: "If I am not mistaken, the question was this: Are wisdom and self-control and courage and justice and piety five names which denote the same thing? Or is there, corresponding to each of these names, a separate underlying reality, a thing with its own peculiar function, no one of them being like any other of them? . . . I should like to know whether this is still your opinion; or if not, I will ask you to define your meaning, and I shall not take you to task if you now make a different statement. For I dare say that you may have said what you did only in order to make trial of me" [Jowett & Ostwald at 53 (349b, 349c)]. What is being tested by Socrates' dialectical examination is not only the truth of Protagoras' claim to know what virtue is (and to be able to teach it to others), but also Protagoras himself. He has made this claim boldly, not only in front of all Athenians in general, but also in front of this specific group of men, here and now, today. Socrates wants to test Protagoras in front of this same audience to see whether his proud claims hold up under critical scrutiny. Both the claims and the person advancing them are to be tested.

Pivotal Moment: Can This Conversation Continue?

Let us now consider something passed over earlier, namely, the critical juncture or turning point in the dialogue, when the initial conversation between Socrates and Protagoras falters and it appears that their discussion is over. This is a crisis in their conversation, and there is no certainty that the rift between the two men will be repaired. How does Plato manage to get these two conversationalists back together? Plato brings into play the audience, the people who have been so far portrayed by Socrates' narrative as enthusiastically and respectfully listening to these two giants spar.

Recall how we came to this pass. Socrates asked Protagoras to explain Protagoras' claim that virtue can be taught. This request calls forth from Protagoras not a brief explanation, but rather a long-winded discourse known as his "great speech," and it is the longest stretch of monologue in this drama. But even after this lengthy attempt by Protagoras to satisfy Socrates, Socrates responds critically. He once again expresses his doubts about virtue being teachable:

> [When] Protagoras finished his *tour de force*, . . . I began to collect myself . . . . I would not have missed the speech of Protagoras for a great deal. For I used to imagine that no human care could make men good; but I know better now. Yet I have still one very small difficulty which I am sure that Protagoras will easily explain, as he has already explained so much. If a man were to go and consult Pericles or any of our great speakers about these matters, he might perhaps hear as fine a discourse; but then when one has a question to ask of any of them, like books, they can neither answer nor ask, and if anyone challenges the least particular of their speech, they go ringing on in a long harangue, like brazen pots, which when they are struck continue to sound unless someone puts his hand upon them. Whereas our friend Protagoras cannot only make a good long speech, as he has already shown, but when he is asked a question he can answer briefly; and when he asks he will wait and hear the answer. And this is a very rare gift. Now I, Protagoras, want

> to ask of you a little question, which if you will only answer, I shall be quite satisfied. . . . Now I want you to tell me exactly whether virtue is one whole, of which justice and self-control and piety are parts; or whether all these are only the names of one and the same thing. That is the doubt which still lingers in my mind. [Jowett & Ostwald at 27–28 (328d–329a, 329b, 329c–d)]

Socrates begins by acknowledging the felicity with which Protagoras speaks, and he even admits that he finds Protagoras' oratory spellbinding. But the way to break the hold that such oratory or rhetoric can have on us is to question it. Socrates begins slowly, with minute concerns. In fact, Socrates emphasizes that his small concerns hardly measure up to the grandiose expressions to which Protagoras treats his audience.[38] To Socrates' expression of his lingering "little" doubt, Protagoras responds: "There is no difficulty, Socrates, in answering" [Jowett & Ostwald at 28 (329d)]. This is the last time during the entire dialogue that Protagoras expresses so sanguine a view of the problem confronting them. In very short order, his "confidence" that he can answer Socrates' questions—or, for that matter, that anyone can answer them—is crushed.

After Protagoras' long speech, Socrates insists that from this point onward, Protagoras should answer Socrates' questions in a more terse manner. [See Jowett & Ostwald at 28 (329a–d).] Protagoras seems agreeable. But after another short speech by Protagoras [see Jowett & Ostwald at 35 (334a–c)], when Socrates again complains that Protagoras' answers are too long for Socrates to be able to follow with his "wretched memory" [Jowett & Ostwald at 36 (334c)], Protagoras in turn expresses his exasperation with Socrates' carping criticism of his half of the conversation: "Socrates, he replied, many a battle of words have I fought, and if I had followed the method of disputation which my adversaries desired, as you want me to do, I should have been no better than another, and the name of Protagoras would not have spread all over Hellas" [Jowett & Ostwald at 36 (335a)].

Protagoras seems tired of answering Socrates' incessant questions, and he begins to resist the entire dialectical enterprise. According to Socrates, "I could see he [Protagoras] was uncomfortable with his previous answers and that he would no longer be willing to go on answering in a dialectical discussion, so I considered my work with him to be finished, and I said so" [Lombardo & Bell at 30 (335a–b)]. Protagoras' mounting resistance precipitates the crisis of this conversation. Shall it go on? Can the conversation continue?

Socrates thinks that it can, but only if Protagoras is willing to give up longwinded speeches ("To me, the mutual exchange of a dialogue is something quite distinct from a public address" [Lombardo & Bell at 31 (336b)]), and instead proceed in the question-and-answer manner that Socrates has proposed. "You know, Protagoras, I'm not exactly pleased myself that our session has not gone the way you think it should. But if you are ever willing to hold a discussion in such a way that I can follow, I will participate in it with you" [Lombardo & Bell at 30–31 (335b)]. Yet, since Protagoras appears to be unable or unwilling to accede to Socrates' request, the conversation appears to be at an end.

At this point, with Socrates ready to leave, the audience intercedes and a compact between the two is reached. [See Jowett & Ostwald at 39–40 (337e–338e).] Callias, the friend of Protagoras, defends his preference for making speeches in response to Socrates' questions. "Protagoras may fairly claim to speak in his own way, just as you [Socrates] claim to speak in yours" [Jowett & Ostwald at 38 (336b)]. Alcibiades, the friend of Socrates, then responds to Callias:

> That, Callias, is not a true statement of the case. For our friend Socrates admits that he cannot make a speech—in this he yields the palm to Protagoras; but I should be greatly surprised if he yielded to any living man in the ability to handle the give and take of argument. Now if Protagoras will make a similar admission, and confess that he is inferior to Socrates in argumentative skill, that is enough for Socrates. But if he claims a superiority in argument as well, let him ask and answer—not, when a question is asked, slipping away from the point and, instead of answering, making a speech at such length that most of his hearers forget the question at issue (not that Socrates is likely to forget, I will be bound for that, although he may pretend in fun that he has a bad memory). And Socrates appears to me to be more in the right than Protagoras. That is my view, and every man ought to say what he thinks. [Jowett & Ostwald at 38 (336b–d)]

This statement by Alcibiades seems to me to be an accurate representation of the situation. If Socrates were merely trying to gain an advantage over Protagoras by coercing him into using a mode of expression preferred by Socrates, this would be unfair treatment of Protagoras and he would be right to complain. But I understand Socrates' claim to be that the answers to his questions about virtue cannot be sought or obtained through making speeches or interpreting poetry; such answers can be gained only by way of the kind of discussion exemplified in Socrates' mode of conversational inquiry. And if this tenet of Socrates' dialectical therapy is true, then engaging in any other form of expression, given the issues posed, is both wasteful and pointless.

Having heard from a proponent of Protagoras (Callias), and then hearing a response to Callias by a proponent of Socrates (Alcibiades), other members of the audience now become involved. Critias, for example, pleads with Socrates and Protagoras not to end this critical examination of one another; then Prodicus speaks to similar effect; and finally, Hippias. All of them implore the two disputants not to leave their discussion unsettled. Hippias essentially summarizes and reiterates the requests of the other members of the audience: "I therefore implore and counsel you, Protagoras and Socrates, to be reconciled and to compromise, under our arbitration, as it were, on some middle course. . . . Both of you must steer a middle course" [Lombardo & Bell at 33 (337e, 338a)].

What has occurred is remarkable; it confirms Socrates' faith (expressed much earlier in the dialogue) that *areté* (virtue, excellence) is not the preserve of some cadre of specialists or of certain ethical experts—at least, not in the city-state of Athens. No, instead, all citizens have the same standing to speak (and to be heard) on such matters of common cause, and all members of the Athenian *polis* have the same right to inquire into these matters. (Recall here Vlastos's comment that Socrates' method "makes moral inquiry a common human enterprise, open to every man. . . . It calls for common sense and common speech."[39])

It is the people of Athens, here in this courtyard, who implore and persuade Socrates and Protagoras not to end the discussion at this point. Socrates does not accept from this group of men, however, their suggestion that the two of them should select an "umpire" or a "moderator" to preside over their conversation [see Jowett & Ostwald at 39–40; and

Lombardo & Bell at 33 (338b–d)]. This person or official would serve, it had been suggested, as a "referee" for their debate. Socrates, instead, appeals to all of the men gathered together as peers, as equals, with as good a claim as anyone to speak about virtue and teaching and what might be proper nourishment for the human soul. No one has a higher standing or a more elevated position from which to judge the fruits of a discussion concerning such matters.[40] (Here I refer again to Cavell's characterization of the procedures followed in ordinary language philosophy, namely, that "you know no better than others what you claim to know. With respect to the data of philosophy our positions are the same."[41])

And so the two controversialists—or conversationalists—finally agree that, since Protagoras is tired of answering Socrates' questions, the procedure will be reversed, and this time Protagoras will ask the questions and Socrates will be put to the test by answering. "Everyone agreed this was the thing to do. Protagoras wanted no part of it, but he had to agree to ask questions, and when he had asked enough, to respond in turn with short answers" [Lombardo & Bell at 34 (338e)].

Speeches and Poems: Unhelpful Tools for Learning

Earlier, I mentioned that Socrates contests the claim of both the sophists and the poets to be moral instructors. The *Protagoras* locates and tests one specific point of contention between Socrates, on the one hand, and the sophists and poets, on the other. In moral teaching or instruction, the sophists use their rhetorical skills, while the poets use their poetical skills. Socrates insists in the *Protagoras* that the education of young people in matters of civic virtue would be better served if it were based not upon their reciting poems or giving speeches, but rather upon their sharing the responsibility for engaging in conversational inquiry. The problem with both oratory and poetry (as alternative ways of acquiring knowledge of virtue) is, according to Socrates, that they do not use or allow questions in the process of teaching and learning. So their deficiency is a lack of instructive questioning or, perhaps, it is a lack of making room for questions—as though neither speeches nor poems invite us to question them.

Let us examine Socrates' claims regarding the purported educational faults of oratory and poetry. When he praises Protagoras' ability to ask and answer questions, and thereby to participate in Socratic conversational inquiry, he goes on to contrast this ability with that of other speakers, including such famous ones as Pericles, as we saw earlier: "If a man were to go and consult Pericles or any of our great speakers about these matters, he might perhaps hear as fine a discourse; but then when one has a question to ask of any of them, like books, they can neither answer nor ask" [Jowett & Ostwald at 28 (329a–b)]. The impression I gain from this description is that speakers (like books)[42] have an established script from which they cannot stray, inflexibly saying only what is set down in the text for them to say; and thereby they avoid responding to any question pressed upon them.

Later in the dialogue, Socrates lodges a similar complaint against poems:

> I said: I wish Protagoras either to ask or answer as he is inclined. But I would rather have done with poems and odes, if he does not object, and come back to the question about which I was asking you at first, Protagoras, and by your help make an end of that investigation. The talk about poetry seems to me like a commonplace entertainment at the banquets of the vulgar who, because they are not able to converse with or amuse one another while they are drinking, with the sound of their own voices and conversation, by reason of their stupidity, raise the price of flute-girls, hiring for a great sum the voice of a flute instead of their own breath, to be the medium of intercourse among them. But where the company are real gentlemen and men of education, you will see no flute-girls, nor dancing girls, nor harp-girls, and they have no nonsense or games, but are contented with one another's conversation, of which their own voices are the medium and which they carry on by turns and in an orderly manner, even though they consume a lot of wine. And a company like this of ours, and men such as we profess to be, do not require the help of another's voice, or of the poets whom you cannot interrogate about the meaning of what they are saying; people who cite them declaring, some that the poet has one meaning, and others that he has another, and the point which is in dis-

> pute can never be decided. This sort of entertainment they decline and prefer to talk with one another, and put one another to the proof in conversation. And these are the models which I desire that you and I should imitate. Leaving the poets and keeping to ourselves, let us try the mettle of one another and make proof of the truth in conversation. If you have a mind to ask, I am ready to answer; or if you would rather, do you answer, and give me the opportunity of resuming and completing our unfinished argument. [Jowett & Ostwald at 51–52 (347b–348a)]

Socrates wishes to return to the mode of inquiry with which he is most comfortable and which he believes to be most beneficial: "I would rather have done with poems and odes, if he does not object, and come back to the question about which I was asking you at first, Protagoras, and by your help make an end of that investigation." Socrates seeks closure here, but he does so only insofar as such closure can be achieved conversationally. Poetry, odes, and speeches will not do.

How else does the *Protagoras* examine speeches and poems as the two main educational or epistemological alternatives competing with Socrates' conversational mode of inquiry as our best means for gaining knowledge? Both speeches and poems are given prominent place by Protagoras himself in his efforts to avoid the painful and humiliating cut-and-thrust of Socratic conversational inquiry. Speeches gain this prominence by virtue of Protagoras' propensity for making them; he indulges in oratory as a way of avoiding conversation with Socrates. Poems gain their own prominence by virtue of the fact that interpreting and understanding an ode by Simonides forms one major portion of this dialogue. The ode is first cited and praised by Protagoras, who then immediately challenges Socrates to state his own understanding of it. This challenge seems a blatant attempt by Protagoras to transfer their contest from the conversational arena to locales more favorable for showing off his considerable critical and interpretive skills, and for thus gaining an advantage over Socrates. [See Jowett & Ostwald at 40–50 (338e–347a).]

Speechmaking and the interpretation of poetry form two extended passages (ten pages each) in a dialogue of only seventy pages. Why are they given such prominence? It seems to me that Plato provides us with these alternative means of gaining knowledge so that we can compare and contrast them with Socrates' method of conversational inquiry. It is not that speeches and poems are empty or useless forms of expression; it is, rather, that they do not afford us the kind of knowledge of people or of propositions that we wish to gain in philosophy—and that Socrates shows us that it is possible to gain through the employment of his method.

Consider, first of all, the matter of speeches. Protagoras has a reputation as a master speechmaker, and he does not disappoint us. I have already mentioned the effect that Protagoras' long speech had on his audience, including Socrates, and I do not think that Socrates is feigning enthusiasm when he says that he was transfixed by it. [See Jowett & Ostwald at 27 (328d).] But Socrates breaks the spell by raising a doubt: "Yet I have still one very small difficulty which I am sure that Protagoras will easily explain, as he has already explained so much." This is Socrates' dialectical therapy at work; it is his way for breaking the hold of spellbinding orators. This aspect of Socrates' practice highlights in turn one of the problems with speeches, namely, that they do not allow their audience an opportunity (by asking questions) to break the spell cast by a speech.[43] In this respect, a speech does not allow its auditors the chance to participate in the inquiry or the argument being sketched by the speaker. Without such interrogation, how can the auditors learn who the speaker is, or what he means? Unless the text itself makes these matters clear, the auditors have no recourse except to engage the speaker in discussion, which is exactly what Socrates attempts to do at the end of Protagoras' speeches.

In a sense, speeches cover too much ground, never pausing to afford their audience the chance to catch their breath or to clear their heads. Any extended stretch of prose, without interruption, risks carrying the audience along without revealing the speaker or the speaker's meaning; indeed, the audience may become enthralled. Or else the audience risks not attending to the specifics of the speech, not actively listening or following the thread of the argument. (We know that Socrates complains to Protagoras that, because of Protagoras' tendency to make speeches, combined with Socrates' poor memory, he simply cannot follow Protagoras' argument.) And sometimes, in order to understand or comprehend the speaker, we in the audience must be permitted to interrupt him. Thus, at one point in their exchange, Socrates has to shout at Protagoras, "Stop, I said; I should like to investigate that" [Jowett & Ostwald at 54 (349e)].

Now consider the matter of poems. If speeches cover too much ground too quickly, without pause for questions, then perhaps we can say that poems are too compressed or condensed; they are not discursive enough. Poems certainly can and do move from topic to topic, but it is a question whether they do so conversationally, that is, in a way that invites the participation of the audience. Socrates' objection to poetry is that poems, like speeches, do not leave room for their audience to question them. As he observes, "[M]en such as we profess to be, do not require the help of . . . the poets whom you cannot interrogate about the meaning of what they are saying; people who cite them declaring, some that the poet has one meaning, and others that he has another, and the point which is in dispute can never be decided." The question of a poem's meaning cannot be decided, Socrates claims. What are we to make of this claim?

In conversation, if something said is unclear or ambiguous, then the participants in the conversation can stop right there to expand upon it, or they can restate it, or they can retract it. (An example of how we can tease out the meaning of a person's expressions, and how we can try out the implications of what a person has said, is depicted in detail through the numerous conversations that compose the *Theaetetus,* as I later discuss in chapter 4.) The flexibility and the fecundity that inhere in conversation may be a part of the reason why Socrates thinks that it is superior to either oratory or poetry as a mode of inquiry.

Protagoras thinks differently. He ventures the opinion that "skill in poetry is the principal part of education; and this I conceive to be the ability to understand which compositions of the poets are correct, and which are not, and to know how to distinguish between them and, when asked, give the reasons" [Jowett & Ostwald at 40 (338e–339a)]. As an example, Protagoras then cites the poet Simonides and one of his odes, and proceeds to offer an interpretation of the ode, at the end of which Protagoras is congratulated by the audience on his virtuoso performance. According to Socrates, "Many of the audience cheered and applauded this. And I felt at first giddy and faint, as if I had received a blow from the hand of an expert boxer, when I heard his [Protagoras'] words and the sound of the cheering; and to tell you the truth, I wanted to get time to think what the meaning of the poet really was" [Jowett & Ostwald at 42 (339d–e)]. Socrates, in desperation, calls upon Prodicus, one of the audience, who is known for his ability to "make . . . charming distinctions," and asks him "to rehabilitate Simonides by the application of your literary art" [Jowett & Ostwald at 42 (340a–b)]. Prodicus obliges. This ploy distracts and confounds Protagoras momentarily, but it is only a way of buying time; Socrates still must come up with an acceptable response to Protagoras' challenge.

Socrates' eventual response, once he has collected his wits, is to parody Protagoras.[44] Start with the fact of Protagoras' claim that the "skill in poetry" with which he is concerned is not the actual making of verses or composing of poems, but rather it is the interpretation of poetry ("the ability to understand which compositions of the poets are correct, and which are not"). Today this ability to give a reading of a poem might be seen as more of a critical skill, and less of a poetical one, but let Protagoras' claim stand for the moment. What is first shown to the group, including Protagoras, is how easy it is for someone—here the culprit is Prodicus—to interpret words from the poem out of context, attributing meanings that may be plausible in the abstract but do not in fact fit the context of this particular poem. This is a way of spoofing Protagoras and his view of what constitutes "skill in poetry." Almost anything can be given or accepted as a "reason" for distinguishing between supposedly correct and incorrect poems, or between supposedly correct and incorrect interpretations. After the bravura performance of Prodicus at the expense of Protagoras, when Protagoras reacts by protesting the perverse way in which Prodicus seemed to be reading the ode of Simonides, Socrates himself remarks: "I also incline to believe, Protagoras, that this was the meaning of Simonides, of which our friend Prodicus was well aware, but he thought that he would make fun and see if you could maintain your thesis" [Jowett & Ostwald at 44 (341d)].

With this prefatory tableau out of the way, Socrates then directly responds to Protagoras' challenge by offering the audience his own interpretation of the same ode earlier cited and discussed by Protagoras. Much of Socrates' reading of Simonides' poem is perfectly plausible—and perfectly awful. (See Jowett & Ostwald at 44–50 [341e–347a].) Sometimes, in his interpretation, Socrates gives an extended paraphrase;

but, at other times, he offers us queries that he puts both to the poem and to the audience. On those occasions when Socrates offers his audience a paraphrase, I take him to be parodying Protagoras, showing how it is possible to say something plausible about the poem without there being any way to refute Socrates' claims of meaning. There is, in Socrates' terms, no way to decide, one way or the other, the meaning of the poem that Simonides created.

For most of Socrates' paraphrases of the poem, we have no basis either for agreeing or for disagreeing with his claims to be paraphrasing correctly or accurately. A glib orator, a facile interpreter, can be very persuasive in this regard (and it is as a defense against such rhetorical glibness or facility that Socrates recommends his dialectical therapy of conversational inquiry). What Socrates says in his paraphrases sounds plausible—that is the most that we can say about his claims. In this respect, he demonstrates the extent to which a person can say something plausible about a poem simply by making up an interpretation out of thin air. (Remember that Socrates is here in exactly the position of inventing an interpretation out of thin air, as a response to the challenge of Protagoras' earlier performance: "And I felt at first giddy and faint, as if I had received a blow from the hand of an expert boxer.") So Socrates' interpretive claims (and Prodicus' perverse suggestions regarding semantics) parody Protagoras' earlier attempt to interpret Simonides' ode. Both Socrates and Prodicus show how a reasonably astute person can take the words of a poem and ascribe meanings to them, all the time giving plausible reasons, without anyone possessing a way of determining or assessing their correctness or incorrectness.[45] As Socrates said before, we cannot interrogate poets about the meaning of what they are saying; instead, "the point which is in dispute can never be decided." [Jowett & Ostwald at 51 (347e)]

Yet, on other occasions, Socrates offers us a way to temper the disadvantages of poetry and its interpretation; he does so by interpolating questions along with his reading of the poem. In these instances, unlike his earlier parodies of Protagoras, Socrates gives an interpretation of Simonides' ode that consists of both reading and quizzing the poem. For example: "Now there is a difficulty in becoming good, and yet this is possible. But to be good is an impossibility—'For he who does well is the good man, and he who does ill is the bad.' But what constitutes 'doing well' in writing? And what kind of activity makes a man good in writing? Clearly, learning it. And what sort of well-doing makes a man a good physician? Clearly, learning the art of healing the sick. 'But he who does ill is the bad.' Now, who becomes a bad physician?" [Jowett & Ostwald at 48 (344e–345a)]. While it is Protagoras who praises the educational benefits of poetry, I think it is Socrates who manages to transform the activity of poetic interpretation into something educational. Socrates' method of learning works by interlacing his interpretation of Simonides with questions for the poet and the poem.

Even as Socrates criticizes Protagoras' penchant for giving speeches and citing poems, he manages to rehabilitate (or to transform) each of these two major forms of expression endorsed by Protagoras. While Protagoras obviously excels at speechmaking, Socrates holds his own whenever he too happens to indulge in speechmaking [see Jowett & Ostwald at 56–62 (351e–356c)]. The difference between Protagoras' speeches and those of Socrates is that a speech from Socrates tends to be interlaced with *questions* to his audience, seeking their assent or dissent and urging them to "join" him in the inquiry. (An important—indeed, crucial—exception to this tendency in Socrates' speeches is the speech that he makes to his jurors at his trial as depicted in the *Apology*.)[46] In both speeches and poems, then, I understand Socrates' performance to undercut Protagoras' performance. It is as though Socrates were refuting him—not rhetorically, and not logically, but dialectically refuting him.[47] I do not think that Socrates' efforts here amount to a kind of juvenile taunt, Whatever you can do, I can do better. Rather, Socrates is showing Protagoras the true resources of speeches and poetry in the hands of a master questioner.

This is, simultaneously, a matter of Socrates revealing the power of conversational inquiry. He is recommending this method to us for the problems that perplex us. I think he is trying to show us that, for the knowledge of people and propositions (expressions) that we seek in philosophical quandaries, the process of questioning and answering is the approach to take. As cited earlier, Socrates says in a passage concluding this portion of the dialogue: "[W]here the company are real gentlemen and men of education, . . . they have no nonsense or games, but are contented with one another's conversation, of which their own voices are the medium and which they carry on by turns and in an orderly manner. . . . This sort of entertainment they decline and prefer to talk with one another, and put one another to the proof in conversation. And these are the models which I desire that you and I should imitate. Leaving the poets and keeping to ourselves, let us try the mettle of one another and make proof of the truth in conversation."

No doubt, this process of conversational inquiry does not work everywhere and every time. It requires, to begin with, "men of education," that is, participants who are able to articulate their thoughts and feelings. But it does promise the possibility of enlightenment for those bold enough to engage in the trying conversation that Socrates directs. We may be confirmed in what we think and say and do, or we may be refuted; but we know that we shall be tested. In Socrates' mode of conversational inquiry, we prove ourselves and the truth of our assertions neither in the abstract nor in a vacuum, but in conversation. For Socratic philosophy, the way to truth and meaning is in media res, and the contexts for making such proofs are provided by our conversation.

A Rueful Conclusion

Who is a candidate for education in the *Protagoras?* And who goes through the fires of disillusion and renewal here? Hippocrates, for one. He is a candidate for education because he starts out woefully unclear about his motive for pursuing Protagoras, and he does learn something from Socrates' questioning. As the result of talking with Socrates, he achieves a modicum of clarity and he takes the lesson to heart. Hippocrates realizes that he had no idea as to what Protagoras offered him in the way of training and, thus, he had no idea why he should associate with Protagoras or pay him for his lessons. It seems apparent, then, that Hippocrates is disillusioned by means of his experience of Socratic conversational inquiry. Still, Hippocrates' accomplishments and status are such that his clarification is neither so difficult nor so telling as to deserve central attention in Plato's dramatic dialogue.

Protagoras, on the other hand, is much bigger game. He is the most famous and most accomplished of the sophists, and he ventures into Socrates' neighborhood. Is Protagoras, then, a candidate for disillusion, for education? I think not. He is not open to disillusion, because he will not open himself up to the kind of self-revelation that Socrates' method of inquiry requires. And, without self-revelation, what chance is there of Protagoras learning what (on the basis of Socrates' examination) he needs to learn?

These two great talkers do clash, of course, and their argumentative confrontation does teach Protagoras a lesson. But Socrates' lesson is imposed by force (and something akin to sleight of hand), and it appears that Protagoras is not open or receptive to the self-knowledge that engagement with Socrates makes possible, because he does not seek such knowledge. I do not say that self-knowledge can never be imposed upon us; I submit, though, that normally self-knowledge is achieved only after an active search for it. Here such knowledge was not sought by Protagoras. Thus, the conclusion of this dialogue merely brings to an end the conversation between Socrates and Protagoras; it does not amount to Protagoras' being disillusioned. Rather, the treatment that he receives at the hands of Socrates only hardens him against Socrates and against the threat he feels in Athens.

Then who else is there to be instructed? Socrates seems to me to be a major candidate for education in this dialogue. As Paul Woodruff puts it, "Socrates' practice of philosophy is an education for everyone, including himself."[48] Is Socrates taken through a process of disillusion and renewal? I think that he is.

Socrates does learn something new, something he did not already know when he began this inquiry with Protagoras. For one thing, he learns that virtue may be teachable, since he believes this to be implied by his conversational inquiry with Protagoras, to the extent that their inquiry suggests that virtue is knowledge. But this implication has not been proven in conversation, and there is work remaining to be done. Socrates acknowledges this rueful conclusion at the end of the dialogue:

> My only object, I said, in continuing with my questions has been the desire to ascertain facts about virtue and what virtue itself is. For if this were clear, I am very sure that the other controversy which has been carried on at great length by both of us—you affirming and I denying that virtue can be taught—would also become clear. . . . Now I, Protagoras, perceiving this terrible confusion,

> have a great desire that it should be cleared up. And I should like to carry on the discussion until we finally ascertain what virtue is, and to investigate whether it is capable of being taught or not, lest haply Epimetheus should trip us up and deceive us in the argument, as he forgot us in the story [which Protagoras told during his long speech]. Even as you were telling the myth, I preferred your Prometheus to your Epimetheus, for of him I make constant use, whenever I am busy about these questions, in Promethean care of my own life in its entirety. And if you have no objection, as I said at first, I should like to have your help in the inquiry. [Jowett & Ostwald at 68, 69 (360e–361a, 361c–d)]

But Protagoras is not interested in pursuing the inquiry further ("at present we had better turn to something else" [Jowett & Ostwald at 69 (361e)]), and the conversation ends here.

But, in the act of questioning and refuting Protagoras, Socrates befriends him, just as Socrates also befriends Protagoras by the act of asking him to question himself, and just as he befriends Hippocrates, too, by examining and testing him. [See, for example, Jowett & Ostwald at 13, 18 (316b–d, 320b–c).] Socrates' aptitude for inquiry is denied to no one—not even to his adversary Protagoras, and certainly not to his friend Hippocrates. This fundamental willingness on the part of Socrates to lend his efforts to anyone genuinely interested in the pursuit of knowledge is proven time and again in the Platonic dialogues. This is a daunting kind of friendship that Socrates shows his conversational partners. But we know that friendship requires candor and admits of disagreements and arguments. A part of the virtue of Socrates that I see displayed in the *Protagoras* is his ability to call upon his capacity for inquiry in aid of anyone—this seems true friendship indeed.[49] He is a stranger to no one deliberately, unless they estrange themselves from him or his methods. This openness or receptivity to others is, in a sense, what gets Socrates in trouble with the Athenians. He is a dangerous man to have around the *polis*.

Socrates' willingness and ability to share himself with others mark him simultaneously as both a teacher and a student.[50] He is talkative, but he does not engage in mere chatter. He talks both as a way of engaging with people and as a way of circulating himself (and his thoughts and ideas) among the people of Athens. This is how he shares himself and his virtues with his fellow citizens. Not only does Socrates not withhold his gift of insight and inquiry from anyone with whom he comes in contact, but also he is perfectly willing to engage in inquiry with anyone inclined to share the burden of doing so. He never withholds himself or his assistance from anyone who has need of it. He never gives up the search for answers.

This last characteristic is important, I think, because it marks the true learner. It is not that a curious or inquisitive person must always *gain* answers, but rather that he or she must always *seek* them, even when those answers do not seem to be forthcoming. Socrates is a candidate for education or instruction in this dialogue in part because he is willing to persevere in the activity of conversational inquiry, to carry on the search in the face of disappointment and disillusion. In fact, I should say that Socrates' success in inquiry is a function of his capacity for not tiring of the work of inquiry (what Richard Poirier, in his splendid book on Robert Frost, calls "the work of knowing"[51]). What distinguishes Socrates from Protagoras (and from Hippocrates) is his ability to call upon his capacity for inquiry, for questioning, whenever he wants it. Hippocrates clearly is not up to pushing himself in the way that Socrates manages to goad him into thought. And Protagoras is also left, by the end of the dialogue, looking for respite. [See Jowett & Ostwald at 68 (360e).] Only Socrates wishes to continue, even in conflict with his social engagements and other commitments. [See Jowett & Ostwald at 69 (361c).] He is prepared to begin anew. He perseveres.

Disillusion need not end in skepticism or cynicism. These are convictions, settled attitudes, that people may have or gain; but they are not necessities, and they are not our fate. As Cavell puts the challenge we face, "The issue on my mind . . . [is] something else, namely, how to accept a therapy of disillusion (or of dismantling) without succumbing to disillusionment, I mean disillusionment as an attitude, something between discouragement and cynicism. (If we see that politics has been one cure for this, and philosophy another, then we should equally see that they have both, or their degradations have, been causes of it too.)"[52] Here, however, the conversation ends for the moment, and we go on our way.

THREE

The Poverty of Socratic Questioning

Asking and Answering in the *Meno*

I understand [philosophy] as a willingness to think not about something other than what ordinary human beings think about, but rather to learn to think undistractedly about things that ordinary human beings cannot help thinking about, or anyway cannot help having occur to them, sometimes in fantasy, sometimes as a flash across a landscape. . . . Such thoughts are instances of that characteristic human willingness to allow questions for itself which it cannot answer with satisfaction. Cynics about philosophy, and perhaps about humanity, will find that questions without answers are empty; dogmatists will claim to have arrived at answers; philosophers after my heart will rather wish to convey the thought that while there may be no satisfying answers to such questions in certain forms, there are, so to speak, directions to answers, ways to think, that are worth the time of your life to discover. (It is a further question for me whether directions of this kind are teachable, in ways suited to what we think of as schools.)

—STANLEY CAVELL[1]

Many people have noted the philosophical richness of the *Meno,* with its compressed treatment of a host of interesting topics. For example, in the Library of Liberal Arts edition,[2] Fulton Anderson begins his

Introduction to the dialogue with words of praise: "The *Meno* is described by Walter Pater as the 'most characteristic dialogue of Plato.' John Stuart Mill calls it a 'gem' among Platonic works, and most aptly, for in no other dialogue of Plato are there exhibited within comparable compass so many facets as the *Meno* contains" [Jowett & Anderson at 7].[3] Given its richness and its compression of topics, we can in this chapter continue to pursue a number of questions that we began to investigate in studying the *Protagoras*. How does anyone become good? Do we become virtuous or excellent because we are born that way, or because we are educated to be good? And, if it is a matter of being taught, who teaches virtue to us? Also, what is the basis or foundation of virtue? Is being good based on knowledge in some way, or is virtue a matter of having true beliefs, correct opinions? Is it mere luck, or is virtue a matter of inspiration, divine or otherwise?

Socrates in the *Meno* does not know the answers to these questions. But, since he is possessed by these questions, perhaps even obsessed with them, he will not let them go unanswered. Or, rather, he does not fail to try to answer them—if, that is, they have an answer. So, as Stanley Cavell suggests in the epigraph to this chapter, "while there may be no satisfying answers to such questions in certain forms, there are, so to speak, directions to answers, ways to think, that are worth the time of your life to discover." What the nature of virtue is or may be, and whether it is possible to teach people virtue, are among the concerns that Socrates and Meno and we investigate in the *Meno,* without knowing how our search for an answer may end. It is an unpredictable inquiry that is portrayed in this dialogue.

The *Meno*'s Progress and Meno's Progress

The dialogue opens with a long discussion between Socrates and Meno; then it shifts to a much shorter exchange between Socrates and Meno's slave, and this exchange is itself briefly interrupted by a short talk again between Socrates and Meno. When Socrates finishes with Meno, he once more turns his attention to the slave; and then, when Socrates finishes with him, another brief conversation occurs between Socrates and Meno. This exchange also is interrupted, when Anytus appears and proceeds to discuss certain matters with Socrates. The dialogue then concludes with yet another extended discussion between Socrates and Meno.

The conversational movement of the *Meno* can be outlined this way:

- Socrates and Meno [pp. 23–38 (70a–82b)]
- Socrates and the Slave [pp. 38–41 (82b–84a)]
- Interlude: Socrates and Meno [pp. 41–42 (84a–d)]
- Socrates and the Slave [pp. 42–43 (84d–85b)]
- Socrates and Meno [pp. 43–49 (85b–89c)]
- Socrates and Anytus [pp. 49–54 (89d–95a)]
- Socrates and Meno [pp. 55–61 (95a–100b)]

This synoptic outline suggests that Meno is the chief character of this drama.[4] We see Meno at three different stages: first, when he meets Socrates and asks him a question; second, after Socrates has discussed some geometric figures with Meno's slave; and, third, after Socrates has discussed virtue and knowledge with Anytus, a passing Athenian politician. I take it that the *Meno*'s progress is portraying Meno's progress, something akin to his growing awareness, and even his gradual education.

A second theme—something besides Meno's growth—develops simultaneously. During the course of this dialogue, Socrates converses with three people, who turn out to be three different types of student. He mainly asks them questions, and his questions elicit different responses differences, that is, in the manner in which these three respond. For example, does any of them welcome the attention that he receives from Socrates? How does he show it? Does any of them come to appreciate the nature of the investigation that he is being invited by Socrates to join? As the *Meno* progresses, then, Socrates teaches three different people by talking with them and questioning them, and we also see how they are affected by the ensuing discussion and by the probing questions. Let me begin with this second theme: the dialogue's presentation of three different types of student.

Three Types of Student

Meno, his slave, and Anytus illustrate different types of student in the sense that these three people are shown to be differently prepared and differently motivated in their discussions with Socrates. In addition, these three are differently situated in terms of their ability or willingness to learn and of how they relate to Socrates.

Meno begins the dialogue by putting to Socrates a question about how virtue is acquired. It is a question that Socrates for some reason does not like, at least in its initial form [see Jowett & Anderson at 23–24 (70a–71b)]. Not answering it directly, Socrates puts Meno's question aside and instead asks him about the nature of virtue, which Meno finds painfully easy: "There will be no difficulty, Socrates, in answering your question" [Jowett & Anderson at 24 (71e)]. For the next few pages of dialogue, Meno then tries unsuccessfully to answer Socrates' "easy" question [Jowett & Anderson at 24–29 (71c–75b)].

Meno's slave, by contrast, initiates nothing. Rather, Meno picks the slave out of a crowd of servants, and Socrates asks him questions [Jowett & Anderson at 38 (82b)]. But, once engaged by Socrates, the slave (at first quite timid) eventually makes a claim to know something. It turns out, however, that the slave's claim is based upon a false inference [Jowett & Anderson at 39 (82e)]. Socrates then corrects this false inference, leaving the slave somewhat abashed. But Socrates, taking the slave in tow, once again leads him through a maze of questions to the correct inference and allows him (as it were) to draw the inference for himself [Jowett & Anderson at 40 (83b–c)]. Emboldened, the slave then answers a further series of questions, which elicit the fact that he still does not understand. He may have made the correct guess when coached by Socrates, but this guess was not based on knowledge or understanding. (True belief is not the same as knowledge.) Socrates' questions get the slave to see, then, that he still does not know what he thought he knew: "Indeed, Socrates, I do not know" [Jowett & Anderson at 41 (84a)].

Anytus comes along later and joins Socrates and Meno while they are engaged, once again, in their common pursuit of the question of the nature and teachability of virtue [Jowett & Anderson at 49 (89e–90a)]. Anytus, who later plays a role in the trial of Socrates, is conveniently pressed into service, just as the slave was. But Anytus is not susceptible to Socrates' searching questions.

Socrates begins by simply asking Anytus, as a friendly bystander, for help: "Who are the teachers of virtue?" [Jowett & Anderson at 49 (90b)]. One might expect Anytus to respond warmly to Socrates' invitation, because he shares Socrates' low opinion of the sophists (who purport to be teachers of virtue), and Socrates casts his question in the form of a request—whether Anytus can help Meno find someone who can teach him (Meno) virtue [Jowett & Anderson at 50 (91a–b)]. Instead of helping Meno, however, Anytus responds by castigating the sophists; he vents his spleen: "By Heracles, Socrates, forbear! I only hope that no friend or kinsman or acquaintance of mine, whether citizen or stranger, will ever be so mad as to allow himself to be corrupted by them [the sophists]; for they are a manifest pest and corrupting influence to those who have to do with them" [Jowett & Anderson at 50–51 (91c)].

It turns out that, as advice for Meno, this invective is not worth much, because when Anytus is pressed on the matter, we discover that his criticism of the sophists is as unfounded in knowledge as was the slave's original inference. Anytus admits that he really is not well acquainted with the sophists [Jowett & Anderson at 51–52 (92b–c)]. This admission puzzles Socrates, as does the cavalier attitude toward knowledge and criticism that it reveals, and Socrates says as much [Jowett & Anderson at 52 (92b–c)]. How can Anytus claim to know that the sophists are corrupt teachers of virtue when he is not acquainted with them? But, unlike the slave, Anytus does not acknowledge his own ignorance in this matter. "I am sure that I know what manner of men these are, whether I am acquainted with them or not" [Jowett & Anderson at 52 (92c)]. Then, to cap it off, Anytus shuns Socrates' suggestion that perhaps some noted Athenians themselves do not know what virtue is, or, at least, that they have been unable to teach their children virtue. Anytus is offended by this suggestion; he finds it slanderous, and he refuses to consider it or to help Socrates investigate the matter [Jowett & Anderson at 53–54 (93c–95a)].

I have said that these three people—Meno, the slave, and Anytus—differ in their cast of mind, their attitude toward learning and education. Part of their difference is their motivation: Meno *wants* to know, he *wants* to learn. The dialogue begins with his querying Socrates, and in a sense Meno's question about virtue is the motivating one of the *Meno*. The fact that Meno does not know how to pursue it on his own, is less important than the fact that the question is his own, that he came up with it by harkening to some doubt or quibble in himself. Is this not what we hope to teach our students to do by way of Socratic questioning—how to pursue their own questions, how to make the most of them?

Meno's ignorance is a part of what Socrates brings out in the first few pages of the dialogue. He shows Meno not only that he (Meno) does not have an acceptable answer to his own question, but, more important, Socrates also demonstrates that Meno does not *realize* this fact about himself when he puts his question to Socrates. This may be one reason why Socrates refuses the question about virtue as it is originally put to him by Meno. He does not refuse the topic of virtue, but he does refuse the tone of Meno's question, the attitude or manner in which it is asked.

Socrates' refusal is as positive a lesson as it is negative, because this refusal leads to a concerted investigation into the nature and teachability of virtue. It does so only, however, insofar as Meno is willing to take up these matters with an attitude that Socrates finds proper. This may strike some people as being hopelessly paternalistic of Socrates, but I take it to be an essential element of what we might call "teaching." Teaching requires that a student be able to participate with the teacher, to see or take or accept what the teacher says as significant, valuable, worthwhile. It also requires a willingness and an ability on the part of the teacher to say, "This is proper; that is not." And the teacher must also be able to show its propriety, to demonstrate it, in his or her actions, to the satisfaction of the student.[5]

Accepting the responsibility for conveying a sense of propriety—in the questions one asks, in the ways in which one pursues them, in the answers that one finds acceptable or satisfying—is essential in teaching.[6] Meno's education in this dialogue consists in the fact that he learns to seek as Socrates seeks, he learns to inquire as Socrates inquires. And yet, paradoxically, learning to follow is learning to lead, or to strike out on one's own. Learning may begin from imitation or emulation; but initiation turns into membership, and with membership comes mastery, and therewith autonomy. This process of growth through the accretion of mastery is the means by which we learn how to go on in our own way.

(I have no explanation for this human phenomenon. I doubt that anyone can explain how or why learning to share the meaning of one's materials or one's medium is a precursor to learning to listen to oneself and to make meaning on one's own. Still, this is what seems to happen among human beings.) Socrates ultimately leaves Meno on his own, to inquire for himself as to these matters that are puzzling him [see Jowett & Anderson at 61 (100b–c)].

While Socrates refuses Meno's opening question as it is initially presented to him, it is equally true that he also shows Meno another way to put the question. He demonstrates for Meno a way to translate his question, a way to understand it, such that Meno's question can be fruitfully followed out and investigated (if not exactly to an answer, then at least to a conclusion). And, despite several setbacks and even reprimands from Socrates, Meno never totally gives up, never leaves the discussion. Certainly, he is daunted by some of Socrates' methods and his tough questions. Often, Meno does not know what to say in response to Socrates, or what to do when the two men find themselves at one of the many impasses they reach in their inquiry into virtue. But then, neither does Socrates always know what to say or do. The point remains that Meno never quits; he perseveres.

Anytus, on the other hand, does not want to know about virtue, and he essentially refuses to listen to whatever Socrates has to say. Eventually, Anytus leaves in a huff over what he imagines to have been Socrates' defamation of some of the famous men and important families of Athens [Jowett & Anderson at 55 (95a)]. (Plato seems here to be relying upon his original audience's presumed knowledge of Anytus' later role in the trial against Socrates, where Anytus presented to the jury the charges leveled by the politicians against Socrates.)[7] Anytus never shows himself to be open to Socrates' questions. Indeed, Socrates' concerns about the possibility of teaching virtue (or about the nature of virtue) leave Anytus cold. He has nothing to do with them.

Furthermore, Anytus has no questions of his own. He hates the sophists with a passion, perhaps a passion as great as Socrates' disdain for them. But Anytus' passion is based on no knowledge, no experience, no acquaintance with the sophists. Anytus knows what he thinks, but not why he thinks as he does; and he seems not to be curious about the "whys" and "wherefores" of his opinions. He has his prejudices, but no inclination to investigate them. With such a student, nothing works; a teacher can do nothing with him. Yet, what if this gap between teacher and student is the fault of the teacher?[8] Then the question becomes whether another teacher can do a better job of inspiring or provoking the student. While this seems at most a faint possibility here, it remains the case that at the very end of the dialogue, Socrates implores Meno (now that he has acquired Socrates' way of inquiring into these matters) to seek out Anytus, so as to try to awaken him to these same questions and concerns [Jowett & Anderson at 61 (100b–c)]. Perhaps Meno can do what Socrates was unable to do.

The slave,[9] situated in the middle of the dialogue, also splits the difference between Meno and Anytus along this typology of students. Meno's slave is neither like his master in initiating any inquiry with Socrates, in wanting to know, nor is he akin to Anytus in not wanting to know. Rather, the slave is like Anytus in his initial passiveness, his self-satisfaction with his state of knowledge, even if it turns out to be a state of ignorance. And yet, the slave is also like Meno in that, once he is provoked by Socrates' questions, he is willing to learn. Thus, the slave starts in a passive mode and then changes into an active learner, an active seeker. If Meno can be said to want to know, and Anytus not to want to know, then the slave can be said to be open to the possible acquisition of knowledge, although he does not know how to begin.

If the slave can be provoked, and Meno can be taught, and Anytus cannot be taught, this range of students suggests another important difference among these three types: their relative receptivity to Socratic questioning. As for Meno, even though he thinks that he knows, he is able to recognize from his inept responses that he does not know, or at least that he needs to be taught. Meno is receptive to Socrates' questions, although it takes him a while to get their drift. (This is shown in a later sequence of exchanges in the dialogue, to which we will return.) With regard to the slave, he does not necessarily think in the beginning that he knows at all; he is quite shy and hesitant in Socrates' presence. But Socrates manages to draw him out, and gradually the slave gains enough confidence to venture an opinion that he claims is based on knowledge, which claim is then shown to be wrong. Dashed, the slave retreats into silence. But he can still be reached by Socrates, who once more by careful questioning draws out the slave and leads him to the correct answer.

Whatever knowledge is gained by Meno and the slave, then, is due not only to Socrates' estimable art of asking the right questions, but also to Meno's and the slave's receptivity. These two students merit praise for their willingness to entertain questions. Meno is the central study here, of course, and his perseverance in the face of Socrates' sustained criticism deserves credit. But the slave deserves some credit too. He may not be a self-starter in the way that Meno seems to be; but, nonetheless, he steadily faces Socrates' relentless questioning and continues to volunteer answers, even when they are offered with trepidation.

Compared either to Meno or to the slave, Anytus is unreceptive to Socrates' questions. It is not that Anytus rejects them out of hand, or that he refuses to listen, because initially he participates with Socrates. But even Anytus' initial responses seem perfunctory [see Jowett & Anderson at 49–50 (90c–91b)]. And after Socrates scorns Anytus' criticism of the sophists (as being unfounded in knowledge), and Socrates then begins to question him as to the ability of important Athenians to teach their children to be virtuous, Anytus becomes churlish. He finds such questions scandalous, an affront to the good families of Athens [Jowett & Anderson at 52–54 (92c–95a)]. He is not receptive to Socratic questions, or to inquiry, or to learning. An unexamined life is just fine with Anytus.

When Two Go Together: Socratic Conversational Inquiry

We have seen how Meno, Meno's slave, and Anytus are differently situated in terms of their ability or willingness to learn, and in terms of how they relate to Socrates. It might also be said, however, that insofar as Socrates tries (with varying degrees of success) to teach these three students how to inquire into matters that they may find puzzling, he is offering them a method of conversational inquiry. In this respect, the *Meno* not only portrays Meno's growth or education, but it also illustrates a method for investigating philosophically a person's concerns, interests, experiences, doubts, and confusions. Earlier in this chapter, I gave a synoptic outline that emphasizes the side of the *Meno* that involves the education of the three types of student. A slightly different outline of the dialogue could be given, however, one that characterizes the movement of the *Meno* in terms of the series of stages in the method of Socratic conversational inquiry. These stages are the following:

- The Ethos of Asking and Answering [pp. 23–31 (70a–76e)]
- We Discover Our Own Ignorance—and Disillusion Ensues [pp. 31–36 (77a–80d)]
- How Is Inquiry into the Unknown Possible? We Must "Re-Collect" Our Knowledge and Use It as Our Guide [pp. 36–45 (80d–86c)]
- A Renewal of the Search, a Renewal of Inquiry [pp. 45–49 (86c–89e)]
- When A Student Does Not Wish to Inquire [pp. 49–55 (90a–95a)]
- Back to the Initial Question: Can Virtue Be Taught? [pp. 55–61 (95a–100b)]

If I am right in thinking that the *Meno* sketches some of the stages in Socrates' way of proceeding, then I would like to examine more closely the sites along the way.

Socrates' way of inquiring into a question requires two or more people to talk with one another. It requires them to share their thoughts and ideas, their words and claims, always trying to express things to their own satisfaction and to the satisfaction of the other person involved in the conversation—and, also, always trying to reveal what they truly believe. In my chapter devoted to the *Protagoras,* I said that Socrates, in his conversational inquiries, typically tests or examines both a person and that person's assertion of knowledge or beliefs. This inquiry seems to be an attempt to understand who the person is (the one who is being examined or tested), and to determine what the proposition (assertion, belief) means, and whether it is true or not. So Socrates' method provides us with the means by which we may get to know both a *person* and a *proposition.*

First. As to our learning about a person: During this intense conversational process, each participant is urged to be candid. As Socrates remarks once to the slave, "Very good; I like to hear you say what you think" [Jowett & Anderson at 40 (83d)]. Why is it so important to Socrates that each participant should say what he or she truly thinks or believes? Some of Socrates' interlocutors do not get it. The sophist Thrasymachus, for example, does not get the point of their candid exchange of views. (He is the person mainly engaged with Socrates in investigating the nature of justice in Book I of the *Republic,* which is the only portion of that long text that portrays Socrates in anything like his typical manner of proceeding conversationally.) During their conversation in Book I, Socrates says: "Nevertheless, we mustn't shrink from pursuing the argument and looking into this, just as long as I take you to be saying what you really think. And I believe that you aren't joking now, Thrasymachus, but are saying what you believe to be the truth." His caustic response to Socrates is: "What difference does it make to you, whether *I* believe it or not? It's *my account* you're supposed to be refuting."[10]

It is true that Socrates does wish to test the validity of Thrasymachus' account of justice, namely, his argument that justice is whatever is in the best interests of the rulers or the powerful people in the *polis*. But, simultaneously, Socrates is interested in examining Thrasymachus himself, and Thrasymachus seems not to realize this. (Or else, Thrasymachus is in denial, trying desperately to save face, ignoring the extent to which he feels himself coming under the uncomfortable scrutiny of an uncompromising judge [Socrates] and jury [Polemarchus and the others who constitute the audience in the *Republic*].) The person making the assertion under examination, having committed himself to articulating this view, must suffer the consequences of what he has said.

But this is not all; there remain additional reasons why Socrates insists upon his conversational partners being candid. In chapter 1, we already looked at the Socratic injunction to "say what you believe," as Gregory Vlastos put it, and again in chapter 2 in conjunction with our reading of the *Protagoras*. Here I shall simply reiterate one of the points made earlier in those two places, namely, that a candid or honest rehearsal of what one thinks or believes is necessary if we truly are to rely upon each participant in the conversation as an equal source of data. As I phrased it in the *Protagoras* chapter, candid or honest recountings of what we think or believe ensure that the data on which we base our conversation are not false or falsified.

There is yet another reason, I believe, for Socrates' repeated insistence that participants be candid in these conversations, a reason that goes beyond the need to collect unfalsified data from each member. It is that the basis of the conversation is friendship. Normally, friends are supposed to tell the truth to one another. Here, in the context of a Socratic inquiry, if we truly are to learn about ourselves and those others who submit themselves to critical scrutiny, we need the sincere help of our friends. Stanley Cavell says, in this regard, that the Socratic "imperative to conversation is meant to capture the sense that . . . we still do not know what 'position' we occupy in society, [and] who we have turned out to be, . . . To know such things is to have a perspective on our lives, on the way we live, and this is precisely the province of what I call, of what interests me in, moral perfectionism. The idea of conversation expresses my sense that one cannot achieve this perspective alone, but only in the mirroring or confrontation of what Aristotle calls the friend."[11] In coming to know ourselves, we require a conversational partner who is willing to volunteer candid insights and opinions, to tell us the truth as he or she sees it.

In two respects—our relationship with the other person engaged in our conversation, and the nature of the context in which our conversation takes place—Cavell articulates further what is involved in the emphasis that Socratic conversational inquiry places on friendship. Initially, he confirms that in coming to make ourselves intelligible, in examining ourselves and our lives, we all need the helpful "perception" or perceptiveness of a friendly critic. Alone, we cannot see what needs to be done. "[T]he aim of moral reasoning in [moral] perfectionism [is] not to assess pluses and minuses of advantage, nor to assess whether the act is recommendable universally, but . . . namely that the one in question make himself intelligible, to others and to himself. Perfectionism concentrates on this moment. . . . [I]t proposes that such muddles essentially stand in need of the perception of a friend . . . [and] it underscores that for one to confront another with her confusion, especially when she has not asked for advice, requires the justification of one's moral standing with her."[12] The person with whom we engage in serious Socratic conversation should have a certain standing with us. A person with such standing is someone to whom we are apt to reveal ourselves in conversation, and to whom we are apt to listen if we are offered candid advice or criticism.

Next, Cavell notes that confronting a person placed under Socratic scrutiny requires a friendly context; otherwise, again, this type of confrontation could not and would not take place. Who would speak up within a conversation where each participant is undergoing inspection, unless each person feels confident that the examination is taking place within friendly confines? Along both these lines, Cavell himself appeals to an example from Socrates: "Socrates' mode is important. He is clearly in disagreement with Euthyphro, as he is discussing disagreement, and I like the notation of his credibly affirming, in that circumstance, friendship with Euthyphro ('What kind of disagreement, my friend, causes hatred and anger?'). The implication is that there the context of moral argument or reasoning, one in which there is a willingness to understand and to be understood, may be difficult to maintain."[13] The Socratic claim, then, seems to come to this: Only in a friendly context are we apt to gain perceptive help with learning, or, in other words (taken from the *Protagoras*), with caring for our soul.

This is one reason why I adduced in chapter 1, in characterizing Socrates' method of inquiry, comments from Gregory Vlastos (calling it a method of moral inquiry) and from Alexander Nehamas (describing it as a method for caring for the self or soul). Socrates' critical attention to the individual person could not take place—it would not work, and it would not be possible—were his conversational inquiry not undertaken within some friendly spirit of camaraderie and good fellowship. Even within such a spirit, it is difficult to induce someone to submit to critical scrutiny and personal examination (witness Protagoras' antipathy toward the Socratic process).

In addition, there is an example in the *Meno* of the importance of the moral "standing" that exists between friends when they are engaged in conversational examination. In response to a question from Meno, Socrates expresses his sense of their friendly engagement in terms of his standing vis-à-vis Meno. Socrates has just given an explanation of what a figure is, and this explanation leaves Meno questioning how enlightening Socrates' explanation would be to someone who truly wants to know what a figure is. Meno challenges Socrates by asking, "[W]hat sort of an answer would you have given him?" Socrates responds: "I should have told him the truth. And if he were a philosopher of the eristic and antagonistic sort, I should say to him: You have my answer, and if I am wrong, your business is to take up the argument and refute me. But if we were friends, and were talking as you and I are now, I should reply in a milder strain and more in the dialectician's vein; that is to say, I should not only speak the truth, but I should make use of the premises which the person interrogated would be willing to admit. And this is the way in which I shall endeavor to approach you" [Jowett & Anderson at 29–30 (75c–d)]. Socrates and Meno are friends (or, Socrates is treating Meno as a friend), and their dialectical conversation proceeds on the basis of this understanding. Their confrontation would not prove fruitful if Socrates tried to "approach" or confront Meno on a less friendly, more antagonistic basis.

This is not to say that Socrates is always and everywhere friendly toward his interlocutors. In the *Gorgias,* while his exchanges with Gorgias are relatively polite and respectful, Socrates' ensuing remarks directed toward Polus, and his later dispute with Callicles, both degenerate into acerbic exchanges.[14] Similarly, in the *Republic,* Thrasymachus basically calls Socrates a liar, a cheat, and a thief—someone, at a minimum, who is duplicitous—and Socrates returns the insult. And, as we have seen, even in Socrates' discussions with Protagoras, their initially friendly conversation gradually deteriorates into fairly open rancor.

These examples from other dialogues make the point that Socratic inquiry is normally meant to take place on the basis of friendship or, at least, of friendly relations. Look again at what happens in the three dialogues I have just mentioned. We said in chapter 2 that Protagoras becomes passive and withdrawn in the second half of the *Protagoras.* In the *Gorgias,* the conversation peters out and Socrates closes the dialogue with a five-page monologue. And, in the *Republic,* at the end of Book I, Thrasymachus leaves the discussion in anger and disgust. So, without friendliness as a basis, Socratic conversational inquiry can deteriorate and eventually break down.

The basic idea of Socratic inquiry is that we are submitting ourselves to examination and criticism (that is, our lives are being subjected to a conscientious effort at critical understanding). This submission of oneself for inspection is daunting. One reason why someone might be willing to undertake such a harrowing experience is that he or she trusts the person with whom he or she is engaging in such an experimental trial. Socrates seeks to earn our trust, or at least to enlist our trust, when he presents himself (as he does in the *Protagoras*) as a "physician of the soul." Equally compelling, in this regard, is the later self-image by means of which Socrates presents himself in the *Theaetetus,* namely, as a "midwife"—again, someone who is a caregiver, someone who is there to succor us during the pains of conversational delivery.

Second. As to our learning about a proposition (that is, a claim of knowledge, or the expression of a belief, or the assertion of an opinion): Socrates' method of inquiry is shared inquiry. It does not work alone; instead, it is meant to work in conversation with someone. Socrates emphasizes this aspect of his inquiry several times throughout the dialogue. For example, he discreetly but firmly draws Meno's attention to the fact that their investigation is a shared effort when he says, "I have no objection to join with you in the inquiry" [Jowett & Anderson at 36 (80d)]. Or, again, Socrates gently reminds Meno of what they are about when he asks, "[S]hall you and I make an effort to inquire together into the nature of virtue?" [Jowett & Anderson at 45 (86c)]

The same is true of Socrates' effort in talking with Meno's slave. "Mark now the further development. I shall only ask him, and not teach him, and he shall share the inquiry with me" [Jowett & Anderson at 42 (84c–d)]. Socrates' discussion with Meno's slave would not work (because it would not demonstrate what Socrates wants to show Meno, and because it would not be educative for the slave), were it not shared by both of them. No self-knowledge would be gained if the expressions investigated did not reveal or disclose the self embodied in the words. Nor could there be refutation, or inconsistency, if the self were not committed to its words, or if the self did not express them candidly.

By having us talk together, Socrates throws us back on ourselves as sources of data and information, of conflict and argument, of thought and judgment. As we have previously seen (in the epigraph to chapter 1), Cavell traces this gesture of self-reliance back to Socrates' response to the Delphic oracle. When the oracle said, "No one is wiser than Socrates," Cavell reminds us that Socrates understood this to mean that he (Socrates) knew that he did not know. What Cavell finds important about this insight, is that there are two complementary inferences to be drawn from Socrates' realization of his own ignorance. First, no one is wiser than we are. No one is in a better position than we are to learn what we wish to learn. Second, and similarly, we are no wiser than anyone else. Our position, even if no worse than anyone else's, also is no better than anyone else's. As to the matters that bother us philosophically, our positions are the same. We are equally ignorant and equally enabled.

According to Cavell, as quoted earlier,

> No man is in any better position for knowing it than any other man—unless *wanting* to know is a special position. And this discovery about himself is the same as the discovery of philosophy, when it is the effort to find answers, and permit questions, which nobody knows the way to nor the answer to any better than you yourself.[15]

> [I]t is a claim that no one knows better than you whether and when a thing is said, and if this is not to be taken as a claim to expertise (a way of taking it which repudiates it) then it must be understood to mean that you know no better than others what you claim to know. With respect to the data of philosophy our positions are the same. This is scarcely a discovery of ordinary language philosophy; it is the latest confirmation of what the oracle said to Socrates.[16]

This philosophical claim complements or completes the earlier lesson of the Socratic method of inquiry, that of the necessary condition of conversational friendship. We need others, to be sure, for what they can do insofar as they confront us as friends. But we also need others because of what they can tell us, for what their testimony can add to the conversation. Since each participant in the conversation is to be treated as an independent and equal source of philosophical data, their data are as valuable and as necessary as our own. They complement us, and our world, which is the common world.[17]

Socrates works together with others because he realizes that, in philosophy, our positions are the same. Or, rather, he realizes that none of us has any special or privileged position from which to speak, from which to prosecute philosophical problems. Such problems include wondering whether we can know anything about the world, or about other people, or about ourselves; whether life is a dream or a nightmare; whether we can discern the difference between good and evil, right and wrong; whether there is such a thing as God; and whether the human soul is immortal, or whether the human spirit dies with the death of the body. These thoughts and concerns are (as, in the epigraph to this chapter, Cavell reminds us) "things that ordinary human beings cannot help thinking about, or anyway cannot help having occur to them, sometimes in fantasy, sometimes as a flash across a landscape"—things that we occasionally find ourselves mulling over in our minds. These questions concern matters that constitute our ordinary human lives and existences; they constitute the human world or the ordinary world, of which we are a part. Again, to cite Cavell, "the ordinary world . . . may not be all there is, but it is important enough: morality is in that world, and so are force and love; so is art and a part of knowledge (the part which is about that world); and so is religion (wherever God is). Some mathematics and science, no doubt, are not."[18]

The ordinary world of our experience is composed of our ordinary thoughts about ordinary things. Or, as G. M. Young was fond of saying, following Frederic William Maitland, in the humanities—such fields as history, law, and philosophy—our work is a function of our ability to recover and study our "common thought about common things."[19] And other people—their views, their minds, their experiences—are as much a source of knowledge and information about these matters as we are. Thus, these are matters about which we can come to agreement, or about which we can discover ourselves to be in disagreement. But they remain matters about which all of us are equally cognizant, equally capable of reflecting on and discussing. Hence, we are both sources of data (advocates, or testifying witnesses) and adjudicators of sense (jurors, or judges).

I mentioned this perspective back in chapter 2, when we were considering the moment in the *Protagoras* when the conversation or debate between Socrates and Protagoras seemed to be breaking down. There, Socrates rejected the proposal by others that the group should seek a referee. Instead, he asked all of the men gathered together to serve as peers, with an equal claim to speak about virtue and teaching and what might be proper nourishment to feed the human soul. Then, too, in an aside to Glaucon during the argument in the *Republic,* Socrates appeals to this very fact of our bifurcated status as participants and adjudicators: "But if, on the other hand, we investigate the question, as we've been doing, by seeking agreement with each other, we ourselves can be both jury and advocates at once."[20] By conversing with one another and asking each other questions, seeking agreement but not fearing disagreement, we truly treat one another as equal sources of judgment and value.

What we wish to learn about in Socratic conversational inquiry is something common to all of us, and in this respect it is something that we share (or that we are capable of sharing). It is a part of our common inheritance as human beings. The specific topic for philosophical attention, for Socratic inquiry, makes little difference; what matters is that the topic is of genuine interest or puzzlement to those of us engaged in the conversational inquiry. In the *Meno,* the inquiry happens to focus upon the nature and the attributes of virtue: what it is, how human beings gain or lose or exemplify it, how it can be transmitted between generations, and so forth. But the question pursued by Socrates might just as easily be the nature and extent of our knowledge; or what piety is and how we act piously or impiously; or what human courage amounts to; or how we become wise and what value or utility human wisdom has for us; or what the nature of happiness is; or how power is a part of human life and society and the ways in which it can be distinguished from justice or law; or any of a number of other topics of inquiry. All of these may be said to name philosophical topics; but they are topics of philosophical thought and discussion because they are common concerns about which we humans periodically and unpredictably come to be struck, confused, intrigued, or puzzled. And then, typically, we humans say something.

Our expressions reveal us; they reveal our interests.[21] Our questions, our doubts, our concerns, our desires, our interests—we express these in words. Perhaps we pose a question, or make a claim, or express a belief, or state an opinion—and someone else wants to know why we think as we do, or what makes us believe what we say we believe. Then a joint Socratic search, a shared journey, is off and running, because a conversational inquiry has begun. And we come to learn not only about the person who made the claim or the assertion under investigation, but also about the claim or the assertion itself. That is, we learn something about the proposition being investigated. And a part of what interests us, in this regard, is the very fact that someone would find this claim or assertion worth making, just here, just now, in the conversation.

I find another similarity between this aspect of Socratic conversational inquiry and "ordinary language philosophy" as exemplified in Cavell's work. Cavell gives the following account of proceeding by means of examining our ordinary expressions:

> I should like to add that identical problems arise in considering the phenomenon of ordinary language philosophy: there the problem is also raised of determining the data from which philosophy proceeds and to which it appeals, and specifically the issue is one of placing the words and experiences with which philosophers have always begun in alignment with human beings in particular circumstances who can be imagined to be having those experiences and saying and meaning those words. This is all that "ordinary" in the phrase "ordinary language philosophy" means, or ought to mean. It does not refer to particular words of wide use, or to particular sorts of men. It reminds us that whatever words are said and meant are said and meant by particular men, and that to understand what they (the words) mean you must understand what they (whoever is using them) mean, and that sometimes men do not see what they mean, that usually they cannot say what they mean, that for various reasons they may not know what they mean, and that when they are forced to recognize this they feel they do not, and perhaps cannot, mean anything, and they are struck dumb.[22]

Being struck dumb, in Cavell's terms, is what Socrates does to people in conversation, when by means of *elenchus* he refutes them, using their own words against themselves. It is the aporetic moment.

In Socratic conversational inquiry, a part of the work of ordinary language philosophy, to which Cavell alludes, already has been done for us through the artistry of Plato. In Plato's dialogues, we already have the "placing [of] the words and experiences with which philosophers have always begun in alignment with human beings in particular circumstances who can be imagined to be having those experiences and saying and meaning those words." In the terms given the speakers by Plato, and in the circumstances in which he has situated those speakers, his dialogues show us ordinary people speaking and acting and thinking in philosophically interesting and provocative ways. If we find these constructions credible, we then witness the drama of our own words coming back to haunt us. As arranged by Plato, and as exemplified in Socrates' elenctic conversations, such drama poses the question: Do we abandon our words? Or, instead, do we leave behind our unexamined lives as we have led them up to now?

In such a context, no one of us is better situated or equipped than anyone else. What we wish to know is exactly something about the human condition as such, our common inheritance. This is one reason why Socrates denies himself to no one.[23] If someone approaches him and asks him a question, this questioner has Socrates' attention. And this also seems to be why he takes his interlocutors when, where, and as he finds them.[24] Yes, Socrates wants to make them better (more acute, more sensitive to the contents and limits of their lives); yes, he wishes to educate them in the ways of his method of inquiry. But, still, he begins with the humble feeling that he can learn from anyone, from everyone. He can. We can too, and we can learn how from Socrates.

Learning to Inquire: Begin with Questions, Seek Definitive Answers

In my second outline of the *Meno,* the first stage is where Socrates tries to teach Meno how to ask and answer questions about virtue. Even when Meno seems to get the hang of the technique, he does not leave the scene, because he still is required by Socrates to give a definition of virtue. This is the second stage in Socratic inquiry. And here, Meno once again fails: he does not manage to give an acceptable definition. When Meno proves unable to do this—although Socrates has already shown him how to do so—he sinks into disillusion. This is the third stage in the process. Socrates then turns to Meno's slave ("Boy" in the dialogue), and takes him through the same process of disillusion. But the Socratic process of conversational inquiry does not stop at disillusion. Rather, having shown the slave that he does not know what he thinks he knows, Socrates proceeds to show him that he does still know enough to enable him (the slave) to answer some questions about arithmetic and geometric figures. And this teaches a lesson to Meno as well, not only because he is an onlooker at this Socratic demonstration, but, more important, because he has been revealed (to himself and to others) to be in the same position as his slave. They both must learn to inquire into the matters puzzling or confounding them, and their inquiry must come from positions in which they have had to admit their own ignorance:

> *Meno:* . . . For my soul and my tongue are really torpid, and I do not know how to answer you. [Jowett & Anderson at 35–36 (80b)]

> *Boy:* Indeed, Socrates, I do not know. [Jowett & Anderson at 41 (84a)]

Meno begins in a state of ignorance, trebled because he is (1) ignorant as to Socrates' method of asking questions; (2) ignorant as to the nature of virtue itself; and (3) ignorant as to his own ignorance about these matters. Meno's main problem is the third point; he does not realize that he is ignorant, so Socrates must make this apparent to him. As Meno's consciousness of his ignorance increases, so too does his receptivity to Socrates' questions—that is, to the doubt that they express. He entertains them more even if he finds himself less able to answer them.

Initially, it appears that Meno refuses Socrates' implicit offer of instruction, because he cannot grasp Socrates' way of asking and answering questions. So, even if Meno wants to learn, it is not at all clear that he shall be able to learn from Socrates. It seems more clear, in fact, that Meno cannot learn from Socrates, because his fumbling answers come to nothing. In contrast, even though Meno's slave does not signal any initial desire to learn, he still shows himself capable of joining in the inquiry with Socrates. (In fairness to Meno, however, it might be said that Socrates' questions put to Meno, about the nature of virtue, are a good deal more difficult than those put to the slave.) As I suggested earlier, "wanting to learn" must also be supplemented with "receptivity," an openness to one's own doubts. We then may ask: In what does Meno's receptivity consist? How does he manage to join together with Socrates to gain an education?

Meno opens the dialogue by asking how virtue is acquired. Socrates suggests that Meno begins with the wrong question. In his opening exchange with Meno [see Jowett & Anderson at 23–24 (70a–71b)], Socrates claims that in order to know the attributes of anything ("quale"), one first must know its nature or essence ("quid") [Jowett & Anderson at 24 (71b)].[25] So the primary question is not how virtue is learned or acquired, but rather what virtue is. Socrates' advice is: Put first things first. It seems possible to question the wisdom of proceeding as Socrates advises, in part because it is not clear how we can determine the essence of an object or of a phenomenon without also determining or knowing its attributes or qualities. So Meno's inquiry into one of the attributes of virtue (how we learn or acquire it) might well make sense to pursue; at least, I do not think that, in the abstract, we can rule it out ab initio.

But we are not working in the abstract here; instead, we are working in the context of this specific dialogue. In order to make this initial question of Meno's a sensible project of inquiry, its proponent, Meno, would have to make an argument that would take account of Socrates' distinction between "quale" and "quid," and he would have to show where Socrates is wrong or misguided in his assumption that the essence of a thing must be defined before we can learn about its attributes. But Meno makes no such argument. He makes no attempt to refute or respond to Socrates' assumption because, as his responses reveal, he does not understand either Socrates' question about the nature of virtue or the assumption behind it.

Meno's opening question to Socrates assumes that both of them already know what virtue is (Socrates' "quid"), and now he is simply asking Socrates to explain one of the attributes of virtue (Socrates' "quale"), namely, is virtue gained by teaching, or is it instead a natural acquisition? Socrates sees the assumption implicit in Meno's question and tries to get Meno to see it too. He does not think that he himself knows what virtue is and, furthermore, he does not think that Meno knows either:

"And I myself, Meno, living as I do in this region of poverty, am as poor as the rest of the world, and I confess with shame that I know literally nothing about virtue; and when I do not know the 'quid' of anything, how can I know the 'quale'? . . . Not only that, my dear boy, but you may say further that I have never known of any one else who did, in my judgment" [Jowett & Anderson at 23–24 (71b–c)].

In the face of this challenge, Meno ignores the assumption implicit in Socrates' distinction between "quale" and "quid" and instead simply proclaims that both Gorgias and he know what virtue is. Socrates remains skeptical of this claim, but urges Meno to prove him wrong: "By the gods, Meno, be generous and tell me what you say that virtue is; for I shall be truly delighted to find that I have been mistaken, and that you and Gorgias do really have this knowledge, although I have been just saying that I have never found anybody who had" [Jowett & Anderson at 24 (71d)]. Meno's response to Socrates is arrogance itself: "There will be no difficulty, Socrates, in answering your question. Let us take first the virtue of a man" [Jowett & Anderson at 24 (71e)]. But Socrates rejects Meno's attempted definition, because it purports to define what virtue is in various entities, while it fails to state what virtue is in and of itself. "How fortunate I am, Meno! When I ask you for one virtue, you present me with a swarm of them, which are in your keeping" [Jowett & Anderson at 25 (72a)].

The Socratic way of inquiring philosophically into matters of common knowledge that continue to perplex us is to formulate an adequate definition of the topic in question. We do this, according to Socrates, by offering definitions of the topic at hand and then testing these definitions for their adequacy. Regardless of whether one agrees with Socrates' attempt to find an acceptable definition of the essence of virtue (and I do not agree with it), it is clear that the main point of his effort in this dialogue is to goad Meno into offering to the two of them Meno's own thoughts. Timidity in this regard is no asset. A refusal by Meno to participate (as Anytus later refuses to help) must end the inquiry. It is Meno's choice.

After Socrates' rejection of Meno's attempted definition, it dawns on Meno that perhaps he does not understand quite as much as he thinks he does about the nature of virtue. The specific doubt that Meno expresses, however, is that he does not yet fully grasp Socrates' *question:* "I am beginning to understand; but I do not as yet take hold of the question as I could wish" [Jowett & Anderson at 25 (72d)]. It takes several more passes at the question, at Socrates' challenge to Meno (to tell him what virtue is), before Meno comes to realize that he does not know how to answer. And it is only after that realization, some pages farther along, that Meno sees that perhaps he does not even know what virtue is.

Having humbled Meno, Socrates tries to show him how his questions might be answered.

> *Socrates:* . . . Could you not answer that question, Meno? I wish that you would try; the attempt will be good practice with a view to the answer about virtue.
> *Meno:* I would rather that you answer, Socrates.
> *Socrates:* Shall I indulge you?
> *Meno:* By all means.
> *Socrates:* And then you will tell me about virtue?
> *Meno:* I will.
> *Socrates:* Then I must do my best, for there is a prize to be won. [Jowett & Anderson at 29 (75a–b)]

> *Socrates:* You are outrageous, Meno, in thus plaguing a poor old man to give you an answer, when you will not take the trouble of remembering what is Gorgias' definition of virtue.
> *Meno:* When you have told me what I ask, I will tell you, Socrates. [Jowett & Anderson at 30 (76a–b)]

It is only at this point in the dialogue, a half-dozen pages into it, that Meno begins to understand that Socrates' questions are different from the one with which Meno began. He is gaining an appreciation of the precision of Socratic questioning and the elusiveness of Socratic definitions, which are what Socrates expects as useful answers.

Since Socrates seems to think that these kinds of questions can have satisfactory answers and that such answers come in the form of definitions, definitions are what he seeks from Meno, and they are the type of answer that Socrates himself tries to supply.[26] This search for definitions is opposed to the kind of answer that the sophists offer: a rhetorical flourish that tells us nothing, that only pretends to be based on knowledge or wisdom. Socrates realizes that Meno expected the original question to have an answer of the kind that Gorgias has taught Meno to anticipate. "[Gorgias] has taught you the habit of answering questions in a grand and bold style, which becomes those who know, and is the style in which he himself answers all comers" [Jowett & Anderson at 23 (70b–c)]. But for Socrates this is a mistaken expectation, because it settles for an answer that is useless or uninformative.

The difference between Socrates' way of answering and Gorgias' way of answering is illustrated when Socrates offers Meno a definition of "what figure [or shape] is" [Jowett & Anderson at 29 (75b)]. Meno finds Socrates' definition ludicrously simple, lacking profundity or philosophical seriousness. This is a part of Meno's ignorance, however, as Socrates goes on to show him. When Socrates proposes a different answer to the question, "What is figure?" (an answer formulated in the style of Gorgias), Meno shouts his approval: "That, Socrates, appears to me to be an admirable answer" [Jowett & Anderson at 31 (76d)]. But Socrates denies the worth of this answer. It may be comforting to Meno, but that is because it fits his preconception of what such an answer should look or sound like. That is why Meno accepts it, not because it is true or useful.

> *Socrates:* The answer, Meno, was in the orthodox solemn vein, and therefore was more acceptable to you than the other answer [that Socrates offered] about figure.
>
> *Meno:* Yes.
>
> *Socrates:* And yet, . . . I cannot help thinking that the other [answer] was the better; and I am sure that you would be of the same opinion if you would only stay and be initiated, and were not compelled, as you said yesterday, to go away before the mysteries. [Jowett & Anderson at 31 (76e)]

The surprise is that Meno does stay, and he is initiated into the intricacies of the Socratic method. It is a method that depends, at one and the same time, on disillusion and something else again.

First Comes Disillusion: Meno and Meno's Slave

The first twenty pages of the *Meno* trace a deepening puzzlement on the part of Meno, as he is initiated into the intricacies of Socratic questioning. This puzzlement eventuates in Meno's disillusion. But Socrates does not end his teaching there. He goes on, rather, to duplicate this disillusion in Meno's slave, and then he further shows both Meno and the slave a way out of their disillusion, by means of their own knowledge and know-how. And this last lesson entails the same moral as the first lesson, namely, that we all—the high, the low, and the middle—share this aspect of the human condition. So, both the disillusion and the know-how shared by Meno and the slave simultaneously name human threats and human promises: they negatively threaten us with all of the problems associated with human limitation and failure, and yet they also positively promise us the powers associated with human possibility and capacity. How are we to negotiate this treacherous terrain? Socrates manages this task by inquiring into these matters in the company of another.

When two go together in the course of Socratic conversational inquiry, we find out that they share, basically, their ignorance and an ability to overcome it, an ability to learn whatever they may need to know. It is the peculiar genius of many of the dialogues of Plato that, as we have seen, they teach two interrelated lessons about human ignorance and limitation:

- You do not know what you think you know.
- You know more (or other) than what you think (you know).

The first is a lesson in disillusion, as I understand it, because it typically concerns a matter about which we all seemingly know, or should know. How is it that we do not in fact know—as Socrates keeps showing us, and then reminding us—something that we think we should (or do) know? It is disillusioning to confront such a question. But the other side of Socrates' teaching is that, given an awareness of our ignorance, we also must acknowledge that we do know more (or other) than what we think we know. So there is hope for us yet; and this I take to be Socrates' second lesson, the "something else" that he offers us.

Let us begin with the first lesson that Socrates teaches: we do not know what we think we know. I said that this discovery leads to disillusion. It is disillusioning to discover that something that we think we know and perhaps even think to be a matter of common knowledge—an epistemological possession that we share in common—is, in fact, something that we do not know at all. Typically, Socrates orchestrates this insight by claiming not to know about a given phenomenon, whereas his interlocutor or student claims to know all about it. Then, when Socrates shows his interlocutor that he (the interlocutor) does not know any more or any better than Socrates himself, the two of them are reduced to the same status, namely, that of not knowing. They have achieved Socratic ignorance. Thus, the operative Socratic insight is that we all start from the same, equal position of ignorance.

But the Socratic position for the initiation of inquiry is not only one of *not knowing,* but also one of *wanting to know.* So, for example, when Meno begins by asking Socrates a question about an attribute of virtue, Meno suggests that he knows what virtue is. And when Socrates ends his response by saying that neither he nor anyone else that he has ever met knows what virtue is, this astonishes Meno. But when his efforts to disprove Socrates are all rejected, with what appear to Meno's satisfaction to be good reasons for rejection, this shakes Meno's confidence. It is meant to do so, of course, because Socrates is trying to show him that Meno's confidence in his own knowledge is misplaced. By asking Meno apparently simple and straightforward questions that he is unable to answer—questions that Meno himself feels to be fair—Socrates reveals to Meno his own confusion and perplexity. Meno thought that he knew what virtue was, but it turns out that he did not.

The maxim found at the Delphic oracle, "Know thyself," is more complicated to apply in practice than we might believe.[27] As to Meno, Socrates' insistence on the idea that any object or phenomenon has a definitive nature or essence, and that we must be able to state a definition of that nature or essence if we claim to know what it is, is the means by which Meno's arrogance is crushed: "Why, did I not ask you to tell me the nature of virtue as a whole? And you are very far from telling me this, but declare every action to be virtue which is done with a part of virtue, as though you had told me and I must already know the whole of virtue, and this, too, when frittered away into little pieces. And, therefore, my dear Meno, I fear that I must begin again and repeat the same question: What is virtue?" [Jowett & Anderson at 35 (79d–e)].

Meno's continued claim to know the nature of virtue, and yet his continued inability to articulate a definition that satisfies either Socrates or himself, one that holds up under their combined critical inspection, disillusions him. His frustration and disillusion are expressed in this way:

> *Socrates:* Then begin again, and answer me. What, according to you and your friend Gorgias, is the definition of virtue?
>
> *Meno:* O Socrates, I used to be told, before I knew you, that you were always doubting yourself and making others doubt; and now you are casting your spells over me, and I am simply getting bewitched and enchanted, and am at my wit's end. And if I may venture to make a jest upon you, you seem to me both in your appearance and in your power over others to be very like the flat torpedo fish, who torpifies [stuns, numbs] those who come near him and touch him, as you have now torpified me, I think. For my soul and my tongue are really torpid, and I do not know how to answer you; and though I have been delivered of an infinite variety of speeches [by the sophists] about virtue before now, and to many persons—and very good ones they were, as I thought—at this moment I cannot even say what virtue is. [Jowett & Anderson at 35–36 (79e–80b)]

Meno's word for having reached this aporetic moment (and subsequent disillusion) is "torpification,"[28] which is unusual, but I think that one can see the kind of experience that he is trying to capture. He feels as though Socrates has cast a spell over him; he is at his wit's end, he is too numb to think or speak. His self-assurance is gone, and he is full of doubt.

This makes two of them. In stating that he now doubts whether he knows what virtue is, Meno has only arrived at the same position of ignorance already reached and acknowledged by Socrates at the beginning of the dialogue. Socrates insists on this need to recognize one's own ignorance as the precondition to joining Meno in an inquiry into the nature of virtue. And, since Meno now shares Socrates' perplexity and his admitted ignorance on the topic of virtue, perhaps they are prepared to inquire further, together. Socrates says: "As to my being a torpedo, if the torpedo is torpid as well as the cause of torpidity [numbness, perplexity] in others, then indeed I am a torpedo, but not otherwise; for I perplex others, not because I am clear, but because I am utterly perplexed myself. And now I know not what virtue is, and you seem to be in the same case, although you did once perhaps know, before you touched me. However, I have no objection to join with you in the inquiry" [Jowett & Anderson at 36 (80c–d)]. Socrates recognizes that his and Meno's condition is a shared one. To call this condition "ignorance" is slightly misleading, because it is as much a kind of knowledge as it is a lack of knowledge. Because of the truthfulness and candor of Socrates' questioning and his willingness to admit his own ignorance, he reveals to himself and to others a perplexity that already existed but that heretofore had gone unknown or unacknowledged. Meno, for example, is now conscious of his ignorance and is able to admit it in front of others. By learning the limits of his knowledge, he has gained something valuable—he has gained knowledge about himself by learning where his knowledge ends. And it is exactly such knowledge of one's ignorance that Socrates finds empowering.

Meno's slave gains knowledge of his own ignorance by means of the same treatment from Socrates that Meno received: questioning leading to perplexity; confusion leading to the slave's tenuous claim to know something; refutation of the slave's claim leading to his disillusion. In the following, Socrates summarizes the slave's initiation into disillusion and what it has gained him:

Socrates: Do you see, Meno, what advances he [the slave] has made in his power of recollection? He did not know at first, and he does not know now, what is the side of a figure of eight feet; but then he thought that he knew, and answered confidently as if he knew, and had no difficulty; now he has a difficulty, and neither knows nor fancies that he knows.

Meno: True.

Socrates: Is he not better off in knowing his ignorance?

Meno: I think that he is.

Socrates: If we have made him doubt, and given him the "torpedo's shock," have we done him any harm?

Meno: I think not.

Socrates: We have certainly, as would seem, assisted him in some degree to the discovery of the truth; and now he will wish to remedy his ignorance, but then he would have been ready to tell all the world again and again that the double space should have a double side.

Meno: True.

Socrates: But do you suppose that he would ever have inquired into or learned what he fancied that he knew, though he was really ignorant of it, until he had fallen into perplexity under the idea that he did not know, and desired to know?

Meno: I think not, Socrates.

Socrates: Then he was the better for the torpedo's touch?

Meno: I think so. [Jowett & Anderson at 41–42 (84a–c)]

The slave would never have been moved to inquire into these matters of geometry and mathematics, had it not been for Socrates. He led the slave to confront and to acknowledge his own ignorance in such matters. It is this confrontation that generates the desire to know or the "wanting to know" that earlier I said is an essential element in making this inquiry possible, and effective. It seems that Meno and his slave find, just as Socrates does, the knowledge of their own ignorance to be empowering.

Recollection as Socrates' Response to Disillusion

If the knowledge of one's own ignorance prepares the stage for further Socratic inquiry, this is only half of the story. As I said above, Socrates offers us dual lessons, only one of which is our disillusion with our own ignorance. Disillusion is hardly apt to motivate us to inquire further—it implies despair, not invigoration, and, if left alone, it leads not to inquiry but rather to a kind of Thoreauvian "quiet desperation." For, if we prove ignorant of things that we (used to) think common knowledge, what point is there in undertaking further inquiry? What point is there in trying to improve ourselves or our knowledge, when it seems desperately out of our reach?

This is what Meno would like to know, and he makes this point after Socrates has led him to disillusion. "And how will you inquire, Socrates, into that which you do not know? What will you put forth as the subject of inquiry? And if you find what you want, how will you ever know that this is the thing which you did not know?" [Jowett & Anderson at 36 (80d)].[29] Faced with their joint perplexity, what are they to do? Meno wants to give up. How can we know what we are looking for—much less recognize it if and when we find it—when we do not know in the first place what its nature or essence is? It is this challenge from Meno that launches Socrates into his celebrated discussion with the slave.

The therapy for disillusion is recollection, according to Socrates, and his discussion with Meno's slave is frequently cited as an early expression of Plato's doctrine of "recollection." This Platonic doctrine attempts to explain how the immortal soul can first possess and then recollect knowledge that it has acquired in its earlier existence and acquaintance with the world (and with the Forms). Socrates puts it: "The soul, then, as being immortal, and having been born again many times, and having seen all things that exist, whether in this world or in the world below, has knowledge of them all; and it is no wonder that she [the soul] should be able to call to remembrance all that she ever knew about virtue and about everything; for as all nature is akin, and the soul has learned all things, there is no difficulty in her eliciting, or as men say 'learning,' out of a single recollection, all the rest, if a man is strenuous and does not faint; for all inquiry and all learning is but recollection" [Jowett & Anderson at 37 (81c–d)]. I can best make sense out of the claim that "all inquiry and all learning [are] but recollection" by understanding it as a figure of speech meant to capture the sense and extent to which our knowledge of any matter comes from the human activity of reconstructing or recapturing it from our own experience.

Socrates and his interlocutors investigate matters of common knowledge, objects or phenomena that are constituents of our ordinary experience and language: virtue, knowledge, belief, courage, wisdom, piety, power, justice, education, and so on. These matters are a part of the experience of all human beings, and our sharing them in our own experience is what makes them appropriate subjects for philosophical (and Socratic) inquiry. As to matters of common knowledge or experience, Ludwig Wittgenstein remarks: "[I]t is . . . of the essence of our investigation that we do not seek to learn anything new by it. We want to understand something that is already in plain view. For *this* is what we seem in some sense not to understand."[30] This is not the most transparent comment ever made on philosophical method, but I understand its denial of wanting to learn anything "new" to be a way of forcing us to face what we share in our experience and life. We are to engage with this common experience first, rather than always looking for something else that supposedly underlies or explains the initial phenomenon confronting us. And we are to engage with our shared human experience by means of calling to mind what we say about our experience. As Wittgenstein puts the idea, "We remind ourselves, that is to say, of the *kind of statement* that we make about phenomena."[31] This activity of inquiry, this calling to mind what we say about things, is a form of recollection. For Wittgenstein, as for Socrates, we reveal ourselves and our minds—and we betray them—in our words and in the kinds of statements that we make. In philosophical activity of this kind, we are engaged in conversational inquiry.

To the extent, then, that we pursue our interest in our experience by proceeding on the basis of ordinary language and experience (as Wittgenstein's and Socrates' philosophical activities do), looking always at what we say and feel and think as the primary data with which philosophy has to work (as, emphatically, Socratic inquiry does), we are not seeking some explanation of these data that appeals to anything outside of them or underlying them. We seek, instead, to understand the data that themselves constitute our lives, our world, our minds, our ideas and ideals. These are what we find ourselves in confusion or perplexity over. Philosophical confusion concerns what we make of our own experience and our own world, or, more typically, what we fail to make of them. And about such things we cannot stop thinking, no matter how much we may try to avoid them or to stifle our thoughts about them. Again, as Cavell reminds us in the epigraph to this chapter, "[They are] things that ordinary human beings cannot help thinking about, or anyway cannot help having occur to them, sometimes in fantasy, sometimes as a flash across a landscape." So, by means of recollection following disillusion, we want to make sense out of the very data of our consciousness or experience.

Socrates sometimes seeks additional data as well as a reorganization or reassessment of the old ones.[32] But the problem remains that we do not yet understand the data that we already have. Paradoxically, they are ours, but they are not ours. We "have" them, but we do not yet "possess" them in any clear or firm sense. What we seek in a philosophical investigation pursued in a Socratic way is a better understanding of the experiential data that we already have in hand.

In this respect, Socrates' call to remembrance, to recollect something that we already know—in the sense that we are already familiar with it, although we do not yet understand it—is a call to make ourselves aware of something. We are not yet as conscious as we should be. Such a conception of the task of philosophical activity pictures us as being in need of coming to our senses. This drive to come to understand ourselves seems to me to be central to Socratic conversational inquiry. So disillusion is understood to lead to recollection, and then recollection is meant to lead to recovery, or renewal, of a certain kind.

Working with What We Have: The Example of Meno's Slave

The slave is chosen from several attendants accompanying Meno, and his only attributes about which Socrates asks are his nativity and his native language. "He is Greek, and speaks Greek, does he not?" [Jowett & Anderson at 38 (82b)] These are all the tools that Socrates requires of him: he needs only to be a native speaker of this natural language. In the exchange between Socrates and the slave, there are at issue certain matters of basic mathematics. But, just as Socrates' method of questioning the slave is similar to that used by Socrates on Meno, the end result is similar too: the slave is refuted in his claim to know. This explicit parallel in the dialogue—between Meno's fate and the slave's fate at the hands of Socrates—seems to me intended to teach the lesson that Meno and the slave are basically in the same position, one of unconscious ignorance, of which each is made aware by means of Socrates' questions.

The exchange between Socrates and the slave begins as follows:

Socrates: Tell me, boy, do you know that a figure like this is a square?
Boy: I do.
Socrates: And you know that a square figure has these four lines equal?
Boy: Certainly.
Socrates: And these lines which I have drawn through the middle of the square are also equal?
Boy: Yes.
Socrates: A square may be of any size?
Boy: Certainly. [Jowett & Anderson at 38 (82b–c)]

This is tepid stuff, and it continues in much the same vein, except that Meno's slave gradually comes to give some answers that require a bit more calculation or thinking.

Socrates: And how many are twice two feet? Count and tell me.
Boy: Four, Socrates.
Socrates: And might there not be another square twice as large as this, and having like this the lines equal?
Boy: Yes.
Socrates: And of how many feet will that be?
Boy: Of eight feet.
Socrates: And now try and tell the length of the line which forms the side of that double square: this is two feet—what will that be?
Boy: Clearly, Socrates, it will be double.
Socrates: Do you observe, Meno, that I am not teaching the boy anything, but only asking him questions; and now he fancies that he knows how long a line is necessary in order to produce a figure of eight square feet; does he not? [Jowett & Anderson at 39 (82d–e)]

Reading this exchange, I cannot agree with Socrates' account of what is happening here: "I am not teaching the boy anything, but only asking him questions."[33] But these are what lawyers would call leading questions (the questions suggest the answers that the questioner wishes the answerer to give), and the slave replies with a few words, essentially assenting to what Socrates has said. This shows nothing about the soul's recollection of prior knowledge (and very few readers take it to do so).[34] What it does show, however, is that Socrates is teaching the slave about two different kinds of knowledge that the slave possesses without knowing it.[35]

First, Socrates is making explicit to the slave certain implications of arithmetic and geometry that follow from the slave's mathematical knowledge, as stated or expressed in the propositions that Socrates puts to him.[36] For example, when the slave says, in response to one of Socrates' formulations, "That is evident" [Jowett & Anderson at 41 (83e)], I find myself wanting to add: *Now* it is evident to you, but only because Socrates has shown you how it can be derived from the preceding propositions that he has stated. For our educational benefit, Socrates is eliciting something implicit in the mathematical knowledge that you have; but it is the teacher's act of *eliciting* these implications that makes them evident to you.

Socrates also is formulating these implications into additional mathematical propositions, to which he then asks the slave's assent. The slave gives it. But this does not show that the slave was himself capable of formulating those same propositions, even though they derived from his own knowledge. He may have recognized the truth of these propositions or implications once they were stated or formulated for him by Socrates, but this does not mean that his knowledge was enough, in itself, to enable him to *state* or to *formulate* these propositions or implications for himself. It was not; he could not do it. Whatever mathematical knowledge he possessed, it was dormant until awakened by Socrates' prompting. (Socrates' role in assisting a person to formulate that person's knowledge or beliefs arises again as a central theme in the *Theaetetus,* as I try to show in chapter 4. It involves what I call "learning to give an account of oneself," including one's words and expressions, or one's thoughts.)

Second, Socrates shows the slave how to go on with certain mathematical series (what happens when one doubles the sides of a square, and so forth). Socrates is doing this, for example, when he asks, "Try and see if you can tell me how much it [the length of a side of a square] will be" [Jowett & Anderson at 40 (83e)]. Gradually, eventually, the slave is able to generate some of his own answers to Socrates' questions. Of course, they are nothing more than basic answers to basic questions. Yet the slave is provoked by Socrates' reminders and exercises. This provocation leads him to reinvigorate his dormant knowledge of mathematics to the point where he can put it to use. Is this not a form of education?

To elicit, to state, to formulate, to show: these activities constitute a portion of the craft of teaching.[37] And generating propositions to which the slave assents, and reawakening his powers of mathematical know-how, however modest they may be—these too are components of teaching.[38]

In making the slave's mathematical knowledge explicit and articulate, Socrates also expands and extends it. In this respect, the slave is learning that knowledge is of a piece. It is systematic, and we can build or extend the system by eliciting its implications and by generating new propositions, formulae, or constructs. Sometimes the system will absorb or incorporate these additions, and sometimes these additions will modify or even revolutionize the system. The relation is symbiotic or internal between the parts and the whole.

All of this activity of renewal—or this process of recollection—is the second lesson that Socrates teaches, as stated earlier, the matching twin to his first lesson in disillusion. This second lesson teaches that we know more (or other) than what we think we know. It is a reminder of our prodigious resources, a call to remember what we have learned and the ways that we have learned them, a call to make ourselves conscious of the techniques and skills and tools that we have at our disposal (if not yet consciously under our control) for making sense of the world and coming to terms with it.[39] Our knowledge and our know-how constitute a system that generates knowledge, not merely collects it, if we realize how to inquire into its connections, relations, and implications and thereby inquire further into the world of our common experience (which is a system, as Kant showed us). (This world of human experience as captured by our language is what Wittgenstein calls our "criteria" and our "grammar" or "grammatical knowledge."[40]) To the extent that we inhabit this system of knowledge, we "know" it already and possess it in a sense. But to the extent that we remain unaware of any aspects of this system, and to the extent that we leave them unmastered or unexplored, then we must recollect these aspects if we are truly to understand them and put them to use. We recollect them by questioning them and by inquiring into them. This is what Socrates teaches the slave, and it is such knowledge that he promises all of us. It is the complement to his other lesson, that of disillusion.

Socrates understands philosophical inquiry to be a matter of traveling from the known to the unknown; you travel from what you know to what you do not know. And if you travel well, then you will end by having domesticated the unknown (insofar as you can do so). Reginald E. Allen is helpful in this regard: "[W]hat is meant by Socrates' claim that all nature is *suggenes*—'akin,' or interconnected— . . . [is] that by learning one single thing, we can recover all the rest (81d). The theory of Recollection is not only a theory of inquiry but also one of inference. A single bit of genuine knowledge can serve as the terminal link in a golden chain by which we can, Zeus-like, draw to ourselves the whole of intelligible reality."[41] But how does a person get from one link in the chain to the other? Or, rather, how do we forge the next link in the chain that we ourselves build through our inquiries?

Socrates' answer is that we begin with what we have, what we possess, what we can do—our knowledge, our skills, our capacities, our aptitudes—and then we pursue our questions and our doubts, wherever they may lead us, applying to them the techniques of knowledge acquisition that we have. Different people may well vary in techniques, skills, or capacities; this matters less, however, than the fact that each person who travels the road toward knowledge must exert himself or herself. The attempt to learn should be vigorous, and it may be strenuous, but most certainly it must be conscientious. As Socrates puts it in his prefatory remark to the exchange with the slave, "there is no difficulty in learning, out of a single recollection, all the rest, if a man is strenuous and does not faint" [Jowett & Anderson at 37 (81d)]. Nor can we be faint-hearted. The work required of us is that of tracing and tying down the numerous links that, bound together, constitute the chain of our knowledge, such as it is.

This last point, about the work of tying down, comes out best in the *Meno* toward its end, after Socrates has finished his discussions with the slave and with the interloper Anytus and is again asking questions of

Meno and joining him in mutual pursuit of the answers. After a long discussion investigating whether or not virtue is knowledge, Socrates seems to suggest that even if virtue is not knowledge, and even if knowledge of virtue is not possible, or at least is not possessed by a person, that person can still act virtuously. [See Jowett & Anderson at 46 (87d).] When asked how this is possible, Socrates says that true opinions, even if they do not amount to knowledge, can often guide our actions correctly; and when they do, they lead to our acting virtuously. "Then true opinion is as good a guide to correct action as knowledge; and that was the point which we omitted in our speculation about the nature of virtue, when we said that knowledge only is the guide of right action; whereas there is also right opinion" [Jowett & Anderson at 58 (97b–c)].

The fact that true opinions are insecure or unsteady does not mean that they are any the less true; rather, it only means that they are less stable than our knowledge. (Less stable because, while we may believe them to be true, we do not know them to be true, so our possession of them is more fleeting.) Socrates then searches for an explanation of this difference between the unsteadiness of true opinions and the steadiness of knowledge, and he finds it in the fact that, according to him, our true opinions, even though true, are not "tied down," whereas knowledge is tied down by the reason(s) we have for it. And being tied down to reason is what makes knowledge so much more valuable than opinion, so much more useful as a guide to our actions.

> *Socrates:* I mean to say that they [certain works of art] are not very valuable possessions if they are at liberty, for they will walk off like runaway slaves; but when fastened, they are of great value, for they are really beautiful works of art. Now this is an illustration of the nature of true opinions: while they abide with us they are beautiful and fruitful, but they run away out of the human soul, and do not remain long, and therefore they are not of much value until they are fastened by the tie of the cause [that is, until they are tied down by giving an account of the reason(s) for them]; and this fastening of them, friend Meno, is recollection, as you and I have agreed to call it. But when they are bound, in the first place, they have the nature of knowledge; and, in the second place, they are abiding. And this is why

> knowledge is more honorable and excellent than true opinion, because fastened by a chain [of reasoning]. [Jowett & Anderson at 58–59 (97e–98a)]

Socrates here says that "this fastening of them [our opinions], friend Meno, is recollection, as you and I have agreed to call it."[42] If this is true, then I understand Socrates' emphasis on recollection as the response to disillusion in this way: When we are led to acknowledge our ignorance by means of the negative side of Socrates' method (his *elenchus*), we are asked not to quit in despair, but rather to renew ourselves in the home of knowledge that we possess. Our common knowledge, our common experience, our ordinary language—these are the things that we all share and possess, and they are our ways of learning what we need to know. They are the structures that we inhabit and the abodes in which we take refuge in this world. Each inquiry is a journey into the unknown from these habitations, but that is exactly why inquiry is necessary, and productive. The world remains to be domesticated (by making ourselves at home in it), just as the world remains to be brought under the rule of reason (insofar as it can be). Our method of inquiry is our way of tying down the unknown, of connecting the unknown with what we already know. We are asked by Socrates to remember what we already know, to test it critically, to reduce it to what we can rely upon, and then to use it as our means of gaining new knowledge. The positive side of Socratic inquiry (his "recollection") is the way that we learn how to tie our opinions down, to anchor them in whatever knowledge we have inherited or accumulated from our parents, from others, from our language and our culture, from our own experience. Socrates teaches us to question things, and then to seek the answers.

"You and I Are Not Good for Much": Poverty and Perseverance

Socrates, in addressing Meno, fears "that you and I are not good for much, and that Gorgias has been as poor an educator of you as Prodicus has been of me. Certainly we shall have to look to ourselves, and try to find someone who will help in some way or other to improve us" [Jowett & Anderson at 57 (96d–e)]. The first twenty pages of the *Meno* take us from questioning to perplexity, from disillusion to recollection. Up to this point in the dialogue, Socrates has been trying to teach his method of inquiry to Meno, first by practicing his art of disillusion on Meno himself, and then by duplicating that feat with Meno's slave. But, since the initial disillusion leaves Meno wondering what the point is to any inquiry into the unknown (Meno's paradox or challenge: "[H]ow will you inquire, Socrates, into that which you do not know?" [Jowett & Anderson at 36 (80d)]), Socrates is forced to respond to Meno's question about the reason for persevering in their inquiry. If we can say that Socrates responds by producing disillusion in the slave too, and then reviving him by showing him (and Meno) that each person still knows much because their knowledge is based upon learning by "recollection," then Socrates has shown that this inquiry into the unknown is worthwhile. So the point becomes one of getting back to the inquiry, and getting back to the inquiry is what we find in the second half of the dialogue.

Yet the second half of the *Meno* is strangely anticlimactic. It reprises many of the questions raised and pursued in the first half (especially Meno's question: Is virtue taught, is it learned by practice, or is it a natural inheritance?), and it adds some new ones (in particular, from Socrates: Is virtue knowledge? If so, then who teaches it?). But a reader can still wonder whether very much progress is made toward reaching any satisfactory answer. In this respect, a reader could find the second half of the *Meno* to be disappointing in its evident failure to do so. Yet, as disappointing as it may be, the second half of the dialogue seems to me to have its own important purposes, chief among them, producing the very disappointment that we feel when the inquiry ends inconclusively.

What this disappointment forces upon us is a recognition that the Socratic method of questioning, even when used properly, does not guarantee satisfying answers. Pursuing Socrates' method is appropriate when we are in doubt, but using his method of conversational inquiry does not mean that we shall ever achieve the knowledge that we seek. This is the poverty of Socratic questioning.[43]

This impoverishment appears at the very beginning of the *Meno,* when Meno first asks his question of Socrates and receives what, to his way of thinking, is a very strange response.

Meno: Can you tell me, Socrates, whether virtue is acquired by teaching or by practice; or if neither by teaching nor practice, then whether it comes to man by nature, or in what other way?

Socrates: O Meno, there was a time when the Thessalians were famous among the other Hellenes only for their riches and their riding; but now, if I am not mistaken, they are equally famous for their wisdom, especially at Larissa, which is the native city of your friend Aristippus. And this is Gorgias' doing; for when he came there, the flower of the Aleuadae, among them your admirer Aristippus, and the other chiefs of the Thessalians, fell in love with his wisdom. And he has taught you the habit of answering questions in a grand and bold style in which he himself answers all comers; and any Hellene who likes may ask him anything. How different is our lot! my dear Meno. Here at Athens, there is a dearth of the commodity, and all wisdom seems to have emigrated from us to you. I am certain that if you were to ask any Athenian whether virtue was natural or acquired, he would laugh in your face and say: "Stranger, you have far too good an opinion of me if you think that I can answer your question. For I literally do not know what virtue is, and much less whether it is acquired by teaching or not." And I myself, Meno, living as I do in this region of poverty, am as poor as the rest of the world, and I confess with shame that I know literally nothing about virtue; and when I do not know the "quid" of anything, how can I know the "quale"? How, if I knew nothing at all of Meno, could I tell if he was fair or the opposite of fair; rich and noble, or the reverse of rich and noble? Do you think that I could?

Meno: No, indeed. But are you in earnest, Socrates, in saying that you do not know what virtue is? And am I to carry back this report of you to Thessaly?

Socrates: Not only that, my dear boy, but you may say further that I have never known of any one else who did, in my judgment. [Jowett & Anderson at 23–24 (70a–71b)]

Socrates wants Meno to understand that, while he cannot offer him an answer of the kind that Meno has been taught by Gorgias to expect, he may be able to offer Meno something else. If it then turns out that Meno takes this "something else" to be a pittance, something that is apt to appear impoverished when compared to the grandiose answers offered by the sophists, that would be Meno's loss. At least, this is the way that I understand Socrates' long response to Meno's opening question, with its emphasis on Socrates' inability to answer in the manner or the style to which Meno seems to have become accustomed. Given Socrates' admission as to a "dearth" of wisdom, he does not, however, simply leave the discussion or give up the question. Rather, what he goes on to do—and this is the life of the dialogue—is to teach Meno a different way to ask the questions that are bothering him and, thus, a way to look for a different kind of answer.

Is this an impoverished view of philosophy and of the wisdom that philosophy makes available to us? To this question, I think that Socrates might answer, Yes. While he is dogged in seeking answers to the questions that we ask ourselves (or, more often, to the questions that he helps us to see that we need to ask ourselves), this does not mean that Socrates therefore believes that final answers are available.[44] A fundamental aspect of his practice is getting us to see that such answers are not available or possible; and yet, despite this fact, we need to continue to seek the answers that we do have available, or that are possible. As Cavell puts it, "Such thoughts are instances of that characteristic human willingness to allow questions for itself which it cannot answer with satisfaction."

Answers to such questions do not come once and for all, but rather serially or sequentially (when they come at all). And what may prove to be a satisfactory answer on one occasion or in one context may prove to be less than satisfactory on another occasion or in another context. This fact—as to the fallibility and specificity of answers, their fitness only for a particular purpose in a given context—may require us to go farther, or to change directions, when certain perennial questions arise once again for us. If we have studied Socrates' example, we should know this much, because doggedness in the pursuit of acceptable answers is what Socrates teaches. (If some people see this as an impoverished way to proceed, then Socrates might grant their point, but only on his understanding of what constitutes both the promise and the poverty of his teaching.)

Socrates and Meno arrive at the following inconclusive conclusion:

> *Socrates:* To sum up our inquiry—the result seems to be, if we are at all right in our view, that virtue is neither natural nor acquired, but an instinct given by God to the virtuous. Nor is the instinct accompanied by reason. [Jowett & Anderson at 61 (99e–100a)]

> *Socrates:* Then, Meno, the conclusion is that virtue comes to the virtuous by divine dispensation. But we shall never know the certain truth until, before asking how virtue is given, we inquire into the actual nature of virtue. I fear that I must go away, but do you, now that you are persuaded yourself, persuade our friend Anytus. And do not let him be so exasperated; if you can conciliate him, you will have done good service to the Athenian people. [Jowett & Anderson at 61 (100b)]

I do not believe that Socrates' concluding comments ("that virtue is neither natural nor acquired, but an instinct given by God to the virtuous"; "that virtue comes to the virtuous by divine dispensation") are meant to be a final answer. Rather, by resorting to this sort of elaborate gesture—that is, virtue just appears on the scene, as though it were a gift from above—Socrates is suggesting that he does not have an explanation of virtue's source. What he offers us in closing is a myth—nothing less, nothing more—and the promise of further inquiry if we seek more enlightenment. "But we shall never know the certain truth until, before asking how virtue is given, we inquire into the actual nature of virtue." Right now, as the matter stands, for all we know, virtue indeed is the gift of God, divine inspiration. This is hardly an account of its source or origin; it is an apostrophe indicating that more work needs to be done before we can render any satisfying account of the source of virtue. As it stands, we do not yet understand virtue well enough to explain its source.

The poverty of Socrates' method is the fact that it does not promise or ensure conclusive results. It may seek them, but it does not promise them. All that it promises is that life is worth questioning, that life repays questioning, and that it is worth our time to pursue the questions that occur to us. Asking questions—some good, some not so good, in terms of their aptness or their timeliness—and then responding to them appropriately, are activities at the heart of this dialogue and at the heart of Socrates' teaching. And by the end of the dialogue, Socrates has shown us that his way of questioning is his faith, his hope for the future. This is what he puts his trust in; this is what he invests himself in.[45]

I have said that the second half of the dialogue is strangely anticlimactic, and yet it seems to have its important purposes. I have tried to discuss in detail one of these purposes in the past few pages, but there is one additional purpose of the second half of this dialogue to which I would like to draw attention. We know that, normally, Socrates does not claim to know anything. So it is startling to find, at the beginning and the end of the second half of the dialogue, two unusually forthright and bold statements of Socrates' beliefs. Here we have him asserting not just one proposition, but two.

His first credo comes at the end of his examination of the slave, when Meno and Socrates are discussing what that examination has shown. The second credo comes at the end of the dialogue, as Meno and Socrates are closing their conversation:

> *Socrates:* And I, Meno, like what I am saying. Some things I have said of which I am not altogether confident. But that we shall be better and braver and less helpless if we think that we ought to inquire than we should have been if we indulged in the idle fancy that there was no knowing and no use in seeking to know what we do not know—that is a theme upon which I am ready to fight, in word and deed, to the utmost of my power. [Jowett & Anderson at 44–45 (86b–c)]

> *Socrates:* I, too, speak rather in ignorance; I only conjecture. And yet that knowledge differs from true opinion is no matter of conjecture with me. There are not many things which I profess to know, but this is most certainly one of them. [Jowett & Anderson at 59 (98b)]

Socrates is willing to say this much: (1) that it is better for us to think that we ought to inquire into things that we do not know; and (2) that knowledge differs from true opinion. These two credos do not promise that knowledge is possible for us, or that we shall gain knowledge if we inquire into that which we do not know. They only say that it is better for us to believe that we ought to inquire, and that knowledge does differ from true belief.

The moral of Socrates' two credos is worked out in detail in his discussion with Anytus, who only appears in the second half of the dialogue. It is not otherwise clear why Plato introduces another interlocutor at this point, but if we understand Anytus to be an exemplar of the negation of Socrates' two credos, then perhaps we shall see the usefulness that Anytus has here.

As I said earlier while discussing Anytus' role as one of the three students, Anytus does not believe in the efficacy of Socratic inquiry. In fact, he barely participates in Socrates' questioning, and he quickly leaves the discussion when he thinks that Socrates is defaming his fellow Athenians. On Anytus' model, inquiry is not good for us, but rather dangerous. Socrates thinks differently. I do not say that Socrates thinks that inquiry is either easy or risk-free, and I doubt that (after his trial) he would deny its dangerous consequences. But I do believe that he would recommend inquiry to us despite its dangers, or perhaps he would have seen the dangers as an inevitable cost of inquiry. In any event, Socrates asks that we believe in the efficacy of inquiry. This is a counsel to perseverance, as it also is one of hope.

Anytus also denies (in practice) Socrates' second credo, the difference between knowledge and true opinion. For example, whereas Anytus may be quite correct in his belief that the sophists are corrupters of youth and that the sophists do not teach virtue to their students, he does not bother to tie this opinion down to the rest of his knowledge by inquiring into it. This cavalier attitude toward the basis of his purportedly true opinion (Anytus' claim to know about the sophists) is what astonishes Socrates: "You must be a diviner, Anytus, for I really cannot make out, judging from your own words, how, if you are not acquainted with them, you know about them" [Jowett & Anderson at 52 (92c)]. Anytus acts as though true opinion—if his opinion of the sophists is true—is just as good, just as solid or reliable, as knowledge. And this Socrates denies.

Anytus' willingness to accept true belief as being as good as knowledge contravenes Socrates' second credo, and it is the point on which the dialogue closes. If we truly wish to tie our opinions down—be they about virtue or some other topic—then, once again, we shall have to inquire into them and the matter at hand. We shall have to question them. For Socrates, and apparently for those of us who try to follow his example in our teaching, there is no other way.

FOUR

The Labor of Socratic Inquiry

Learning in the *Theaetetus* to Give an Account of Oneself

There is another point also in which those who associate with me are like women in child-birth. They suffer the pains of labour, and are filled day and night with distress; indeed they suffer far more than women. And this pain my art is able to bring on, and also to allay.

—SOCRATES SPEAKING ABOUT HIS ART OF MIDWIFERY[1]

And thus there are some things which all creatures, men and animals alike, are naturally able to perceive as soon as they are born; I mean, the experiences which reach the soul through the body. But calculations regarding their being and their advantageousness come, when they do, only as the result of a long and arduous development, involving a great deal of trouble and education.

—SOCRATES INSTRUCTING THEAETETUS[2]

When we examined the *Protagoras*, I began by noting that Socrates found something surprising in his experience—namely, his fascination with Protagoras and his consequent neglect of Alcibiades, something that it was worthwhile for him to relate to his conversational companion. And it was from this point of interest that the dialogue began, with Socrates narrating to his friend the events and exchanges that constituted Socrates' discussions with Hippocrates and Protagoras. The

Theaetetus begins, instead, with something that is said to be unsurprising, but only in the sense that the phenomenon in question happens to be typical of the person under discussion. What is found unsurprising is the heroism of Theaetetus. And, despite its being found unsurprising, this phenomenon is something of interest; so it is worth remarking. The dialogue begins, then, with a brief commentary emphasizing that Theaetetus is an outstanding person. This is how we come to have the short introductory tableau between Eucleides and Terpsion.

Terpsion has been searching for Eucleides (to no avail) in the Athenian marketplace, and Terpsion is on his way back home when coincidentally he bumps into Eucleides, who is returning to Athens with sad tidings. Terpsion soon learns the bad news:

> *Eucleides:* I ran into Theaetetus, who was being taken to Athens from the army at Corinth.
>
> *Terpsion:* Alive or dead?
>
> *Eucleides:* Alive, but only just. It's partly that he's suffering from some wounds, but he's getting more trouble from the disease that's broken out in the army.
>
> *Terpsion:* Dysentery?
>
> *Eucleides:* Yes.
>
> *Terpsion:* That means he's in danger. What a man for this to happen to!
>
> *Eucleides:* Yes, Terpsion, a fine person. Actually, I've just been listening to some people waxing positively lyrical about what he did in the battle.
>
> *Terpsion:* Yes, that's not at all out of the way; it would have been far more surprising if he hadn't been like that. [McDowell at 1 (142a–c)]

Theaetetus' good character being established, Eucleides then recalls that Socrates had spoken about him in praiseworthy terms and had predicted great things of him, if Theaetetus managed to stay alive: "[A]s I was coming back, I recollected with admiration how prophetically Socrates had spoken about him—as of course he did on other subjects too. It was shortly before his death, I think, that Socrates came across him, when Theaetetus was a boy. He met him and had a discussion with him, and he was extremely impressed by Theaetetus' natural gifts. When I went to Athens, he [Socrates] repeated to me what they'd said in their discussion, which was well worth hearing; and he said that Theaetetus was absolutely bound to become famous, if he lived to be grown up" [McDowell at 1–2 (142c–d)]. It is by means of this commentary by Eucleides and Terpsion that we gain entry to the discussion, "well worth hearing," that took place long ago between Socrates and Theaetetus. We then proceed to overhear this long-ago discussion as it is read aloud and reenacted (not narrated) in the ensuing text.

This opening of the *Theaetetus* presents us with an interesting mixture of understatement and dramatic tension. As the dialogue gets under way, we learn that Theaetetus lingers near death, and the drama in this moment, while unemphatic, is heightened as the remarks of Eucleides recall the days shortly before Socrates' own death. Being registered here by Plato, in a few economical strokes, are not only the tragic passing of Socrates and the likely prospect of Theaetetus' death, but also (as it were) our shunned knowledge of our own mortality. A somber shading hangs over this dialogue from its inception.

In addition, without histrionics, Plato represents the good character of Theaetetus as something worthy of comment and even veneration. Yet, if Theaetetus deserves such praise, then how much more deserving is Socrates? As worthy as Theaetetus is, so is Socrates, who tested and confirmed the genuineness of Theaetetus. And from what we know about Socrates and the rigors of his testing, his approval will not have been awarded in a cavalier way. His approval could be earned only by Theaetetus having subjected himself to the fire of Socratic examination. The lesson of a person learning to submit to the rigors of a Socratic examination is foreshadowed, as it were, in the opening of the *Theaetetus*.

With Whom Is It Worth Talking? Who Is Worth Teaching?

As the scene shifts to the discussion proper between Socrates and Theaetetus, the *Theaetetus* poses the question, "Who is worthy of Socrates' attention?" This is the initiating theme of the dialogue. "Worthiness" as a topic of interest has already been prepared for us by the preliminary tableau between Eucleides and Terpsion. Now, as Socrates appears on the scene, this text provokes us to ask, "Who has earned the right to talk with Socrates, and to participate in the work, the struggle, of Socratic inquiry?"

> *Socrates:* If I cared more about the people in Cyrene, Theodorus, I'd be asking you about its affairs and its people—whether any of the young men there are taking an interest in geometry or any other way of cultivating wisdom. But as things are, I'm less fond of them than I am of the Athenians, and so I'm keener to know which of our young men are thought likely to turn out well. So I keep a look-out for that myself, as far as I can, and I ask other people about it too—anyone with whom I see that the young people like to associate. . . . So if you've come across anyone worth talking about, I'd be glad to hear it.
>
> *Theodorus:* Yes, Socrates, there is a boy I've come across among your compatriots: it'll be well worth my saying, and your hearing, what he's like. [McDowell at 3 (143d–e)]

It is possible that this passage alludes to Socrates' defense statement in the *Apology*. Remember, prefacing this passage is Eucleides' recollection, "It was shortly before his death, I think, that Socrates came across [Theaetetus]." In the *Apology*, some of Socrates' jurors were upset that his attentions to his fellow citizens seemed abrasive and uncivil. But in his defense statement, Socrates defends his actions. He there makes the point that his examinations of his friends and neighbors are undertaken out of concern for their well-being. Socrates wants his friends and neighbors to understand themselves better; he wants them to understand better what is important in life, what is worth pursuing. It is as a summation of this overriding concern that Socrates remarks (famously), "An unexamined life is not worth living" (*Apology* [38a]).

The opening of the *Theaetetus* recapitulates this aspect of Socrates' defense statement. Socrates' fondness and concern for his fellow citizens are captured by the fact that he asks Theodorus not about the Cyrenians, but rather about the Athenians. And he wants to know specifically about their intellectual vigor and moral vitality. So Socrates asks Theodorus whether there are among those Athenians whom Theodorus knows—especially the youth of Athens (to whom Theodorus likely is teaching geometry)—some who are spending time caring for their souls. Are there, as Socrates puts it, "any of the young men there [who] are taking an interest in geometry or any other way of cultivating wisdom?" Cultivating wisdom (seeking knowledge) matters most for Socrates because, as we saw in the *Protagoras,* wisdom or knowledge is the sustenance of the human soul.[3] And cultivating wisdom (seeking knowledge) matters because, as Socrates indicates in the *Republic* and elsewhere, it is our "want" of education, our lack of "cultivation" of our souls, that most threatens us and our well-being.

For Socrates, the question "Who is taking an interest in any field that requires the cultivation of wisdom?" evolves into the question, "Who among the young men is interesting?" So in the opening of the *Theaetetus* we find Socrates asking Theodorus to name those of his students who are "worth talking about." Theodorus' response takes Socrates at his word, yet Socrates converts Theodorus' response to his own purposes. When Theaetetus serendipitously appears on the scene, Socrates asks Theodorus to invite him over to be introduced: "You make him sound an excellent person. Do ask him to come and sit here with me" [McDowell at 4 (144d)].

When Theaetetus joins the two men, Socrates then invites Theaetetus to engage in an investigation. While the purported project is to investigate Theodorus' claim that Socrates and Theaetetus are similar or alike, the inquiry soon is revealed to be more a matter of examining both Socrates and Theaetetus personally, by means of posing and answering questions. So the dialogue becomes a conversational inquiry typical of Socrates.

> *Socrates:* Still, if each of us had a lyre, and he'd said they were tuned alike, would we have believed him [Theodorus] straight away, or would we have investigated whether he was speaking as an expert in music?
>
> *Theaetetus:* We'd have investigated.

> *Socrates:* But what if he praised the mind of either of us for virtue and wisdom? Wouldn't it be worthwhile for one of us, when he heard that, to do his best to inspect the one who'd been praised,

> and for the other to do his best to show himself off? [McDowell at 4, 5 (144e, 145b)]

This personal inspection is about to begin.

The Action of the *Theaetetus*: Discussions and Digressions

One major topic of the *Theaetetus* is the nature of knowledge. Socrates asks early and often, "What is knowledge?" [see Levett & Burnyeat at 5 (146a)]. The bulk of the dialogue consists of Socrates discussing with Theaetetus (but sometimes also with Theodorus) a number of views about the nature of knowledge, none of which they find satisfactory. It is because of this focus, and because of the extent of the inquiry and its persistence, that the *Theaetetus* has been hailed as the beginning text in Western epistemology.[4] Robin Waterfield says (in the preface to his translation of the dialogue) that, prior to this time, while various Western philosophers had made scattered remarks about the problems of human knowledge, epistemology was not itself an established or separate field of philosophical study. Plato's dialogue changed that. "[T]he *Theaetetus* establishes the study of knowledge as a branch of philosophy in its own right, distinct from, especially, ontology" [Waterfield(3) at 9].

As Myles Burnyeat is careful to note, however, the *Theaetetus* "is a dialogue, not a treatise."[5] Despite the position that it holds in Western epistemology, Plato's treatment does not proceed as might a modern treatise on the subject.[6] Socrates and Theaetetus inquire into the nature of knowledge by investigating several theories of knowledge, the implications and ramifications of which end up comprising a large and disparate set of considerations and themes. The *Theaetetus* is not a finely tuned or polished presentation of acceptable and unacceptable views on knowledge, nor is it a steady review of the terrain constituting our concept of it. Rather, the dialogue moves in several directions, sometimes casually, sometimes frenetically, first looking here, then looking there, then returning to its first theme, then starting a third, and so on. Bernard Williams, in his brief commentary introducing the Hackett edition of the *Theaetetus,* calls it "one of the more discontinuous [of Plato's dialogues] in its argument" [Levett & Burnyeat at xx]. This characterization is accurate, I think, but it should not be taken pejoratively, as though Plato failed when he made the dialogue discursive or digressive. For, rather than being a flaw, this characteristic discontinuity or digressiveness is one of Plato's achievements in writing this dialogue: he shows the discontinuity in fruitful philosophical inquiry. The Platonic lesson (illustrated by Socrates' method of conversational inquiry) helps us to gain an appreciation for the fact that philosophy cannot be forced. It cannot be managed quickly—at least, not if the philosophical activity being pursued has therapeutic aspirations, as does Socrates'.[7]

Socrates uses his method of conversational inquiry to explore the prolific structures of ordinary experience, ordinary language, and ordinary life. The idea driving such work is the thought that philosophical concerns arise on their own naturally in the stream of life (or in the stream of our consciousness), and accordingly they must be allowed to unfold, to yield their secrets, on their own terms and at their own pace.[8] We are to respond in kind to such concerns. This style of philosophy is pursued, I believe, by Socrates as well as by Ludwig Wittgenstein and philosophers such as Stanley Cavell, all of whom seem to be interested in the activities and events of ordinary life. And they take seriously the data afforded us in ordinary language. For these thinkers, genuine philosophical activity includes the investigation of our open secrets, our everyday commonplaces, and the realities of our ordinary lives. But philosophically satisfying investigation of these realities and commonplaces and secrets requires that they arise in their natural contexts. Socrates, for one, provides these contexts conversationally, as it were, during the course of his inquiries. (Similarly, Wittgenstein provides them by imagining fictional as well as factual contexts that he calls "language-games.") And in allowing these matters to unfold naturally, Socrates observes one natural progression by seeking to disillusion his conversational companion, through elenctic refutation, before proceeding to his reconstructive effort of recollection or renewal. (In Wittgenstein's later philosophy, we find a similar sense of priority or progression, expressed as follows: "One must start out with error and convert it to truth. . . . To convince someone of the truth, it is not enough to state it, but rather one must find the *path* from error to truth.")[9]

Let us begin by setting the stage in the *Theaetetus*. In addition to Socrates, there are two main participants: Theaetetus and Theodorus. Theaetetus is a young man of Athens, and he happens to be a student of Theodorus, a middle-aged or older geometrician from Cyrene. Socrates does not know Theaetetus, but (as we have seen) it is through Theodorus that Socrates makes his acquaintance and then subjects him to a thorough examination. The sequence of speakers in the dialogue is the following:

1. Eucleides and Terpsion [pp. 1–2 (142a–143c)]
2. Socrates and Theodorus [pp. 3–4 (143d–144d)]
3. Socrates and Theaetetus [pp. 4–26 (144e–161a)]
   a. Theodorus' interjection: he declines to participate [p. 6 (146b)]
   b. Socrates' first speech: His Art as Midwifery [pp. 10–13 (148e–151d)]
4. Socrates and Theodorus: an interruption [pp. 26–28 (161a–162b)]
5. Socrates and Theaetetus: back again [pp. 28–31 (162c–164e)]
6. Socrates and Theodorus (and Theaetetus) [pp. 31–32 (165a–165b)]
7. Socrates and Theaetetus [pp. 32–33 (165b–165e)]
8. Socrates' second speech (as Protagoras' advocate or defender) [pp. 33–36 (166a–168c)]
9. Socrates and Theodorus: Theodorus is challenged to participate fully [pp. 36–55 (168c–183c)]
10. Socrates and Theodorus and Theaetetus [p. 56 (183d–184b)]
11. Socrates and Theaetetus [pp. 57–93 (184b–210d)]

Notice that (except for the introductory exchange between Eucleides and Terpsion, and the two stretches where Socrates offers us an extended speech [see 150b–151d and 166a–168a]) the dialogue consists of unbroken conversation among Socrates, Theaetetus, and Theodorus. As much as any Platonic dialogue, the *Theaetetus* embodies philosophical inquiry as a matter of conversing with one another about the topics at hand. But what are the topics at hand? I have already said that the nature of knowledge is an important theme of the dialogue, central to its action, yet this characterization proves to be not very helpful, because of the expectations it evokes. The way in which Plato and Socrates pursue this theme is not (as I have also said) in the style of a typical treatise on knowledge. Instead, the dialogue early on becomes extremely diffuse, and it often is unclear how the diverse points being discussed relate to one another (or, much less, how they relate to the overall theme of the nature of knowledge). On one view of philosophy, this procedure seems wrong: it appears to fail to close singlemindedly with its topic, failing to focus exclusively on it. This way of proceeding also seems not to bring the inquiry or analysis to a conclusion.

Admittedly, the *Theaetetus* is diffuse, as it also is inconclusive. It considers many different matters, not always indicating clearly how they relate to one another or to the overriding concern of formulating an adequate definition of knowledge. The dialogue also never arrives at a satisfactory account of the nature of knowledge. (Some commentators characterize this aspect of the dialogue in terms of its being "negative," or of its having wholly "negative" results. On their view, the dialogue shows what knowledge is not, or what knowledge could not be.[10]) So, while the *Theaetetus* eliminates some initially plausible or attractive theories of knowledge, it does not tell us what knowledge is. But this view of how philosophy should proceed assumes that our "overriding concern" is to formulate an adequate definition or account of knowledge. And what if it is not? What if Plato wishes to teach us something other than how best to conceive of the nature of knowledge?

To the extent that the *Theaetetus* is digressive—willing to follow the argument wherever it may lead—then this is a part of its lesson. Perhaps one of Plato's points about conversational inquiry is that it is not meant to be, and cannot be, single-mindedly directed toward a sole argument or conclusion. If we feel otherwise when we are engaged in philosophical reflection, then we may be imposing false or misleading requirements upon ourselves. The alternative that Plato proposes (through Socrates' example) is that conversational inquiry is episodic, recurrent, provisional: it is always something to which we can return.[11] And, in a sense, conversational inquiry is always something calling us back, inviting us to return. As I said in chapter 1 (citing and relying upon Gregory Vlastos; see note 3), Socrates in his conversational inquiries displays the virtue of always being willing to reexamine the matter at hand, notwithstanding however many times he may have examined it in the past. Renewing the search, recollecting the data, reviewing any matters once felt to be settled (or perhaps earlier found to be wanting), persisting in the hunt for an acceptable definition or a satisfying account; this is what Socrates does.

Since conversational inquiry is a joint undertaking, however, the progress and the digressions in any Socratic discussion are a function not only of Socrates' contributions to the investigation but also of those of his conversational partner. In this regard, it seems to me that the conversations in the *Theaetetus* differ from those that we have studied in the *Protagoras* and the *Meno,* due in part to the different attitudes of the conversational partners with whom Socrates is speaking. In the *Protagoras* and the *Meno,* there are the two relatively friendly interlocutors—Hippocrates and Meno, respectively. They both express themselves (at least initially, before they are disillusioned by Socrates) with more self-assurance than does either participant in the *Theaetetus.* And, as to the more combative interlocutors in these two earlier dialogues—Protagoras and Anytus, respectively—I think that, in their conversational exchanges with Socrates, it is fair to characterize Protagoras and Anytus as displaying more arrogance than does either Theaetetus or Theodorus. So, overall, I would say that Hippocrates and Protagoras, as well as Meno and Anytus, speak with more conviction, with more confidence, than do Theaetetus and Theodorus. One way of registering this difference would be to say that Hippocrates and Protagoras and Meno and Anytus are more dogmatic than Theaetetus or Theodorus.

Conversely, it may be better to say that Theaetetus and Theodorus are more cautious in their expressions and claims. This could mean that they are more intellectually honest or scrupulous in the claims that they are willing to make. But it also is possible that this difference in tone or attitude marks the fact that the two earlier dialogues usually feature claims to know something (for example, what virtue is, or whether virtue is teachable, or who can teach us, and so forth). And the epistemic claims made by Hippocrates and Protagoras, and by Meno and Anytus, are *pressed* in their discussions with Socrates, until he disabuses them of their illusions. On the other hand, the claims of Theaetetus and of Theodorus in the *Theaetetus* are not so much *asserted* by them as they are *extracted* from them by Socrates. He has to pry their expressions out of Theaetetus and Theodorus. And their expressions (or, their "claims," to the extent that Theaetetus and Theodorus make any claims) also seem to be of a different kind. These two interlocutors do not express themselves in terms of what they know, but rather in terms of what they think or believe, as a way of trying to express their inchoate thoughts or ideas.

If Theaetetus and Theodorus are simply attempting to put their thoughts into words, then it would appear that these expressions by Theaetetus and Theodorus are mostly being uttered without the accompanying claim that each man is asserting that he *knows* them to be true. In this respect, these are claims of meaning more than they are claims of knowledge. And their refutation by Socrates is not so much a showing that Theaetetus or Theodorus does not know what he thinks he knows; rather, their refutation is more in the nature of a showing that the words of these two interlocutors cannot be meant here and now, at this time in this context. So the illusions being removed from Theaetetus or Theodorus are illusions of meaning more than they are illusions of knowledge. (In noting earlier that the initial theme in the *Theaetetus* deals with the question of the worth of talking with someone, I had in mind the connection between this theme and the companion theme of the possibility that we may be speaking emptily. The worth of talking with someone leads us to explore the further question of when what we say is not worth saying, or hearing. It is on such occasions that, despite our having the illusion of meaning something by what we say, or the illusion of saying something meaningful, what we have said is, in fact, empty.)

In the *Theaetetus,* Socrates' goal seems less to be one of effecting the refutation or humiliation of Theaetetus or Theodorus than it is one of effecting the joint recognition that his conversational companion at the moment does not mean what he thinks he means by what he is saying. Or, it might also be said that Socrates in the *Theaetetus* attempts to show Theaetetus and Theodorus that they do not want to say what they have just now said—once, that is, they are brought to see what it means. In this respect, neither Theaetetus nor Theodorus truly knows himself, because neither knows what he is saying. In particular, Socrates effects the disillusion of Theaetetus by way of a patient and rather mild exercise in the deflation of his words. Some of his favorite thoughts and opinions are nothing more than what Socrates calls "wind-eggs," empty expressions, "phantoms," or illusory conceptions. The process of teasing out the meaning of what these two people are saying tends to effect deflationary or disillusioning results in Theaetetus. (This is less true in regard to Socrates' efforts with Theodorus.)

I do not mean to suggest, however, that Socrates' method of conversational inquiry changes vis-à-vis either Theaetetus or Theodorus; his method remains confrontational. To ask them both to express themselves clearly and coherently is to challenge them to make themselves intelligible. Cavell has said more about this aspect of Socrates' characteristic manner of proceeding, and he also suggests why someone might feel affronted by being faced with such critical scrutiny: "About Plato's or Socrates' arguments I might say that I am no more generally convinced by them than their interlocutors often seem to be. What to my mind is permanent in them, fresh every day, is the perception that the assertions of our fellow citizens, including ours to them, or to ourselves, need to be confronted, questioned, stopped, in ways that are apt to strike their proponents as violent. We are, after all, telling them that they do not know what they are saying."[12] It seems to me that Socrates, by the manner of his treatment of Theaetetus and Theodorus, implicitly acknowledges in this dialogue (more so than in the earlier two dialogues) just how difficult it is to criticize fairly and responsibly another person's theories, or even one's own intellectual positions.

Any person's thoughts and ideas on any particular subject are apt to be inchoate and unschematic, somewhat piecemeal, and irreducible to a formula. Recognizing this fact here, Socrates spends more time on the activity of drawing out the implications of the views initially expressed by Theaetetus, namely, that knowledge is perception, or that knowledge is true belief or true opinion. Socrates also engages in developing the multiple possibilities, the multiple possible meanings, of this view of knowledge, which is, I suppose, one way in which he is able to demonstrate the pregnancy of meaning and thus his assistive art of the midwife. It is this very process of teasing out the meanings that leads this dialogue to tend toward digressiveness. To develop an idea, to explain one's meaning, requires one to digress. And the *Theaetetus* pays more attention than do the *Protagoras* and the *Meno* to the difficulty of eliciting and developing the thoughts and ideas of the various protagonists undergoing Socrates' critical scrutiny.

In the *Theaetetus,* what I have earlier called the negative lesson of Socrates' method (that is, that we do not know what we think we know) is shown in the deflation that our words and assertions receive at the hands of Socrates and his critical questioning. We are, however, also shown in the *Theaetetus*—powerfully so, I believe—what I am calling the positive lesson involved in the Socratic method: namely, that we know more (or other) than we think we know. Responding to the pressure of personal testing, we learn that perhaps we can do more to elaborate our thoughts and our ideas than we might otherwise think we can. But, in order to do this, we have to digress.

All of these conversational activities serve the purpose of enabling Socrates to perform his criticism in a scrupulous manner, one that he can claim to be intellectually fair; and they also allow him to demonstrate what constitutes someone giving an account of something. Sometimes, the interlocutor on the spot is asked to explain or justify a claim that he has made, or an assertion that he has entered into the conversation; but, at other times, "giving an account" becomes a matter simply of making an adequate statement of some position or view or theory. It is practice in this daunting activity—making a statement, giving an account—that governs the action of the *Theaetetus* as a whole.

Giving an Account of Oneself by Saying What One Means

There are many ways to collate the conversational moments and movements in the *Theaetetus,* but I suggest that we group them into three major sections of unequal length. After the brief exchange between Eucleides and Terpsion, there are (1) the series of exchanges between Socrates and Theaetetus or Socrates and Theodorus for the first 40 percent of the dialogue [Levett & Burnyeat at 3–36 (143d–168c)]; then (2) the long discussion between Socrates and Theodorus for the next 20 percent of the dialogue [Levett & Burnyeat at 36–55 (168c–183c)]; and finally (3) an extended conversation between Socrates and Theaetetus for the final 40 percent of the dialogue [Levett & Burnyeat at 57–93 (184b–210d)].

Let us begin by looking at what I am calling the first major section, which comprises sequences 2–8 in my structural outline of the sequence of speakers in the *Theaetetus*. There is something odd about the first major section, in contrast to the second and third major sections. As to the other two major sections, each comprises a single set of speakers (sequences 9 and 11, respectively), whereas the first main section contains eight shifts of voice or speaker. Why does it take this dialogue fully 40 percent of its length to get going, to achieve some momentum and direction? And what is it that gets settled or stabilized such that, in the remaining 60 percent, there occurs much less variation in speakers and much more compression in the exchanges? It seems that, as the intensity of the conversation heats up, capturing the attention of both the discussants and us, the readers, the conversation invites fewer interruptions and digressions.

The action of the *Theaetetus,* through all three major sections, revolves around the idea that each participant in the conversation has to give an account of himself.[13] Three people here—Socrates, Theodorus, and Theaetetus—discuss matters that require each of them to account for what he claims to think about something. Socrates is the model for giving such an account, and throughout the dialogue he leads the discussion mainly by expanding on what he and the other two have said. Both early and late in the dialogue, then, we find Socrates characteristically questioning his own remarks in a search for ambiguities or falsehoods or misleading implications. Or, sometimes, he interrogates what Theaetetus or Theodorus has said to him in response to one of his questions. Or, at other times, Socrates offers to explain something, either to Theaetetus or to Theodorus ("And shall I tell you what is the explanation of that?" [Levett & Burnyeat at 10 (149b)]). Socrates then proceeds to clarify the matter by means of an argument, an example, a story, a speech, a myth, or a dream.

The instances of these activities are too numerous to cite individually; they would weigh too heavily on the progress of my narrative. Yet, just because they proliferate throughout the dialogue, they are apt to be overlooked. Still, if we scan the pages of the *Theaetetus* alert to such offers of explanations of meaning and requests for clarification, we shall see that the dialogue is replete with them. What do they mean or portend? Individually, they mean whatever happens to be their point in the particular context in which they arise. Cumulatively, they have a larger function. The entire movement of the *Theaetetus* becomes driven by this need to explain oneself (what one means by what one has said), or this need to receive an explanation from someone else of what he said or thinks or believes.

We have, for example, this early exchange between Socrates and Theaetetus:

> *Socrates:* That is certainly a frank and indeed a generous answer, my dear lad. I asked you for one thing and you have given me many; I wanted something simple, and I have got a variety.
> *Theaetetus:* And what does that mean, Socrates?
> *Socrates:* Nothing, I dare say. But I'll tell you what I think. [Levett & Burnyeat at 6–7 (146d)]

Here, Socrates is teaching Theaetetus how to respond to his question. He teaches this lesson by explaining what he meant by what he has just said—his desire for a simple answer. And Socrates demonstrates the meaning of "giving an account" by giving an account of his meaning.

Socrates inquires into (among other things) the meaning of our words. This effort is driven by his recognition that, in examining our words, we are simultaneously examining ourselves. (Wittgenstein's later philosophy, and ordinary language philosophy as represented in the work of J. L. Austin, and the writing of Stanley Cavell, all thrive on the same recognition.) Our concepts, the meanings of our words, give us access to ourselves. On Socrates' understanding, then, his method of conversational inquiry is as much a matter of gaining self-knowledge as it is one of gaining knowledge of the implications and possibilities of our words as they are used in our language. The two are intertwined, or symbiotic, such that knowledge of one is necessarily knowledge of the other.

Yet these matters require clarification. Our knowledge of ourselves is shunned, or deadened; and our knowledge of our language waits to be activated.[14] This joint task of understanding our language and the task of self-clarification are matters about which I spoke in my first chapter, when I talked about Socrates' personal testing being aimed, in Cavell's phrase, at "making ourselves intelligible to ourselves and to others." In opening ourselves up to Socratic scrutiny, the Socratic process requires that we explain ourselves. By participating in the conversational process, we thus make ourselves vulnerable to such a personal examination. Socratic questioning requires us to give or produce our reasons, our explanations, our stories, our examples, our accounts, and the like in part because these things reveal us. These *logoi* tell us who and what we are. And, of course, the threat is that they may reveal us to be leading incoherent and unexamined lives of illusion.

During the course of Socrates' conversational inquiries, his singular request is that we clarify ourselves by clarifying our words. This aspect of Socrates' procedure is brought out immediately after he gets Theaetetus to consent to being examined. Remember, we began with the brief exchange between Eucleides and Terpsion; then we witnessed Socrates asking Theodorus who among the Athenian youth was worth knowing. Theodorus responded that Theaetetus was an exceptional youth, whereupon Socrates sought out Theaetetus and asked him to submit to being examined. Theodorus' recommendation of Theaetetus not being sufficient warrant, according to Socrates, we need something more if we are to evaluate properly Theodorus' claim that Theaetetus is a promising youth, that he is worth getting to know.

> *Socrates:* But supposing it were the soul of one of us that he [Theodorus] was praising? Suppose he said one of us was good and wise? Oughtn't the one who heard that to be very anxious to examine the object of such praise? And oughtn't the other to be very willing to show himself off?
>
> *Theaetetus.* Yes, certainly, Socrates.
>
> *Socrates:* Then, my dear Theaetetus, now is the time for you to show yourself and for me to examine you. [Levett & Burnyeat at 5 (145b)]

But how is Theaetetus supposed to reveal himself, his soul (*psyché*), to Socrates?

Theaetetus reveals himself by giving an account of himself and letting Socrates check his computations. He does not account for himself by telling us the story of his life, his biography, for this is not what Socrates wants. Rather, the idea is to study Theaetetus under the pressure of

Socrates' examination by questioning. This amounts to personal revelation by way of inquiry. Socrates asks questions of Theaetetus, who is supposed to answer them, which answers Socrates will then test, which testing will then lead to more questions from Socrates and more responses from Theaetetus. Thus, we shall know Theaetetus by his works and his words.

It is at this juncture that Socrates broaches his "difficulty," namely, what is knowledge? And Socrates implores Theaetetus to help him with this question. "Now this is just where my difficulty comes in. I can't get a proper grasp of what on earth knowledge really is. Could we manage to put it into words?" [Levett & Burnyeat at 6 (145e–146a)] (Waterfield translates the last sentence as follows: "Are we in a position to give an account of it?" [Waterfield(3) at 20 (145e–146a)]) Theaetetus' initial response is to give Socrates several examples, such as craftsmen who are knowledgeable in their crafts, and this response sends Socrates into a frenzy. Such an answer is "absurd" [Levett & Burnyeat at 7 (147b)]. He explains to Theaetetus that he wanted "a short and commonplace answer" [Levett & Burnyeat at 7 (147c)]; and a few lines later, he reiterates that he wants a "simple, commonplace statement" [Levett & Burnyeat at 8 (147c)]. Subsequently he again puts the challenge to Theaetetus in these terms: "You must put your whole heart into what we are doing—in particular into this matter of getting a statement of what knowledge really is" [Levett & Burnyeat at 9 (148c–d)]. (Waterfield renders this line as follows: "[D]o your absolute best to express your thoughts, especially about what knowledge in fact is" [Waterfield(3) at 25 (148d)].) Socrates concludes by demanding, "[N]ow I want you in the same way to give one single account of the many branches of knowledge" [Levett & Burnyeat at 10 (148d)].

Soon thereafter (still within the first major section of the dialogue, and just after Socrates has offered Theaetetus the characterization of his method as one of "midwifery"), we get another revealing exchange between these two concerning the kind of examination to which a person is subjected when he or she undergoes Socratic examination.

Socrates: Now if you and I were professional savants [that is, sophists], who had already analysed all the contents of our minds, we should now spend our superfluous time trying each other out; we should start a regular Sophists' set-to, with a great clashing of argument on argument. But, as it is, we are only plain men; and so our first aim will be to look at our thoughts themselves in relation to themselves, and see what they are—whether, in our opinion, they agree with one another or are entirely at variance.

Theaetetus. That would certainly be my aim, anyway.

Socrates: And mine. That being so, as we are not in any way pressed for time, don't you think the thing to do is to reconsider this matter quietly and patiently, . . . "analysing" ourselves, and asking what are these apparitions within us? [Levett & Burnyeat at 18 (154d–155a)]

Before we can argue about the truth or validity of our various thoughts, we have to know what they mean. This is, Socrates says, a "matter [of] quietly and patiently . . . 'analysing' ourselves," and he effects such analysis by means of the questions he asks of himself and of others. Specifically, "our first aim will be to look at our thoughts themselves in relation to themselves, and see what they are—whether, in our opinion, they agree with one another or are entirely at variance." Fortunately, Theaetetus is prepared to submit to such an examination, uncomfortable as it may turn out to be. And, of course, Socrates himself is prepared to carry out the rigors of such an investigation. (That is a part of his virtue, his seemingly unlimited willingness to submit himself to inspection and critical scrutiny or testing. This signifies his passion for philosophy.[15])

That others are not so willing is shown in an exchange between Theodorus and Socrates. Theodorus makes the point that followers of Heraclitus would not submit to such an examination, and thus that Socratic examination would not succeed with them:

Theodorus: [The Ephesians, followers of Heraclitus] are just like the things they say in their books—always on the move. As for abiding by what is said, or sticking to a question, or quietly answering and asking questions in turn, there is less than nothing of that in their capacity. . . . If you ask any one of them a question, he will pull out some little enigmatic phrase from his quiver and shoot it off at you; and if you try to make him give an account of what he has said, you will only get hit by another, full of strange turns of language. You will never reach any conclusion with any of them, ever; indeed they never reach any conclusion with each other, they are so very careful not to allow anything to be stable, either in an argument or in their own souls. . . .

Socrates: I dare say, Theodorus, you have seen these men only on the field of battle, and never been with them in times of peace—as you don't belong to their set. . . .

Theodorus: . . . As I was just going to say, you will never get these men to give an account of themselves, willingly or unwillingly. What we must do is to take their doctrine out of their hands and consider it for ourselves, as we should a problem of geometry. [Levett & Burnyeat at 51 (179e–180b, 180c)]

The irony of this exchange is that Theodorus himself proves to be reluctant to submit to such scrutiny, by Socrates or by anyone else. Accordingly, a portion of the action of the *Theaetetus* is Socrates' calling Theodorus to account.

By the end of the dialogue, Socrates is still at it, still engaged in the examination of self or soul begun so many pages earlier. So, for example, by the time he broaches the question of whether "elements" are unknowable while their compounds or complexes are knowable, he finds that, once again, we must turn to self-examination on the matter at hand. "Let's take and examine them [that is, elements and compounds] then. Or rather let us examine ourselves, and ask ourselves whether we really learned our letters in this way or not" [Levett & Burnyeat at 82 (203a)].

Self-examination, as practiced by Socrates, comprises several steps. First, there is the asking of questions; these questions have to be such that they elicit useful, productive answers. Next, there must be the answers, their actual expression or articulation. Even when we have a question and an answer, however, we are not finished; in fact, we have just begun. Because we then must go on, either to revise or expand upon the initial answer, or else to test it further and critically assess it. This critical questioning may require that we return to the task of articulation, or it may require that we further express ourselves on the matter at hand, or that we also question ourselves. One never knows beforehand where our conversational inquiry will take us. We do know, however, that this activity of "giving an account" or "making a statement" demands continued attention, reiteration, recounting, revision, recollection, and countless other actions. Through this process, we explore the implications of what we say, and the possibilities of what we think and do. This is another way of saying that, through this process, we educate ourselves by means of the Socratic method of conversational inquiry. As Socrates puts it to Theaetetus, in the epigraph to this chapter, "[T]here are some things which all creatures, men and animals alike, are naturally able to perceive as soon as they are born; I mean, the experiences which reach the soul through the body. But calculations regarding their being and their advantageousness come, when they do, only as the result of a long and arduous development, involving a great deal of trouble and education." It is the whole intricate structure of human exposition that Socrates repeatedly calls "making a statement" or "giving an account" (which is one meaning of the central Greek term, *logos*).[16] This is the core way that he teaches both Theodorus and Theaetetus to respond to his questions. But to engage properly in such an examination, the person being examined has to have the ability to give an account and the willingness to make a statement. And both of these issues are raised in the examinations of Theaetetus and Theodorus.

Theodorus the Kibitzer: Provoking Him to Participate

The central activity of getting or giving an account is extended, then, to Socrates' two conversational companions—both Theaetetus and Theodorus are called upon to account for themselves. In Theaetetus' case, it is his *aptitude* for giving an account that is tested and tutored by Socrates. In Theodorus' case, on the other hand, it is his *attitude,* his willingness to give an account, that is tested and tutored.

I have already mentioned that, in this dialogue, Socrates' power to disillusion his interlocutors has a different force because of the nature of the people with whom he is in conversation. Unlike Protagoras (an accomplished sophist who is sure of himself), and unlike Meno (a student unaware of his own limitations), in the *Theaetetus* we have Theodorus and Theaetetus. Theodorus is an experienced geometrician, middle-aged (or, at least, between the ages of Theaetetus and Socrates), and a casual adherent of Protagorean theories, although he displays no intense commitment to these theories. Theodorus is a passive fellow, unwilling to compete in the rough-and-tumble of Socratic inquiry. Theaetetus, however, is much more willing than Theodorus to contest with Socrates. But Theaetetus is still a mere youth who looks to Socrates and Theodorus for instruction and correction, and who doubts his own ability to give Socrates the kind of answers that the older man is looking for. These facts make both Theodorus and Theaetetus much less ripe for disillusion than were Protagoras and Meno. Moreover, disillusion may not be called for if a person is not initially committed to the words that express a purported illusion. And who among these people is committed to the words of this dialogue? Who among them is a proponent of the views expressed, willing not only to put them forward, but also to defend them?

Theodorus is more than a nominal actor in the dialogue, although he receives less attention from Socrates than does Theaetetus. Theodorus is, initially, the means by which Socrates meets Theaetetus. But, introductions having been effected, Theodorus does not then simply fade out of the picture. Instead, he sticks around to overhear the sequence of exchanges between Socrates and Theaetetus and occasionally to offer a comment or a question of his own. These interjections range from brief asides to momentary stays in the discussion or minor digressions. Theodorus is a kibitzer, and he freely gives Socrates and Theaetetus his advice, without being willing to participate actively in the prosecution of the inquiry. So why is Theodorus a part of this dialogue? Why does Plato bother? What does the example of Theodorus show? And what does he help us to learn?

Theodorus' reluctance to participate in Socrates' examination of the self and soul affords us a contrast to Theaetetus along one dimension of educability, namely, that of a student's willingness to submit himself to the rigors of the educational process. As to the hard work entailed by Socratic inquiry and examination, Theaetetus welcomes it; he is not daunted by the effort required. Theodorus, on the other hand, wants nothing to do with Socratic inquiry and the work that it entails.

He does not want to be put to the test. It is not that Theodorus, an experienced geometrician, is unable to give an account in the form required by Socrates (although Theodorus pretends that that is a part of his reluctance); it simply is not credible that a person of Theodorus' accomplishments could not generate the accounts sought by Socrates, if he (Theodorus) really wanted to oblige him (Socrates). Rather, what becomes painfully evident as the dialogue unfolds is that Theodorus is not up to the rigors of the task.

The reluctance of Theodorus is established very early in the dialogue, as soon as Socrates turns his attention to Theaetetus and begins asking his persistent questions: "Now this is just where my difficulty comes in. I can't get a proper grasp of what on earth knowledge really is. Could we manage to put it into words? What do all of you say? Who'll speak first? . . . Well, why this silence? Theodorus, I hope my love of argument is not making me forget my manners—just because I'm so anxious to start a discussion and get us all friendly and talkative together?" [Levett & Burnyeat at 6 (145e–146a)]. Socrates' solicitude could not be more manifest, but Theodorus begs off, excusing himself purportedly because he is too old for this kind of thing. "No, no, Socrates—that's the last thing one could call forgetting your manners. But do make one of the young people answer you. I am not used to this kind of discussion, and I'm too old to get into the way of it. But it would be suitable enough for them and they would profit more by it. For youth can always profit, that's true enough. So do go on; don't let Theaetetus off but ask him some more questions" [Levett & Burnyeat at 6 (146b)]. Age has its privileges, I suppose, and Socrates does turn his attention to Theaetetus. One thing at a time; Theodorus can wait.

While Theodorus' plea gets him off the hook, his avoidance of discussion is not very attractive; in fact, it establishes something unpleasant about his character. Putting aside Theodorus' shirking of this opportunity to engage Socrates in conversation, what kind of a friend to Theaetetus does Theodorus prove to be? Not much. Under the guise of being too old for this sort of thing, Theodorus pushes Theaetetus forward and tells Socrates, "Here, take your best shot at him."

As I said, Socrates for the moment accepts Theodorus' plea and turns his attention to Theaetetus. The ensuing conversation continues for another twenty pages, complicating Theaetetus' initially straightforward claim that "knowledge is perception," and eventually culminating in an elaborate formulation of Theaetetus' insight, which is said to derive from Protagoras and others, such as Heraclitus and Homer. At this point, when Socrates has finally achieved a plausible statement of Theaetetus' theory, the following exchange occurs:

> *Socrates:* [addressing Theaetetus:] This [epistemological theory], then, it appears, is what our efforts have at last brought forth—whatever it really is. And now that it has been born, we must perform the rite of running round the hearth with it; we must make it in good earnest go the round of discussion. For we must take care that we don't overlook some defect in this thing that is entering into life; it may be something not worth bringing up, a wind-egg, a falsehood. What do you say? Is it your opinion that your child ought in any case to be brought up and not exposed to die? Can you bear to see it found fault with, and not get into a rage if your first-born is stolen away from you?
>
> *Theodorus:* Theaetetus will put up with it, Socrates. He is not at all one to lose his temper. But tell me, in Heaven's name, in what way is it not as it should be?
>
> *Socrates:* You are the complete lover of discussion, Theodorus, and it is too good of you to think that I am a bag of arguments, and can easily pick one out which will show you that this theory is wrong. But you don't realise what is happening. The arguments never come from me; they always come from the person I am talking to. All that I know, such as it is, is how to take an argument from someone else—someone who *is* wise—and give it a fair reception. So, now, I propose to try to get our answer out of Theaetetus, not to make any contribution of my own. [Levett & Burnyeat at 26 (160e–161b)]

This is droll. Socrates has just managed to elicit a detailed accounting of Theaetetus' theory of knowledge. But now, when Socrates is preparing to turn to the matter of testing and criticizing this theory, Theodorus sticks his nose in. What gall! "Theaetetus will put up with it, Socrates." Who is Theodorus to vouch for Theaetetus?

Socrates is appropriately caustic in his response: "You are the complete lover of discussion, Theodorus." Yes, Theodorus loves discussion so much that he refuses to participate, yet he is eager to volunteer Theaetetus for the examination. Unlike Theodorus, of course, Theaetetus will "put up with it," because he (Theaetetus) is willing to submit himself to the labor of Socratic inquiry. At this point, then, Theodorus receives polite deference from Theaetetus and amused sarcasm from Socrates.

Notice, however, that Theodorus' attitude has changed slightly. He is no longer withdrawn from the discussion. This marks a significant movement on his part. Before, Theodorus was disinclined to discuss these matters with Socrates; now, despite himself, despite his cowardice, Theodorus cannot help but be intrigued. He implores Socrates: "But tell *me,* in Heaven's name, in what way is it not as it should be?" [Emphasis added.] Theodorus will not take part, but, all the same, he wants to know the results of the discussion. Theodorus is selfishly willing to profit from the efforts of Socrates and Theaetetus.

This change in attitude leaves Theodorus vulnerable, and Socrates presses his advantage here, ever so slightly, engaging him in a brief discussion of Protagoras' theory. But it is not a full-blooded examination of Theodorus and his beliefs, and Theodorus once again retreats behind the privilege afforded him by his age:

Socrates: . . . [W]hat are we to say, Theodorus? . . .

Theodorus: Protagoras was my friend, Socrates, as you have just remarked. I could not consent to have him refuted through my admissions; and yet I should not be prepared to resist you against my own judgement. So take on Theaetetus again. He seemed to be following you very sympathetically just now.

Socrates: Now, Theodorus, supposing you went to Sparta and were visiting the wrestling-schools. Would you think it right to sit and watch other men exercising naked—some of them not much to look at—and refuse to strip yourself alongside them, and take your turn at letting people see what you look like?

Theodorus: Why not, if I could persuade them to leave the choice to me? Similarly I am hoping to persuade you to allow me to be a spectator and not drag me into the arena now that I am grown stiff; but to take on someone who is younger and more supple.

Socrates: Well, Theodorus, what you like I'll not dislike, as the saying goes. So we must again resort to our wise Theaetetus. Come, Theaetetus. Think, to begin with, of what we have just been saying, and tell me . . . . [Levett & Burnyeat at 27–28 (161d, 162a–c)]

Theodorus is acknowledging his friendship with Protagoras while simultaneously denying that this friendship puts him under any obligation to answer Protagoras' critics or to protect his memory. Still, I suppose that to the extent that Theodorus displays any virtue, he at least is candid about his willingness to slip through the bonds of common courtesy and mutual hospitality if his hosts will let him do so. "Why not, if I could persuade them to leave the choice to me?" This is refreshingly candid. Of course, he is not beneath making an appeal to Socrates on the basis of his advanced age. Again, Socrates lets Theodorus off the hook; not, I think, because he is fooled by Theodorus' plea, but rather because he is not yet prepared to skewer him. Socrates is biding his time. And, besides, Theodorus is not yet ready, as tempting a target as he may present. Instead, Socrates returns to the unfinished business of assessing the truth or falsity of the theory of knowledge that he and Theaetetus have just been developing: "So, now, I propose to try to get our answer out of Theaetetus."

Shortly thereafter, Theodorus has another opportunity to participate actively in the discussion, but again he declines. When Socrates and Theaetetus finish further elaborating Protagoras' theory of knowledge, and they find it still lacking in certain respects, Socrates says: "I don't think this would have happened, my friend [Theaetetus], if the father of the other tale [that is, Protagoras] were alive. He would find plenty of means of defending it. As things are, it is an orphan we are trampling in the mud. Not even the people Protagoras appointed its guardians are prepared to come to its rescue; for instance, Theodorus here. In the interests of justice, it seems that we shall have to come to the rescue ourselves" [Levett & Burnyeat at 31 (164e)]. This provokes Theodorus to respond: "I think you must. It is not I, you know, Socrates, but Callias, the son of Hipponicus, who is the guardian of Protagoras' relics. As it happened, I very soon inclined away from abstract discussion to geometry. But I shall be very grateful if you can rescue the orphan" [Levett & Burnyeat at 31 (164e–165a)]. Although Theodorus claims to be interested in Protagoras' theory ("I shall be very grateful if you can rescue the orphan"), he takes no responsibility for defending it. He claims to have been a friend of Protagoras, but by declining Socrates' invitation to intervene at this point in the dialogue and rescue Protagoras' theory, Theodorus denies or avoids the obligations of friendship. Theodorus seems to have no sense of honor or responsibility.

At this point, Socrates stops humoring Theodorus and starts instructing him in his duties. "Good, Theodorus. Now, will you give your mind to this rescue work of mine—what little I can do? Because one might be driven into making even more alarming admissions than we [Socrates and Theaetetus] have just made, if one paid as little attention to the words in which we express our assertions and denials as we are for the most part accustomed to doing. Shall I tell you how this might happen? Or shall I tell Theaetetus?" [Levett & Burnyeat at 32 (165a)] To this invitation, Theodorus finally accedes, albeit grudgingly: "Tell us both, Socrates; but the younger had better answer. It will not be so undignified for him to get tripped up" [Levett & Burnyeat at 32 (165a–b)]. Even now, Theodorus is looking to protect his own reputation from the humiliation of Socratic examination and refutation. He timidly agrees to defend and explain Protagoras' theory, and even then his agreement is premised upon a kind of dual responsibility, one that he shares with Theaetetus, for the defense. This is progress of a kind. Theodorus is gradually coming to play an active role in the inquiry.

The dénouement comes a few pages later, when Socrates shames Theodorus into taking part:

> *Socrates:* . . . Well, Theodorus, here is my contribution to the rescue of your friend [Protagoras]—the best I can do, with my resources, and little enough that is. If he were alive himself, he would have come to the rescue of his offspring in a grander style.
>
> *Theodorus:* That must be a joke, Socrates. It was a very spirited rescue.
>
> *Socrates:* You are kind, my friend. Tell me now, did you notice that Protagoras was complaining of us, in the speech that we have

just heard [a speech made by Socrates as an advocate for Protagoras], for addressing our arguments to a small boy and making the child's nervousness a weapon against his ideas? And how he disparaged our method of argument as merely an amusing game, and how solemnly he upheld his "measure of all things" and commanded us to be serious when we dealt with his theory?

Theodorus: Yes, of course I noticed that, Socrates.

Socrates: Then do you think we should obey his commands?

Theodorus: Most certainly I do.

Socrates: Look at the company then. They are all children but you. So if we are to obey Protagoras, it is you and I who have got to be serious about his theory. It is you and I who must question and answer one another. Then he will not have *this* against us, at any rate, that we turned the criticism of his philosophy into sport with boys.

Theodorus: Well, isn't our Theaetetus better able to follow the investigation of a theory than many an old fellow with a long beard?

Socrates: But not better than *you,* Theodorus. Do not go on imagining that it is my business to be straining every nerve to defend your dead friend while you do nothing. Come now, my very good Theodorus, come a little way with me. Come with me at any rate until we see whether in questions of geometrical proofs it is really you who should be the measure or whether all men are as sufficient to themselves as you are in astronomy and the other sciences in which you have made your name.

Theodorus: Socrates, it is not easy for a man who has sat down beside you to refuse to talk. That was all nonsense just now when I was pretending that you were going to allow me to keep my coat on, and not use compulsion like the Spartans. So far from that, you seem to me to have leanings towards the methods of Sciron. The Spartans tell one either to strip or to go away; but you seem rather to be playing the part of Antaeus. You don't let any comer go till you have stripped him and made him wrestle with you in an argument. [Levett & Burnyeat at 36–37 (168c–169b)]

Here the charade ends. Socrates confronts Theodorus with his cowardice in hiding behind his age and turns the age factor against him. "Look at the company then. They are all children but you. So if we are to obey Protagoras, it is you and I who have got to be serious about his theory." When Theodorus tries to wiggle out of this argument by proposing Theaetetus in his place, Socrates quashes that sham plea too: "But not better than *you,* Theodorus." In other words, Theodorus is fully capable of following the thread of the argument in Socrates' exhausting inquiries, and nothing will exempt him from his obligation to participate in the inquiry under way concerning the nature of knowledge.

Theodorus concedes defeat. But this does not mean that he is happy about it, or that he submits willingly.

> *Theodorus:* All right. I resign myself; take me with you where you like. In any case, I see, I have got to put up with the fate you spin for me, and submit to your inquisition. But not further than the limits you have laid down; beyond that I shall not be able to offer myself.
>
> *Socrates:* It will do if you will go with me so far. [Levett & Burnyeat at 37–38 (169c)]

And he does.

While Socrates does not convert Theodorus, he at least gets him to participate in the discussion. For the next twenty pages—the second major section of the dialogue—Socrates and Theodorus explore some of the implications and possibilities of Protagoras' theory of knowledge as well as the associated theory of Heraclitus ("All is flux"). They also discuss a number of other topics, including the differences between the philosopher and the practical man. To get Theodorus to go this far, with a reasonable semblance of willingness, even enthusiasm, is a victory for Socrates, albeit a limited one. It approximates his goal of engaging each capable person in the rigors of conversational inquiry. And this Socratic engagement with Theodorus pays some dividends.

One such dividend is that Theodorus actually gets caught up in the excitement of the hunt. For instance, at one point in the second major section of the dialogue, as Socrates and Theodorus are exploring the increasingly tangled aspects of Protagoras' theory, we catch a glimpse of Theodorus exhorting Socrates to further questioning.

> *Socrates:* . . . Now I think we ought to begin by examining the other party, the fluent fellows we started to pursue. If they appear to us to be talking sense, we will help them drag us over to their side, and try to escape the others. But if those who make their stand for the whole appear to be nearer the truth, we will take refuge with them from the men who "move what should not be moved." And if it appears that neither party has a reasonable theory, then we shall be very absurd if we think that insignificant people like ourselves can have anything to say, after we have rejected the views of men who lived so long ago and possessed all wisdom. Think now, Theodorus, is it of any use for us to go forward upon such a dangerous venture?
>
> *Theodorus:* We can't refuse to examine the doctrines of these two schools, Socrates; that couldn't be allowed.
>
> *Socrates:* Then we must examine them, if *you* feel so strongly about it. [Levett & Burnyeat at 52 (181a–c)]

The change in Theodorus' attitude is presented even more starkly in Jowett's translation, where Socrates is given to say: "Then examine we must, since you, who were so reluctant to begin, are so eager to proceed" [Jowett & Copi at 46 (181b–c)].

Still, however, the attitudinal change in Theodorus does not last long. What he has been eager to explore is the Heraclitean philosophy ("All is flux") held by the Ephesians, a group of Greeks whom he has just been loudly berating. "As I was just going to say, you [Socrates] will never get these men [the Ephesians] to give an account of themselves, willingly or unwillingly. What we must do is to take their [Heraclitean] doctrine out of their hands and consider it for ourselves, as we should a problem in geometry" [Levett & Burnyeat at 51 (180c)]. But Theodorus does not consider himself a follower of Heraclitus. (Waterfield notes that "Theodorus, a quasi-Protagorean, is definitely not a Heraclitean" [Waterfield(3) at 79 n. 2].) So, Theodorus' newfound enthusiasm for inquiry, his willingness to investigate these matters, seems premised on the fact that he is not investigating his own words or beliefs but rather the doctrines of another, Heraclitus. This makes the activity impersonal. The inquiry now stands as an objective study of an impersonal doctrine, just "as we should [study] a problem in geometry." There is no hope of self-revelation, and no promise of disillusion, in such an impersonal situation.

Socrates tries to correct this, as much as he can, by exhorting Theodorus to say what *he* thinks: "[B]ut don't let this be only what *I* think. You commit yourself as well, so that we may come to grief together, if need be" [Levett & Burnyeat at 52 (181c)]. But Theodorus steadfastly refuses: "Heaven knows, *I* can't answer that. I suppose *they* would say, in both ways" [Levett & Burnyeat at 53 (181e); second emphasis added]. It is shortly after this exchange that Theodorus is relieved to learn that his limited bargain to participate in the discussion has been fulfilled.[17]

> *Socrates:* Then we are set free from your friend [Protagoras], Theodorus. We do not yet concede to him that every man is the measure of all things, if he be not a man of understanding. And we are not going to grant that knowledge is perception, not at any rate on the line of inquiry which supposes that all things are in motion [that is, Heracliteanism]; we are not going to grant it unless Theaetetus here has some other way of stating it.
>
> *Theodorus:* That's very good hearing, Socrates, for when these matters were concluded I was to be set free from my task of answering you, according to our agreement, which specified the end of the discussion of Protagoras' theory. [Levett & Burnyeat at 55 (183b–c)]

A page later, Theodorus makes his last comment [see Levett & Burnyeat at 56 (184b)], and he remains silent for the rest of the dialogue.

Theodorus' suggestion that this marks "the end of the discussion of Protagoras' theory" is wrong. Socrates, upon taking up the matter once again with Theaetetus, proceeds directly to another extended consideration of the implications and possibilities of Protagoras' theory. [See Levett & Burnyeat at 56–60 (184b–186e).] What has happened is that Theodorus has gone as far as he is willing to go in investigating the underpinnings of the Protagorean theory, and this limit seems to be drawn at the edges of the overlap (if any) between the theories of Protagoras and Heraclitus. And this means that, beyond this point, Theodorus is not interested in investigating his own beliefs, his own thoughts, about knowledge or about Protagoras' theory ("Man is the measure of all things"). I take this to show that Theodorus is not committed to these ideas in the sense that they are *his*; they do not constitute a part of his self. He is not a true believer in Protagoras' theory; or, if Theodorus is a Protagorean of some sort, then his adherence to this philosophy is not adamant. These ideas do not define him or who he is, as they do define Protagoras and who he is.[18]

Although, as Socrates shows, Theodorus has the aptitude or ability to discuss these matters, and he certainly has the experience and sobriety required for a serious discussion, he is not *interested* in engaging in such a task. He wants the "orphan" saved—but not enough to himself rescue the orphaned doctrine of Protagoras, although he would be glad if someone else would. "As it happened, I very soon inclined away from abstract discussion to geometry. But I shall be very grateful if you [Socrates] can rescue the orphan." Theodorus absolves himself from making the effort.

Since Theodorus is not committed to these ideas or theories, he is not disillusioned by their refutation. Their refutation is not *his* refutation, not his humiliation. Compare, for example, Socrates himself in this regard, who is embarrassed by his own actions when they lead him astray. Because Socrates' words and actions during his inquiries are his—he owns them, or owns up to them—and because he purports to be following his muse in what he does philosophically, the results are his responsibility. Socrates is committed to his own activities and practices, his method of conversational inquiry. So, whereas the deflation of the Protagorean theory of knowledge is not a personal deflation for Theodorus, the misuse of Socrates' method reflects poorly on Socrates himself. Thus, Socrates can be disillusioned, but there can be no disillusion for Theodorus.

There is a second comparison to make here, not between Theodorus and Socrates, but instead between Theodorus and Theaetetus. In this extended discussion, the unwilling student (Theodorus) contrasts unfavorably with the willing and even eager student (Theaetetus). They exemplify one kind of educational failure and success, not in terms of their ability to give accounts of something (if anything, Theodorus the geometrician would seem to be more accomplished than Theaetetus at this), but rather in terms of their attitude toward the inevitable work or labor required by Socratic conversational inquiry.

Theaetetus: A Willing Pupil

Even though Theodorus makes several appearances in the *Theaetetus,* for the most part they amount only to relatively minor interjections or interruptions, ranging from brief asides to momentary stays in the discussion. As we know, Theodorus is a kibitzer. Not so, Theaetetus; he is Socrates' main partner. Theaetetus begins the search in the first major section, when he defines knowledge as being a matter of perception; and he concludes the dialogue in the third major section, an extensive closing exchange that completely omits Theodorus. I estimate that, altogether, Theaetetus appears in 80 percent of the dialogue. And even when Theodorus takes center stage, I get the impression that Socrates sometimes uses Theodorus simply as an object-lesson to show Theaetetus what he should avoid doing.

Unlike Theodorus,[19] when it comes to being willing to engage in the difficult give-and-take of Socratic examination, Theaetetus has nothing to learn. A teacher could not ask for a more willing student. "Well, I ought to answer, Socrates, as you and Theodorus tell me to. In any case, you and he will put me right, if I make a mistake" [Levett & Burnyeat at 6 (146c)]. If, at the beginning of the dialogue proper, Theaetetus hesitates to join in the discussion with Socrates, his hesitancy does not arise from any unwillingness to participate but rather from the fact that Theaetetus is not sure that he can satisfy Socrates with his answers. This is the rub for Theaetetus. Socrates, accordingly, offers Theaetetus lessons in how to give an account of himself.

> *Socrates:* So when the question raised is "What is knowledge?", to reply by naming one of the crafts is an absurd answer; because it points out something that knowledge is of when this is not what the question was about.

Theaetetus: So it seems.

Socrates: Again, it goes no end of a long way round, in a case where, I take it, a short and commonplace answer is possible. In the question about clay, for example, it would presumably be possible to make the simple, commonplace statement that it is earth mixed with liquid, and let the question of whose clay it is take care of itself.

Theaetetus: That seems easier, Socrates, now you put it like that. But I believe you're asking just the sort of question that occurred to your namesake Socrates here and myself, when we were having a discussion a little while ago. . . . [Theaetetus describes their answer on mathematical powers.]

Socrates: Excellent, my boys. I don't think Theodorus is likely to be had up for false witness.

Theaetetus: And yet, Socrates, I shouldn't be able to answer your question about knowledge in the same way that I answered the one about lengths and [mathematical] powers—though you seem to me to be looking for something of the same sort. So Theodorus turns out a false witness after all. [Levett & Burnyeat at 7–8, 9 (147b–d, 148b)]

In the very next exchange, Theaetetus continues to profess his inability to supply Socrates with the kind of answer that he expects from Theaetetus (an answer that Socrates thinks it possible [and Theaetetus thinks it impossible] to produce).

Socrates: Then do have confidence in yourself and try to believe that Theodorus knew what he was talking about. You must put your whole heart into what we are doing—in particular into this matter of getting a statement of what knowledge really is.

Theaetetus: If putting one's heart into it is all that is required, Socrates, the answer will come to light.

Socrates: Go on, then. You gave us a good lead just now. Try to imitate your answer about the [mathematical] powers. There you brought together the many powers within a single form; now I want you in the same way to give one single account of the many branches of knowledge.

> *Theaetetus:* But I assure you, Socrates, I have often tried to think this out, when I have heard reports of the questions you ask. But I can never persuade myself that anything I say will really do; and I never hear anyone else state the matter in the way that you require. And yet, again, you know, I can't even stop worrying about it. [Levett & Burnyeat at 9–10 (148c–e)]

Even with putting his heart into it, as Theaetetus clearly does, it is not that easy to achieve the result sought by Socrates. Courage and honesty and enthusiasm Theaetetus has in abundance, as everyone in this dialogue testifies: Socrates, Theodorus, Eucleides, and Terpsion. Still, while these character traits may be necessary for pursuing the task of Socratic conversational inquiry, they are not sufficient. Something more must be entered into the equation.

This fact comes into prominence when the sincerity and the genuineness of Theaetetus' philosophical impulse are noted. At a couple of points in the dialogue, the authenticity of Theaetetus' desire to know, his wonder at philosophical problems, is remarked. For example, consider the statement quoted above: "And yet, again, you know, I can't even stop worrying about it." Despite his inability to contribute fruitfully to the inquiry, Theaetetus cannot leave such questions alone. He is unable to ignore them. Later, Theaetetus also avers: "Oh yes, indeed, Socrates, I often wonder like mad what these things can mean; sometimes when I'm looking at them I begin to feel quite giddy" [Levett & Burnyeat at 19 (155c)]. To this remark, Socrates responds: "[T]his is an experience which is characteristic of a philosopher, this wondering: this is where philosophy begins and nowhere else" [Levett & Burnyeat at 19 (155d)].

When in a state of wonder, how are we to proceed? While Theaetetus knows what Socrates wants from him, it is *delivering* it to Socrates that gives Theaetetus pause. And, as noted, he is honest enough to admit this to himself as well as to Socrates: "But I can never persuade myself that anything I say will really do; and I never hear anyone else state the matter in the way that you require." Is such an answer capable of being generated? And if such answers are possible, how does one gain the ability to formulate them?

In the *Theaetetus,* Socrates demonstrates the possibility of giving such answers by generating several different definitions of knowledge and investigating them critically by means of interrogation, all by way of giving accounts of them (including their implications and possibilities). As Socrates is giving these accounts, he is simultaneously teaching both Theaetetus and us (Plato's readers, the audience) how these accounts—these definitive answers—are created. Thus, Socrates demonstrates how giving an account of one's views (and of oneself) is done.

Teaching Theaetetus How to Give an Account

The bulk of the *Theaetetus* is given over to the art of formulating and criticizing answers to the kind of questions that are at the heart of Socrates' conversational investigations. Socrates demonstrates his method of inquiry, his art, in the following response:

> *Socrates:* Well, my dear lad, this has been a long yarn; but the reason was that I have a suspicion that you (as you think yourself) are pregnant and in labour. So I want you to come to me as to one who is both the son of a midwife and himself skilled in the art; and try to answer the questions I shall ask you as well as you can. And when I examine what you say, I may perhaps think it is a phantom and not truth, and proceed to take it quietly from you and abandon it. Now, if this happens, you mustn't get savage with me, like a mother over her first-born child. . . . So begin again, Theaetetus, and try to say what knowledge is. And don't on any account tell me that you can't. For if God is willing, and you play the man, you can. [Levett & Burnyeat at 13 (151b–c, d)]

According to Socrates' account here, his art consists in two operations: first, he attempts to "deliver" the other "pregnant" participant of his struggling expression. Second, once the expression or locution is uttered (is born), Socrates subjects it to testing. "Now my art of midwifery is just like theirs in most respects. The difference is that I attend men and not women, and that I watch over the labour of their souls, not their bodies. And the most important thing about my art is the ability to apply all possible tests to the offspring, to determine whether the young mind is being delivered of a phantom [an illusion], that is, an error, or a fertile truth" [Levett & Burnyeat at 11–12 (150b–c)]. What Socrates hopes to pass along to Theaetetus is this art, this ability to deliver others (or oneself, if it comes to that) of their views and opinions, and then to test them for their reality or illusoriness. This is the fundamental action of the *Theaetetus.*

When Socrates directs Theaetetus to make another attempt at saying what knowledge really is, Theaetetus responds in his usual spirit of goodwill:

> *Theaetetus:* Well, Socrates, after such encouragement from *you,* it would hardly be decent for anyone not to try his hardest to say what he has in him. Very well then. It seems to me that a man who knows something perceives what he knows, and the way it appears at present, at any rate, is that knowledge is simply perception.
>
> *Socrates:* That's a good straight answer, my son. That's the way to speak one's mind. But come now, let us look at this thing together, and see whether what we have here is really fertile or a mere wind-egg. [Levett & Burnyeat at 13 (151d–e)]

Rather than proceeding to test Theaetetus' initial expression to determine its fertility, Socrates instead relates Theaetetus' remark immediately to Protagoras: "But look here [Theaetetus], this is no ordinary account of knowledge you've come out with: it's what Protagoras used to maintain. He said the very same thing, only he put it in rather a different way" [Levett & Burnyeat at 14 (151e–152a)].

We should stop to appreciate the oddness of this moment. For it is odd, in at least two ways. First, what Theaetetus so far has managed to say about knowledge hardly amounts to an "account." He has gotten the barest of statements out of his mouth, and Socrates is already lauding him ("this is no ordinary account"). It is difficult to see what all the excitement is about. But Theaetetus' remarks are a beginning, and that is all that Socrates needs in order for him to work his magic, to practice his craft. This is what I think we are meant to see here. Theaetetus has provided Socrates with the kind of statement—"a short and commonplace answer"—that he had sought earlier. So these types of answer are possible, and we have shown that they are possible by producing one.

Yes, and no. This statement by Theaetetus is an answer of a sort, but, standing alone, it hardly constitutes an *account*—of knowledge or of anything else. And this is the initial oddness about this moment that I think we are meant to notice. Theaetetus' statement, on its own, cannot satisfy us. But, worked on, labored over, treated with Socrates' art of midwifery, the transformed statement may serve as an adequate account of knowledge. We are *capable* of producing satisfactory accounts, *if* we learn how to go about creating them, how to go on with them. And how is that done? How do we accomplish this feat?

We can learn how from Socrates, because he teaches us his art of accountancy. (Just as, differently situated, Thoreau teaches us his art of accountancy in *Walden*.)[20] The first major section of the dialogue is devoted to teaching Theaetetus the secrets of Socrates' art,[21] his midwifery. Given, then, that we are supposed to learn something here from Socrates, I want to relate this point to the perceived second oddity concerning what Socrates does in response to Theaetetus' beginning statement. The second odd thing is that Socrates proceeds not by testing Theaetetus' remark, but rather by connecting it to another person, attributing Theaetetus' theory to Protagoras. Why does Socrates proceed this way?

This is a part of what I understand Socrates' art to encompass. What previously I called the discursiveness of the *Theaetetus*, is a function of Socrates' willingness and ability to digress, to follow out his own remarks and the remarks of others, to pursue their implications and to trace their possibilities.[22] In regard to Theaetetus' view of knowledge, one implication of his initial statement is its connection with Protagoras' theory. Admittedly, the two are differently expressed. Still, what this apparent difference comes to mean, within the crucible of Socrates' art, is that we shall have to show how one statement (that is, Theaetetus') can be translated into the other expression of Protagoras' theory,[23] or, we might say, how one statement can be shown to derive from the other. And this activity—of connecting the two, or of deriving one from the other, or of showing how one implies the other—is exactly what Socrates here proceeds to undertake: "But look here [Theaetetus], this is no ordinary account of knowledge you've come out with: it's what Protagoras used to maintain. He said the very same thing, only he put it in rather a different way. For he says, you know, that 'Man is the measure of all things: of the things which are, that they are, and of the things which are not, that they are not.' You have read this, of course?" [Levett & Burnyeat at 14 (151e–152a)].

Socrates is, in this instance, engaging in rather obvious understatement. Protagoras' theory hardly is "the very same thing" as Theaetetus' view of knowledge. To claim, as to Protagoras' theory, that "he put it in rather a different way," is seriously to understate the differences between the two. But then part of the challenge in the remaining discussion will be to make stick Socrates' alleged connection between the two, to make this claimed connection stand up to critical scrutiny and testing. And, in fact, this aptly characterizes the ensuing activity for the majority of the dialogue, extending from the first major section on through the second and into the third. During all of this conversation, while Socrates speaks both with Theaetetus and Theodorus, the main item of discussion remains Protagoras' theory and its purported relationship with Theaetetus' expression concerning the nature of knowledge.

Earlier I said that Theaetetus, in responding to Socrates' request that he "try to say what knowledge is," comes up with this definition: "knowledge is simply perception." Socrates takes over the management of this definition by immediately taking out of Theaetetus' hands any responsibility for giving an account of his initial definition. (Is this because Socrates already realizes that Theaetetus cannot get any further with giving an account of what this definition means or implies?) Socrates then begins his own account of the matter, by attributing this theory of knowledge to Protagoras ("Man is the measure of all things"), and also by associating certain aspects of the theory with Heraclitus, Empedocles, and Homer [Levett & Burnyeat at 15 (152e)]. At this juncture, Socrates offers his own interpretation of Protagoras' theory of knowledge ("my friend, you must understand our theory in this way") [Levett & Burnyeat at 16 (153d)].

How are we to understand Socrates' motivation here? His actions are driven by Theaetetus' frequent comments that he (Theaetetus) does not understand what Socrates means by what he is saying. So, for example, we have the following:

> *Theaetetus:* What do you mean by that, Socrates?
> *Socrates:* I'll tell you; . . . . [Levett & Burnyeat at 14 (152d)]

> *Theaetetus:* But what do you mean?
> *Socrates:* Let us follow what we stated a moment ago, and posit that . . . . [Levett & Burnyeat at 16 (153e)]

> *Theaetetus:* What do you mean? What sort of ridiculous things?
> *Socrates:* Let me give you a simple example of what I mean, and you will see the rest for yourself. [Levett & Burnyeat at 17 (154b–c)]

In responding to Theaetetus' repeated requests for clarification, sometimes Socrates tells him something more; sometimes Socrates follows out a previous statement by positing something else; and sometimes Socrates gives Theaetetus an example (adding that then Theaetetus will be able to "see the rest for" himself). All of these activities—telling, following out, positing, giving examples—constitute Socrates' pursuit of the implications and possibilities of something that had previously been said by him. This is Socrates teaching Theaetetus how to give an account of his words.

Gradually, Theaetetus seems to get the hang of it: "Well, Socrates, if I answer what seems true in relation to the present question, I shall say 'No, it is not possible'; but if I consider it in relation to the question that went before, then in order to avoid contradicting myself, I say 'Yes, it is'" [Levett & Burnyeat at 17–18 (154d)]. This is a careful, cautious answer, full of nuance and a sense of what kind of answer is appropriate for which kind of question. "That's a good answer, my friend, by Jove it is; you are inspired" [Levett & Burnyeat at 18 (154d)]. Theaetetus is making progress. Yet, even with all that, he still has much to learn.

These are difficult matters, and they demand of both the teacher and the student their renewed effort and perseverance.

Socrates: . . . But aren't you beginning to see now what is the explanation of these puzzles, according to the theory which we are attributing to Protagoras?

Theaetetus: I don't think I am, yet.

Socrates: Then I dare say you will be grateful to me if I help you. [Levett & Burnyeat at 19 (155d)]

Socrates: Now what does this tale really mean, from our point of view, Theaetetus? How does it bear on what we were saying before? Do you see?

Theaetetus: Not really, Socrates.

Socrates: Look here, then, let us see if we can somehow round it off. What it is trying to express, presumably, is this. . . . [Levett & Burnyeat at 20 (156c)]

Socrates claims, in expounding Protagoras' theory, to be helping Theaetetus "to discover the veiled truth in the thought of a great man" [Levett & Burnyeat at 19 (155e)]. But this is possible only if Theaetetus is one of those people who can appreciate the details noted (and the distinctions drawn) by Socrates. Such a person is guided by a sense of wonder or of puzzlement, by a desire to know.[24] "[T]his is an experience which is characteristic of a philosopher, this wondering: this is where philosophy begins and nowhere else" [Levett & Burnyeat at 19 (155d)]. But, as Socrates also acknowledges, it is this very desire to know, this anxious questing after answers, that causes us pain.

Socrates is willing to live in such a conflicted position. He has both the courage of his desire to know, and the candor to admit that he still does not know the answers to the questions causing him pain. He is caught between the hardheaded dogmatists and the more subtle cynics and sophists, who think they have the answers for what Socrates is seeking. But neither of their answers satisfies him. He chooses neither to dismiss nor to swallow either of the proffered answers. Rather, he continues to test and to inquire into the matters that puzzle him. This careful balance is not easy to accomplish. It would be so much easier (as Socrates knows) to play the all-knowing prosecutor,[25] yet he refuses to reduce his method of inquiry to this level. Remember: "As it is, you see, we may easily find ourselves forced into saying the most astonishing and ridiculous things, as Protagoras would point out or anyone who undertook to expound his views" [Levett & Burnyeat at 17 (154b)]. This vulnerability or susceptibility to making extravagant statements or claims when one is pressed critically, is a risk that Socratic inquirers must run.

In conducting our critical searches, Socrates teaches us to resist the human temptation to criticize unfairly. For example, when he concludes his initial account of Protagoras' theory [Levett & Burnyeat at 21 (157c)], he could leave the matter there, with his exposition of Protagoras' theory as it stood; if he did so, it would be difficult to fault Socrates. He had been as fair to Protagoras as one reasonably could expect of a critic engaged in an emotionally charged dispute. Socrates, however, acts differently:

> *Socrates:* Well, Theaetetus, does this look to you a tempting meal and could you take a bite of the delicious stuff?
>
> *Theaetetus:* I really don't know, Socrates. I can't even quite see what you're getting at—whether the things you are saying are what you think yourself, or whether you are just trying me out.
>
> *Socrates:* You are forgetting, my friend. I don't know anything about this kind of thing myself, and I don't claim any of it as my own. I am barren of theories; my business is to attend you in your labour. So I chant incantations over you and offer you little titbits from each of the wise till I succeed in assisting you to bring your own belief forth into the light. When it has been born, I shall consider whether it is fertile or a wind-egg. But you must have courage and patience; answer like a man whatever appears to you to be true about the things I ask you. [Levett & Burnyeat at 21 (157c–d)]

Is any part of the "tempting meal" sufficiently attractive to Theaetetus? Does Theaetetus find himself inclined to say what Socrates has given him to say, in the guise of expounding Protagoras' theory? Will Theaetetus assent to any of these sayings, and thus permit Socrates to begin testing them for their truth or falsity? "When [your own belief] has been born, I shall consider whether it is fertile or a wind-egg." Will Theaetetus adopt these expressions of Protagoras' theory as his own? That is the critical question Socrates now puts to Theaetetus.

If Theaetetus makes these words his own, then we shall have identified something about what he is willing to say and to believe. And, by means of discovering what he is willing to say, we shall have revealed something about Theaetetus' self or soul. His expressions betray his self.[26] In this way, Theaetetus can learn how to give an account of himself, how to take account of himself, how to make an accounting of what he thinks and believes, by auditing what he is willing to utter, to offer to the world. This is why Socrates emphasizes (at the end of this exchange) that whatever discovery is to be made here, is a function of Theaetetus' character,[27] his courage and his candor in giving his answer to Socrates' questions. "But you must . . . answer like a man whatever appears to you to be true about the things I ask you." Any failure of nerve threatens the entire project of Socratic examination.

For nearly ten pages, Socrates explicates and examines Theaetetus' initial statement about knowledge and perception. At this stage, Theaetetus appears sufficiently satisfied with Socrates' account of this theory of knowledge to accept Socrates' reformulation of it (as does Theodorus, the friend of Protagoras, or at least an adherent of Protagoras' theory[28]).

> *Theaetetus:* All right, go on with the questions.
>
> *Socrates:* Tell me again, then, whether you like the suggestion that good and beautiful and all the things we were just speaking of cannot be said to "be" anything, but are always "coming to be."
>
> *Theaetetus:* Well, as far as I'm concerned, while I'm listening to your exposition of it, it seems to me an extraordinarily reasonable view; and I feel that the way you have set out the matter has got to be accepted.
>
> *Socrates:* In that case, we had better not pass over any point where our theory is still incomplete. What we have not yet discussed is . . . . [Levett & Burnyeat at 21–22 (157d–e)]

Theaetetus is willing to accept Socrates' restatement and elaboration as they stand, but it is Socrates who will not let the matter rest there. He insists on investigating matters further, checking all of the issues that remain outstanding and untested. Socrates teaches self-criticism, so it is he who is not satisfied with his own account. Here, he recognizes that he still cannot claim to know what knowledge is, based simply upon his own account of the Protagorean theory of knowledge. Instead, Socrates tests his own account by examining its implications.

For anyone who adopts Protagoras' theory that knowledge is perception, for example, there is the problem of "false perceptions":

> *Socrates:* You realise, I suppose, that it would be generally agreed that all these cases appear to provide a refutation of the theory we have just expounded. For in these conditions, we surely have false perceptions. Here it is far from being true that all things which appear to the individual also are. On the contrary, no one of the things which appear to him really is.
>
> *Theaetetus:* That is perfectly true, Socrates.
>
> *Socrates:* Well then, my lad, what argument is left for the person who maintains that knowledge is perception and that what appears to any individual also is, for him to whom it appears to be?
>
> *Theaetetus:* Well, Socrates, I hardly like to tell you that I don't know what to say, seeing I've just got into trouble with you for that. But I really shouldn't know how to dispute the suggestion . . . .
>
> *Socrates:* But there's a point here which *is* a matter of dispute, especially as regards dreams and real life—don't you see?
>
> *Theaetetus:* What do you mean? [Levett & Burnyeat at 22 (157d–e)]

Socrates once more must show Theaetetus the way. And Socrates does; not because he is an adherent of the Protagorean theory of knowledge, but rather because he is trying to investigate in a fair yet critical way the truth or falsity of that theory of knowledge. In doing so, he is trying to keep an open mind. For Socrates, when one is a critic of a theory whose truth has not yet been determined, philosophical criticism is in part a matter of being fair-minded.[29]

In asking Theaetetus, "[W]hat argument is left for the person who maintains that knowledge is perception?" Socrates is testing one's resources, or one's resourcefulness, seeing whether the materials are there and the capability is there out of which one can make an adequate response. He is looking for additional argument—an extension of his initial account of knowledge. This argument or extension will enable us to square the Protagorean theory of knowledge with our awareness that we sometimes have false perceptions (that is, that perception is not always veridical).

> *Socrates:* You see, then, it is not difficult to find matter for dispute, when it is disputed even whether this is real life or a dream. . . .
> *Theaetetus:* That certainly is so.
> *Socrates:* And doesn't the same argument apply in the cases of disease and madness, except that the periods of time are not equal?
> *Theaetetus:* Yes, that is so.
> *Socrates:* Well now, are we going to fix the limits of truth by the clock?
> *Theaetetus:* That would be a very funny thing to do.
> *Socrates:* But can you produce some other clear indication to show which of these beliefs are true?
> *Theaetetus:* I don't think I can.
> *Socrates:* Then you listen to me and I'll tell you the kind of thing that might be said by those people who propose it as a rule that whatever a man thinks at any time is the truth for him. I can imagine them putting their position by asking you this question . . . . [Levett & Burnyeat at 23 (158c–e)]

Theaetetus still stands in need of instruction in how to give an account of himself; and Socrates continues to be prepared to teach him this art. The rest of the text shows this learning and this teaching as they take place. The dialogue sketches, then, the progress of Theaetetus as student and Socrates as teacher.

Theaetetus Learns How to Give an Account

What progress does Theaetetus make? He begins to learn how to give an account by himself. So, for example, Theaetetus begins, even with occasional lapses, to make insights. And he also begins to catch or capture Socrates' meaning:

> *Socrates:* Well, now let us apply this same statement to you and me and things in general. Take, for example, Socrates ill and Socrates well. Shall we say Socrates in health is like or unlike Socrates in sickness?
>
> *Theaetetus:* You mean the ill Socrates as a whole compared with the well Socrates as a whole?
>
> *Socrates:* You get my point excellently; that is just what I mean. [Levett & Burnyeat at 24 (159b)]

Theaetetus now begins to generate answers to Socrates' questions, answers that are interesting and productive:

> *Socrates:* So we must again resort to our wise Theaetetus. Come, Theaetetus. Think, to begin with, of what we have just been saying, and tell me if you are not yourself astonished at suddenly finding that you are the equal in wisdom of any man or even a god?—Or do you think the Protagorean measure isn't meant to be applied to gods as much as to men?
>
> *Theaetetus:* I most certainly don't. And, to answer your question, yes, I am very much astonished. [Levett & Burnyeat at 28 (162c)]

We soon reach the point where Socrates not only is praising Theaetetus for his efforts but also is urging him on with his work, inviting him to go ahead and do more: "Very good indeed, Theaetetus; and it would not be right for me to stand in the way of your progress by raising objections to what you say. But look, there is another difficulty coming upon us. You must think now how we are going to fend it off" [Levett & Burnyeat at 29 (163c)].

Theaetetus is making progress. He has not, of course, developed fully as a Socratic inquirer, but it is a mark of Socrates' masterful teaching that he is able to bring Theaetetus along at Theaetetus' own pace. A good teacher uses different techniques for different students in different situations. By this I mean that the choice of a teaching technique depends upon the quality and readiness of the student as well as the pedagogical situation at hand (that is, the resources available, the nature of the materials being studied, and so forth).

It is not until the third major section of the dialogue [see Levett & Burnyeat at 56–93 (183d–210d)] that Theaetetus settles into his role as a Socratic inquirer. At this point, two important things happen. First, Theodorus drops out of the dialogue. His last locution comes just after he is "set free" from his agreement with Socrates to investigate Protagoras' theory [see Levett & Burnyeat at 55 (183b–c)]. Doing without Theodorus reduces to some extent the discursiveness or digressions in the *Theaetetus*. Of the three major parts in this dialogue, the third section is the most compressed and focused even though it covers the most territory, in that it considers all three separate theories of knowledge.[30]

Second, Theaetetus takes a more active role in the investigations, at Socrates' urging: "But perhaps it would be better if you [Theaetetus] stated the answers yourself, rather than that I should busy myself on your behalf" [Levett & Burnyeat at 57 (184e)]. This is all the authorization that Theaetetus requires. Now, subsequent to the rigorous lessons taught him in the first major section, and subsequent to his observation of the exchanges between Theodorus and Socrates in the second major section, Theaetetus is ready to participate as a full partner. This change or development is signalled in two respects: Theaetetus is more assertive; and he is more quizzical or questioning in regard to his (and Socrates') assertions. For example:

Socrates: You follow me exceedingly well, Theaetetus. These are just the things I am asking about.

Theaetetus: But *I* couldn't possibly say. All I can tell you is that it doesn't seem to me that for these things there is any special instrument at all, as there is for the others. It seems to me that in investigating the common features of everything the soul functions through itself.

Socrates: Yes, Theaetetus, you would say that, because you are handsome and not ugly as Theodorus would have it. For handsome is as handsome says. And besides being handsome, you have done me a good turn; you have saved me a vast amount of talk if it seems to you that, while the soul considers some things through the bodily powers, there are others which it considers

> alone and through itself. This was what I thought myself, but I wanted you to think it too. [Levett & Burnyeat at 58–59 (185d–e)]

Theaetetus' response to Socrates shows both discrimination and caution: he is willing to respond, but he is willing to say only so much. Theaetetus is more capable of putting his thoughts or ideas into words and asserting them, and testing their consistency or their implications or their consequences. Accordingly, Theaetetus is willing to be saddled or burdened only with the specific words that *he* feels *he* can say here and now. And he is learning that, in order to give an account of himself, this ability depends upon his saying only what he does mean (or can mean) at this specific moment in these particular circumstances.[31]

There is a newfound maturity in Theaetetus' expressions and a new gravity in his voice, as though his hardwon experience with Socrates' critical examination has sobered him (which is not to say that Theaetetus had been reckless or wanton). This maturity, this soberness, begins where we have seen it before in these circumstances: namely, with disillusion. Socrates' critical inquiry has led Theaetetus to the realization that his original theory of knowledge, his original story ("tale") that knowledge is simply perception, is not adequate.

> *Socrates:* Then, Theaetetus, perception and knowledge could never be the same thing.
>
> *Theaetetus:* No, apparently not, Socrates; we have now got the clearest possible proof that knowledge is something different from perception. [Levett & Burnyeat at 60 (186e)]

Theaetetus expresses disappointment in this regard, but this realization does not devastate him. Disillusioning Theaetetus (as well as Theodorus, to the extent that he too can be disillusioned) is more a matter of deflating him than it is of refuting him. Or, rather, the refutation of Theaetetus takes place by means of deflating his words, showing them to be empty, mere "wind-eggs."

Getting Theaetetus to be more committed, getting him to consider and choose more carefully his words, his claims to know, is one of Socrates' aims.

Socrates: Your opinion, my dear lad, is correct. Now look back to the beginning. Wipe out all that we have said hitherto, and see if you can see any better from where you have now progressed to. Tell me again, what is knowledge?

Theaetetus: Well, Socrates, one can't say that it is judgement in general, because there is also false judgement—but true judgement may well be knowledge. So let that be my answer. If the same thing happens again, and we find, as we go on, that it turns out not to be so, we'll try something else.

Socrates: And even so, Theaetetus, you have answered me in the way one ought—with a good will, and not reluctantly, as you did at first. If we continue like this, one of two things will happen. Either we shall find what we are going out after; or we shall be less inclined to think we know things which we don't know at all—and even that would be a reward we could not fairly be dissatisfied with. Now what is this that you say? [Levett & Burnyeat at 60–61 (187a–c)]

Theaetetus expresses here a new sobriety concerning his chances at coming up with something that so far has escaped every other person who has tried to articulate a theory of knowledge. He admits that what he now says may "not . . . be so." It is not that he treats his own words or claims lightly. It is, rather, that he realizes, in all humility, that he may not be able to articulate an adequate theory of knowledge or to explain it satisfactorily. If this proves to be so, however, then he will try again.

Theaetetus now is committed not only to the process of inquiry in a way not true of him before, but also to the task of weighing and testing his words. At first, Theaetetus simply was a good sport, willing to play along with the examination and sufficiently interested in Socrates to answer his questions with goodwill. But now Theaetetus also displays patience, as asked of him earlier [see 157d], and a persistence unlike what we had seen before in the dialogue. What follows in the wake of this new recognition by Theaetetus of his powers and limitations? It is not that he magically or miraculously becomes a master of the Socratic technique of question-and-answer. Rather, Theaetetus moves from inability to ability, from incompetence to competence, in the activity of giving an account.

Toward the end of the dialogue, Socrates turns over to Theaetetus the lead in their discussion.

> *Socrates:* Come now, you answer.
> *Theaetetus:* Well, my answer will be that . . . . [Levett & Burnyeat at 73 (195e)]

In the final twenty or thirty pages of the dialogue, there is a new assurance in Theaetetus. It is not that he now thinks he has all the answers. Rather, he becomes more assured in his ability to come up with an account of the matter at hand, and in his ability to inquire into it. Now, he can express what he needs to say, and he can assess what he has said. We even, on occasion, find a new boldness in Theaetetus [see, for example, Levett & Burnyeat at 64 (189d)], just as we occasionally find him now exhorting Socrates: "Then do be bold, please. And if you [Socrates] don't keep from using these words, we'll forgive you all right" [Levett & Burnyeat at 74 (197a)].

Ten pages later, we find Theaetetus following his own advice: "I don't feel at all certain; but as you keep telling me to answer up with a good will, I will take a risk and say they are different" [Levett & Burnyeat at 84 (204b)]. A page later, Socrates acknowledges this change in him: "You are putting up a good fight anyway, Theaetetus" [Levett & Burnyeat at 85 (205a)]. And, toward the end of the dialogue, we even find Theaetetus translating or rephrasing Socrates' words, which is something that Socrates has been doing to Theaetetus the entire time:

> *Socrates:* Then have you forgotten that at first when you were learning to read and write that is just what you and the other boys used to do?
> *Theaetetus:* You mean we used to think that sometimes one letter and sometimes another belonged to the same syllable, and used to put the same letter sometimes into its proper syllable and sometimes into another?
> *Socrates:* Yes, that is what I mean. [Levett & Burnyeat at 89 (207d–e)]

Theaetetus has learned not only how to give an account but also how to examine the account given to him by another (here, Socrates). The lesson is over.

Socrates: Well now, dear lad, are we still pregnant, still in labour with any thoughts about knowledge? Or have we been delivered of them all?

Theaetetus: As far as I'm concerned, Socrates, you've made me say far more than ever was in me, Heaven knows. [Levett & Burnyeat at 92 (210b)]

Theaetetus is spent. So, too, is Socrates.

If the dialogue closes on this note, we are not quite in a position to do the same. Before we can complete our treatment of this dialogue, I want to look more closely at the nature of the art practiced by Socrates, drawing from his example a moral or two for our further edification.

Conversational Criticism as Delivery

When Theaetetus tells Socrates that he is willing to try to answer Socrates' questions, but doubts that he is capable of producing adequate or satisfactory answers, Socrates responds by reassuring him. Your worries, your anxieties, Socrates says, "are the pains of labour, dear Theaetetus. It is because you are not barren but pregnant" [Levett & Burnyeat at 10 (148e)]. It is not that Theaetetus is without answers; he has them. He needs to learn how to produce them, however, and this means learning what Socrates and his questions ask of Theaetetus. So, rather than being unable to answer, Theaetetus' pain and anxiety reveal him to be pregnant with thoughts and ideas. Only, he needs help in delivering them, and this help is a part of what Socrates provides.

Recall an earlier passage when Socrates addresses Theaetetus: "And now that it has been born, we must perform the rite of running round the hearth with it; we must make it in good earnest go the round of discussion. For we must take care that we don't overlook some defect in this thing that is entering into life; it may be something not worth bringing up, a wind-egg, a falsehood. What do you say? Is it your opinion that your child ought in any case to be brought up and not exposed to die? Can you bear to see it found fault with, and not get into a rage if your first-born is stolen away from you?" This suggests that the primary goals for Socrates are twofold: first, the delivery of the person under scrutiny of his thoughts or opinions; and then, second, the testing of those thoughts or opinions. That set of dual aims is what Socrates' practice of being a midwife to our souls is meant to achieve.

As summarized, the Socratic procedure consists of two operations. The first operation responds to the need to bring forth an expression (that is, the delivery of the utterance). "This, then, it appears, is what our efforts have at last brought forth—whatever it really is." Let it not be forgotten, however, that these efforts comprise twenty pages of hard work; they represent Socrates' tenacious effort to elicit an adequate expression from Theaetetus.

One aim of my numerous descriptions of Socrates' performance in this chapter has been to capture the great effort that he puts forth to articulate adequately the glimmer of a theory, the bare inkling of a thought. *This* is what Socrates extracts from the inarticulate but willing Theaetetus. When Theaetetus avers, timorously, that perhaps "knowledge is simply perception," that is just the tip of the iceberg. It has taken Socrates ten pages to get Theaetetus to see what kind of an answer Socrates wants to his question, "What is knowledge?" But then it takes another ten pages for Socrates to work this first, timid try into something worth contesting. So, the first twenty-five pages of the dialogue (including the two introductory sections) are devoted to the articulation of Theaetetus' initial try at a theory of knowledge (and, of course, to its development in the thought of Protagoras, who is granted priority).[32]

The second operation in the procedure that Socrates follows in the *Theaetetus* is the testing of the expressions and elaborations just rendered. Once offered, they must be rigorously tested. "And now that it has been born, we must perform the rite of running round the hearth with it; we must make it in good earnest go the round of discussion. For we must take care that we don't overlook some defect in this thing that is entering into life; it may be something not worth bringing up, a wind-egg, a falsehood."

The two operations in Socrates' process of investigation are not completely separable, of course, for some aspect of testing surely is included within the very attempt to articulate better (or to elaborate further) the thoughts and expressions initially put forward. A person's original thought may be true or fruitful, but that possibility becomes dubious if we learn that neither that person nor we can do anything with it. If we discover that we cannot go on with a thought or expression, that it fails to connect with the rest of our knowledge or experience, that we cannot successfully trace its implications or consequences (and so forth), then that in itself is an important discovery. So, in the act of articulating and elaborating the views expressed by Theaetetus (and attributed to Protagoras), Socrates already is testing them (implicitly, as it were).

Explicit testing also appears in the *Theaetetus,* and it comes in the form of the fairly frequent expressions of surprise that someone's words have failed. Upon examination, we find that the words to which our attention is just now being drawn have led us to an inconsistency, or to a contradiction, or to a clear falsehood. Moments such as these frequent the pages of the *Theaetetus:*

Socrates: Then apparently we get an impossible result when knowledge and perception are identified?
Theaetetus: It looks like it. [Levett & Burnyeat at 30 (164b)]

Theaetetus: Well, I draw a conclusion that contradicts my original suppositions.
Socrates: And that is the kind of thing that might have happened to you more than once, you wonderful fellow. [Levett & Burnyeat at 32 (165d)]

Socrates: A fine way this turns out to be of making our answer right. We were most anxious to prove that all things are in motion, in order to make that answer come out correct; but what has really emerged is that, if all things are in motion, every answer, on whatever subject, is equally correct, both "it is thus" and "it is not thus"—or if you like, "becomes," as we don't want to use any expressions which will bring our friends to a stand-still.
Theaetetus: You are quite right.
Socrates: . . . The exponents of this theory need to establish some other language; as it is, they have no words that are consistent with their hypothesis—unless it would perhaps suit them best to use "not at all thus" in a quite indefinite sense.

Theaetetus: That would at least be an idiom most appropriate to them. [Levett & Burnyeat at 55 (183a–b)]

This is the Socratic moment when someone is refuted. His or her words have been found empty, or inconsistent, or contradictory, or self-defeating, or otherwise deficient—nothing more than a "wind-egg." Both Socrates and Theaetetus fall victim at different times to this defeat. As mentioned above, however, Theodorus does not seem to share these failures of expression. This is why I believe that Theodorus never suffers or entertains disillusion. Since he never produces his own words, or words that he is willing to own, he cannot be refuted and disillusioned, as can the other two participants in this dialogue.

One might ask how disillusion, or refutation, is possible in the case of Socrates, for we have just seen that Socrates claims a dispensation from this condition, on the ground that, as he puts it to Theodorus, "[t]he arguments never come from me; they always come from the person I am talking to" [Levett & Burnyeat at 26 (161b)]. Does Socrates' claim amount to a denial of his responsibility for the words that he uses to express and elaborate the theories of Theaetetus and Protagoras? I do not think it can.

Here I call attention to the inaccuracy of Socrates' self-characterization when it relates to his own capacity for being disillusioned. I think there is something untoward in his self-description. Take another look at what Socrates says. His complaint is that Theodorus "think[s] that I [Socrates] am a bag of arguments, and can easily pick one out which will show you that this theory is wrong" [Levett & Burnyeat at 26 (161a–b)]. Is this an accurate characterization of Socrates and his method of inquiry? To say that he is "a bag of arguments" suggests that Socrates carries these arguments around with him and produces them at the appropriate moment in a dispute or an investigation. And this image carries with it the implication that Socrates' arguments are ready-made, not tempered by the heat of the moment but rather mass-produced for any occasion.

I do not think that this implication captures the reality of Socrates' art, his ability to *generate* an argument that speaks to the situation or problem at hand. What this implication fails to credit is his familiarity or experience with the matters at hand. Socrates is responsive in philosophical argument—and fertile in being philosophically imaginative—not because he happens to be a human information-retrieval system par excellence, but rather because he is thoroughly experienced in exploring the questions arising during his discussions with other people. Here again I appeal to Gregory Vlastos's description of Socrates' practice of continuing to review and to reexamine aspects of an argument. As Vlastos puts the matter, "Previous reflection has led him to many conclusions, and he does not put them out of his mind when jumping into a new argument. There they all are, and not in a vague or jumbled-up form, but in a clear map, on which he constantly relies to figure out, many moves in advance, the direction in which he would like to press an argument. . . . Nor is it only a matter of re-examining previously reached conclusions; it is no less a matter of hoping for new insights which may crop up right in this new argument and give the answer to some hitherto unanswered problem."[33]

Given Socrates' familiarity with the matters being discussed (be they about knowledge, or courage, or wisdom, or piety, or virtue, or justice), he has definite thoughts and ideas to offer. And because his previous reflections on these matters have led him to certain conclusions or beliefs, his mind certainly is not a tabula rasa. Rather, Socrates' mind is fully populated with a variety of ideas. "There they all are, and not in a vague or jumbled-up form, but in a clear map, on which he constantly relies to figure out, many moves in advance, the direction in which he would like to press an argument." But, nevertheless, these thoughts or ideas remain *provisional*. They are conclusions to which he has given only tentative assent. Having once arrived at them, he may yet depart from them. It all depends upon the evidence adduced and the direction that the argument or discussion takes. Socrates is open to persuasion or further discovery, but he comes to the conversation fully tested, experience in hand. (This sense of Socrates having a vast conceptual landscape at his fingertips, is an achievement that I believe Socrates shared with Wittgenstein. Here I am thinking of a remark Wittgenstein once made in his notebooks, to the effect that "I am showing my pupils details of an immense landscape which they cannot possibly know their way around."[34])

Socrates' prior experience with these matters means that, depending upon what crops up in the discussion, he can respond in any number of different ways. How he responds will depend upon how an argument is put, or what story is told, or what claim is made, or which image is invoked. I said earlier in this chapter that Socrates' practice assumes that philosophy is not an activity to be hurried or rushed. We cannot artificially accelerate the therapeutic solution to our philosophical problems. Accordingly, with all the things that Socrates has managed to learn during his countless conversations with others, and all the things that he has grappled with in trying to examine himself and others and subjecting everyone to critical scrutiny, he has a comprehensive competency on which to call when he is put in the position of responding to someone else's claim or assertion or theory. But he responds at that time to the topic and its aspect as they arise in the natural course of the conversation.[35] (The context for the point that Socrates wishes to make, or for the remark that he wishes to enter, has to be appropriate.)[36] Whichever aspect of the topic that Socrates finds prompting or profitable, that is what he pursues in the ensuing conversational investigation. And, as I already have remarked, one consequence of this Socratic trait is the characteristic discursiveness (or the digressions) that we find in Socrates' conversational inquiries, including in the *Theaetetus*.

The characterization of Socrates attributed to Theodorus (namely, that Socrates is "a bag of arguments") may express an appreciation for the fact that Socrates is far more cognizant of the theories and assertions of others than his claims of ignorance might otherwise lead us to believe. After all, Socrates does produce these ready-made arguments from "the wise," as he calls them, and I suppose that this fact might be counted against his denying that he is simply a grab-bag of canned arguments. And Socrates does show a remarkable familiarity with the theories of Protagoras, even quoting or paraphrasing several times from Protagoras' book, *Truth*. He also demonstrates an acquaintance with the thoughts and works of Heraclitus and Empedocles and Parmenides as well as with the poems of Homer.

Positively speaking, Socrates' activity of citing to other philosophers who have expressed thoughts similar to Theaetetus' initial statement is a valuable contribution to the Socratic effort to "give an account." Scattered throughout the *Theaetetus* are quotations from, and citations to, other thinkers and writers. These quotations and citations are a way of establishing a cultural framework, both historical and philosophical, within which to situate Theaetetus' initial definition of knowledge. In this respect, Socrates' activity serves both to integrate Theaetetus' comment into the larger cultural and philosophical context as well as to individuate Theaetetus' expression within that horde of competitors and critics. Locating Theaetetus' remark in this way (putting it, as it were, on the cultural map) is one way of exploring its implications and possibilities. Accordingly, to give an account of the theory that knowledge is perception can be, in part, to situate it historically and philosophically in its culture or world,[37] and this is exactly what Socrates does.

Negatively speaking, Socrates' complaint that Theodorus ought not to treat him as though he were "a bag of arguments" is a criticism not of Socrates but of Theodorus. *His* passivity in the face of argument, *his* lack of participation in the dialogue, is the feature that distinguishes Theodorus. Socrates is admonishing Theodorus not to treat him (Socrates) as though he were the sole source of responses or arguments, not to turn to him automatically whenever the discussion flags or the investigation becomes blocked. It is possible, Socrates is pointedly saying, that you yourself, Theodorus, could contribute here; *you* could do something positive to help our joint investigation of this matter. The acerbity of Socrates' remark should not be ignored.

This entire discussion leads me to ask: How are we to characterize the activity of Socrates in giving or constructing his account? (This is, I have claimed, the central activity of the *Theaetetus*.[38]) It seems to me correct for Socrates to say that he does not himself come up with the originating statement that gets the dialogue moving. Socrates does not express it; rather, Theaetetus does. So the original idea comes from Theaetetus, which remark Socrates takes over and then, without necessarily making it his own, elaborates to such an extent that it is probably unrecognizable to the person (Theaetetus) who originated the idea.

In the passage which I have been parsing (that is, the exchange between Socrates and Theodorus), the Levett and Burnyeat translation casts Socrates' statement in terms of his not being a bag of "arguments." But the Jowett translation puts it differently: Socrates there claims not to be a bag of "theories" [Jowett & Copi at 24 (161a)]. It is more plausible to me that Socrates is not a theoretician and thus cannot be likened to a bag of theories, than it is that he is not an arguer, not a source of arguments (which I think he is). In fact, Socrates later concedes that he is given to argument, or at least to heated discussion, when he calls himself garrulous. “I'm annoyed at my own stupidity—my own true garrulousness. What else could you call it when a man will keep dragging arguments up and down, because he is too slow-witted to reach any conviction, and will not be pulled off any of them?” [Levett & Burnyeat at 72 (195c)].

Yet a different rendering of this same passage can be found in Robin Waterfield's translation. There, Waterfield casts Socrates' denial in terms of his not being a “repository of ideas” [Waterfield(3) at 47]. On this rendering, the “ideas” do not come initially from him.[39] It is possible that this denial suggests only the thought that Socrates is not the source or origin of these ideas; perhaps this is true. Certainly, Socrates' citations to Protagoras, Heraclitus, and Homer suggest that many of the ideas he discusses originated with others. In fact, he speaks of his offering Theaetetus “tit-bits” and “a tempting meal,” and chanting “incantations” over him, as though he, Socrates, were merely the servant offering delicacies to the hungry guest, Theaetetus.

All of this I am willing to acknowledge. But, in the face of Socrates' repeated claims of ignorance, I think it must be recognized that Socrates does all the rest of the work, mostly on his own, without the urging or the assistance of either Theaetetus or Theodorus.[40] It is Socrates who enlarges, modifies, corrects, amends, distinguishes, states exceptions, develops arguments, constructs answers, generates definitions, draws distinctions, and responds both to his own questions and to the puzzled queries of his two interlocutors. These creations are his and his alone. If they were not, it would not be possible for him to be embarrassed or ashamed, as he frequently says he is by something that he has said.

> *Socrates:* Shame. I am afraid our criticism might be a very cheap affair. [Levett & Burnyeat at 56 (183e)]

> *Socrates:* I should be ashamed to see us forced into making the kind of admissions I mean while we are still in difficulties. If we find what we're after, and become free men, then we will turn round and talk about how these things happen to other

> people—having secured our own persons against ridicule. [Levett & Burnyeat at 66–67 (190e–191a)]

> *Socrates:* Well, then, don't you think it is a shameless thing that we, who don't know what knowledge is, should pronounce on what knowing is like? [Levett & Burnyeat at 74 (196d–e)]

Is Socrates' embarrassment warranted? Is his fear—that criticism of these theories of knowledge "might be a very cheap affair"—justified?

Conversational Criticism as Fair Testing

The anxiety Socrates expresses—that what he does may cast him in a shameful light—is appropriate insofar as the Socratic method of conversational inquiry is an exercise in personal assessment. It is a means for inquiring into who we are and what we stand for (or what we stand by). In this regard, however, Socrates is concerned to give his interlocutor a fair hearing ("All that I know, such as it is, is how to take an argument from someone else—someone who *is* wise—and give it a fair reception"). This Socratic concern for a fair hearing seems to me to be vindicated in his critical practice (as it also stands in ironic contrast to the treatment that Socrates receives from his critics in the *Apology*). Socrates is fair in his criticism because he makes the effort to be.

Consider Socrates' critical practice in terms of the attention and care that he pays to Protagoras' theory. Socrates carefully parses the Protagorean theory into a variety of formulations, all of which he considers to be implied by this theory. Each formulation or implication seems to derive from a general statement, which Socrates puts this way: *Everything is what it is, only in relation to something else.* "That is the meaning of the theory we have been expounding" [Levett & Burnyeat at 25 (160b–c)]. This theory is a version of relativism. And this, concludes Socrates, is what the various theories of Protagoras, Heraclitus, and Theaetetus come to. "Then that was a grand idea of yours when you told us that knowledge is nothing more or less than perception." In this respect, then, the theories of Protagoras, Heraclitus, and Homer coincide with Theaetetus' theory [Levett & Burnyeat at 26 (160d–e)].

Some critics would stop here, but not Socrates. At this point the work of Socratic inquiry is just beginning, because all we have at this moment is a well-developed expression of Theaetetus' (and Protagoras') theory of knowledge. It has not yet been tested. Socrates makes this clear when he declares that this theory is Theaetetus' "first-born child," the result of Socrates' acting as a midwife [Levett & Burnyeat at 26 (160e)]. It remains to put Theaetetus' progeny to the test.

Socrates is ready to test the truth of Theaetetus' theory, but Theodorus interrupts the discussion for several pages [see Levett & Burnyeat at 26–28 (160e–162c)]. After this digression, Socrates then turns to Theaetetus and begins his assessment. But Socrates does so first by taking Protagoras' version of the theory [see Levett & Burnyeat at 28–31 (162c–164d)], and Socrates begins by mustering the best defense he can in response to Protagoras' critics, including himself. "Protagoras, or anyone speaking on his behalf, will answer us like this" [Levett & Burnyeat at 28 (162d)]. So Socrates' initial test of Protagoras' theory constitutes a response to his own criticisms, voiced earlier, of Protagoras' theory. Can there be a more scrupulous critical handling of the theory of an acknowledged antagonist? (I am referring to the sophist Protagoras as Socrates' antagonist, not to the student Theaetetus.)

Then Socrates reverses direction, once more imagining possible ways to explain the relativistic theory of knowledge proposed by Protagoras, Heraclitus, and Theaetetus. "Here . . . is another way in which we might consider whether knowledge and perception are the same or different things" [Levett & Burnyeat at 29 (163a)]. After several more pages of considerations and criticisms, Socrates concludes that this relativistic theory of knowledge is not true. It is an illusion, not real. "And so the tale of Protagoras comes to an untimely end; yours [Theaetetus'] too, your tale about the identity of knowledge and perception" [Levett & Burnyeat at 31 (164d)].

Even now, however, Socrates does not declare victory. Instead, he begins yet again to consider what might be said in the theory's defense, in trying to account for its apparent attractiveness to Protagoras, Heraclitus, and Theaetetus. Socrates tries, in other words, to come to the rescue of Protagoras' theory [see Levett & Burnyeat at 31–36 (164e–168c)]. He does this in part by posing a new puzzle for Theaetetus and himself:

"Is it possible for a man who knows something not to know this thing which he knows?" [Levett & Burnyeat at 32 (165b)]. In doing so, Socrates is scrupulous to avoid getting involved in what he calls a million questions from "mercenary skirmishers of debate" [see Levett & Burnyeat at 32–33 (165b–e)]. These skirmishes would not necessarily be good-faith attempts to understand the Protagorean-Theaetetean theory; rather, they would be scoring mere debaters' points, without being guided by a passion to seek the truth of the matter in a fair way. To elaborate and explain the Protagorean theory sympathetically, Socrates adopts the guise of being an advocate for Protagoras, imagining as it were what Protagoras might say on behalf of his own theory [see Levett & Burnyeat at 33–36 (166a–168c)]. (Protagoras was deceased at the time.) What I have been calling the first major section of the *Theaetetus* closes with Socrates' reconstruction of Protagoras' position.[41]

All this is done on behalf of granting Protagoras and Theaetetus what Socrates calls a "fair reception" to their thoughts or theories. I call attention to two final matters with respect to Socrates' example of fair-minded criticism.

(1) First, contrast Socrates' example of appropriate critical deportment and behavior with that of the sophists. Were Socrates to be on the receiving end of critical attention from Protagoras, the most famous sophist, it is unlikely that Protagoras would be as fair-minded. Or as Socrates puts it, "I imagine, he [would] come to grips with us, and in no respectful spirit either" [Levett & Burnyeat at 33 (166a)]. And, throughout the dialogue, Socrates refers in unfavorable terms to the sophists as a group: they are "professional savants" [Levett & Burnyeat at 18 (154d)]; "mercenary skirmishers of debate" [Levett & Burnyeat at 32 (165d)]; "experts in contradiction" [Levett & Burnyeat at 74 (197a)]; "expert[s] in refutation" [Levett & Burnyeat at 78 (200a)]. Sophists may get results; they may win arguments, but only at the expense of extending to their opponents fair treatment. And, when Socrates catches himself following their example, he refuses to go any further: "We seem to have been adopting the methods of professional controversialists: we've made an agreement aimed at getting words to agree consistently; and we feel complacent now that we have defeated the theory [of Protagoras] by the use of a method of this kind. We profess to be philosophers, not cham-

pion controversialists; and we don't realise that we are doing just what those clever fellows do" [Levett & Burnyeat at 31 (164c–d)]. For a responsible critic, in that way lies corruption.

What is the alternative, then, for a fair-minded critic? It may be useful to identify, in a summary way, a few of the most salient features of his critical art.

(a) First, Socrates proceeds not by way of immediately trying to refute or otherwise disconfirm the theory or belief elicited from his companion. Rather, he tries initially to develop it further, to articulate and elaborate it, pursuing its implications and possibilities. The governing idea here is, I believe, one of trying to find the right words in which to formulate the position to be examined and tested.

(b) Second, this activity of development entails that the fair-minded critic be willing to follow the argument wherever it may lead. This means that such a critic must be willing to entertain digressions in the argument, allowing for a certain amount of discursiveness. The critic must lend the argument his or her ears: listen to what is being said, and how, when, and where it is being said. This requires time, or patience, both of which Socrates recommends to us as necessities of his art of self-examination.

For example, when Socrates describes the character of the philosopher a fair minded one, a critical one—he says that such a person has the "leisure" to follow an argument or a puzzle wherever it may lead us, in the pursuit of truth. A lawyer, on the other hand, or another "practical" person, does only what he has time to do and what he has been paid to do. The philosopher is not corrupted by having to request compensation—another major distinction between Socrates and the sophists, who, as we know, demanded payment for their teaching services. And discursiveness in an argument also is necessary to the extent that we want a position or a theory to develop naturally and on its own terms. If a theory or belief is to be truly tested, then it must be permitted to speak in its own voice.

(c) Finally, however, this willingness to entertain digressions or discursive developments of a position must be kept in balance with the need to close with that position, to conclude at some point in the conversation. A critical exploration can be extensive, but it cannot be interminable. We need to reach an end, even if the end proves to be inconclusive. Reaching an end is a matter of reaching a terminus, but, then, a terminus may serve as the starting point for yet another discussion.

> *Socrates:* But we had better leave it there; all this is really a digression; and if we go on, a flood of new subjects will pour in and overwhelm our original argument. So, if you don't mind, we will go back to what we were saying before. [Levett & Burnyeat at 47 (177b–c)]

> *Socrates:* So I am afraid we might not understand even what he [Parmenides] says; still less should we attain to his real thought. Above all, I am afraid that the very object of our discussion, the nature of knowledge, might be left unexamined amid the crowd of theories that will rush in upon us if we admit them; especially as the theory we have now brought up is one which involves unmanageably vast issues. To treat it as a side-show, would be insult and injury; while if it is adequately discussed, it is likely to spread out until it completely eclipses the problem of knowledge. We must do neither. What we must do is to make use of our midwife's art to deliver Theaetetus of the thoughts which he has conceived about the nature of knowledge. [Levett & Burnyeat at 56 (184a–b)]

The controlling idea is not one of treating a topic of discussion exhaustively (for it does not seem possible to exhaust any of the topics of Socratic conversation), but rather one of seeing it through to a conclusion, no matter how tentative or provisional the conclusion may prove to be.[42] "Would you like us to have a review of them, or shall we let them be, and return to the argument? We don't want to abuse this freedom to change our subject of which we were speaking just now" [Levett & Burnyeat at 44 (173b)].

I said that I had two thoughts to offer in regard to Socrates' example of fair-minded criticism, and the first has been to notice the contrast in critical styles between the sophists and Socrates. The second thought goes to the motivation behind these two styles of critical deportment.

(2) How is a critic to proceed if he or she is to be fair to all concerned? For the sophists (as represented by Protagoras), Socrates says that criticism is a matter of attacking and refuting the other. "'Show a little more spirit, my good man,' he [Protagoras] will say, 'and attack my actual statement itself, and refute it, if you can'" [Levett & Burnyeat at 34 (166c)]. This may be the way in which the sophists criticize someone, but it is not Socrates' way in the *Theaetetus*. (In some of Plato's dialogues—for example, the *Gorgias*—this other nonfriendly approach might be an accurate description of Socrates' method of treating his conversational companions.) For Socrates, fairness in criticism requires a more gentle touch, a kind of resuscitation of lost or misplaced opinions and ideas, a welcoming attitude toward unwanted or unheeded thoughts. "In the interests of justice, it seems that we shall have to come to the rescue ourselves. . . . Now will you give your mind to this rescue work of mine—what little I can do? Because one might be driven into making even more alarming admissions than we have just made, if one paid as little attention to the words in which we express our assertions and denials as we are for the most part accustomed to doing" [Levett & Burnyeat at 31, 32 (164e, 165a)].

I am suggesting, then, that Socrates sets an example of the critic as friend, as a person of goodwill. We noticed in our discussions of both the *Protagoras* and the *Meno* that Socratic conversational inquiry normally anticipates that "when two go together" in conversation, their inquiry is based upon friendship, or friendliness. Certainly, this is seen in the image of Socrates as a midwife, helping his conversational partners to deliver their thoughts and expressions. Socrates' example in the *Theaetetus* gives us to understand the aim of the scrupulous critic as a person who pays better "attention to the words in which we express our assertions and denials." This is in one respect what Socrates has been doing in this dialogue. He is delivering us of our words and then testing those words, out of his goodwill toward us and toward these interesting issues or ideas, just as he has instructed Theaetetus to act and speak in this manner of critical friendliness and candor. But many people might not understand this to be Socrates' motivation in his critical activities. "Do you know, people have often before now got into such a state with me as to be literally ready to bite when I take away some nonsense or other from them. They never believe that I am doing this in all goodwill; they are so far from realising that no God can wish evil to man, and that even I don't do this kind of thing out of malice, but because it is not permitted me to accept a lie and put away truth" [Levett & Burnyeat at 13 (151c–d)].

Youth and Old Age: Eulogy for Theaetetus, Elegy for Socrates

The *Theaetetus* opens not with Socrates or either of the two main characters; rather, it opens with a conversation between Eucleides and Terpsion, as we saw earlier. Terpsion has been searching for Eucleides, who has just returned from the harbor, where he met Theaetetus, badly wounded and not expected to live. They both lament his likely death, and Eucleides allows that "he is a noble fellow" [Jowett & Copi at 1 (142b)]. To my mind, in this brief colloquy between Eucleides and Terpsion, the frame for the rest of dialogue is established. By way of a brief eulogy for the then-adult Theaetetus, now badly wounded in battle, we learn of his many virtues, including his bravery, nobility, and honor. [See Levett & Burnyeat at 1–2 (142a–d).] Above all, Theaetetus is hailed as a splendid leader, a noble warrior for the Athenians. And, in the next scene in the dialogue, harkening back to Theaetetus' youth and his first meeting with Socrates when Socrates prophesied a glorious adulthood for him if he managed to live long enough, we find that even Theodorus himself sings the praises of Theaetetus [see Levett & Burnyeat at 3–4 (143e–144d)]. Why does Plato bother to open the dialogue this way?

I cannot help but think that it serves his purpose to emphasize that this extended exchange between Theaetetus and Socrates took place in the past, and that now the uncertain future beckons us on. So the dialogue begins in an evocative mood, and for me it retains its melancholy as the theme of age gets subtle play throughout. Theodorus, for example, pleads his age as the reason why he seeks "to persuade you [Socrates] to allow me to be a spectator and not drag me into the arena now that I am grown stiff; but . . . take on someone who is younger and more supple." But Theaetetus seems equally incapacitated by his lack of age, his lack of experience, at least according to Socrates: "Yes, because you are young, dear lad; and so you lend a ready ear to mob-oratory and let it convince you" [Levett & Burnyeat at 28 (162d)]. Socrates, as we know, ends up by using Theodorus' age against him, shaming him into giving the defense of Protagoras a try [see Levett & Burnyeat at 37 (168d–169a)]. And Theaetetus' youth is also turned to advantage, because his lack of experience means that he brings freshness and a lack of guile to the discussion.

Nevertheless, a pall hangs over this dialogue. I find myself concurring, in this regard, with Robin Waterfield's remark that the "*Theaetetus* is a kind of homage to Socrates" [Waterfield(3) at 132]. It is a homage not only to Socrates' memory but also to his method of conversational inquiry—a method of learning and teaching that I believe to be a means of cultural transmission between generations. Socrates does not seem able to transmit his vision of philosophy and his love of the active, inquiring life to Theodorus, but in that failure there is no tragedy. Theodorus has lived a full life, and he is not a member of the next generation. It is different for Theaetetus, who is among those who will come after Socrates. The urgent question for Socrates and his generation is, "How will they manage to succeed us?" And so, "Theaetetus, if ever in the future you should attempt to conceive or should succeed in conceiving other theories, they will be better ones as the result of this enquiry. And if you remain barren, your companions will find you gentler and less tiresome; you will be modest and not think you know what you don't know. This is all my art can achieve—nothing more" [Levett & Burnyeat at 92–93 (210b–c)].

The positive side of Socrates' art is that it helps us to express better what we think and feel and believe. If we test our thoughts, feelings, and beliefs by way of a Socratic examination, they are apt to become better formulated or articulated. Yet, in the testing, they may turn out to be nothing but wind-eggs, illusions. This is the negative side of Socrates' art. Still, even if we prove barren of fertile thoughts and ideas, then at least this dose of self-scrutiny should teach us modesty and humility. And that lesson is itself worthwhile.[43]

Socrates closes with a declaration of the poverty of his method: "I do not know any of the things that other men know—the great and inspired men of today and yesterday. But this art of midwifery my mother and I had allotted to us by God; she to deliver women, I to deliver men that are young and generous of spirit, all that have any beauty. And now I must go to the King's Porch to meet the indictment that Meletus has brought against me; but let us meet here again in the morning, Theodorus" [Levett & Burnyeat at 93 (210c–d)]. His mother delivered women of their infants, while Socrates delivers men of their beliefs and opinions. And both test the adequacy of what their arts have delivered. Socrates' faith is that by cultivating our capacity for questioning, members of the next generation can succeed to the work, the task, of learning their way around the world (and themselves). And they can work at coming to some kind of understanding of the world (and themselves). They may learn to arrive at conclusions—provisionally, tentatively. But, then, they also may learn to depart from them. The journey is all. Or, rather, as Shakespeare put it, "Men must endure / Their going hence, even as their coming hither; / Ripeness is all."[44]

Now, however, there is this troublesome indictment to be answered. Socrates must, again, give an adequate response. This is the next labor that faces him.

FIVE

Learning to Find Ourselves at a Loss

How Does Philosophy Begin?

[P]hilosophical ideas reveal their good only in stages, and it is not clear whether a later stage will seem to be going forward or turning around or stopping, learning to find oneself at a loss.

—STANLEY CAVELL[1]

[O]ur lives inherently possess the power—as well as betray the need—to criticize themselves. But since most of us, most of the time, do not consult what we say as in criticism of our lives, the implication is that we ordinarily live in partial oblivion of what we say and do at every moment . . . . This is a version of what Socrates names the unexamined life.

—STANLEY CAVELL[2]

If Stanley Cavell is correct in thinking that "philosophical ideas reveal their good only in stages," then I might trace the developing stages in my idea of Socratic conversational inquiry as follows: In the *Protagoras*, we see Socrates argue for treating conversation as the preferred way to care philosophically for our soul, or our self. Food for the soul—which I take to include self-knowledge as well as knowledge of others and of the world—is to be gained by means of conversing with people and examining them, asking them who they are and what they can teach us, what we can learn from them. Then, in the *Meno,* we learn how properly to ask and answer questions that can afford us the dual lessons of disillusion and renewal. We gain these lessons by engaging in Socrates' elenctic conversation. And finally, in the *Theaetetus,* we study how to elicit knowledge of ourselves, by means of giving an account of what we mean by what we say. Our assertions or expressions reveal us, as they also expose us to testing and criticism. The two-part process of Socrates' critical art encompasses the delivery of our words and the fair testing of those words and expressions.

So far, so good. It is at this stage that I turn from the *Theaetetus* to the *Apology,* in looking to complete my account of Socrates' method of conversational inquiry. In making this transition, however, I wish to mention one of the continuities between the *Theaetetus* and the *Apology*. In my reading of the *Theaetetus,* I have emphasized the extent to which learning who we are is a function of learning what we mean by what we say and do. In this regard, the *Theaetetus* teaches us how deaf or deadened we can be to the meaning of what we say and do. As Cavell puts it, "we ordinarily live in partial oblivion of what we say and do at every moment." We live unconscious lives of unexamined illusions. And Socrates wishes to make us conscious of this fact; he tries to help us become conscious of the illusions under which we live.

Implicit in the *Theaetetus* is the suggestion that, for Socrates, learning to elicit the meaning and the implications of our words and deeds prepares us to learn the still more daunting task of drawing out the meaning and the implications of our lives. This suggestion becomes explicit in the *Apology*. There, Socrates begins by exploring the implications of something said, a statement made by the oracle at Delphi. He tells his jurors in the *Apology* that he was confounded to learn that the Delphic oracle had characterized him as being the wisest of men, whereas this appellation conflicted with Socrates' own estimate of himself. To learn more about the meaning of this divinely inspired statement became Socrates' mission. Yet, during the course of his explorations of the implications of this strange saying by the oracle, Socrates began to learn more about himself and his situation. He came to realize that he had been sleepwalking through life, largely oblivious to what he was saying and doing in his everyday activities. And Socrates also came to appreciate that the same was true of most of his fellow citizens in Athens.

Few, if any, of them knew what they were doing, or what their lives meant, or what the implications of their daily actions might be. Accordingly, it became incumbent upon Socrates to examine the meaning and the worth of our "unexamined" lives. Or so he says in his defense statement recorded in the *Apology*.

In this sense, Socrates' conversational inquiry becomes a method for achieving self-awareness. We become aware of what we are saying and doing—and aware of what those things mean or imply—through the self-examination and self-criticism practiced by us as we undergo the rigors of Socratic inquiry and refutation. But self-criticism is not an activity that comes naturally to most people. Becoming self-critical has to be learned; it must be acquired. But can this activity of self-criticism be taught? Or is self-criticism something that we must learn on our own? Even though the method of Socratic conversational inquiry may be a means of self-criticism (and, thus, a way of gaining self-knowledge), does this entail that Socrates' method is a teaching method? Is engaging in Socratic conversational inquiry a way to teach anything? In what sense is Socrates' method of inquiry educational? Who or what teaches us to inquire into our lives? And does Socrates teach us, or is it his method that teaches us?

Learning to Inquire into Our Lives

The *Apology* is Plato's representation of Socrates' account of his life.[3] Socrates has been called to the court of justice to defend himself, to explain why he should not be found guilty of the charges lodged against him by certain influential members of the Athenian *polis*.[4] These charges have been brought against Socrates because he insists on behaving as an irritating gadfly toward his fellow citizens, someone who talks too much and who does not quit his investigations until he has reached the end of his questions.

Socrates loves to talk with people;[5] he is addicted to it. And, since he talks as a way of inquiring into the lives of his conversational partners (as well as into his own life), his penchant for talking with others has gotten him into trouble. Socrates examines people at any time and anywhere, and his questions cause them embarrassment. In addition, his unrelenting examinations have humiliated these people in front of other important citizens, and even the youth of Athens. Is Socrates merely a pest, a social deviant or malcontent? Or is he something worse, something destructive to the fabric of Athenian society? *He* thinks he is a true friend to the citizens of Athens even if, at the moment, they do not realize this.

Trying to convince his jurors that he is a true friend of the city and its people, Socrates defends the way that he has conducted himself in Athens; he does so defiantly. First, he denies the charges lodged against him: that he has been irreligious, and that he has corrupted young Athenians. Far from being impious, Socrates contends that he has conducted his life in conformity with the instructions of the gods (insofar as they have been made known to him by the oracle at Delphi). And, rather than corrupting the young, Socrates has not attempted to teach them at all. Instead, he has turned his attention to the elders of Athens, and he has tried to encourage them to learn what is most important in life instead of frittering away their time on insignificant matters and concerns. But, according to Socrates, this attempt to goad the people of Athens into a life of inquiry has not proceeded on the basis of any claim by him to be able to teach these people the important things in life. No, Socrates is not in a position to teach others; he readily admits that he knows nothing about such matters. Socrates himself is ignorant. Being aware of his ignorance, Socrates is motivated to try to learn about these matters, about what he needs to know in order to live his life well. He *wants* to live virtuously and in accordance with the dictates of the gods. Far from being irreligious, Socrates claims that his actions display a reverence for life, an appreciation for the importance of living well; and his actions also reveal his piety for following the dictates of the gods to the extent that he understands them. In addition, far from being someone who presumes to be able to teach others, Socrates considers himself a student. This is why Socrates spends his life talking with others and asking them questions. He hopes *they* will teach *him*, not the other way around.

Toward the end of his defense speech,[6] Socrates anticipates a hypothetical question being posed to him by his jurors, to the effect that if he would simply exile himself (and, thus, stop annoying people with his discomfiting investigations), he not only could live out his life in peace, but perhaps the jurors also would overlook his past indiscretions. This suggestion is unacceptable to Socrates. He refuses to conform to the desires of his fellow citizens. He believes that the gods have told him to act in a different way, and to do otherwise would itself be an instance of impiety.[7]

Socrates feels compelled by his devotion to the gods (and to their dictates) to examine his own life and the lives of other people with whom he comes into contact. If he were to stop searching for the answers to the questions that greatly trouble him—questions that should equally trouble his self-satisfied neighbors and fellow citizens—then life as it is led in Athens would go unexamined. And, as we know, for Socrates, an unexamined life is not worth living:

> Perhaps someone will say, "Why cannot you withdraw from Athens, Socrates, and hold your peace?" It is the most difficult thing in the world to make you understand why I cannot do that. If I say that I cannot hold my peace because that would be to disobey the god [according to the Delphic oracle], you will think that I am not in earnest and will not believe me. And if I tell you that no greater good can happen to a man than to discuss human excellence every day and the other matters about which you have heard me arguing and examining myself and others, and that an unexamined life is not worth living, then you will believe me still less. But that is so, my friends, though it is not easy to persuade you. [Church & Cumming at 45 (37e–38a)]

Socrates does not undertake the arduous task of examining a person's life out of any petty curiosity. His motivation is not that of a voyeur. What drives Socrates is a desire to learn the truth about such matters. Or so he frequently declares: "Then listen, Gorgias, for I am quite sure that if there ever was a man who entered on the discussion of a matter from the pure desire to learn the exact truth, I am such a person; and I should say the same about you."[8] Socrates expects the same commitment, the same unwavering focus, from the people who are willing to talk with him and to join him in his investigations.

In his defense statement in the *Apology,* Socrates speaks of feeling compelled to respond to something that was bothering or confusing him. His lack of clarity may be due to a lack of education (something that, at the beginning of Book VII of the *Republic,* the allegory of the cave is said to portray—"our education or lack of education").[9] For all we know, initially Socrates may have been just like everyone else in Athens, in the sense that he was living comfortably, smug in the satisfaction of being an adult male leading an ordinary life. What led Socrates, then, to begin his disruptive investigations? Apparently, it was a fortuitous question asked by Chaerephon, a longtime friend, while visiting the oracle at Delphi; the answer awoke Socrates from his dogmatic slumbers and launched him on his educational journey: "You remember Chaerephon. From youth upwards he was my comrade; and also a partisan of your democracy, sharing your recent exile and returning with you. You remember, too, Chaerephon's character—how impulsive he was in carrying through whatever he took in hand. Once he went to Delphi and ventured to put this question to the oracle—I entreat you again, my friends, not to interrupt me with your shouts—he asked if there was anyone who was wiser than I. The priestess answered that there was no one" [Church & Cumming at 25 (20e–21a)].

Rather than being flattered by the priestess's statement, or accepting its truth with assurance, Socrates was confused by the oracle's declaration that no one was wiser than himself. On the one hand, Socrates knew "very well that I am not wise, even in the smallest degree" [Church & Cumming at 26 (21b)]. Aware of his own ignorance, he did not presume that this self-awareness qualified him to be a wise person. On the other hand, "It cannot be that he [Apollo] is speaking falsely, for he is a god and cannot lie" [Church & Cumming at 26 (21b)]. So Socrates found himself left with a puzzle: "What can the god mean by this riddle? . . . For a long time I was at a loss to understand his meaning" [Church & Cumming at 26 (21b)]. Being stopped, confused, puzzled, is what is called "the aporetic moment." "Then, very reluctantly, I turned to investigate it in this manner: I went to a man who was reputed to be wise, thinking that there, if anywhere, I should prove the answer wrong, and meaning to point out to the oracle its mistake" [Church & Cumming at 26 (21b–c)]. Confusion in Socrates engendered an effort to clarify.

When Socrates sought out the first person for questioning (that is, "a man who was reputed to be wise"), he learned that this man did not know what he claimed to know. "When I conversed with him I came to see that, though a great many persons, and most of all he himself, thought that he was wise, yet he was not wise. Then I tried to prove to him that he was not wise, though he fancied that he was. By so doing I made him indignant, and many of the bystanders" [Church & Cumming at 26 (21c–d)]. Then Socrates questioned another man, and the process of disillusion repeated itself. Humiliated by their inability to answer Socrates' questions satisfactorily, these people turn on him. "Next I went to another man who was reputed to be still wiser than the last, with exactly the same result. And there again I made him, and many other men, indignant. . . . I found that the men whose reputation for wisdom stood highest were nearly the most lacking in it, while others who were looked down on as common people were much more intelligent" [Church & Cumming at 26–27 (21d–e, 22a)].

We humans mostly fail to realize our own ignorance. This human failing is what Cavell is referring to, I take it, when he says in the epigraph to this chapter that "we ordinarily live in partial oblivion of what we say and do at any moment." Remaining oblivious to the meaning and implications of our lives is one more indication of our fundamental lack of education. When the *Republic* speaks of our "want" or "lack" of education, it invokes an image of the cave, a condition of deprivation. Here, in the *Apology*, people once again are characterized as "lacking" something; here, it is wisdom or knowledge that we lack (Socrates says, "I found that the men whose reputation for wisdom stood highest were nearly the most lacking in it"). These two "lacks"—of education described in the *Republic*, and of wisdom noted in the *Apology*—amount to the same thing.

Most of us remain in our darkened caves, thinking that we know the truth, when in fact we are entranced and enchained by chimeras, mere shadows cast on the walls. So we forsake our educational opportunities, for the sake of what? Our pride, perhaps, or our dignity? Socrates tells us that, as a result of his disillusioning inquiries, "there again I made him, and many other men, indignant." Our anger or resentment masks our want of education. What might make us aware of our captivity?

Impious Activities, Corrupt Teachings?

For Socrates, our failures of awareness are "lacks" that can be addressed by a process of education. Yet, until we become aware of these "lacks," it is unlikely that we will seek any sort of education. (As depicted in the *Republic*'s allegory of the cave, we begin and continue our ordinary existence unaware of the fact that we are captive in the cave of our illusions.) Socrates wants to make us aware, but he does so at a grave risk to his life. "From this examination [of other people], Athenians, has arisen much fierce and bitter indignation, and as a result many prejudices about me. . . . But be assured it is certainly true, as I have already told you, that I have aroused much indignation" [Church & Cumming at 27, 34 (22e–23a, 28a)]. Again, as with the allegory of the cave in the *Republic,* removing our illusions (that is, leaving the cave and exposing our untrained eyes to the harsh sunlight) causes us pain. Consequently, we "are indignant, as drowsy persons are when they are awakened" [Church & Cumming at 37 (31a)]. And yet, for Socrates the pesky gadfly, the effort to remove our illusions is worth it. Hence, we have his categorical claim, late in his defense statement, that "an unexamined life is not worth living" [Church & Cumming at 45 (38a)].

Others in Socrates' society disagree, so he is brought up on charges in the Athenian court of law. As we know, two accusations are made against him: Socrates engages in philosophic activity that is impious and irreligious; and he corrupts the youth of Athens by teaching them to follow this same philosophic activity, at the risk of polluting their souls and turning them against the official religion. These twin charges form the core of the indictment against Socrates.

Socrates takes these charges very seriously, and a measure of his seriousness is that he proposes to answer them twice. Socrates claims that he *has* to answer twice, because in fact there are *two* indictments. The first is the formal one recently brought against him by his enemies. The second indictment is, however, not a formal legal pleading, but rather an informal one: it consists of the list of rumors and offenses whispered behind his back these many years by scandalmongers and by those people who are suspicious of Socrates' activities and his generally scandalous behavior on the streets and in the marketplace of

Athens. And although this second one may consist of gossip about him, its very informality and fluidity may make it the harder of the two indictments to refute.

So this is why Socrates portrays himself as answering two indictments, and why his defense statement takes the form that it does. First, immediately after the opening section of the *Apology* (where Socrates apologizes for the form of his defense statement, and where he asks his jurors to ignore "the manner of my speech"), he devotes himself to answering the "old" accusations made against him informally by society gossips [see Church & Cumming at 23–29 (19a–24b)]. And then, second, he makes the transition immediately thereafter to considering and answering the "new" accusations made against him (the formal charges lodged by Meletus, Anytus, and Lycon) [see Church & Cumming at 29–34 (24b–28a)].

From Socrates' perspective, the recent allegations depend for their force and credibility upon the older ones. These older accusations are the charges that worry Socrates the most, both because they have been around the longest without having been answered or refuted (and, hence, they may have gained a certain plausibility simply from their longevity); and because they are only tacit or implicit charges (thus it is more difficult to confront and refute them, since they never have been explicitly formulated). Socrates tells his jurors that these old accusations have taken on a veneer of respectability, because they likely were absorbed by his jurors while many of them were still children (and, hence, were vulnerable to gossip and hearsay). So now these old accusations pass among most Athenians for what has come to be deemed common knowledge.

> I have to defend myself, Athenians, first against the older false accusations of my old accusers, and then against the more recent ones of my present accusers. For many men have been accusing me to you, and over very many years, who have not spoken a word of truth; and I fear them more than I fear Anytus and his associates, formidable as they are. But, my friends, the others are still more formidable, since they got hold of most of you when you were children and have been more persistent in accusing me untruthfully, persuading you that there is a certain Socrates, a wise man, who

> speculates about the heavens, who investigates things that are beneath the earth, and who can make the worse argument appear the stronger. These men, Athenians, who spread abroad this report are the accusers whom I fear; for their hearers think that persons who pursue such inquiries never believe in the gods. Besides they are many, their attacks have been going on for a long time, and they spoke to you when you were most ready to believe them, since you were all young, and some of you were children. And there was no one to answer them when they attacked me. The most preposterous thing of all is that I do not even know their names: I cannot tell you who they are except when one happens to be a comic poet. But all the rest who have persuaded you, from motives of resentment and prejudice and sometimes, it may be, from conviction, are hardest to cope with. For I cannot call any one of them forward in court to cross-examine him. I have, as it were, simply to spar with shadows in my defense, and put questions which there is no one to answer. [Church & Cumming at 22–23 (18a–d)]

Starting, then, with the disadvantage of having to try to defend himself against innuendo and rumors spread long ago and, until now, not having had a forum in which to confront his nameless accusers, Socrates is reduced to the tactic of having to formulate—and then refute—the old accusations against him. Accordingly, Socrates goes through the act of stating how they might be formulated, were they to be reduced to the form of a written indictment: "Let us begin from the beginning, then, and ask what is the accusation that has given rise to the prejudice against me, on which Meletus relied when he brought his indictment. What is the prejudice which my enemies have been spreading about me? I must assume that they are formally accusing me, and read their indictment. It would run somewhat in this fashion: 'Socrates is guilty of engaging in inquiries into things beneath the earth and in the heavens, of making the weaker argument appear the stronger, and of teaching others these same things.' That is what they say" [Church & Cumming at 23 (19a–c)]. There are three charges here: (1) Socrates improperly inquires into matters better left unexplored; (2) he makes the weaker argument appear to be the stronger argument; and (3) he corrupts others by teaching them these improper inquiries and manipulative methods of argument. The first two indict Socrates for wrongful behavior in regard to his own philosophic activities, while the third alleges that he compounds the mischief from his misbehavior by passing it on to others. I want to examine these charges in turn.

Is there anything impious in Socrates' philosophic activities? He thinks not, for several reasons. There are, to begin with, the dual reasons to which Socrates appeals throughout his defense statement: First, all of his philosophic inquiries have come only at the behest of the god Apollo, who spoke through the oracle at Delphi. So how can following Apollo's command be impious? And, second, in his inquiries Socrates always has heeded his own inner voice or divine guide. So, again, how can following divine guidance be impious?

> It would be very strange conduct on my part if I were to desert my station now from fear of death or of any other thing when the god has commanded me—as I am persuaded that he has done—to spend my life in searching for wisdom, and in examining myself and others. That would indeed be a very strange thing. Then certainly I might with justice be brought to trial for not believing in the gods, for I should be disobeying the oracle, and fearing death and thinking myself wise when I am not wise. [Church & Cumming at 35 (28e–29a)]

> I have a certain divine guide, which is what Meletus has caricatured in his indictment. I have had it from childhood. It is a kind of voice which, whenever I hear it, always turns me back from something which I was going to do, but never urges me to act. It is this which forbids me to take part in politics. [Church & Cumming at 38 (31c–d)]

These remarks suggest that Socrates' philosophic activities have been undertaken in a manner solicitous of the deities, not in defiance of them or their dictates.

There is, however, yet another reason why Socrates believes his activities illustrate his own piety; this reason has to do with the fact that he sees them as aimed at helping his neighbors. What could be impious about that?

> Athenians, I am not arguing in my own defense at all, as you might expect me to do, but rather in yours in order [that] you may not make a mistake about the gift of the god to you by condemning me. . . . It seems to me that the god has attached me like [a gadfly] to the state, for I am constantly alighting upon you at every point to arouse, persuade, and reproach each of you all day long. You will not easily find anyone else, my friends, to fill my place; and if you are persuaded by me, you will spare my life. . . . And you may easily see that it is the god who has given me to your city; for it is not human, the way in which I have neglected all my own interests and allowed my private affairs to be neglected for so many years, while occupying myself unceasingly in your interests, going to each of you privately, like a father or an elder brother, trying to persuade him to care for human excellence. [Church & Cumming at 37 (30d–e, 30e–31a, 31a–b)]

In order to parse the complications in Socrates' assertions here, it will be useful to consider separately the first two charges made against Socrates, namely, that he inquires into matters better left unexplored, and that he makes the weaker argument appear to be the stronger one.

The first charge suggests that Socrates is unconcerned with matters of ordinary life, and that instead he devotes his energies to researching esoteric matters concerning the heavens or "under the earth" rather than matters of everyday human interest and concern. Remember that Socrates is trying to refute the charge that "there is a certain Socrates, a wise man, who speculates about the heavens, who investigates things that are beneath the earth." On Socrates' understanding of himself, nothing could be further from the truth. For Socrates, *his* interests have always been tied to the things of this life and this earth. He further complains: "These men, Athenians, who spread abroad this report are the accusers whom I fear; for their hearers think that persons who pursue such inquiries never believe in the gods." The accusation that Socrates is only interested in metaphysical or ethereal matters is preposterous.

In the *Protagoras*, for example, Socrates' aim is to investigate whether anyone qualifies to serve as a teacher of human virtue. Anyone who does qualify would, on Socrates' accounting sheet, count as a "physician of the soul."[10] From one perspective, of course, this concern for a person's spiritual state of health can seem sublime, otherworldly, but Socrates offers his conversational companions and himself an alternative perspective: one that sees such Socratic concerns for matters of human health and welfare (be they physical or spiritual) as fundamental and, hence, practical. As Socrates characterizes his actions in his defense statement, "As long as I have breath and strength I will not give up philosophy and exhorting you and declaring the truth to every one of you whom I meet, saying, as I am accustomed, 'My good friend, you are a citizen of Athens, a city which is very great and very famous for its wisdom and power—are you not ashamed of caring so much for the making of money and for fame and prestige, when you neither think nor care about wisdom and truth and the improvement of your soul?'" [Church & Cumming at 35–36 (29d–e)] No topic, no issue, could be more practical, more pressing, than the state of one's soul. And it is to determine the state of one's soul that Socrates undertakes his painstaking, and indeed painful, examinations. (This comports with the claim made by Gregory Vlastos, to the effect that Socrates is engaged fundamentally in *moral* inquiry.)

Socratic conversational inquiry concerns nothing less than how we humans are to conduct ourselves, our lives and our affairs. Or so Socrates believes. Still, he realizes that his jurors are apt not to credit his claim that his actions are motivated by his selfless concern for the health of others as well as for his own moral health. This is why Socrates says, "And if I tell you that no greater good can happen to a man than to discuss human excellence every day and the other matters about which you have heard me arguing and examining myself and others, and that an unexamined life is not worth living, then you will believe me still less. But that is so, my friends, though it is not easy to persuade you." (It is more likely than not that Socrates is arguing his defense to a hostile audience.)

The alternative perspective offered by Socrates is illustrated in the first book of the *Republic*, just as his exchange with the sophist Thrasymachus reaches its climax. There, Socrates punctuates the seriousness of the conversation—as well as the gravity of his dialectical activities and his resolve to seek an answer to the questions that both Socrates and Thrasymachus have raised about the meaning or nature of justice—by castigating the sophist. Thrasymachus, having made some provocative comments about the unjust being better than the just, appears ready to walk away from their conversation, in cavalier disregard for testing the claim that he has just entered. Socrates' acerbic rejoinder to Thrasymachus stops him in his tracks: "'You can't just pelt us with words, so to speak, and then leave before adequately demonstrating—or before finding out yourself—whether or not they're true. Or do you think that what you're attempting to define is a trivial matter, and not how anyone can live his life in the most rewarding manner?'" [Waterfield(1) at 27 (344d–e)] So the issue broached in Socrates' defense statement in the *Apology* is similarly joined and pursued in the *Republic,* namely, "How should we live?"[11]

And yet Socrates' old enemies—his old accusers—take his single-minded devotion to our mental and moral health, to ascertaining the state and standing of our souls, to be laughable. They portray Socrates as though he were otherworldly, concerned only about matters not of this world, matters both impolitic and irreligious. So it is that at one point during his presentation to the jury, Socrates imagines the following challenge being voiced to him: "'Are you not ashamed, Socrates, of leading a life which is very likely now to cause your death?'" [Church & Cumming at 34 (28b)]. It is in response to this challenge—a challenge that misconstrues at a stroke Socrates' activities—that Socrates, in his defense statement, takes it upon himself to set the record straight. "[I]n the comedy of Aristophanes [*The Clouds*] you yourselves saw a man called Socrates swinging around in a basket and saying that he walked on air, and sputtering a great deal of nonsense about matters of which I understand nothing at all. I do not mean to disparage that kind of knowledge if there is anyone who is wise about these matters. I trust Meletus may never be able to prosecute me for that. But the truth is, Athenians, I have nothing to do with these matters" [Church & Cumming at 23–24 (19c–d)]. Socrates cannot recognize himself in this portrayal. How can his efforts be seen as frivolous? Or metaphysical? Or meanspirited?

In view of the challenge that these accusations create for Socrates, however, he responds with a challenge of his own, one addressed to his jurors. He appeals to them to verify whether or not he has ever conducted himself in these ways. "[A]lmost all of you are yourselves my witnesses of this. I beg all of you who have ever heard me discussing, and they are many, to inform your neighbors and tell them if any of you have ever heard me discussing such matters at all. That will show you that the other common statements about me are as false as this one" [Church & Cumming at 24 (19d)]. This appeal to the shared civic knowledge of his activities is one reason why Socrates seems to expect his jurors to determine that the "old" accusations against him are patently false. (We readers of this dialogue may wonder whether it is reasonable to imagine that Socrates' jurors would appreciate what he is trying to accomplish here. Can his audience grasp the distinction that Socrates is trying to draw between the concerns expressed and explored by philosophers such as Thales and Heraclitus and Anaxagoras, on the one hand, and the quite different concerns for our moral health and standing that Socrates expresses and explores, on the other?)

In responding to the claim that his philosophic activity is impious and irreligious, Socrates does not present himself as a knower or a sage. He is not claiming to be a wise man with a message to deliver to the great unwashed (or unlearned). Indeed, Socrates differs in this respect from his predecessors in Greek philosophy (for example, Thales, or Anaxagoras, or Heraclitus, whose views are considered and critically investigated in the *Theaetetus* [see 160d–e]). For his predecessors, it might be correct to say that they claimed for themselves the authority of a wise man or thinker, but while Socrates has a message to share, he delivers it only from a position of poverty, one of professed ignorance. "My dear Meletus, do you think that you are prosecuting Anaxagoras? You must have a very poor opinion of these men [the jurors], and think them illiterate, if you imagine that they do not know that the works of Anaxagoras of Clazomenae are full of these doctrines [that Meletus and the other accusers attribute to Socrates]. And so young men [supposedly] learn these things from me, when they can often buy them in the theater for a drachma at most, and laugh at Socrates were he to pretend that these doctrines, which are very peculiar doctrines, too, were his own" [Church & Cumming at 32 (26d–e)]. Socrates' inquiries proceed instead from a kind of bitter knowledge: *he* claims *not* to know. He is not a dreamer whose head is in the clouds (contra Aristophanes); rather, he is a seeker, a searcher.[12] Moreover, any claim that Socrates may make during the course of his investigations, his conversations, is entered provisionally. It is put forth as a candidate not for acceptance or acclamation but rather for testing and critical scrutiny. Socrates has few doctrines to offer his conversational companions, and none that he wishes them to accept uncritically. Everything that Socrates says is to be tested.

As to the other philosophical activity of which Socrates stands accused, does he, in fact, attempt to make the weaker argument appear to be the stronger? This claim accuses Socrates of using rhetorical devices to make the weaker argument appear stronger. His defense statement in the *Apology* does not give much attention to this second accusation, and I think it is fair to say (following Alexander Sesonske) that Socrates does not fully respond to this charge.[13] Yet, having said this, it also needs to be recorded that Socrates gives us at least two reasons to disbelieve the justice of this charge.

First, Socrates indicates throughout the *Apology* that he speaks the whole truth, that he does not attempt to cover up or hide anything. On my reading of Socrates' defense statement, one implication of this claim to veridicality is the implied suggestion that Socrates does not finagle with appearances. Simply put, he does not attempt to make the weaker appear to be the stronger. "What I have told you, Athenians, is the truth: I neither conceal nor do I suppress anything, trivial or important" [Church & Cumming at 29 (24a)]. For Socrates, the truthfulness of his statements is a function of the fact that his claims and remarks are not produced by rhetoric or rhetorical flourish.

At the very beginning of his defense statement, for example, when Socrates first addresses the jury, he combines the two claims that he shall speak the truth to them and that he shall not engage in rhetorical tricks: "[M]y accusers . . . have scarcely spoken one single word of truth. Of all their falsehoods, the one which astonished me most was their saying that I was a clever speaker, and that you must be careful not to let me deceive you. I thought that it was most shameless of them not to be ashamed to talk in that way. For as soon as I open my mouth they will be refuted, and I shall prove that I am not a clever speaker in any way at all—unless, indeed, by a clever speaker they mean someone who speaks the truth. . . . My accusers, I repeat, have said little or nothing that is true, but from me you shall hear the whole truth. Certainly you will not hear a speech, Athenians, dressed up, like theirs, with fancy words and phrases. I will say to you what I say, without artifice" [Church & Cumming at 21 (17a–c)]. I read this opening statement to be, if not a direct denial of the second charge against him, then at least an explicit denial by Socrates that he is a rhetorician or that he uses rhetorical devices in making his statement to the jury.

But there is another reason for understanding Socrates' defense statement as implicitly denying the charge that he makes the weaker argument appear stronger. Socrates says again and again that he does not take money for doing what he does. "I have never withheld myself from anyone, young or old, who was anxious to hear me converse while I was making my investigation; neither do I converse for payment, and refuse to converse without payment" [Church & Cumming at 39–40 (33a–b)]. Is it relevant to the second charge against Socrates that he does not ask for (or accept) payment from his hearers? I think it is. In this respect, Socrates is distinguishing himself from the sophists, who are the other teachers notorious in the Greek city-states. Socrates' suggestion is, I take it, that since he does not get paid for what he does philosophically or pedagogically, he has no incentive to manipulate his arguments, no reason to make the weaker appear to be the stronger. "There would have been a reason for it, if I had gained any advantage by this, or if I had been paid for my exhortations; but you see yourselves that my accusers, though they accuse me of everything else without shame, have not had the shamelessness to say that I ever exacted or demanded payment. To that they have no witness. And I think that I have sufficient witness to the truth of what I say—my poverty" [Church & Cumming at 37 (31b–c)].

If Socrates has no economic incentive to twist the facts, it also appears that he has no political incentive for making the weaker argument appear the stronger. For, remember, Socrates makes a point of saying that he is not politically active, in part because his inner voice, his divine guide, tells him not to become politically involved. But Socrates also realizes that it would not be prudent for him to take part in Athenian politics—not, that is, if he is to conduct himself fearlessly in questioning whomever he meets wherever he goes.

> Perhaps it may seem strange to you that, though I go about giving this advice privately and meddling in others' affairs, yet I do not

> venture to come forward in the assembly and advise the state. You have often heard me speak of my reason for this, and in many places: it is that I have a certain divine guide, which is what Meletus has caricatured in his indictment. [Church & Cumming at 38 (31c–d)]
>
> Now do you think that I could have remained alive all these years if I had taken part in public affairs, and had always maintained the cause of justice like a good man, and had held it a paramount duty, as it is, to do so? Certainly not, Athenians, nor could any other man. [Church & Cumming at 39 (32e)]

I must admit that I am skeptical about Socrates' claims regarding his apparent disavowal of rhetoric.[14] His defense statement is not quite so transparent and unrhetorical as he himself seems to think it is. And Sesonske gives additional reasons for thinking that Socrates does sometimes make the weaker argument appear the stronger.[15]

Be that as it may, to my mind there remains an additional reason for Socrates to claim that he does not manipulate arguments: his wish to distance himself from the sophists. Let me next turn to this last aspect of Socrates' defense against the old accusations, since its consideration also allows me to assess the third and final accusation lodged against Socrates by his old accusers, namely, that he teaches others his philosophical activities and thereby corrupts those others, especially the young men of Athens.

Corrupting Others by Teaching Them?

The citizens of Athens were angry at Socrates, and it seems unlikely that they would have taken kindly to his suggestion that his critical examinations should be understood as a "gift" from the god Apollo. Socrates as an annoying "gadfly," the Athenians might understand;[16] but Socrates as a gift from the gods?

And how did the Athenians feel toward the sophists? The sophists were not popular either. We catch glimpses of this social unpopularity throughout several of the Platonic dialogues. For example, we can gather as much from the testimony of Anytus, who not only is one of Socrates' accusers in the *Apology* but also is deposed by Socrates during the *Meno*. It is in the *Meno* where, under Socrates' searching cross-examination, Anytus demonstrates his antipathy toward the sophists, and he seems unashamed or unrepentant when Socrates demonstrates that Anytus has formed this negative opinion on the basis of very little actual experience. Similarly, in the *Protagoras* and the *Gorgias*, we catch glimpses of the tense relations between Athenian society and the sophists. Protagoras and Gorgias were among the most famous of the sophists, and, in the dialogues that bear their names, they freely acknowledge their unpopularity in Athens. Indeed, both proceed cautiously and do not wish to draw too much attention to themselves or to their teaching activities with the youth of Athens. Protagoras even says as much, when he is introduced to Socrates. At the beginning of the dialogue, Protagoras notes that Socrates treats him with more respect and consideration than he usually receives from people when they learn that he is a sophist.

> Thank you, Socrates, for your consideration of me. For certainly a foreigner finding his way into great cities, and persuading the flower of youth in them to leave the company of others, kinsmen or strangers, old or young, and live with him, under the idea that they will be improved by their association with him, ought to be very cautious. Great jealousies are aroused by his proceedings, and he is the subject of many enmities and conspiracies. Now the art of the Sophist is, as I believe, of great antiquity, but in ancient times those who practiced it, fearing this odium, veiled and disguised themselves under various names, . . . I take an entirely opposite course and acknowledge myself to be a Sophist and instructor of mankind. Such an open acknowledgment appears to me to be a better sort of caution than concealment. Nor do I neglect other precautions, and therefore I hope, as I may say, by the favor of heaven that no harm will come of the acknowledgment that I am a Sophist. [Jowett & Ostwald at 13–14 (316c–317c)]

The relations between the Athenians and the sophists were uncomfortable, then, and it makes sense to me that the accusers of Socrates were counting on the general disfavor in which the sophists were held to bolster their case against Socrates. But what in particular about their charges against Socrates made his old and new accusers believe that they could defame him with the sophistic tag?

There are a number of ways in which what Socrates does and what the sophists teach seem to be comparable activities. In chapter 1, I quoted R. L. Nettleship's lecture notes on the *Republic,* where Nettleship describes how the sophists interacted with the Athenians. I want to return to Nettleship's remarks, as they help us to understand how others might perceive Socrates and the sophists as proceeding along similar pedagogical paths. Nettleship tells us, "The sophists were more or less professional men; they made their living by teaching, and from the necessities of the case they had to address themselves to a certain public and to strive to get influence over it, just as a modern press-writer has to consider for whom he writes, and, to a certain extent, has to adapt his style and matter to his public."[17] As to the sophists, Nettleship indicates that "[n]early all of them taught rhetoric; that is to say, the power of using language as an instrument in life."[18] So the sophists taught rhetoric, and this entailed teaching their students how to use language. Compare Socrates' work. The bulk of his time in the Platonic dialogues is devoted to inquiring into how we use words such as "virtue" or "excellence" (*areté*), or "justice" (*diké*), or "courage" or "temperance" or "self-control" (*sophrosyné*), and the like. Perhaps the single most important activity undertaken by Socrates and his conversational companions during the early and middle dialogues is the process of formulating and examining and testing definitions of various words. Nor, in this regard, is it irrelevant that Socrates professes to respect the ability of Prodicus, one of the sophists who takes part in the discussions narrated in the *Protagoras*. Prodicus made a career out of drawing fine distinctions in meanings, and in this regard, Socrates and Prodicus seem more akin than dissimilar.

Another central activity undertaken by Socrates is that of stating, developing, and testing arguments. (Gregory Vlastos observes, "Almost everything Socrates says is wiry argument; that is the beauty of his talk for a philosopher" [Jowett & Ostwald at xxxi].) So how does this aspect of Socrates' philosophical activity differentiate him from the sophists? The emphasis that the sophists placed on rhetoric, oratory, and persuasion is a portion of the sophists teaching people how to argue effectively.

(We might ask: Is this where people get the claim that the sophists—and, I suppose, Socrates—possess an art whereby their students are taught how to make "the weaker argument appear to be the stronger"?)

Finally, we might say that the core of Socrates' activities is to get his listeners and conversational companions to think about what is most important in life. He wants us to reflect on how we should live. Surely his maxim—"the unexamined life is not worth living"—expresses a moral concern, at least in part, for the condition or quality of our lives, and hence a concern for the state of our souls. In chapter 1, as noted earlier, I adduced Vlastos's characterization of Socrates' method of inquiry as being a matter of "moral inquiry." Remember here that Nettleship describes the sophists in these terms: "[T]he teaching of the sophists was a moral education, an education in things which have to do with life."[19] What other concern is more central to Socrates' entire project than this one?

Along any of these dimensions of comparison, then, it seems that Socrates appears to be akin to the sophists. These strong similarities are what Socrates' accusers were counting on; they place Socrates within the fold of the sophists. Given the historical and social context of ancient Athens, it would be more surprising if the jurors did *not* take Socrates to be just another sophist corrupting their youth. I conclude that the threat is quite real that he may be taken for a sophist by his jurors.[20] It is, therefore, against such a background that we should try to understand the logic behind various portions of Socrates' defense statement in the *Apology*, and especially those portions that relate to the third accusation, namely, that Socrates corrupts the young—just as the sophists corrupt the young.

In order not to be mistaken by his jurors for a corrupting sophist, Socrates employs three arguments in refutation of the last charge lodged against him: (1) unlike the sophists, Socrates does not ask for payment, nor does he accept payment from his conversational partners, no matter what the outcome of their joint and mutual explorations; (2) unlike the sophists, Socrates neither teaches others rhetoric nor uses rhetoric against them during their discussions and explorations (instead, Socrates' philosophical practice relies upon something he calls "dialectic," the point of which is not to fool his conversational companions or to manipulate them, but rather to lay bare the unspoken assumptions and the logical implications of the arguments they are considering); and (3) unlike the sophists, Socrates does not teach. Socrates grants that he may influence others, but he has no knowledge that he wishes to share.

I believe these three lines of argument are intended to separate Socrates from the sophists. Accordingly, certain portions of his defense statement seem to illustrate further this attempt by Socrates to set himself apart. Early in his defense, for example, he draws a line in the sand for his jurors, a line that distinguishes him from the sophists: "[I]f you have heard that I undertake to educate men, and make money by so doing, that is not true either, though I think that it would be a fine thing to be able to educate men, as Gorgias of Leontini, and Prodicus of Ceos, and Hippias of Elis [three prominent sophists] do. For each of them, my friends, can go into any city, and persuade the young men to leave the society of their fellow citizens, with any of whom they might associate for nothing, and to be only too glad to be allowed to pay money for the privilege of associating with themselves" [Church & Cumming at 24 (19e–20a). This early attempt by Socrates to differentiate himself from the sophists places most of its emphasis on what I was calling his first line of defense, namely, that, unlike the sophists, Socrates does not ask for payment. But this early claim also bears more than a hint of Socrates' third line of defense, namely, that he does not teach anyone anything: "if you have heard that I undertake to educate men, . . . that is not true either, though I think that it would be a fine thing."

Later in his defense statement, Socrates asks why people feel anger and resentment toward him. He suggests, in response, that their anger is a transference of their anger at themselves. They are, Socrates says, "ignorant pretenders to knowledge," and so they hate being humiliated while undergoing his probing cross-examinations:

> [T]he persons who are cross-examined get angry with me instead of themselves, and say that Socrates is an abomination and corrupts the young. When they are asked, "Why, what does he do? What does he teach?" they do not know what to say. Not to seem at a loss, they repeat the stock charges against all philosophers, and allege that he teaches people to disbelieve in the gods, and to make the worse argument appear the stronger. For, I suppose, they would not like to confess the truth, which is that they are shown up as igno-

> rant pretenders to knowledge that they do not possess. So they have been filling your ears with their bitter prejudices for a long time, for they are ambitious, energetic, and numerous; and they speak vigorously and persuasively against me. [Church & Cumming at 28 (23c–e)].

If these charges are indeed the standard ones leveled by indignant citizens against philosophers, it is no wonder that Socrates wishes to distance himself, on the one hand, from traditionalists such as Thales, Parmenides, Heraclitus, and Anaxagoras, and, on the other hand, from the new sophists such as Protagoras, Gorgias, Prodicus, Hippias, and Thrasymachus.

It is only when Socrates has finished responding to both the old and the new sets of charges lodged against him, that he returns to his denial that he teaches anyone anything. The specific context this time for Socrates' denial is one in which his accuser, Anytus, has asked that Socrates (if convicted) be put to death. Socrates now turns his thoughts to his jurors and their likely state of mind. Given the gravity of the charges, and the possibility that the death penalty may be imposed, he imagines that his jurors will be anxious, and conflicted. Conflicted because, if his jurors were to acquit him, they might still see Socrates as a threat to their children. You are worrying (Socrates tells his jurors) that "if I escape, all your sons will be utterly corrupted by practicing what Socrates teaches" [Church & Cumming at 35 (29c)].

Here, finally, Socrates asks his jurors to consider what it is that he actually practices or teaches when he engages other people (including, but not limited to, the youth of Athens) in discussion and argument. He characterizes his practice or teaching in the following terms:

> If he disputes my words and says that he does care about these things [that is, wisdom and truth and the improvement of one's soul], I shall not at once release him and go away: I shall question him and cross-examine him and test him. If I think that he has not attained excellence, though he says that he has, I shall reproach him for undervaluing the most valuable things, and overvaluing those that are less valuable. This I shall do to everyone whom I meet, young or old, citizen or stranger, but especially to citizens, since

> they are more closely related to me. This, you must recognize, the god has commanded me to do. . . . For I spend my whole life in going about and persuading you all to give your first and greatest care to the improvement of your souls, and not till you have done that to think of your bodies or your wealth. And I tell you that wealth does not bring excellence, but that wealth, and every other good thing which men have, whether in public or in private, comes from excellence. If then I corrupt the youth by this teaching, these things must be harmful. But if any man says that I teach anything else, there is nothing in what he says. [Church & Cumming at 36 (29e–30a, 30a–b)]

But notice what it is that Socrates admits to doing. He urges his conversational partners, first and foremost, to devote their time and energy to pursuing and attaining excellence, to improving their souls: "I spend my whole life in going about and persuading you all to give your first and greatest care to the improvement of your souls." Socrates is not offering his partners in conversation a philosophical doctrine or theory to be memorized. Rather, he is exhorting them to improve themselves, to teach themselves whatever it is that they feel the need to know.

What excellence is, or what it takes to attain *areté,* Socrates does not say.[21] All that he knows, and all that he teaches, is that virtue or excellence is the thing in life most worth caring about. And it is the task of a lifetime to investigate this matter and to attempt to attain whatever constitutes human virtue or excellence. "If then I corrupt the youth by this teaching, these things must be harmful. But if any man says that I teach anything else, there is nothing in what he says." On my reading of this passage, Socrates' denial of teaching serves two purposes.

First, Socrates' denial categorically separates him from the sophists. Unlike Socrates, the sophists claim that they know what virtue or excellence is, and that they are capable of teaching it to others, as Nettleship suggests in his description of them as moral educators. Protagoras explicitly makes this claim in the early portion of the *Protagoras,* although he proves to be unable to defend it. In addition, the same claim is attributed by Meno to Gorgias at the very beginning of the *Meno*. Socrates, on the other hand, claims only to teach the worth of moral investigation, the importance of being concerned about one's moral health and the state of one's soul. He thereby locates an object of study and effort, to be sure, but he does not prescribe how one is to prosecute such a study. Nor does he indicate the likely result of our undertaking such a study. All of these further things are unknown to Socrates, as they are to us. His professed ignorance as to these further matters is real and unfeigned.[22]

Second, Socrates' denial of teaching puts the burden for pursuing such a study squarely on the shoulders of those with whom he is conversing. His denial of teaching is his way for getting other people—those with whom he comes into contact through his dialectical conversations and examinations—to accept their responsibility for conducting their own education.

> [T]hroughout my whole life, both in private and in public, . . . you will find I have always been the same and have never yielded unjustly to anyone; no, not to those whom my enemies falsely assert to have been my pupils. But I was never anyone's teacher. . . . I am ready to ask questions of rich and poor alike, and if any man wishes to answer me, and then listen to what I have to say, he may. And I cannot justly be charged with causing these men to turn out good or bad, for I never either taught or professed to teach any of them any knowledge whatever. And if any man asserts that he ever learned or heard anything from me in private which everyone else did not hear as well as he, be sure that he does not speak the truth. [Church & Cumming at 39–40 (33a–b)]

Throughout Socrates' adult life, at least since the revelation of the oracle at Delphi, he puts on no airs in public, and he conducts no special lessons or sessions in private. He presents the same face, the same persona, to everyone. "I am ready to ask questions of rich and poor alike, and if any man wishes to answer me, and then listen to what I have to say, he may." This is the core of Socratic conversational inquiry: Socrates asks questions, someone else answers, and then Socrates responds critically.

Is this process didactic? Sometimes, but not always. When Socrates talks with Meno's slave and appears to elicit from the slave his recollected knowledge of geometry, the process of question-and-answer does seem to me to be straightforwardly didactic. For example, many of Socrates' questions to the slave are leading ones. And some of the exchanges in the *Protagoras* between Socrates and Hippocrates, and even some exchanges with Theaetetus in that later dialogue, strike me as didactic exercises.

Other examples of didactic exchanges can be found in the *Republic.* Most of the books after Book I in that dialogue seem to comprise didactic exercises. In his "Introduction" to his translation of the *Republic,* A. D. Lindsay offers the thought that in the books following Book I, "Socrates is no longer examining the opinions of others. He is leading the conversation to an end already apprehended by himself. He is no longer an inquirer but a teacher. His companions cease to argue as Thrasymachus had argued. Glaucon and Adeimantus still take some real share in the conversation, but after their first long statements they play the part, not of rival disputants, but of slow-witted pupils for whom the master sometimes goes too fast."[23] Lindsay summarizes this change in the *Republic:* "When it begins it is dramatic, a representation of the historical Socrates. It becomes a dialogue which conveys Plato's teaching" [Lindsay, xv].

Yet the central aim of Socratic conversational inquiry does not seem to me to be one of didactic transmission of information or technique. In many of the exchanges between Socrates and Protagoras, for example, or between Socrates and Theaetetus, the ongoing process of question-and-answer does not appear to progress by means of didactic steps. This is one reason why Protagoras hates this Socratic method so much; he cannot predict its results or control the process; instead, *it* controls *him.* On the other hand, Theaetetus seems to be thrilled by this process of nondidactic inquiry. He also is, perhaps, a little intimidated by it all, but he basically seems fascinated by the world that he finds Socrates opening up for him. Meno, on yet a third side, seems merely benumbed by Socrates' nondidactic process of question-and-answer. He confesses to Socrates: "My mind and my mouth are literally torpid, and I have no answer for you, despite the fact that I've spoken at length about excellence on countless occasions."[24] But whether it is Protagoras or Theaetetus or Meno who is vying with Socrates, in most instances I read the two participants in these conversations as sincerely seeking answers to questions for which, at the present time, they are unsure there even is an answer. Their attitude appears to be either one of befuddlement and confusion, or one of pain and anxiety, and the outcome of their searches is in doubt.

Even when Socrates's technique is not didactic—or, perhaps better, especially when the process is not didactic—we may learn from it.[25] We may, that is, *if* we are willing and able to face Socrates' questions and to generate a response that will allow him to respond in kind. But we learn whatever we learn *from the process of inquiry itself,* not by absorbing some pet theory or doctrine from the master.[26] And learning is not guaranteed to us.

In this regard too, Socrates is unlike the sophists. Protagoras and Gorgias, for example, are apt to guarantee that we will become better people simply by associating with them and learning lessons from them. In the case of Socratic inquiry, learning may happen; but, then again, it may not. As much as we "lack" education, our educational need may not be satisfied. Learning, clarification, edification need not occur. And since learning is not necessary (in the sense that it need not occur), then too the results of engaging in inquiry are not calculable or predictable. "[I]f any man wishes to answer me, and then listen to what I have to say, he may" [Church & Cumming at 40 (33b)]. But that is up to the interlocuter to decide; it is not something that Socrates can ensure or guarantee. Nor does he want to do so. It remains up to us to navigate and assimilate the powers and the limitations of Socrates' method.

If Socrates does not teach other people, then he cannot corrupt them. If these others become corrupt, then (in looking to blame someone) they must look only to themselves. It is not Socrates' influence or teaching that corrupts them. Their own failures of self-education leave them vulnerable to the possibility of becoming corrupt. If they do not care about the state or the improvement of their souls—and instead care for money or power or prestige or fame—whose fault is that? Not Socrates'.

Paradoxical Denials: Recognizing the Need to Inquire

Socrates thrives on paradox.[27] His conversations are laced with paradoxical comments and formulations, and others before me have noted this aspect of the figure of Socrates in Plato's dialogues.[28] Still, it may be useful to restate some of the most salient paradoxical points: A master teacher, Socrates denies that he teaches anyone anything. A sage, Socrates disclaims possessing any knowledge, and instead professes his ignorance. Seeking someone who can teach human virtue or excellence to the next generation, Socrates discovers that virtue or excellence may not be teachable. Seeking knowledge, Socrates concludes that we cannot provide an adequate account of what knowledge is. Inquiring into the nature of virtue or of excellence, Socrates is led by Meno, his conversational companion, to consider whether the activity of inquiry is impossible. Himself a victim of persecution and irresponsible denunciation by his enemies, at the end of his trial Socrates declares that a good man cannot be harmed. "[N]o evil can happen to a good man, either in life or after death" [Church & Cumming at 48–49 (41c–d); see also 36–37 (30c–d)].

Evidently, these paradoxes are related to whatever it is that we are meant to learn from Plato's presentation of Socrates in his dialogues. There are two paradoxes central to our concerns here. First, there is Socrates' denial that he is a teacher, or that he teaches anyone anything. Second, there is Socrates' denial that he is wise, or what Vlastos calls "Socrates' disavowal of knowledge."[29] How are we understand these twin paradoxical denials by Socrates?

I have argued earlier that Socrates' denial of being a teacher is meant to distance him from the sophists. His denial also is intended to get us to recognize our own responsibility for teaching ourselves whatever we need to know. As Ralph Waldo Emerson puts the idea, "Truly speaking, it is not instruction, but provocation, that I can receive from another soul."[30] Pedagogical provocation may take the form of someone cajoling us, or exhorting us, or reproaching us, or inspiring us: all of these things (and more) Socrates does.

If it remains the case, however, that making up for our lack of education is our own responsibility, then this may be one reason why Socrates insists so vehemently that he does not teach anyone. He does not want the responsibility for undertaking the work of learning to be shifted away from us and onto him. (Such a shift onto Socrates is, I suppose, what his new accusers expect from the jurors in reaching their verdict.) The sort of knowledge that Socrates and we are pursuing through the means of conversational inquiry is knowledge that can be generated only through our active participation in the process of inquiry itself. Similarly, as Alexander Nehamas points out with regard to the discussion of knowledge and recollection in the *Meno,* "[this] model of recollection . . . is crucial in emphasizing the necessity of working out a proof or of reaching any sort of understanding through and for oneself."[31] We have seen throughout this book that Socratic conversational inquiry involves learning not only about propositions but also about people. This kind of personal knowledge is generated through the means afforded us by Socrates' critical art. Sometimes his critical art demands of us that we be midwives; at other times, it requires of us that we be physicians of the self or soul. In either event, no one else can do this for us. Furthermore, it seems to me that the knowledge that we participants are able to gain regarding the persons engaged in our critical conversation, is a function of the extent to which Socratic conversational inquiry affords us access to knowledge of the self.[32]

Socrates' other paradoxical denial—that he is wise, his profession of his own ignorance as to the matters at hand—seems to me to serve not only an epistemological function but also a pedagogical one. Epistemologically speaking, this disavowal is Socrates' way of preventing himself from saying something that he cannot then and there fully mean. Pedagogically speaking, this same disavowal is Socrates' way of saying that some work needs to be done; specifically, that we need to inquire further into the matter at hand.[33]

In the *Apology,* for example, Socrates describes the examinations of the Athenian politicians, poets, and artisans that he undertook as a result of the cryptic saying of the Delphic oracle ("no one is wiser than Socrates"). There, Socrates makes the point that his examinations of these people always seemed to end in their refutation. Despite their reputations for being wise or knowledgeable, it turned out that these people did not know what they claimed to know. "I found that the men whose reputation for wisdom stood highest were nearly the most lacking in it, while others who were looked down on as common people were much more intelligent." The ignorance of these politicians, poets, and artisans varied between two types.

First, in some instances (mainly, with the politicians and poets), it turned out that, upon examination, these politicians and poets did not know or understand what it was they did in their own professions. The poets, for example, could not account for the meaning of the poems they composed: "Almost any one of the bystanders could have talked about the works of these poets better than the poets themselves" [Church & Cumming at 27 (22b)]. They were capable of putting words together in a pleasing way, yet, it turned out, this poetic knack was not based upon any knowledge or understanding of their art. "So I soon found that it is not by wisdom that the poets create their works, but by a certain instinctive inspiration, like soothsayers and prophets, who say many fine things, but understand nothing of what they say" [Church & Cumming at 27 (22b–c)].

In other instances, however, Socrates found that the person involved in conversation with him really did know or understand the particular field of practice in which that person worked. This seems to have been the case most often in his examination of the artisans. "Finally, I went to the artisans, . . . and I was sure that I should find that they knew many fine things. And in that I was not mistaken. They knew what I did not know, and so far they were wiser than I" [Church & Cumming at 27 (22c–d)]. Unfortunately, the artisans did not recognize the limits of their knowledge, and this illustrates the second kind of ignorance that Socrates discovered among his fellow Athenians. The artisans seemed to think, simply because they were knowledgeable in their respective areas, that somehow this expertise was transferrable. In other words, these artisans believed that they also possessed knowledge of politics and education and virtue and justice. And this claim turned out to be false, as they discovered when Socrates refuted them. "Each of them believed himself to be extremely wise in matters of the greatest importance because he was skillful in his own art: and this presumption of theirs obscured their real wisdom" [Church & Cumming at 27 (22d–e)].

In both instances, then, where Socrates refuted his fellow Athenians in their claims to know, he found them to be suffering from a misplaced pride in their purported wisdom.[34] In the case of the politicians and poets, they thought that they knew when they did not know. In the case of the artisans, they thought their knowledge of their craft bestowed upon them a more general wisdom about matters of politics and virtue and education and justice. In both instances, these people made their human knowledge seem more complete or comprehensive, as though we humans were gods or were capable of a god's knowledge of the world, a kind of divine wisdom.

But we humans do not possess divine wisdom. Human wisdom or knowledge is more modest, and it exists on a humble scale or level. Socrates realizes this aspect about human knowledge, which is why he is more circumspect than his interlocutors in what he claims to know. For example, again in the *Apology,* Socrates acknowledges: "I have gained . . . [my] reputation, Athenians, simply by reason of a certain wisdom. But by what kind of wisdom? It is by just that wisdom which is perhaps human wisdom. In that, it may be, I am really wise. But the men of whom I was speaking just now must be wise in a wisdom which is greater than human wisdom, or else I cannot describe it, for certainly I know nothing of it myself, and if any man says that I do, he lies and speaks to arouse prejudice against me" [Church & Cumming at 25 (20d–e)].

Socrates is careful to draw his claim to knowledge exactly at the limits with which he feels comfortable. It is "perhaps human wisdom" that Socrates possesses; and he acknowledges only that, in this regard alone, "it may be" that he is in fact "really wise." These unassertive terms do not express overconfidence or boastfulness. Instead, they suggest a cautious speaker who is trying to say exactly what he means, and to mean everything he says—and no more than that.[35]

If Socrates' wisdom is "just that wisdom which is perhaps human wisdom," then the men with whom he converses "must be wise in a wisdom which is greater than human wisdom, or else I cannot describe it." They lay claim to a kind of wisdom with which Socrates is unfamiliar. But he is willing to examine them and their claims to know; and if, during his examination, he happens to refute them in their claims—if he happens to expose their inconsistencies to themselves and to the world—whose fault is that? After all, who went before the world in the first place, proclaiming their knowledge? Not Socrates, surely; "for certainly I know nothing of it myself, and if any man says that I do, he lies and speaks to arouse prejudice against me."

This seems to me to be one reason why Socrates, in his defense, invokes the god at Delphi on his behalf: "I will bring the god of Delphi to be the witness of my wisdom, if it is wisdom at all, and of its nature"

[Church & Cumming at 25 (20e)]. Socrates himself is not willing to say, flatly, that he is wise. But, "if" he possesses any wisdom, then perhaps we (his audience, his jurors) will consider on his behalf the testimony of Apollo as to the nature of the wisdom that Socrates possesses. For Socrates has only human knowledge, human wisdom, and that is a relatively impoverished thing.

Human knowledge is, according to Socrates, provisional and tentative.[36] We know something from one side, from one perspective; yet, if we then take another path, a different route, to what we think is going to be the same spot—suddenly, we find ourselves lost in the woods. Anything that we may claim to know, is corrigible. It is subject to being corrected, revised, amended, or, ultimately, even rejected, refuted.

This does not make Socrates a skeptic. As far as I know, he never denies the possibility of human knowledge, or the possibility that any particular person may know what he thinks he knows, or what she claims to know. And the fact that Socrates continually urges us to inquire further indicates his nonskeptical belief that we might gain knowledge if we are willing to work at acquiring it. All that Socrates insists upon is the fact that this possibility of gaining knowledge, of coming to learn or know something, *be tested*. Any claim to know must be treated critically; it must be openly investigated in joint and mutual conversation among any number of speakers and auditors. This is what Socrates' vision of human knowledge is built upon: a dialectical process of producing and revising and testing and amending and investigating and criticizing "just that wisdom which is perhaps human wisdom."

Against this conception of a vulnerable yet accessible kind of human knowledge, Socrates contrasts a kind of knowledge commonly sought or claimed by others. This misleading model is figured in our tendency to speak as though we possess knowledge that only a god could have. Socrates does not make this claim himself, yet others do so. "But the men of whom I was speaking just now must be wise in a wisdom which is greater than human wisdom, or else I cannot describe it, for certainly I know nothing of it myself." Claiming a knowledge "greater than human wisdom" is, I take it, to claim divine knowledge.[37] Socrates will have none of it: "certainly I know nothing of it myself." This, then, is how I understand Socrates' disavowal of knowledge: His denial is his way of putting off an answer to the question pressing upon him until he feels himself better prepared, better able, to formulate a response. Until then, we had best look into the matter more deeply and, in the meantime, reserve our judgment.

Socrates' disavowal asks us to take stock of the situation in which we find ourselves. His paradoxical denial of knowledge is Socrates' gesture for getting us to stop ourselves *before* we claim to know all about some subject (say, the nature of virtue, or what knowledge is, or how excellence is taught, or courage, or temperance, or self-control). Before we barge ahead and claim to know all about it, even before we have investigated it (whatever the "it" happens to be when we are pulled up short by Socrates' paradoxical denial of knowledge), we are asked by his method of inquiry to stop and take an inventory of our supposed knowledge in this area. In this respect, his disavowal also emphasizes the sequence or priority of events: First comes inquiry, then (possibly) comes claiming to know. Primary, though, is the need to engage in a search, which Socrates hopes will be jointly undertaken by himself and his conversational companions.

The corollary of Socrates' denial of knowledge and claim of ignorance is the need to inquire, the need to seek to learn what we need to know. It is in this respect that I meant my characterization concerning Socrates' disavowal of knowledge being not only an epistemological claim but also a pedagogical one. How does Cavell put this idea here? "Heidegger writes philosophy according to the myth of having read everything essential, Wittgenstein according to the myth of having read essentially nothing. They push from opposite sides against the question that the project of a philosophical curriculum is to answer: What must I know to say what I must say?"[38] Before we can speak, we need to investigate. Once the inquiry is over, then we may be in a position to say what we must say. But, until then, we must hold our tongues.[39]

Living one's life under the scrutiny of Socratic examination requires us to make ourselves intelligible to ourselves and to others. (This formulation borrows from and builds upon Cavell's ideas concerning moral confrontation and assessment.) It seems to me that this kind of investigation or inquiry is meant to lead us to a knowledge of ourselves, an understanding of who we are and what we do. This is the kind of knowledge or understanding that only we can generate and confirm during the course of our investigations. So, while Vlastos wishes to claim that Socrates' elenctic method depends upon a common or shared moral knowledge,[40] I would suggest that Socrates' method of conversational inquiry can produce moral knowledge only in the respect that it is a matter of our coming to learn something about ourselves. It can be moral knowledge that Socratic conversational inquiry makes available to us only because that method of inquiry leads to personal knowledge (that is, knowledge of persons), which is a kind of self-knowledge.[41]

Finding Ourselves at a Loss

For Socrates, philosophical inquiry becomes necessary not when someone discovers that he or she knows something, but rather when he or she does *not* know something. This recognition of ignorance marks, for Socrates, our need for philosophical inquiry. Stopping; finding ourselves at a loss; and realizing our ignorance; these are the stages that initiate Socratic conversational inquiry.

Late in the *Meno,* when Socrates has begun to examine Meno's slave about geometry, Socrates turns to Meno and says: "Meno, can you see where our friend here has got to on his journey towards recollection? At first, he didn't *know* which line would produce the figure with an area of 8 square feet—just as he doesn't yet know the answer now either; but he still *thought* he knew the answer then, and he was answering confidently, as if he had knowledge. He didn't think that he was stuck before, but now he appreciates that he *is* stuck and he also doesn't think he knows when in fact he doesn't know" [Waterfield(2) at 120 (84a–b)]. An awareness of our own ignorance seems to be a necessary precondition to our being willing to undertake the rigors of Socratic inquiry. It is one of the fundamental functions of Socrates' dialectical conversation to make us aware of our own ignorance. We seem to recognize that we are at a loss only when we become stuck, stopped by Socrates' questions; this is "the aporetic moment." In Socrates' process of inquiry, he first wishes to get us stuck, to stop us, so that we can realize our own ignorance, which is the nature of our true situation. As Socrates says to Meno about his slave's initiation into the method of conversational inquiry, "Have a look then, and see what he'll discover even under these circumstances as he undertakes the enquiry with me, with his puzzlement as our starting-point" [Waterfield(2) at 120 (84c)].

There is some further discussion between Socrates and Meno:

> *Socrates:* Do you think he'd have tried to enquire or learn about this matter when he thought he knew it (even though he didn't), until he'd become bogged down and stuck, and had come to appreciate his ignorance and to long for knowledge?
>
> *Meno:* No, I don't think he would, Socrates. [Waterfield(2) at 120 (84c)]

Philosophy is called for, not in the fullness of our knowledge, but rather in our discovery that we are empty of knowledge. In recognizing our own ignorance, philosophy is called forth from us. For Socrates, this is not a moment of possession, but rather one of poverty. And it calls for action.

The action called for is inquiry. We are asked to inquire into the matter that is causing us pain or hope or wonder or confusion, and we are asked to do so philosophically. For Socrates, questions asked of ourselves and of one another, are the means by which to inquire into any matter philosophically. So the philosophical moment begins with a question, but some people do not harken to the philosophical moment. Some miss it entirely, others consciously avoid it, and still others waste it.[42] These people apparently are unable or unwilling to find themselves at a loss, to stop and think and inquire, before they claim to know. Or, it is possible that these people do not *want* to know. Or, more likely, they would rather remain smug and secure in what they presume to be their already-acquired "knowledge."

What does it take for someone to welcome the opportunity presented by a Socratic inquiry? Paul Woodruff says that, in this regard, much depends upon the resources of the person who is presented with such an opportunity: "Socrates denies that he is a teacher, and the people he questions often deny that they have anything to learn from him. These denials are tinged with irony, of course, but they contain a grain of truth: Socratic education puts the responsibility for learning on the learner. Nothing is more important to this kind of education than the resources that learners bring to it: their experience, their conceptual and logical abilities, and their desire to know the truth."[43] Some of Socrates' interlocutors seem less than excited about the opportunity that is being offered to them. Here I am thinking specifically of men such as Hippocrates and Anytus and Theodorus, all of whom we have met in the dialogues. Whether they are friends of Socrates (as Hippocrates is), or simply acquaintances (as Theodorus is), or even an enemy (as Anytus was to become), all of them seem unwilling to undertake a philosophical search. Plato uses these people as figures of comparison, to contrast with the other conversational companions in the dialogues.

In the *Protagoras,* Hippocrates is enthusiastic and engaged in his conversation with Socrates. Still, Hippocrates does find himself at a loss, because he does realize that he cannot explain, to anyone's satisfaction, why it is that he wants to become a student of Protagoras. Yet, pondering this question, he cannot advance the conversation any further. For example, Hippocrates is unable to judge who might qualify as a "physician of the soul." And, as to the major question ("Who can teach us?") in the dialogue, Hippocrates has little or nothing to contribute. For this issue, we must wait for the verbal sparring between Socrates and Protagoras, both master teachers, both of whom also are candidates for the title, "physician of the soul."

In the *Meno,* there is engaged and enthusiastic conversation between Socrates and Meno, and even some between Socrates and Meno's slave. Such conversational give-and-take enables us to make some philosophical progress in the dialogue. But, when Socrates turns to Anytus for help in the inquiry, in marked contrast, Anytus refuses to participate in any useful way.

In the *Theaetetus,* Theodorus contrasts with Theaetetus in regard to finding himself at a loss. Theodorus cannot be bothered to enter the conversation, to contribute to the search, and he is at best a reluctant participant, wary of Socrates' probing questions and seeking early release from the examination. Theaetetus, on the other hand, welcomes the discovery of finding himself lost and emptyhanded. Also, it is Theaetetus who gives Socrates the chance to practice his midwifery skills by delivering Theaetetus of his various thoughts concerning the nature of knowledge.

Joe Sachs, in his translation of the *Theaetetus,* makes a connection between being able to find ourselves at a loss, and our having a sense of wonder: "The richest, most direct, and most extensive presentation of the philosophic activity in Plato's writing is the *Theaetetus.* The question that guides that dialogue is about knowledge, but the question that Socrates asks first is about young men who care about philosophy (143D). It is in the *Theaetetus* that Socrates makes the famous claim that philosophy begins in wonder (155C), and forms of the word 'wonder' occur in the dialogue more than twenty times."[44] It also is in the *Theaetetus* where we find the implicit question, "Who is a student worth teaching?" This suggests that Socrates is prepared to act as a teacher for anyone worth teaching, yet we already have seen in our considerations of the *Apology* that Socrates is adamant in denying that he teaches anyone anything. Is there a way to resolve this apparent conflict in how Socrates is portrayed?

Woodruff notices and deftly sketches the difficulty posed here by Socrates' paradoxical denial of being a teacher: "Still, Socrates is more teacher than he admits; he has firm beliefs himself about the rough outlines of knowledge and human virtue (his main subjects of inquiry); and he often questions people to bring them to see that they too must accept such beliefs, on pain of inconsistency with their deepest commitments. Socrates speaks humbly enough, but his aim is not modest: it is to transform people's lives by coaxing them into thinking as a philosopher thinks. And Plato, in writing about this, faces hard questions about the value of the education for which Socrates stands."[45] Socrates denies being a teacher, yet he seems willing to help those people who show themselves to be worth teaching—people, that is, willing to be stopped at an aporetic moment and to find themselves at a loss. He will engage with us so long as we are willing to stop and talk with him awhile.

To teach is not necessarily to lecture or to demonstrate or to prove; in some contexts, teaching may simply be a matter of helping someone see something for himself or herself. According to Lesley Brown, "When Socrates purported to think that an absence of conventional teachers proves a thing unteachable, perhaps he was testing Meno, testing him to see if he had retained the lesson from the experiment with the slave, that true teaching—certainly in the ethical sphere—is when you are helped to work out something for yourself, not when some paid teacher or other authority figure tries to din it into you."[46] Socrates himself does not know the answer to our problems or our puzzles. He is traveling with us on this same road, this path of inquiry. He has not reached a destination somewhere ahead of us, at which he awaits our arrival. He is there with us, walking together, inquiring together into these difficult and puzzling matters.[47] His companionship is his example, which he gives to us. And his example, which he sets for us, is that which teaches us Socratic lessons. As J. Peter Euben states, "we teach who we are."[48]

If, by his examinations and his example,[49] Socrates teaches us how to inquire into our lives, then how might we learn such lessons? This question does not primarily concern Socrates' ability to teach; rather, this question concerns our ability to learn. Are we prepared to inquire into these matters and to think about what we find? What is required at this point is some indication of *our* readiness and willingness to undertake the rigors of such inquiries.

What I have been calling the lesson of disillusion amounts to the first glimmer of hope for ourselves. "So when I went away, I thought to myself, 'I am wiser than this man: neither of us knows anything that is really worth knowing, but he thinks that he has knowledge when he has not, while I, having no knowledge, do not think that I have. I seem, at any rate, to be a little wiser than he is on this point: I do not think that I know what I do not know'" [Church & Cumming at 26 (21d)]. We are, in this respect, "a little wiser" than the other person "on this point." In what does our wisdom consist? It is that we *know* that we are ignorant; we are alive to it. Thus, this awareness of our lack of knowledge now can drive us to seek knowledge about the things that are causing us pain or confusion or puzzlement. For Socrates, such personal insight forms the core of our self-knowledge. It is such a recognition that drives Socrates' inquiries into the nature of things. As Cavell puts it, "No man is in any better position for knowing it than any other man—unless *wanting* to know is a special position."[50] What is our position here? Do we share Socrates' passion for the search?

As Socrates says in the *Gorgias,* he wants our company on this journey that affords us the possibility of gaining a joint education.

> Then join with me and be my companion on the journey to the place where, as the argument shows, you will be happy both in life and in death.... Then at length, when we have really practiced virtue together as we should, we may, if it seems appropriate, apply ourselves to politics or deliberate about whatever else may attract us; for then we shall be better fitted for such deliberation than we are now. It would be disgraceful for men in what appears to be our present condition [of ignorance] to put on airs as though we amounted to something, we who never hold twice the same opinion about the same subjects, and that, too, though they are of the greatest importance. Such are the depths to which our lack of true education has brought us. [Helmbold at 107 (527c, d–e)]

As we currently stand, we are not fit to talk politics, or to propose educational reforms, or to presume to teach others about virtue. We do not ourselves yet know what politics is, or what education is, or what virtue is, and whether it is even teachable. But an inquiry into such matters may equip us in this regard, since it is through Socrates' conversational inquiry that we may learn more about the nature of politics and education and virtue. To vie with each other in putting forward our best thoughts on such matters and exerting ourselves to our best efforts—that is the result for which Socrates devoutly hopes. And, if we were to reach it, it would be a case of our "hav[ing] really practiced virtue together as we should." For the genius of Socrates' method is that, in order to reach the result or goal that he projects, one must put oneself through the fire of personal commitment and effort required by philosophical inquiry.

Socrates is willing to risk the ignominy of refutation, the discovery that he still does not know about such matters. Refutation does not produce in him either disgust or indignation, although it does lead to his being disillusioned. Yet he seems to find this experience to be invigorating:

> So, then, I shall continue the discussion as seems best to me; but if anyone of you thinks that any statement of mine is contrary to the truth, he should take issue with me and refute it. For it is by no

> means from any real knowledge that I make my statements; it is, rather, a search in common with the rest of you, so that if my opponent's objection has any force, I shall be the first to admit it. . . . But since you, Callicles, are unwilling to help me finish the argument, at any rate please listen and take issue with me whenever I seem to be going wrong. And if you will be kind enough to refute me, I'll not be annoyed with you, as you have been with me; on the contrary, you'll be nominated my greatest benefactor. [Helmbold at 80–81 (506a, b–c)]

How is it that Socrates welcomes refutation? And why does he keep insisting that "it is by no means from any real knowledge that I make my statements?" What does this apparent denial mean?

It means that Socrates recognizes that he still has a lot to learn. "People say that I am 'a wise man.' For the bystanders always think that I am wise myself in any matter wherein I refute another. But, gentlemen, I believe that the god [at Delphi] is really wise, and that by this oracle he meant that human wisdom is worth little or nothing. I do not think that he meant that Socrates is wise. He only made use of my name, and took me as an example, as though he would say to men, 'He among you is the wisest who, like Socrates, knows that his wisdom is really worth nothing at all.' Therefore I still go about testing and examining every man whom I think wise, whether he be a citizen or a stranger, as the god has commanded me" [Church & Cumming at 27–28 (23a–b)].[51]

Socrates takes the Delphic oracle as a mandate to inquire further, to continue to investigate that which puzzles him. I suppose that this helps to account for his saying, near the end of the *Gorgias,* "It would be disgraceful for men in what appears to be our present condition [of ignorance] to put on airs as though we amounted to something."

Earlier in the *Gorgias,* Socrates allows that coming to know something is akin to chaining or tying things down:

> These points, as I am stating them now, have already been set forth in our previous discussion and there fastened down and chained (if I may put it rather bluntly) by arguments of adamant and steel—or so it would appear. If you or someone yet more vigorous are not able to break through them, then it will be impossible for anyone

> to speak correctly on such a subject in any way other than the way I am speaking now. Remember that my position has always been the same: though I have no real knowledge of the truth of these matters, yet just as on the present occasion, I have never encountered anyone who was able to maintain a different position in such a discussion and not come off covered in ridicule. Accordingly, I must assume that matters stand as stated; . . . . [Helmbold at 84–85 (508e–509b)]

Until proven otherwise, by further inquiry and argument, the matters stand as stated. Why? Because they have not yet been refuted, even though they have been subjected to a thorough vetting within Socrates' methodical inquiry. Provisionally, for the moment, we may take them to be true.

What does human knowledge look like? It looks like *this*. *This* is human knowledge. This is the best that we can do in this regard. Again, for Socrates, knowledge is tentative, subject to correction. Tying down these opinions, relating them and connecting them (through inquiry and argument) with the rest of what we believe to be true, is the best criterion that we have for telling whether or not they are true—that is, for telling whether or not they constitute knowledge. This is not divine, unchanging knowledge; but, then, we are not gods.

As I mentioned in chapter 1, a similar image of human knowledge is evoked in the *Meno*. There, when Socrates is trying to account for the difference between true belief and knowledge, he tells Meno that true beliefs, while useful for guiding our behavior, "tend not to stay for long; they escape from the human soul and this reduces their value, unless they're anchored by working out the reason. And this anchoring is recollection, Meno, my friend, as we agreed earlier. When true beliefs are anchored, they become pieces of knowledge and they become stable" [Waterfield(2) at 139 (98a)]. We have inquired of these matters, and they have survived our testing and examination: they are "there fastened down and chained (if I may put it rather bluntly) by arguments of adamant and steel—or so it would appear." Where "fastened down and chained"? *There,* in the discussion; they are "set forth in our previous discussion."

Does this make these thoughts and ideas, these opinions, incontrovertible? Not at all. They are knowledge only insofar as they manage to survive our further testing and examination. This is why Socrates says that these opinions are true, "or so it would appear." We never get beyond the provisional assurance of the truth of these matters. They "appear" to us now to be true, because, through our means of conversational inquiry, we have fastened them down and chained them to everything else that we know or believe to be true. Still, they may lead us to an inconsistency or to a contradiction. Then, if they do, we shall have refuted them. At this point, they shall no longer count as knowledge.

Nonetheless, if we wish to take our bearings and proceed with our researches into the truth of these matters, "then it will be impossible for anyone to speak correctly on such a subject in any way other than the way I am speaking now." The next inquiry begins here, where we have tentatively concluded our labors, with these words. Socrates places his faith or confidence in this process of inquiry and disillusion. It is a process of continual testing and examination during the course of our conversation. The inquiry goes on for as long as the discussion goes on. Beyond the fruits of any particular discussion, and any specific tying down of our opinions, Socrates does not know, nor does he claim to know.

As we find Socrates saying in the *Charmides,* another dialogue of search, "'But Critias,' I replied, 'you are talking to me as though I professed to know the answers to my own questions and as though I could agree with you if I really wished. This is not the case—rather, because of my own ignorance, I am continually investigating in your company whatever is put forward. However, if I think it over, I am willing to say whether I agree or not. Just wait while I consider.'"[52] For something to be investigated, it needs to be presented to us for inquiry. And for this to occur, we need to converse, putting our words and our thoughts and our lives on the line. Philosophy in the form of Socratic conversational inquiry begins anew every time that we accept this invitation to join him. Do we gather?

Epilogue

Realities of the Classroom

> *Given the intention and the opportunity of constructing a course of study, the realization of the best course of study is to be discovered only in practice, which means only in the experience of the particular people, and in the particular places, it is to occupy. . . . My second guiding point is this. Given teachers with something to love and something to say and a talent for communicating both, you can afford to forget for a moment about curriculum. Whatever such teachers say is an education. And there are books the reading of which is also an education.*
>
> —STANLEY CAVELL[1]

Readers of this book might ask, in relation to my discussion of Socrates and his method of conversational inquiry, "How much of this material do you manage to use in your law school classes?" I use all of it, when the occasion and the materials being studied call for it. Knowing when Socratic conversational inquiry is called for, and when not, is a part of my formative experience as a teacher in law school and in the humanities. Invoking such a manner of teaching, and method of learning, is a matter of judgment, as are most of the important matters connected with any profession or craft or art.

Socratic teaching requires me to question and criticize my students, and to entertain their own questions and criticisms of me. This interplay of questioning and answering can, I believe, lead to moral inquiry, insofar as it entails or includes an examination of our lives as we are leading them. Such an examination becomes, at least in part, a conversational inquiry into who we are and what we claim to be. This interplay can also lead to self-knowledge, as it almost inevitably invites a kind of disillusion in the student—a growing awareness of the illusion of knowledge, the illusion that one knows more than he or she truly understands. It is bracing to discover how little we do know, so long as that insight is paired with the further realization that we have the ability, the resourcefulness, to learn more than we currently know. So, we may know less than we think we know; but we also realize that we might learn more than we currently know. Learning the limits of our knowledge, the extent of our current ignorance, is one element of self-knowledge that Socratic teaching makes available to us.[2] And, as such, it is intentionally founded upon the aim of teaching one's students by disillusioning them.

I would expect some readers to express skepticism regarding the notion that law teachers engage in "moral inquiry" with their students; or that teachers in a professional school (or, for that matter, in the humanities) should, as a part of their course of instruction, aim at generating "self-knowledge" in their students. Nonetheless, during my career as a teacher, I have in various essays defended such audacious thoughts or claims. I have, for example, written about the sense in which teachers can display virtue (or fail to do so) in their actions in the classroom, thus teaching (or failing to teach) by their example.[3] And, in a discussion of teaching law—Jurisprudence in particular—I have spoken about the ways in which law teachers can aspire legitimately to base their teaching upon the goal of self-knowledge. Indeed, I claim that there is a sense in which teachers of such subjects neglect at their peril, and at the peril of their students, a recognition of the extent to which our knowledge of law is based upon self-knowledge.[4] And, again with respect to law students, I have argued that courses in Legal Ethics or in Professional Responsibility must wrestle with questions of self-knowledge, questions asking us who we are and what we are becoming when we turn ourselves into lawyers.[5]

I mention these earlier writings of mine not out of any misplaced confidence that my essays have in any way established my various claims about such matters. Issues involving teaching and moral inquiry and self-knowledge are unsettled, and they must remain so. They are among those concerns that W. B. Gallie once characterized helpfully as "essentially contested."[6] Rather, in this Epilogue, I want to say something more specific about how I manage to use Socrates' method of conversational inquiry in my teaching in law school.

How I Teach in Law School

I use different teaching styles in large and small classes. (By "large," I mean classes of forty or more students, while seminars or classes numbering less than twenty students are "small.") Since many dynamics of teaching change as class size changes, here I am referring specifically to teaching large classes. For a class in Property, Estates and Trusts, Land Use, or Legal Ethics, typically I prepare by doing several things. First, I read intensively the cases, statutes, problems, and other materials assigned for class, thinking about what makes them tick, how they work, and what I wish to point out about them. Second, I also focus upon ambiguities or potential problems in the materials, things that I expect the students to question or to be bothered or confused by. Third, I think about how we as a class can manage to cover all of these topics—how I can say what I want to say and also hear and respond to what the students want to say—in the fifty or seventy-five minutes allotted. Finally, I think about how I should structure my thoughts and questions on the materials, and the thoughts and questions that are apt to be expressed by the students, and how to present and coordinate the points that I want to bring out and the points that they are apt to make, in a way that makes them comprehensible for the students. Otherwise, while the particular point or question that anyone might raise may make sense in isolation, I cannot be confident that it will make sense in sequence, as it comes up during the class. Thus, this is another part of what I try to anticipate. (I am organizing these matters for my benefit intellectually, so that I understand them, and pedagogically, so that I can teach them.) It is a challenging task.

Thus, I find myself thinking not only about what needs to be said and done, but also about how any of this can be achieved. Of course, I realize that some of these matters will take care of themselves, because any class, as it unfolds or works itself out, will inevitably achieve insights and provoke problems that "just happen." They are not wholly planned or always anticipated and perhaps not even much under my control. The insights and problems that we in the class discover from our discussion and its give-and-take are in this respect incalculable, and probably are better for that. But this incalculability is itself a condition of teaching, something that needs to be considered (even if not calculated). To my mind, the only way to honor this condition of teaching is for a teacher to place his or her faith in the unknowable workings of the classroom, to recognize the limits of what one can do, and to welcome the gifts that education brings. The ensuing mystery is one not only of teaching and learning, but also of the process of inquiry itself: how it proceeds from doubt or question or concern to interrogation and investigation, perhaps tentative and often intuitive, and finally to insight or revelation (but then also, sometimes, defeat). Much of what goes on in a class—be it good, bad, or mediocre—is serendipitous.

A teacher cannot just place his or her faith in classroom dynamics, or just wait for the intellectual sparks to fly. "Spontaneous combustion" is a rare occurrence in the classroom, and it still requires the right conditions. Thus, a teacher must think about how conditions favorable to its appearance might be created.[7] In law school, we create favorable conditions, we investigate our assigned materials, and we provoke discussion by asking questions of our students. This practice is akin to what Socrates did when he asked questions of his interlocutors, who then asked questions of him. This example of education by interrogation, by criticism and argument, has come to seem paradigmatic for much of Western education. So it is that, in considering how what I want to happen in my class is to be achieved, I think about how my lesson plan can be accomplished by means of asking questions.

Asking questions of our students in law teaching proceeds on the belief that they have carefully read these materials and thought about them prior to class. This last point is important in a couple of respects. First, it illustrates that the law school teaching context is one in which we claim that all of us are able to participate (as is mostly the case in the Platonic dialogues, for they assume the radical equality among inquirers in conversation with Socrates) and that we all are engaged in the materials at hand. These may be fictions, of course, but they are convenient, operative fictions upon which we take action. We teach as though they were the case. The assumption of mutual preparation also illustrates that the questions asked—either those of the teacher or those of the students—make sense only within a given context. Such preparation helps to ensure that the teacher and the students share a context in which the questions asked will make sense to all of them. The process of preparing ourselves for class makes us more commensurate and more communicative, more capable of sharing the process of conversational inquiry and education.

The preparatory process that I have described typically takes place over a series of days, even weeks, but most intensively for me the night before a class and again in the hours immediately preceding a class. This is a process of priming myself to perform, to enact in front of my students an intellectual drama of enthusiastic yet daunting engagement with the materials.[8] But the enactment is not solely my own, nor is the engagement mine alone. I may be a major player in the class, but I am not the only one on stage, and the students are not there simply as my audience. I am not there to perform a soliloquy; I am there to help the students understand the texts that address the knots of nested human desires and needs with which we wrestle in our law and legal system. I can do this best not by lecturing to them, but rather by investigating these materials in tandem with them as we jointly question and analyze, role-play, or otherwise work through the materials together.

At the end of this preparatory process, I come into the classroom, set down my books and notes, and bring the class to order. I am the director of the show. I may begin with a question, and it may range from a broad one ("What is the importance of possession to property claims?" or "Why do we put so much weight on the fact of possession in Property law?") to a specific one ("What is the holding in Pierson v. Post?"[9] or "Who won in Pierson v. Post and why did he win?"). Or I may simply ask, "Who has Pierson v. Post ready?"

More often than not, however, I do not begin with a question of any kind. Rather, I start by lecturing, sketching the background of the lesson for the day, perhaps reviewing briefly what was said and done in the previous class, perhaps starting a new topic or continuing an old one. What is important to me is that I give the students a sense of the universe of understanding and discourse into which our specific topic for the day fits. They need this kind of holistic frame-setting, if each separate and discrete class session is to make the most sense for them in sequence, and I try to provide the requisite continuity for them. This is not to say that I sketch anew the entire universe every time that we begin a new topic.

Students learn better if the class begins by my setting the context for the day's work. In addition, whatever thoughts, developments, and refinements that I have worked out for myself, I want to share with my students so that we have some common ground on which to approach the day's materials. Consequently, I try to give them some sense of where these materials fit into the "big picture" of Property or Estates and Trusts or Land Use. This context-setting proceeds hand-in-hand with introductory and contextual materials set out in the casebook or the photocopies that we are using for the class. I depend upon the book to have done much of this work, and thus depend upon the students to have absorbed enough of this information such that occasional reminders from me are sufficient to create a world in which the specific cases, problems, and questions for the class make sense.

Having set the context, introduced the topic, or described a bridge that gets us from yesterday's class to the present, I begin. Who can state the case? What was its holding? What did the court give as the relevant facts? Did the court miss the relevance or implication of any of the facts that it stated in its opinion? Did it overemphasize or underemphasize some fact, value, or policy? What was the rule of law that the court gave as its ratio decidendi? Was the rule well stated, or well applied, or well understood by the court? Does the student stating the case (or any other student in class) think that the court's arguments or reasons for its analysis and judgment were well stated or well founded? Why or why not? What was the crucial aspect of the case, both in the court's view, and in the student's view? What were the equities between the parties? Can we, in this class, design a better decision? What can we include in the law that the court excludes, or what can we remove from the law that the court finds itself unable to jettison? And what does such inclusion or exclusion do to the body of law that we are studying?

More often than not, I do not proceed very far with these questions, because the student volunteering to discuss the case has said something incorrect. Usually, when one of my students starts to relate what happened to initiate this case, or describes how the courts disposed of this case, I find some significant misstatement of fact or law, or some omission of fact or procedure. As a result, I stop the student: "Bob, you said that Mr. Post was chasing the fox, but you didn't say where this chase took place, or how Mr. Post undertook this chase. Do you remember where the chase took place? How it was done?" Or, I may interject: "Susan, you say that the majority holds that you don't have to actually possess the fox, but can merely chase and seriously wound it, in order to gain title to it. Is that really what this case holds? Why or why not?" To such questions, I usually get one of two responses.

On the one hand, the student may understand, or may think that he or she knows, what I am referring to in my interjection, and then he or she tries to respond. Sometimes the student is right, sometimes wrong. If, in what the student offers the class in response, the fact or procedure or rule that I am looking for is stated, then I follow up with, "Why do you think I asked that question? What is important or significant about this fact (or procedure or rule)?" This tends to get the student thinking about what he missed in the case, or what she failed to see when she prepared the case for class. Often, my follow-up question is answered not by the student who originally recited the case, but by another student who has been listening to our exchange and who suddenly sees what now needs to be said. On the other hand, if the fact, procedure, or rule that I am looking for is not stated by the original student in response to my initial question, then my follow-up question is apt to be, "Can anyone else see what I'm looking for here? Can anyone else help us?" The floor is then open to another volunteer.

In response to my original interjection, however, I may get back a blank stare, or a quizzical look, or even a glare. The student either does not know what I am looking for or else does not care. Then the student usually refuses to proceed further or may even refuse to acknowledge my follow-up question, and simply refrains from participating further. Then I begin again, seeking another student who can tell me what I want to know.

Asking Questions, Expecting Answers

This is all that I wish to describe of my teaching in law school, although it consists of more than this, especially toward the end of our class session. At that later time, I usually move into a different mode and bring fragments of the day's class together, perhaps comparing and contrasting things said throughout the period. Or else I remind the students of something we had said the day or week or month before, and then show them its relevance to what we have just this day discussed. But all that I want for the moment is the act of teaching just described, where I am questioning (and to some extent antagonizing) my students, and they are responding (or failing to respond, or choosing not to respond). I call it "teaching by disillusioning the student." How does it work?

Let me start with my questions. Many times, I am looking for specific answers or responses.[10] On the holding of a case, for example, I often have a particular way in which I think the holding should be stated. While I recognize that there is a certain amount of leeway, I do not permit just any statement to stand, either as offered by my students or as suggested to me by the teacher's manual drafted by the editors of the casebook. If I receive, in response to one of my questions, a statement of the holding that by my lights is incorrect, then I try again to elicit it, either from the same student or from another. Eventually, I may offer my own statement of the holding, and then I go on to parse it, explaining to my students why I have included what I did, and why I omitted what they may think is an important aspect or element of the case.

At other times, however, I am not looking for any particular answer, and, in fact, I am asking my question because I myself do not know the answer but think that the question is somehow "a good one"—perhaps because it tends to provoke thought, or at least argument, or perhaps because the kinds of answers that it tends to evoke have proven to be useful ones on which to reflect. And often, when I ask a question to which I do not know the answer, I ask it because I really want to learn what my students are making out of these matters (and, indirectly, out of the course as a whole) as well as seeing how my students are developing as lawyers.

In these two different situations in which I ask questions—where I know the answer or at least where I expect a certain answer to be given, and where I do not know the answer or at least do not expect any particular answer to be given—I think about them as two fundamentally different scenes of instruction.[11] In one scene, I am engaging in an "exercise," in which we are essentially rehearsing answers that I have heard before, answers that I want and expect to come in front of the class, answers that usually do not surprise me at all. At other times, however, I am seeking to glean information from my students by asking them questions to which I do not know the answers, in which case I think about the scene of instruction as being a matter of "true inquiry" or "investigation." Notice, however, that this is what we are doing in the classroom from *my* perspective alone; this is not the way in which I want my students to view the matter.

If students in my class were to realize that we were merely "rehearsing" answers, they would be contemptuous of the process. They might demand: "If you, Eisele, know the answers, then simply tell them to us!" The threat here is that the students may lose interest in our class. For what is the point of going through an inquiry or an investigation if it is merely an exercise? To teach in this way seems not only inefficient but also dishonest and disrespectful.

It is at this point, I believe, where we must consider what we are doing as teachers and why we do it. As a teacher, I do not want to take the experience of learning by self-discovery away from my students, which might occur if I act or signal that, for me, this is all routine, a mere "exercise," a matter of putting the students through their paces. Simply because I am not surprised by certain answers to certain questions does not mean that the answers themselves are unsurprising or that the students are not surprised by them. We teachers are not there, at the front of the classroom, to display our knowledge; rather, we are there to help our students gain their own learning experience. We are not there to discover what we can do; rather, we are there to help the students discover what they can do for themselves, by themselves, with some initial help or provocation from us.

When I ask my students questions to which (I think) I know the answers, I conceive of myself, in this regard, as still going through an inquiry when I do this, a true inquiry or investigation, but it is an inquiry that is both the same and slightly different from the one my students are going through. Let me try to describe their inquiry first.

I focus their attention in class on the materials at hand and ask questions about those materials, thereby trying to get them to discover what they can make out of them. We all are engaged in the same process of making something legally recognizable and effective out of the materials the law gives us, but the responsibility is mainly theirs to do so. As some law teachers are notorious for saying (in my generation, it was Professor Kingsfield of *The Paper Chase* fame), "We law teachers don't teach you the law, you students do that; we teach you how to think." In certain contexts this claim is simply fatuous (when, for example, it is an attempt on the teacher's part to escape responsibility). In other contexts the claim is downright false. Our students already know how to think, and they already have minds of their own. (If they did not, they would not be in law school. More to the point, if they did not already know how to think in general, then we could not teach them anything in law school.) We teach them, rather, *ways* to use their minds; we show them *how* they may wish to think (if they choose do so so). We are demonstrating for the edification of our students—and, thus, we are training them in—*techniques* of thinking. We are displaying ways of applying legal materials in developing the thinking skills that the students already possess.

When properly invoked, then, Socratic teaching can serve as a useful reminder that it is primarily the law students' responsibility to discover what these materials come to mean legally. Our teaching can only partially and incompletely convey what these materials mean (and what they can be made to mean). The primary lesson is not a matter of learning about what we teachers have managed to make out of the law (as a resource or a repository of legal problems and legal problem-solving material), but rather of learning what our students are capable of making out of the law.

At the same time, however, the students are watching both their fellow students and me, their teacher, even as they focus on the materials at hand. I may be criticizing their attempts at lawmaking at any time during their performances, their recitations in front of the class, and I am also giving performances of lawmaking myself, for their edification.

So too are their fellow students. Thus, the students must try to watch me and to see what I am doing, even while they themselves recite or watch another student recite. (This duality of focus is one reason why it is imperative for them to prepare the assigned materials prior to class.)

My inquiry and observation are similarly fragmented, but they have slightly different objects of attention. I am looking at the materials to see what becomes of them under the attention that we give them in class, and I am watching the students as they recite. I am also watching something else as well, however; I am watching myself teach them, and watching them learning. I am trying, then, to take in or focus on the class as a whole—the class conceived of as a unit of human activity and education—not me and them, but *us*.

This last is an object of my attention because I have particular lessons or goals that I want to cover during the class, and I do not wish to lose sight of them by losing myself in the class discussion. If I do lose track of the overarching lesson plan, while the imaginative interplay and discussion may be immediate and rewarding, the long-term losses may turn out to be severe.[12] Thus, I am trying to do three things at once: to see what we are making of the materials at hand, to watch the students perform, and to determine how we are doing as a class. That complicated constellation of pedagogical interests is one reason why I too had better be well prepared when I get to class. From my perspective, then, what distinguishes the two scenes of instruction—"exercises" from "true inquiries"—is not the presence or absence of these three teaching goals, but rather their mix or balance within the particular scene of instruction that at the moment happens to be unfolding.

When I ask my students questions to which I do not know the answers, I am looking for enlightenment about the materials that we are studying at the moment, be they Property or Estates and Trusts or Land Use. But their responses can also tell me a lot about what kind of lawyers my students are becoming (or are failing to become), and their responses also can make me pleased or worried about the progress of the class. In this regard especially—asking questions with unknown answers—the risk to class progress can be great. The danger is that, if I choose to let the students pursue the implications of a question whose answer I do not know, I myself do not know the parameters of the discussion that may ensue, and so I do not know what bridges there may be from that discussion to the remainder of my lesson plan. Further, when I ask questions of my students to which I do know the answers, I am apt to be primarily interested in learning what they are making out of themselves as lawyers and only secondarily interested either in the materials that we are studying at the moment or the immediate progress of the class. These matters can change in their primacy, however, depending upon the extent to which the answers do or do not surprise me, do or do not conflict with my expectations.

My response, then, to my students who might feel contempt for what we are doing in class, were they to see that at least some of the time, my questions are meant to "rehearse" answers that I know already, is the following. "Yes, often I do know the answers to the questions I ask. But you do not; or, at least, I cannot be sure that you do, until I have learned that you know the answers. I cannot learn this by lecturing to you. My lecturing to you, my giving you the answers, would not help you, because law is not a matter of having answers; it is a matter of gaining answers, of creating answers, out of the materials that the law affords to lawyers. This skill—the ability to gain or to create answers out of legal materials—cannot be tested or ascertained by my giving you the answers. What I want to know is whether *you* have this skill."

Students may learn any number of important lessons in this way. They may learn, for example, that for all of the terrible ambiguity and vagueness in the law, there are on some occasions in some areas of the law some definite answers to some definite questions—for instance, in my Property course, in problems that can arise in landlord-tenant law, or in future interests and the dread Rule Against Perpetuities, or in my Legal Ethics course when we discuss certain conflicts of interest. It is not so in my Property course, on the other hand, when we discuss much of Takings law, or in my Legal Ethics course when we address some disclosure-of-client-confidences problems. Some legal materials permit more definite answers than others, given sufficiently definite questions or problems raised in a sufficiently definite factual setting. This lesson is something about the law that it is worthwhile for the students to learn.[13] Other lessons are harder to swallow. In particular, as noted earlier, when I hear my students say something wrong or misleading in response to one of my questions, I stop them.[14] Why do I do this?

I want my students to learn, first and foremost, that they do not know something that they think they know. This is an important lesson. Yet, it is equally important not to take the lesson too far, or not to draw the wrong inference. The right inference is, "I thought I knew, but I did not, in fact, know, when I said that I knew. How could this have happened to me?" This lesson humbles the speaker, at least momentarily, and makes the speaker go back over the grounds or bases for his or her claim to have known, checking and rechecking the facts—in other words, giving them some more thought. This cautionary tale is all to the good; it may make our students more thoughtful. And it may even make them more circumspect as to what they claim to know. This too is all to the good; we lawyers could use some humility, and some hesitancy, in claiming to know things. But one of the wrong inferences to draw would be this: "Since I don't know here and now what I claimed to know, then I never can know; I never can (or should) claim to know anything." This would be an absurd conclusion to draw from this experience, and yet it is the frame of mind that in philosophy we find expressed as skepticism.

I shall say later why I think that skepticism is an incorrect inference to draw from this humbling experience, but for the moment, there is something else that I as a teacher hope to gain from this kind of questioning. I want a recognition on the part of the students that the way out of this fix is through themselves, not through me. I realize that I can provide some temporary relief for their befuddlement, and, given sufficient cause, I often will step in and offer an argument or a fact or a rule that may settle the concern raised by my question. This is only a temporary solution; nothing I do or say can save my students from the professional challenges they have ahead of them.[15] The way out is through themselves, and not through me. This is the second lesson I expect them to learn from this form of questioning.

As so much in the foregoing chapters has suggested, it is in my view the peculiar genius of the Socratic dialogues of Plato that they teach these same two lessons: you don't know what you think you know; and you know more (or other) than what you think (you know).[16] The first, a lesson in self-knowledge, results in what I am calling "bitter knowledge," knowledge gained by disillusion.[17] The disillusion is a lesson taught by defeating the expectations and hopes of the student. To the extent that a student begins a class by thinking that he or she already knows how to deal with the materials or the problems or the questions given, this is arrogance. It needs to be defeated, and it is defeated by the method of Socratic questioning.

It is not enough to leave the matter there, however; that would leave the student crushed or defeated, and such an attitude is not what we are seeking in education, either in law school or in any other school. Disillusioning a student is not enough in and of itself. Something else is needed. This "something else," which I am claiming is a necessary part of the Socratic method of conversational inquiry, is engendering renewed effort out of disillusion, which I will discuss later.

The Value of Disillusioning Students: Bitter Knowledge

Here, however, I want to concentrate on what I said was our "drawing the right inference" from the experience that I described above: where I stop a student who is trying to answer one of my questions ("You do not know what you think you know"). This is, I claim, a failure of self-knowledge.[18]

In drawing the right inference from this failure, it is important to recognize that this form of Socratic questioning takes place in a context where the student volunteers to state the case or to recite some particular problem. I mentioned this fact in passing while generating my description of how I teach, but I did not emphasize it too much, exactly because I wanted to see whether or not it would seem significant to my reader if I did not. (I suspect that it did not.) For, after all, we teachers have the power to call on our students to state cases or recite problems in class. Why does it matter whether we exercise that power, or whether instead the students volunteer?

It matters because if the students are called on, then they really have not put themselves in the position of having claimed to know. And that position is the one that I very much want them to be in—that is, it is the position I want *them* to have put themselves in when they are speaking and acting in my class. If indeed I call on a student, then he or she may or may not know the answer. But the mere fact that he or she does not know it does not teach the lesson that I specifically want to impart; rather, it shows only that the student does not happen to know a particular piece of information at that moment. But this we already acknowledge. At any given time in the classroom, any student's not happening to know a particular piece of information does not refute that student at all, because he or she never claimed to know it in the first place. It was I who put the burden of answering on that student's shoulders.

The situation that I want to create in the classroom is where the student, for all the world to see, is claiming to know something. In this context, that claim says something personal about the claimant; it almost functions as a proud boast to expertise, to professional accomplishment, before his or her peers, all of whom are also trying to attain professional status. In such a context, I am confident that the claim to know will be both strenuously tested (or contested) and vehemently defended. That is good; I want that commitment of the self to the self's words, just as Socrates wanted it too, in his conversations that turned into elenctic refutations that brought about humiliation.[19]

When I stop the student who claims to know and I ask him or her questions, I do not know whether he or she can answer them—that is, my questions are genuine, good-faith efforts to determine whether the student who has volunteered to speak really knows what he or she is talking about. When students claim to know, but then discover that they do not know, they are chagrined. They have made a mistake, and a serious one; it can lead to disillusion. But not just any mistake leads to disillusion. What is it specifically about this kind of conversational teaching by questioning that has this power to disillusion a person?

First, as I have been saying, is the fact that the students volunteered to speak. They claimed to know in this situation.[20] Theirs is a claim to know both something about the world and something about themselves: "I know that I know something about the world." It is particularly disillusioning for them to learn in *this* situation that they do not know. "I have mistaken both the world and myself." What else is there? What else might I more easily or more fully know than my particular chosen professional world (here, the legal materials assigned for mastery)? And whom else might I more easily or fully know than myself?[21]

There surely is some pride expressed in a placing of the self in front of one's peers, and the subsequent shame, when one discovers that one does not know, has the power to make the volunteer feel embittered and disillusioned. Then, too, there is the public nature of the humiliation. Having one's errors and mistakes handed back to oneself on a platter is more difficult to dismiss or deny than would be the private correction of one's errors, say, during a tutorial. Finally, in addition to the lack of self-knowledge that such refutation shows, and the lack of professional mastery that it displays, and the public nature of the humiliation that it performs, there also is this: the student is rejected for all to see by someone whom most students respect—the teacher. Is this not an adequate reason for disillusion? I think it is.

Socrates' method of teaching by way of conversational inquiry can be understood as being both empowered by and enjoined by the Delphic maxim, "Know thyself."[22] And, insofar as we proceed in the manner of questioning that I have been describing, the maxim also befits law teaching. By means of Socratic questioning, we force students to recognize something about themselves, something unpleasant but undeniably true. It is this fact of combined unpleasantness and undeniable truth that makes such self-knowledge bitter.[23] This way of teaching law forces our students to acknowledge their ignorance in three different ways, all of which can lead them to learn.

First, done this way, teaching is based upon forcing the student to see something about himself or herself. If I actually *show* a student that he or she has said something wrong, or has gotten something incorrect, then I am forcing a piece of self-knowledge on that student. My students must recognize this about themselves—that this is what they did, or that that is what they said—and they must do this before we can continue the conversation or discussion. (This is one reason why I interrupt them.) This is frustrating teaching, but it also is very powerful teaching because it blocks the students' natural urge to go on with their training. Such teaching tends to foster self-knowledge not because it makes self-knowledge any less bitter or any easier to swallow, but rather because it makes self-knowledge unavoidable, even necessary.

The second way in which this teaching produces self-knowledge is that it compels the student to see that he or she has misread or mistaken something. The materials that we use in the law are primarily written—

case reports, statutes, administrative regulations, scholarly journals, and the like. The second lesson in self-knowledge taught Socratically is that these objects may not be what they appear to be, and so we must proceed cautiously in reading them and trying to understand them. This is usually what we teach when we ask students to state the holding of a case, for example, because commonly we expect them to be misled by something in the written opinion. This is not the same as saying that we are deluding ourselves about the world; that would be another lesson about us, not about the world. Illusions in the world are not delusions we create, but rather are aspects of the world that fool us into thinking that they are something that they are not.[24] (Mirages and other optical illusions are the paradigm instances of this second type of problem.)[25]

The third lesson in self-knowledge taught Socratically is in a sense the most difficult and galling one because it is the most threatening for our students at this point in their careers. It forces them to see that their teacher does not accept their answers. Since the teacher represents the profession to which they aspire, this amounts to the profession's rejection of them as well as the teacher's. To have this evidence of rejection of one's legal skills (especially in front of one's peers) is devastating. It says to the aspirant: you have failed to act as a professional would act.

All of this talk about the Socratic method being a means to self-knowledge can seem disturbingly smug, as though Socrates' method were some sort of antiseptic tool rather than what it is: a personal confrontation with one's way of thinking, seeing, and speaking. Who are these teachers who think that they have the right to cause the student disillusion and humiliation? This question places the discomfort in the wrong light. As I understand it, Socratic teaching does not proceed as a matter of right. Rather, it proceeds as a matter of need. The only justification for teaching this way, as well as the sole good of teaching this way, comes from a belief that it is a necessary response to certain human constants.

As Stanley Cavell suggests, "disillusion is what fits us for reality," but the justification for such teaching "must be . . . based on a true knowledge of what our illusions are."[26] And is it? The Socratic method of questioning and answering is directed toward discovering self-ignorance, and Socratic conversational inquiry is bent on revealing that fact. I think that Socrates' method is, in this respect, based upon "a true knowledge of what our illusions are." I believe that ignorance of the self is a shared condition of human beings, and I would venture to say that our continued susceptibility to a kind of unconscious ignorance, and also our pride or even arrogance in our powers of knowing, trace a continuous theme in human experience and human history. These attributes of fallibility and frailty have always been with us. They are, in this sense, necessary parts of the structure of our lives and experience.[27] Since we cannot escape them, we must learn not only to live with them but also how to deal with them. And the Socratic method of conversational inquiry is one way of dealing with them. (I do not say that it is the only way.)

This leaves pending a concern over the element of humiliation in such teaching. Is it really necessary to humiliate students in order to teach them that they do not know what they think they know? I would say, "Yes, and No." Humiliation must not imply any kind of ridicule, either by a teacher or by the other students. Socratic conversational inquiry is based (as we have seen) on an assumption of there being a radical equality among its participants, not upon any misuse of an imbalance of power that may exist between teacher and students. Teaching that countenances ridicule (Socratic or otherwise) is destructive, not productive. But "humiliation" has a root in humility. To teach humility in what one claims to know—a training to some caution in what one claims to know, and how one expresses it, and how one states what one means in claiming to know what one knows—is a noble enterprise. It remains a goal that encompasses values that are at the core of Western education and philosophy.

Engendering Renewed Effort out of Disillusion

Despite the considerable merits of teaching by disillusioning one's students, I do not mean to suggest that it is unproblematic; teaching in this way is a troubling experience. We may find ourselves, in this regard, again learning from Plato. His brief statement of the "myth of the cave" in the *Republic* is perhaps Western culture's paradigmatic image of the duality of the experience of disillusion.[28] The educational effort to drag the captives from the shadows of the cave into the glaring sunlight is painful and depressing; it is resisted by those who find the old reality less painful and more real. Yet, the captives do want enlightenment, and, yes, they do want the release and the freedom that knowledge of reality will give them. But the shock and misery of this educational effort seem almost unendurable. (T. S. Eliot once wrote that "human kind / Cannot bear very much reality.")[29] Something is gained in the educational effort, but something else is just as surely lost, and the gain may seem bitter comfort for the loss.[30]

One positive aspect of disillusion is our realization that we were mistaken about something. In this way we "come to know" through the explicit process of ridding ourselves of illusions that, until now, may have prevented us from seeing what is true. Yet one negative aspect is that we also realize that we were mistaken about something. In this way we "come to know" through the explicit process of admitting that we got something wrong about the world. This realization disappoints us, and perhaps we even despair of ever getting the world right.

Such disappointment or despair over our ability to know, such disillusionment, leads naturally to skepticism. I said earlier that skepticism is one wrong inference to draw from the experience of being disillusioned,[31] but it seems almost inevitable that our students will draw such an inference. For what person—subjected to the day-after-day criticism of one's claims to know the law in any particular case, or what a statute says, or how to apply a specific rule, or any number of other things about the law—would not become jaded and skeptical? Despair and humiliation in learning through disillusion are manifest. In response, I can only suggest that these experiences are both natural and necessary. We humans tend to become infatuated with what we know (or what we think we know), and we find it disenchanting to learn that we do not know what we think we know. Still, any humiliation suffered by a student should not be taken as though the refuted student were different from the rest of us. Rather, the point of Socratic elenctic questioning is to show not where we all differ, but where we all are the same. We humans share the condition of, on occasion, not knowing what we claim to know. (This is one respect in which we all are radically equal, as Socratic conversational inquiry asks us to recognize.) We who teach Socratically are saying that there is something that we all share, call it "human ignorance" or "human vanity," or a combination of the two. The point is: this is a permanent part of our human condition, not something of which we can rid ourselves once and for all. Consequently, we had better learn how to deal with it. Socrates dealt with it by his method of conversational inquiry through questioning and answering.

The negative and the positive sides of the experience of Socratic conversational inquiry are taught or conveyed simultaneously. How is the positive side of this lesson made available to us by means of Socratic questioning and answering? When I stop a student who is trying to respond to one of my questions, what do I encourage that student to do? In the face of my rejection and criticism, I ask him or her to try again. I ask my students to look at the case again and to see what it says (or implies), to look at themselves and see what they are doing, or to listen to themselves and hear what they are saying. I ask them to hold themselves in front of the class and in front of their materials and to examine what they are doing with these colleagues and with these materials. What is most important is that the mistake or miscue not be allowed to pass unnoticed; its being wrong or inapt or improper must be acknowledged.

In return for this acknowledgment, I shall listen to them seriously and respond fairly. That is the reciprocal commitment I make. If they will try again, then so shall I. We may all learn that the mistake was not the students' but *mine,* that I mistook the truth or propriety of what they were trying to say, or that I misunderstood the materials that we are discussing at the moment. In a teaching method based upon being disillusioned and humbled, it is not the students alone who are threatened with being humiliated or refuted in front of everyone. This is a risk that any teacher must take who wishes to engage in the Socratic contract with students.

How, specifically, do I reciprocate? How does my willingness to reciprocate operate? There are three aspects of positive learning and student encouragement that come to the fore in the process of my agreement with my students to stop, look, and listen again. First, in asking them to return to the class materials, I am implicitly placing faith in them to do correctly now something that they had failed to do initially. No matter how many times my students fail to respond correctly, I trust that eventually the vast majority of them will develop the ability and skill to read and understand legal materials. When we do the hard work repetitiously in law school, class after class, day after day, going through the materials slowly and steadily, always looking to the students to help us understand those materials, we teachers do so in the sure and certain hope that they will grow into their roles. Their gradual accretion of "know-how" may be imperceptible at times, but it is there and it is undeniable. Most of the students have learned the means and the methods by which to become lawyers. They have learned to do the things that lawyers do. With the help of a teacher's encouragement, the students also learn that they have the tools necessary to get the matter right.

The positive Socratic message—"You know more (or other) than what you think (you know)"—is based upon just such confidence in our shared abilities to make ourselves and our world understood, to get things right by means of our shared media (most especially, through our language). As I put the matter earlier, the students already have much of what they need in order to know how to read and understand the law or how to derive or generate answers from the law. They have much of the social and intellectual competencies that we expect of young adults, and these competencies are the bases of the powers wielded by any competent lawyer.

Thus, it is right to say, as James Boyd White does, that law teaching (at least, such teaching that claims to be Socratic) "will assume, what is true of all of our readers [and students], that he or she has a full competence at the social and linguistic practices by which our world is defined. It is thus on our knowledge of language as practice and art or on our shared social and linguistic competence, that we will most rely [in our teaching]; this is not infirmity, but strength, for this is the knowledge we most securely have."[32] Ludwig Wittgenstein's emphasis that our knowledge of language, our possession of our words, is measured by whether or not (and to what extent) we know "how to go on" with our words,[33] also exemplifies the fact that we rely on the social and intellectual competencies that we all possess by means of our native languages. A similar point came out during our discussions of the *Protagoras*, where a group of auditors gathered to hear and assess the discussion between Socrates and Protagoras, and they ended up cobbling together a suitable compromise that saved the conversation from self-destructing. And we also saw this point being made in the *Theaetetus*, where the youthful Theaetetus proved to be as competent as the older Theodorus in responding to the stimulus of Socrates' probing questions. But perhaps this point comes across most clearly in the *Meno,* where Socrates engages anyone as a potential student—from high-born to lower-born, from Anytus and Meno to Meno's slave—so long as the person can speak Greek and therefore participate in conversational inquiry.

As to the refuted student's second lesson, that the world has fooled him or her, the student also learns (conversely) that the world is readable. At least on some occasions in some contexts, the world does give us an answer. This is one reason why skepticism is not the right inference to draw from a student's experience of being refuted. Even though the world fools us repeatedly, or even though we manage to misread the world—we get it wrong—this does not mean that we never can get it right. What needs to be done, as soon as possible, is to get each student back on track by asking him or her to recite again, or by recognizing the student the next time he or she volunteers. The hope is that this time the student will be able to display to the teacher and to the class what he or she has learned.

As to the third lesson, that the refuted student has been rejected by the teacher as well as by the law profession, the positive side is that the teacher befriends the student again by welcoming his or her renewed effort. And the teacher must continue to keep open the possibility that it is the teacher, and not the student, who is wrong. The reciprocity implicit in recognizing that making mistakes works both ways goes a long way toward teaching this lesson. If the students will try again, I shall try again. If they will listen, I shall listen. If they will look and see, then I too shall look and see. As Gregory Vlastos makes the point (to which I have alluded again and again throughout this book), Socrates is endlessly ready to review and to revisit any topic supposedly settled or exhaustively explored in some earlier conversation. This means that, like Socrates, I must continue to befriend my students;[34] I must continue to solicit their opinions and views, to welcome them, and to give them a fair hearing in the forum of the classroom.

This befriending of our students must be done not only because it is entailed by the ethics of the situation, but also because we have no other way in which to teach them what they need to learn. Without this, there can be no transmission of law from one generation to the next.

Cavell showed us this earlier: "If my teacher of French will not accept what I say and do as what he says and does, perhaps treating my American accent with tacit contempt, then I will not learn French (from him). But what happens if 'my elders,' all of them (those bigger people from whom . . . I learn to use words), will not accept what I say and do as what they say and do? Must they? Is it only natural for them to? Is it their responsibility? . . . I would like to say: If I am to have a native tongue, I have to accept what 'my elders' say and do as consequential; and they have to accept, even have to applaud, what I say and do as what they say and do."[35] If we are to have laws among us, and if our students are to learn the language of the law, then at some point our students must take what we law teachers say and do as consequential. But then, too, so must we law teachers take what our students say and do as consequential.

A class driven by questions both asked of the students and directed back to the teacher is based upon the assumption that everyone present has read and studied the materials and is prepared to venture some sort of opinion or response. (This is, of course, a variant of Socrates' prescription, "say what you believe.") While we may not all have the same experience with these materials, and while we probably do not all begin with the same proficiency, the project is one of inducing all of us to enlarge and enhance our skills of lawmaking and law construal by doing the actual work required of a legal professional.[36] The classroom instruction is not meant to make us "the same" in how we think about and handle the law, but it is supposed to make us more commensurate, more capable of speaking and thinking and working together, more capable of communicating, than we otherwise were at the beginning of the class. This is, in my view, just another version of Socrates' or Plato's idea (first mentioned in my Preface) that our minds function best when they work in a circle of minds and voices, circulating our ideas, and perhaps socializing ourselves, and certainly exposing ourselves to examination and testing.

"[I]n a world so perplexingly contrived as this is," as G. M. Young said in honoring Frederic W. Maitland, "a frank and joyous acknowledgement of ignorance is the only way of wisdom."[37] I have said that Socratic teaching begins in questioning that leads to disillusion, which seems to me to be a certain kind of wisdom, as does its converse in the renewal that follows disillusion. If, following Socrates and Emerson and Wittgenstein, we are convinced that illusion in human life is a necessary and in some sense unavoidable aspect of human experience, then teaching Socratically holds an impoverished kind of promise. The promise is that it claims to possess "a true knowledge of what our illusions are," and it locates them in the very structure of human life and language. The poverty of the Socratic method, however, is that all it promises us is that there is work to be done; that we need to persevere in trying to learn and understand ourselves as well as others and the world around us; and that all of these tasks begin by knowing ourselves. For Socrates, the work is never finished. Still, it has a beginning, and that origin is in self-knowledge. Self-knowledge is the root, the home, of human wisdom.[38] But is not this what Plato portrays Socrates as saying in the *Apology?*

NOTES

ONE Introduction

1. Stanley Cavell, "Foreword: An Audience for Philosophy," in *Must We Mean What We Say? A Book of Essays* (New York: Charles Scribner's Sons, 1969), xxviii.

2. Gregory Vlastos reports something similar in his experience of tracing the Platonic dialogues from their early stage into their middle stage. Characterizing the change in Socrates' behavior from one set of Plato's dialogues to another set, Vlastos says: "By the time this has happened the moralist of the earlier dialogues has become the metaphysician and epistemologist of the middle ones. The metamorphosis of Plato's teacher into Plato's mouthpiece is complete." Gregory Vlastos, "Postscript to 'The Socratic elenchus,'" in *Socratic Studies*, ed. Myles Burnyeat (Cambridge: Cambridge University Press, 1994), 37. I should also mention that similar imagery is invoked by Myles Burnyeat when he characterizes a shift or return to an earlier Socratic activity in the relatively late dialogue, the *Theaetetus*. About this shift in Socratic activity, Burnyeat says: "Socrates himself, instead of being a mouthpiece for Platonic views, is restored to something like his original role as the man who knows nothing on his own account but has a mission to help others by his questioning." Myles Burnyeat, "Socratic Midwifery, Platonic Inspiration," in *Essays on the Philosophy of Socrates*, ed. Hugh H. Benson (Oxford: Oxford University Press, 1992), 58.

3. Vlastos gives a splendid description of this "provisional" nature of the conclusions reached by Socratic inquiry. Vlastos characterizes Socrates in terms of his always being ready to "re-examine" the positions and the propositions arrived at in his discussions:

> You would think this hardly the time and place to re-open this issue, but Socrates is quite willing. And I suggest that he is always willing; that he goes into every discussion in just this frame of mind. Previous reflection has led him to many conclusions, and he does not put them out of his

> mind when jumping into a new argument. There they all are, and not in a vague or jumbled-up form, but in a clear map, on which he constantly relies to figure out, many moves in advance, the direction in which he would like to press an argument. But clear as they are, they are not finally decided; every one of them is open to review in the present argument, where the very same kind of process which led to the original conclusion *could* unsettle what an earlier argument may have settled prematurely, on incomplete survey of relevant premises, or by faulty deductions. Nor is it only a matter of re-examining previously reached conclusions; it is no less a matter of hoping for new insights which may crop up right in this new argument and give the answer to some hitherto unanswered problem. And if this is the case, Socrates is not just the fighter he appears to be on the surface, intent on vindicating predetermined results by winning just one more victory in an ordeal of combat. He is the investigator, testing his own ideas in the course of testing those of his interlocutor, watching the argument with genuine curiosity to see whether it will really come out where it should if the results of previous arguments were sound, and scanning the landscape as he goes along, looking for some new feature he failed to notice before.

Gregory Vlastos, "Introduction: The Paradox of Socrates," in *The Philosophy of Socrates: A Collection of Critical Essays,* ed. Gregory Vlastos (Garden City, N.Y.: Anchor Books, 1971), 11–12; reprinted with slight changes, in Gregory Vlastos, "The Paradox of Socrates," *Studies in Greek Philosophy,* Volume 2: *Socrates, Plato, and Their Tradition,* ed. Daniel W. Graham (Princeton: Princeton University Press, 1995), 11–12.

4. When I began law teaching, I was helped to see this gap between pedagogical promise and practice in law school upon reading Bill Heffernan's essay on the sophistic basis of legal education. See William Heffernan, "Not Socrates, But Protagoras: The Sophistic Basis of Legal Education," *Buffalo Law Review* 29 (1980): 399–423. There is an extensive literature commenting on the gap that exists in the United States between the ideal of teaching like Socrates and how in fact much of legal education is conducted. This literature is fully cited and ably summarized by Milner Ball. See Milner S. Ball, *Called by Stories: Biblical Sagas and Their Challenge for Law* (Durham, N.C.: Duke University Press, 2000), 219 n. 27.

5. Vlastos, "Paradox," in *Philosophy of Socrates,* 1; reprinted with slight changes, in *Studies in Greek Philosophy,* 2:4.

6. Alexander Nehamas, *The Art of Living* (Berkeley: University of California Press, 1998), 6–7.

7. Vlastos, "Paradox," in *Philosophy of Socrates*, 19; reprinted in *Studies in Greek Philosophy*, 2:17.

8. Ibid., 20; 17.

9. Ibid.

10. Myles Burnyeat has commented on "the somewhat elusive notion that the real reward of Socratic inquiry is a certain kind of self-knowledge." After describing a number of steps toward self-knowledge that a participant in the process of Socratic inquiry is directed or forced to take by means of Socrates' questioning, Burnyeat concludes: "Self-knowledge, then, is not only the goal of Socratic education. It is also, right from the beginning, a vital force in the process itself, which involves and is sustained by the pupil's growing awareness of his own cognitive resources, their strengths and their limitations." Burnyeat, "Socratic Midwifery," in *Essays on Socrates*, 59–60.

11. Stanley Cavell, "Knowing and Acknowledging," in *Must We Mean What We Say? A Book of Essays* (New York: Charles Scribner's Sons, 1969), 239–40.

12. "If you speak Greek and are willing to talk and reason, you can be Socrates' partner in searching." Gregory Vlastos, "The Socratic elenchus," in *Socratic Studies*, ed. Myles Burnyeat (Cambridge: Cambridge University Press, 1994), 7. This ancient insight also finds expression in Aristotle's *Nicomachean Ethics* as well as in his *Politics*. Cavell tells us that in Aristotle's *Politics*, there is an "early emphasis on the possession of language as the condition of the association of human beings in a polis." Stanley Cavell, *Cities of Words: Pedagogical Letters on a Register of the Moral Life* (Cambridge, Mass.: Belknap Press of Harvard University Press, 2004), 356–57.

13. Stanley Cavell, "Notes after Austin," in *Encounters*, ed. Kai Erikson (New Haven: Yale University Press, 1989), 118–19.

14. Nehamas, *Art of Living*, 6.

15. Ibid., 2.

16. Ibid., 43.

17. Cavell contrasts his conception of moral perfectionism with teleological and deontological theories of morality in the following way. First, as to teleology and deontology, Cavell states:

> A favored way of approaching the field of moral theory is to contrast two major theories: one of them, called deontological, takes the notion of the right as fundamental, independent of the good, and emphasizes the assessment of human action by its responsiveness to obligation and the motive of duty; the other of them, called teleological, takes the notion of the good as fundamental, deriving from it the notion of right, and stresses the

> consequences or utility of actions rather than their motives, emphasizing the assessment of human action by its responsiveness to the call to maximize the pleasure or happiness at a person's or a group's disposal. The most influential theory of the good is that of utilitarianism, represented most famously by John Stuart Mill in the nineteenth century; the principal theories of the right are associated with the names of Kant and Hegel.

Cavell, *Cities of Words,* 9. He goes on to draw the differences or distinctions between these two main theories of morality and his third view, called moral perfectionism: "[M]oral perfectionism . . . [is] a register of the moral life that precedes, or intervenes in, the specification of moral theories which define the particular bases of moral judgments of particular acts or projects or characters as right or wrong, good or bad." Ibid., 2. "This aspect or moment of morality—in which a crisis forces an examination of one's life that calls for a transformation or reorienting of it—is the province of what I emphasize as moral perfectionism. I do not conceive of this as an alternative to Kantianism or utilitarianism (Kant and John Stuart Mill both have deep perfectionist strains in their views) but rather as emphasizing that aspect of moral choice having to do, as it is sometimes put, with being true to oneself, or, as Michel Foucault has put the view, caring for the self." Ibid., 11. Michel Foucault and "caring for the self" also are studied in Nehamas's book, *Art of Living.*

18. Cavell, *Cities of Words,* 24.

19. Ibid., 25.

20. Ibid., 49.

21. Cavell, "Foreword: An Audience for Philosophy," in *Must We Mean What We Say?,* xxviii.

22. Eva Brann, "Plato's Theory of Ideas," in *The Past-Present: Selected Writings of Eva Brann,* ed. Pamela Kraus (Annapolis, Md.: St. John's College Press, 1997), 116 n. 9: "For Socrates *methodos* means a *path* of inquiry to be followed (*Republic* 533B), not a preset investigatory *procedure.*" In a different essay, Brann also says: "[I]t is a contradiction in terms to speak of 'the Socratic method.'" Eva Brann, "Statement on Educational Policy," in *Past-Present,* 350. Gregory Vlastos makes a similar point in an early passage of his essay on the *elenchus:* "In marked contrast to 'Socrates' speaking for Plato in the middle dialogues, who refers repeatedly to the 'method' (*methodos*) he follows . . . , the 'Socrates' who speaks for Socrates in the earlier dialogues never uses this word and never discusses his method of investigation. He never troubles to say why his way of searching is the way to discover truth or even what this way of searching is." Vlastos, "The Socratic elenchus," in *Socratic Studies,* 1.

Seth Benardete seems to agree with Brann and Vlastos when he remarks, "There cannot be a method (*methodos*) of thought in the thoughtful going after (*metienai*) of thought." Seth Benardete, "Strauss on Plato," in *The Argument of the Action: Essays on Greek Poetry and Philosophy,* ed. and intro. Ronna Burger and Michael Davis (Chicago: University of Chicago Press, 2000), 409. A similar conclusion is stated, after a thorough catalogue of the reasons for taking such a position, by Thomas Brickhouse and Nicholas Smith: "Socrates has no method, if by 'method' we mean to identify an orderly procedure which follows patterns that must be learned and mastered before one is able to achieve effective results. There is no 'cook-book' for the Socratic *elenchos,* nor could a step-by-step procedure ever be set forth." Thomas C. Brickhouse and Nicholas D. Smith, *Plato's Socrates* (New York: Oxford University Press, 1994), 10. That Socrates has no script that he can teach his interlocutors to memorize and to follow in their investigations, seems to me to be correct. Perhaps this means that the best that Socrates can do is to goad us to inquire into our lives, into the things that matter to us. At this point, however, Socrates must leave us to respond as best we can.

Based on my understanding of Socrates' characteristic way of proceeding in his version of conversational inquiry, however, I believe that there is something habitual and methodical in Socrates' practice. Making out the structure or characteristic rhythm of his conversational inquiry is a central goal of this book. Compare Cavell's remarks: "Perhaps more shocking, and certainly more important, than any of Freud's or Wittgenstein's particular conclusions is their discovery that knowing oneself is something for which there are methods—something, therefore, that can be taught (though not in obvious ways) and practiced." Stanley Cavell, "The Availability of Wittgenstein's Later Philosophy," in *Must We Mean What We Say?,* 66–67. The topic of Socrates' method is usefully discussed by a number of scholars from a variety of perspectives in a recent collection: Gary Alan Scott, ed., *Does Socrates Have a Method? Rethinking the Elenchus in Plato's Dialogues and Beyond* (University Park: Pennsylvania State University Press, 2002).

23. Myles Burnyeat has argued that there are dual aspects (i.e., positive and negative aspects) of Socrates' method of inquiry. With regard to the *Meno,* for example, which discusses a notion of human knowledge based upon a particular kind of recollection, Burnyeat suggests that "the doctrine of recollection" in that dialogue serves as "a theory of the Socratic method, designed to explain how the dialectical process of eliciting an interlocutor's beliefs and testing them for consistency need not be wholly negative and destructive; if the discussion is pursued with sincerity and determination, Socratic inquiry can lead to knowledge." Burnyeat, "Socratic Midwifery," in *Essays on Socrates,* 57.

24. Concerning the "aporetic" moment, the notion of *aporia* is carefully discussed in Robin Waterfield's "Introduction" to his recent translation of the *Meno:*

> [T]he dialogues of search tend to end in *aporia* ("having no resources," "having no way to progress," "being in an impasse," "being stuck"), as Socrates traps his interlocutors into infuriating self-contradiction. An impasse is more precise than "confusion," as the word is often translated; it refers to the state of mental frustration which results when you have followed a train of thought as far as it can go, and it has failed to take you where you wanted or expected, and you can see nowhere else to go. Socrates clearly believed that *aporia* was good for the soul . . . . Our basic and worst sin, he thought, is believing that we know something when we really do not, and *aporia,* unlike plain ignorance, is a state where we are compelled to be aware of our ignorance and will hopefully be motivated to do something about it (though, oddly, few of the characters in the aporetic dialogues evince much interest in continuing their education).

Plato, *Meno and Other Dialogues: Charmides, Laches, Lysis, Meno,* trans. and intro. Robin Waterfield (Oxford: Oxford University Press, 2005), viii, hereafter cited as Waterfield(2). Additional references to *aporia* and the aporetic moment can be found in Waterfield's "Introduction," at pp. xvii, xxviii, xxx, xxxviii, and xlii.

Myles Burnyeat notes an interesting change or shift in the "aporetic moment" when it occurs in the *Theaetetus:* "Where earlier dialogues had valued perplexity merely as a necessary step towards disencumbering someone of the conceit of knowledge [citations omitted], the *Theaetetus* treats it as a productive state, the first stirring of creative thought." Burnyeat, "Socratic Midwifery," in *Essays on Socrates,* 58. Gareth Matthews concentrates on the aporetic moment, and on the notion of *aporia* from the pre-Socratics through Plato to Aristotle, in his good book on Socratic perplexity. There, Matthews contends that "what gets called *aporia* . . . [in the] early and middle dialogues is the state of bewilderment that puzzles of a certain sort naturally induce." Gareth Matthews, *Socratic Perplexity and the Nature of Philosophy* (Oxford: Oxford University Press, 1999), 30. Thus, "for Socrates, at least as he is portrayed in the early definitional dialogues, philosophy begins in the astonished recognition that he is not able to solve some basic puzzle—perhaps not a puzzle about the cosmos, but rather a puzzle about ethics, and in particular, a puzzle about how to develop satisfactory definitional analyses of one of the individual virtues in a way that captures correctly its relation to virtue as a whole." Matthews, *Socratic Perplexity,* 29.

25. Gregory Vlastos, "Socrates' Disavowal of Knowledge," *Philosophical Quarterly* 35 (1985): 1–31; reprinted with changes in *Socratic Studies,* ed. Myles Burnyeat (Cambridge: Cambridge University Press, 1994), 39–66.

26. Stanley Cavell's numerous studies of ordinary language philosophy as well as his subsequent pursuits of the "ordinary" emphasize the importance of this philosophical appeal to our largely dormant abilities and resources. In once more revisiting this topic, Cavell has cast his thoughts in the following way:

> [M]y motivating question [in several of his early essays] was less how we know what we say and mean (which was the point on which criticism[s] of those two papers were centered) than it was the question of what it betokens about our relation to the world, and others, and myself, that I do in fact, to an unknown extent, inescapably know (barring physical or psychic trauma), and that I chronically do not know or cannot say what I mean, and that I can know further by bethinking myself of what I would rather or might or must or could say, or not say, or rather not. Few philosophers would now, I believe, deny that the ability to speak a language carries with it the ability to perform these linguistic feats, but I assume most do not attach the importance I continue to do to the bearing of this ability on the questions of self-knowledge and of skepticism.

Stanley Cavell, "Preface to Updated Edition of *Must We Mean What We Say?*," in *Must We Mean What We Say? A Book of Essays,* Updated Edition (Cambridge: Cambridge University Press, 1976, updated ed. 2002), xviii.

27. Also relevant here are the earlier remarks by Myles Burnyeat, which I quoted in notes 23 and 24.

28. I again refer to Myles Burnyeat's remarks regarding recollection as an aspect of Socrates' method. As well, it is worth noting again Burnyeat's characterization of Socrates' method as being a means of achieving a kind of self-knowledge (in addition to its being a matter of working with, or relying upon, self-knowledge). See notes 10 and 23.

29. As Nehamas makes clear, "Plato's emphasis on the permanence of *episteme* is anything but irrelevant." Alexander Nehamas, "Meno's Paradox and Socrates as a Teacher," in *Virtues of Authenticity: Essays on Plato and Socrates* (Princeton: Princeton University Press, 1999), 20.

30. Plato, *Meno,* trans. Benjamin Jowett and intro. F. H. Anderson (Indianapolis: Bobbs-Merrill Co., 1949), 58–59 [98a], hereafter cited as Jowett & Anderson.

31. In his essay on "Meno's Paradox," Nehamas makes the valuable point that it is the activity of fastening or "tying down" (through reasoning, or

explaining, or giving an account) that transforms true beliefs (*doxa*) into knowledge (*episteme*). Nehamas also points out that this activity is the core of what Socrates (or Plato) meant by "recollection." Nehamas, "Meno's Paradox and Socrates as a Teacher," in *Virtues of Authenticity,* 7, 14, 17.

32. Vlastos, "The Socratic elenchus," in *Socratic Studies,* 7 (see also 136). In his book on Socrates the ironist, Vlastos puts the methodological point of this injunction this way: "its operative force was *to exclude debate on unasserted premises.*" Gregory Vlastos, *Socrates, Ironist and Moral Philosopher* (Ithaca: Cornell University Press, 1991), 14.

33. Stanley Cavell, "Existentialism and Analytical Philosophy," in *Themes Out of School: Effects and Causes* (San Francisco: North Point Press, 1984), 217.

34. Gary Alan Scott, *Plato's Socrates as Educator* (Albany: State University of New York Press, 2000), 11 (see also 13).

35. I have elsewhere discussed in more detail the sense in which Socrates teaches virtue (and other matters) by his example. See Thomas D. Eisele, "Must Virtue Be Taught?," *Journal of Legal Education* 37 (1987): 495–508. The topic of teaching-by-example comes up once again in this book in chapter 5, where I invoke Euben's perceptive remark that "we teach who we are." J. Peter Euben, *Corrupting Youth: Political Education, Democratic Culture, and Political Theory* (Princeton: Princeton University Press, 1997), 42.

36. See Richard Kraut, *Socrates and the State* (Princeton: Princeton University Press, 1984), 294–304 ("§12. Does Socrates think that he teaches?").

37. Nehamas, "Meno's Paradox and Socrates as a Teacher," in *Virtues of Authenticity,* 12. More generally, Nehamas claims that "Socrates' primary concern was what he called 'the care of the self'. . . , where that self was, above all, his own. . . . Socrates was therefore much less of a teacher of others than we have tended to believe." Alexander Nehamas, "Introduction," in *Virtues of Authenticity: Essays on Plato and Socrates* (Princeton: Princeton University Press, 1999), xxx.

38. Vlastos, "Paradox," in *Philosophy of Socrates,* 7–9, 11–13; reprinted with slight changes, in *Studies in Greek Philosophy,* 2:9–10, 12. These roles are neither mutually exclusive nor exhaustive. Vlastos adds more roles to the mix (i.e., those of the ironist and the moral philosopher) in his book, *Socrates, Ironist and Moral Philosopher,* passim.

39. The conflict and tension between Socrates and the sophists do not mean that he shared nothing with the sophists. Indeed, some people have claimed that Socrates was himself sophistic, or that he was someone who inherited the problems of the sophists and who worked with those problems in his own way. Laszlo Versényi makes this claim in *Socratic Humanism,* where he spends a substantial portion of his book describing the sophists, in part as a

way of showing that the sophistic tradition was inherited by Socrates, as it also was something with which Socrates struggled. "As Socrates' philosophy grew out of, built on, and corrected the shortcomings of the work of his immediate predecessors, the Sophists, it will be helpful to preface our study with a discussion of the Sophists' activities." And: "The greatest accomplishment of the Sophists consisted in their return to man, and in this, too, Socrates follows them. Although the solutions they proposed to man's problems were inadequate, the fact that they made these problems once again the central concern of philosophy prepared the ground for the work of Socrates, the greatest Sophist and wisest man of them all." Laszlo Versényi, *Socratic Humanism* (New Haven: Yale University Press, 1963), 2, 69.

The similarity between Socrates and the sophists having been noted, however, it remains important to give full weight to the differences that distinguish him from the sophists. As to this latter point, Versényi offers us the following catalogue of distinguishing traits:

> While the Sophists in many instances "preferred probability to truth," which they relinquished as unobtainable, and in consequence concentrated on persuasion rather than enlightenment, on obtaining the uncritical consent of the many rather than the intelligent agreement of the few, Socrates did the opposite. He not only insisted on truth but showed a way of getting at it through one's own critical reflection and thus devised a true form of education. The Sophists gave lectures. Socrates merely questioned. The Sophists gave verbal exhibitions on education, virtue, and human excellence. Socrates exhibited them by embodying them in his life. In view of all of this, it is not surprising that, while Sophistic teaching resulted in external education, a cure from without, Socrates brought about internal improvement in men, a true "therapy of the soul."

Versényi, *Socratic Humanism*, 74.

40. In the preceding note, I mentioned that Laszlo Versényi emphasizes the initial continuity between Socrates and the sophists. Here, I also want to draw attention to the fact that Martha Nussbaum, in her pivotal work on Greek tragedy and philosophy, makes a somewhat similar claim regarding Plato and the Greek tragic poets preceding him. Nussbaum contends that there exists significant continuity (at least initially) between the earlier poets and Plato in his ethical dialogues featuring Socrates. "Plato's ethical thought, I shall argue, is continuous with the reflections about *tuché* that we have uncovered in tragedy, responding to the same urgencies, giving shape to the same human ambitions. It is bolder and more single-minded in its pursuit of progress, but not without

its own sense of the human cost of progress." Martha Nussbaum, *The Fragility of Goodness: Luck and Ethics in Greek Tragedy and Philosophy* (Cambridge: Cambridge University Press, 1986), 87. By noting these continuities, I seek to increase the plausibility of my effort to understand Socrates and his activities by placing them within the context of those people with whom he associates and against whom he defines himself.

41. Henry Teloh, *Socratic Education in Plato's Early Dialogues* (Notre Dame, Ind.: University of Notre Dame Press, 1986), 7. About these three groups of people who have some claim to be teachers of virtue, Alexander Nehamas makes a similar point (referring specifically to the *Meno*): "[t]hree classes of possible teachers of *areté* are brought up in the *Meno:* sophists, notably successful citizens, and, in a rather cursory way, poets (89e–96b)." Nehamas, "Meno's Paradox and Socrates as a Teacher," in *Virtues of Authenticity,* 10. Nehamas adds, however, that when Socrates and Meno actually consider these possible pedagogical contenders, all three groups are either disqualified or summarily dismissed as true teachers of *areté*.

42. Richard Lewis Nettleship, *Lectures on the* Republic *of Plato,* ed. Godfrey R. Benson (London: Macmillan & Co., 1897, 2d ed. 1901, 1961), 20–21, 24–25. Martha Nussbaum amplifies our understanding of the status that philosophers and poets had in ancient Athens:

> It is also important to bear in mind that, in the fifth and early fourth centuries, it was the poets who were regarded as the most important ethical teachers. For one thing, some of the major figures whom we call philosophers and include in our histories of Greek philosophy were themselves poets, and wrote placing themselves in a poetic tradition: Xenophanes, Parmenides, and Empedocles are the most salient examples; the first and last are major figures in the history of Greek ethics. But it is equally important to remember that figures whom we usually classify and study as poets were unhesitatingly judged by their contemporaries to be philosophers, if by this one means seekers for wisdom concerning important human matters. . . . Plato's interlocutors, when in search of illumination about virtue or choice, turn naturally to the words of Homer, Hesiod, Simonides, Pindar, the tragic poets; rarely, if ever, to the words of anyone whom we list as a philosopher. It is obvious from the dialogues alone that the well-educated Athenian of the late fifth century has enormous confidence in the wisdom of these figures; Polemarchus, Callicles, and Critias, Protagoras and Prodicus—gentleman and professional sophist alike revere them. Platonic philosophy has to define itself, above all, in opposition to these texts, which embody a deeply shared tradition of reflection about excellence, praise,

> and blame. It is no surprise that the interlocutors of the *Republic* agree that epic and dramatic poems have the strongest *prima facie* claim to form the center of the new city's curriculum.

Nussbaum, *Fragility of Goodness,* 124. We also have John Finley's characterization of the Greek intellectual background during the fourth and fifth centuries B.C. As to the Greek poets and the sophists, Finley says:

> One must remember that the Greeks had no organized priesthood and no accepted theology, and that through the formative centuries of their development they further lacked any such sense of scientific law as in modern times supplies the basis of thought. The poets rather, as Aristophanes says, were the teachers of Greece—a fact which shows once more how thoroughly the national mind was formed on broad truths of the sort that wisdom and observation can supply. For, barring theology or science as the foundation of thought, such insights into the nature of social and individual life necessarily remained the chief means whereby men saw themselves in relation to the world. . . . [T]he poets remained true to their calling as interpreters of civic standards and human experience to the people. It is essential merely to recognize that, when after the middle of the fifth century the sophists to some degree took over the poets' earlier function in society, they could not and did not abandon the latter's essential attitude of mind. The Greeks still relied not on scientific or religious truths but on truths drawn from human observation, and, however novel the precise views of the sophists may have been, the character of those views was inevitably generic.

John Finley, *Thucydides* (Cambridge, Mass.: Harvard University Press, 1942), 39–40 (see also 40–44).

43. For a development of this theme, see Thomas D. Eisele, "'Never Mind the Manner of My Speech': The Dilemma of Socrates' Defense in the *Apology,*" *Legal Studies Forum* 14 (1990): 253–88.

44. *Plato's Theaetetus,* trans. and intro. Joe Sachs (Newburyport, Mass.: Focus Publishing Co., 2004), 5, 4, hereafter cited as Sachs.

45. In noting that several of Plato's works are not dialogues, Myles Burnyeat mentions in passing that "the *Apology* . . . is a forensic speech." Myles Burnyeat, "Plato," *Proceedings of the British Academy* 111 (2001): 1–22, 5 n. 7. And, as Richard Kraut further notes, "The *Apology* consists almost entirely of a courtroom speech and is not happily classified as a dialogue, although there is some interchange when Socrates examines one of his accusers." Richard Kraut,

"Introduction to the Study of Plato," in *The Cambridge Companion to Plato,* ed. Richard Kraut (Cambridge: Cambridge University Press, 1992), 33 n. 8.

46. Whitehead's remark is this: "The safest general characterization of the European philosophical tradition is that it consists of a series of footnotes to Plato. I do not mean the systematic scheme of thought which scholars have doubtfully extracted from his writings. I allude to the wealth of general ideas scattered through them." Alfred North Whitehead, *Process and Reality* (New York: Free Press, 1979), 39.

47. Burnyeat, "Plato," *Proceedings of the British Academy,* 4–5.

48. Euben, *Corrupting Youth,* 42.

49. From a slightly different perspective, I think that John Cooper makes a point very similar to my claim about reading a Platonic dialogue:

> A book must keep on saying the same words to whoever picks it up. Most books—perhaps those of Parmenides and some other early philosophers among them—attempt the impossible task of telling the reader the truth, with the vain idea that, through putting their words into their heads, they will come to possess knowledge of it. Plato's dialogues are writings—books—too; like all books, once written, their words are fixed for all time and all readers. But because they demand that the reader interpret and reinterpret the meaning of what is said, going ever deeper in their own questioning and their own understanding both of the writings themselves and of the truth of the subjects addressed in them, these writings speak in a unique new way to the reader. It may remain true that only a mind, and no book, can contain the knowledge of anything important. But a Platonic dialogue makes a unique claim to do what a book *can* do to engage a person effectively in the right sort of search for truth.

John M. Cooper, "Introduction," in Plato, *Complete Works,* ed. with intro. and notes John M. Cooper (Indianapolis: Hackett Publishing Co., 1997), xx–xxi.

50. Jacob Klein, *A Commentary on Plato's* Meno (Chapel Hill: University of North Carolina Press, 1965), 6. Is not a commentary on Plato's texts an instance of such participation? A commentary normally consists of imaginative responses to—and extrapolations from, and interjections with, and extensions of—the conversations displayed in those texts. Martha Nussbaum also comments on the way in which our participation in Plato's dialogues is encouraged: "The *Protagoras,* for example, puts before us the responsiveness of dialectical interaction, ... We see an active, ongoing discussion, rather than a list of conclusions or a proclamation of received truths. Furthermore, the dialogue sets up, in its open-endedness, a similarly dialectical relationship with the reader,

who is invited to enter critically and actively into the give-and-take, much as a spectator of tragedy is invited to reflect (often along with the chorus) about the meaning of the events for his own system of values." Nussbaum, *Fragility of Goodness*, 126.

51. Klein, *Commentary*, 7.

52. Ibid., 8–9.

53. Ibid., 20.

54. Cavell, *Cities of Words*, 7.

55. See generally Cavell, "Foreword: An Audience for Philosophy," in *Must We Mean What We Say?* Decades later, Cavell said about his earlier essay, "I once claimed that the only audience of philosophy is one performing it." Cavell, *Cities of Words*, 331.

56. Cavell, *Cities of Words*, 7.

57. See generally Nehamas, *Art of Living*, passim.

58. Bernard Williams, *Plato: The Invention of Philosophy* (New York: Routledge, 1997, 1999), 44–45.

59. Ibid., 45. Myles Burnyeat, in his lecture on Plato, cites with approval this remark by Bernard Williams, saying, "This seems to me a good way to start thinking about Plato's unique place in the history of philosophy." Burnyeat, "Plato," *Proceedings of the British Academy*, 4. By the end of his lecture, however, Burnyeat adds his own addendum to Williams's original formulation:

> Plato's ability to move between two worlds [a transcendent realm and the world we are born into], giving each its due, is evident on every page of his writing. James Mill, like Cicero, remains firmly down here on earth. Plotinus is constantly eager to get away to a better place. Plato, inspiration for all three, illuminates both poles of the universe into which he draws his readers. That is why he is altogether larger, more imaginative, richer in ideas, more amusing and more inspiring (even to those who are not philosophically minded), more fruitful to think with, more challenging, more outrageous—in short, more philosophical—than any of the diverse followings that came after him. Plato remains a powerful presence because he opens our mind to thoughts it was not aware it needed.

Burnyeat, "Plato," *Proceedings of the British Academy*, 22.

60. Sachs, *Plato's Theaetetus*, 4.

61. Ibid., 4, 5. Seth Benardete offers us a similar characterization of how a Platonic dialogue works: "Something happens in a Platonic dialogue that in its revolutionary unexpectedness is the equivalent to the *periagogé*, as Socrates calls it, of philosophy itself. This turnaround has a peculiar structure. It has to

be experienced and can never be formulated in such a way as to allow one anything more than anticipation of an equivalent turnaround in another dialogue. There cannot be a method (*methodos*) of thought in the thoughtful going after (*metienai*) of thought." Benardete, "Strauss on Plato," in *Argument of the Action*, 409.

TWO Who Can Teach Us?

1. Plato, *Protagoras*, trans. Benjamin Jowett, rev. trans. Martin Ostwald, ed. and intro. Gregory Vlastos (Indianapolis: Bobbs-Merrill Co., 1956), 69 [362a], hereafter cited as Jowett & Ostwald.

2. Plato, *Protagoras and Meno*, trans. and intro. W. K. C. Guthrie (Harmondsworth: Penguin Books, 1956), 10, hereafter cited as Guthrie.

3. I cannot say that this judgment is universally shared. For example, I was surprised to find the following remark made by Richard Kraut: "Even when [a Platonic] dialogue conveys no drama and no real opposition of viewpoints—as in such earlier works as the *Protagoras* and *Gorgias*—it continues to serve this further purpose [of reminding the reader that insight comes through discussion and not mere reading]." Kraut, "Introduction to the Study of Plato," in *Cambridge Companion to Plato*, 27. Since I find the two named dialogues to be among the most dramatic, lively, and philosophically engaging presentations of Socratic conversational inquiry, I am at a loss to understand Kraut's finding them undramatic and presenting no real opposition of philosophical viewpoint. (I should add that his observation is given in passing, entered as an aside, and nothing further in his discussion hinges upon it.)

4. Myles Burnyeat, "Foreword," in B. A. F. Hubbard and E. S. Karnofsky, *Plato's Protagoras*, trans. B. A. F. Hubbard and E. S. Karnofsky (Chicago: University of Chicago Press, 1982), vii, hereafter cited as Hubbard & Karnofsky.

5. Plato, *Protagoras*, trans. and intro. C. C. W. Taylor (Oxford: Oxford University Press, 1996), ix, hereafter cited as Taylor. See also Plato, *Protagoras*, trans. with notes and commentary C. C. W. Taylor (Oxford: Clarendon Press, 1976).

6. Michael Frede, "Introduction," in Plato, *Protagoras*, trans. Stanley Lombardo and Karen Bell (Indianapolis: Hackett Publishing Co., 1992), x, hereafter cited as Lombardo & Bell.

7. Hubbard & Karnofsky, xi, xv.

8. Nettleship, *Lectures on the* Republic *of Plato*, 7.

9. "Virtue" is *areté* in the transliterated Greek, and sometimes it is said that this term might better be translated as "excellence." See Aristotle, *Nico-*

machean Ethics, trans. and intro. Martin Ostwald (Indianapolis: Bobbs-Merrill Co., 1962), 303, 304. See also Bruno Snell, *The Discovery of the Mind: The Greek Origins of European Thought,* trans. T. G. Rosenmeyer (Cambridge, Mass.: Harvard University Press, 1953), 158; and David Luban, "Epistemology and Moral Education," *Journal of Legal Education* 33 (1983): 636, 650. In one fairly recent translation of the *Protagoras,* the rendering of *areté* as "excellence" is followed systematically. See Hubbard & Karnofsky, xiii and passim. On the other hand, another fairly recent translation continues to follow the traditional rendering of *areté* as "virtue." See Lombardo & Bell, xxxv–xxxvi and passim.

Alexander Nehamas has suggested that neither "virtue" nor "excellence" is an adequate rendering of *areté.* "'Virtue' is simply too narrow a concept, while the more recent 'excellence' is, I believe, too weak, colorless, and vague." Nehamas, *Art of Living,* 77. In a series of intriguing paragraphs, Nehamas goes on to recommend that we might do better to construe *areté* as meaning either "success" (or, he says, "the quality or qualities that account for it"), or something "outstanding" or "notable." "We could do no better, I suggest, than to think of it [*areté*] as that quality or set of qualities that makes something an *outstanding* member of the group to which it belongs. *Areté* is the feature that accounts for something's being *justifiably notable.*" Ibid., 77, 78.

10. Are we searching for knowledge, or for answers? Are they the same thing, or different? It seems to me that Socrates assumes that knowledge always can be displayed in the answers we give to his questions. Thus, sometimes it appears that Socrates is searching for knowledge to be cast in the form of a certain type of answer (e.g., a lexical definition). But it may turn out that the knowledge we want or need in such a case cannot be provided by such an answer. Compare Alexander Nehamas's comment that "Socrates' belief in the priority of definition is much less radical than we have often tended to suppose." Alexander Nehamas, "Socratic Intellectualism," in *Virtues of Authenticity: Essays on Plato and Socrates* (Princeton: Princeton University Press, 1999), 36.

11. In this regard, Alexander Nehamas has suggested that the norm for Plato's Socratic dialogues is the following: "The first thing to note is that, as in most of Plato's Socratic dialogues, it is the interlocutor of Socrates, Euthyphro himself, and not Socrates who makes a point of initiating their discussion. Contrary to what most people think, it is not Socrates who stops people in the street and, out of the blue, asks them to define virtue and to justify their lives but someone else who draws him into conversation." Nehamas, *Art of Living,* 36 (with citations to relevant sources).

12. In contrasting the unassertive way in which Ludwig Wittgenstein begins his *Philosophical Investigations* (i.e., with a quotation from Saint Augustine), Stanley Cavell says: "The assertions of Augustine's memories are not,

rhetorically, accosting, or insisting, as, say, Socrates' interlocutors are in stopping him on the street with their accostive certainties." Stanley Cavell, "Notes and Afterthoughts on the Opening of Wittgenstein's *Investigations*," in *Philosophical Passages: Wittgenstein, Emerson, Austin, Derrida* (Cambridge, Mass.: Blackwell Publishers, 1995), 129 (italics omitted).

13. Plato, *Euthyphro,* in *Euthyphro, Apology, Crito,* trans. F. J. Church, rev. trans. and intro. Robert D. Cumming (Indianapolis: Bobbs-Merrill Co., 1948, 2d ed. 1956), 1 [2a], hereafter cited as Church & Cumming.

14. Plato, *Meno,* in Jowett & Anderson, 23 [70a].

15. Frede, "Introduction," in Lombardo & Bell, x.

16. Stanley Cavell, *In Quest of the Ordinary: Lines of Skepticism and Romanticism* (Chicago: University of Chicago Press, 1988), 83–84.

17. Ibid., 87.

18. See Vlastos, "Socrates' Disavowal of Knowledge," 1–31; reprinted in *Socratic Studies,* 39–66.

19. Frede, "Introduction," in Lombardo & Bell, xxxii. John M. Cooper, in the collected edition of the Hackett translations of Plato's works, offers an additional thought on the matter of Socrates' narration of the events and utterances in the *Protagoras:* "Thus both speakers get their comeuppance—Socrates for denying that virtue is teachable, Protagoras for denying that it is wisdom. The whole matter has to be rethought. At the end, we are sent back to the beginning, to go over the old ground once more, as Socrates himself has just done in retelling the events of the day to his unnamed friend and to us readers." John M. Cooper, "Editorial Note to *Protagoras,*" in Plato, *Complete Works,* ed. with intro. and notes John M. Cooper (Indianapolis: Hackett Publishing Co., 1997), 747 (italics omitted).

20. Frede, "Introduction," in Lombardo & Bell, xxxii–xxxiii.

21. Robert Frost, "The Figure a Poem Makes," in *Selected Prose of Robert Frost,* ed. Hyde Cox and Edward Connery Lathem (New York: Collier Books, 1966, 1968), 18: "The figure a poem makes. It begins in delight and ends in wisdom. . . . It begins in delight, it inclines to the impulse, it assumes direction with the first line laid down, it runs a course of lucky events, and ends in a clarification of life—not necessarily a great clarification, such as sects and cults are founded on, but in a momentary stay against confusion." The figure a Platonic dialogue makes is similar: it begins in doubt (rather than delight), it inclines to the chase of an inquiry or a quest, it assumes direction with the first line laid down, it runs a course of lucky events, and it ends in disillusion (which is, indeed, a clarification of life—not necessarily a great clarification, but a clarification nonetheless), itself a momentary stay against illusion.

22. It may be worth mentioning that while the Jowett and Ostwald translation introduces the explicit phrase, "I know," as attributed to Socrates' companion, the original Greek does not contain this phrase. Other translations support the idea that the Greek text implies that Socrates' companion thinks the answer to his question is "obvious." See, e.g., Taylor, 1; Lombardo & Bell, 1; and Hubbard & Karnofsky, 1.

23. This claim of mine does not say all that might be said about Plato's selective use of the technique of narration in some of his dialogues. In discussing, for example, the tension that exists in Plato's works between authority and an openness to correction, Ruby Blondell makes a number of interesting observations about the advantages and disadvantages of both the "direct dialogue" and the "narrated dialogue" forms of drama:

> Direct dramatic form seems more honest than reported dialogue, since it removes the narrator's mediating voice to create an effect of dramatic transparency, as if we were eavesdropping. This is in part why direct mimesis encourages audience identification more than narrative does . . . . But in another way, this apparent honesty is specious, since the effect of immediacy, of honest reportage, belies the manipulations of the author behind the scene. In the preamble to *Theaetetus,* Eukleides explains that in his transcription of the original conversation [between Socrates and Theaetetus] he omitted such phrases as "he said" out of convenience (143bc). The moment serves to remind us that even direct dramatic form is always controlled by an underlying authorial and/or editorial voice. The decision to elide overt narrative control is itself a form of control, a fact to which we are alerted by Plato's marking of Eukleides' decision. In this respect, the *narrated* dialogues are paradoxically more honest, in so far as they constantly remind us that the account is shaped by a voice other than that of the participants. This in turn serves to remind us of the author who stands behind the narrator, not necessarily to agree with him, but (necessarily) to create and control him.

Ruby Blondell, *The Play of Character in Plato's Dialogues* (Cambridge: Cambridge University Press, 2002), 43–44.

24. W. K. C. Guthrie emphasizes what he calls "this stylistic device" in his translation of the *Protagoras,* when he calls the dialogue "a dramatic masterpiece," and Guthrie further says about it: "Much of the secret of this [dialogue being enjoyable and readable] lies in the stylistic device of the reported dialogue. The dialogue form conveys the dramatic sense of actual presence,

whereas the fact that the dialogue is not presented directly, but narrated by Socrates to a friend, allows also for a lively description of scene and actors. . . . In the *Meno,* where the dramatic element plays a smaller part, this device is not used. We read the whole dialogue like the text of a play. With the *Protagoras* we seem, not simply to read the play, but to see it acted." Guthrie, 7. (I should also mention that, at a presentation of an earlier draft of this chapter, Gene Garver emphasized to me in conversation the narrated aspect of the *Protagoras.*)

25. The request by Socrates' companion to be told the meaning of this strange happening—namely, that while Socrates has just come from Alcibiades, Socrates barely paid any attention to him—provides additional motivation for what comes later in this dialogue. The companion demands: "What is the meaning of this? Has anything happened between you and him? For surely you cannot have discovered a fairer love than he is, certainly not in this city of Athens." The added surprise is that, indeed, Socrates *has* found a "fairer" object of his attentions, someone more attractive than Alcibiades. At this point, Socrates proceeds to explain to his companion how he finds himself more attracted to Protagoras than to Alcibiades. So, in this respect, Socrates instructs his companion. Protagoras is fairer in Socrates' eyes than Alcibiades (as we learn by listening to Socrates' story) because Protagoras can offer Socrates something—knowledge, or wisdom—that Alcibiades cannot. How this can be true, and the sense in which it is true, are both topics of the story that Socrates then narrates.

26. It is interesting to compare this brief exchange with an earlier passage in the *Protagoras* (at the very beginning of the dialogue). When Socrates' companion thinks that he already knows the answer to the opening question ("Where have you been?"), the Lombardo and Bell translation has the companion implore Socrates not to speak, not to tell him anything. "Where have you just come from, Socrates? No, don't tell me" [Lombardo & Bell at 1 (309a)]. Here, however, where Socrates promises the companion a "strange" story about the arrival of Protagoras and Socrates' "interview" with the famed sophist, the companion implores Socrates to "tell" him all about it. Thus, again, Plato carefully sets the stage for the ensuing narration by Socrates.

27. Recall Stanley Cavell's remark that narrative works "as part of a mode or genre of telling." I notice that the imagery of telling and listening permeates the opening lines of the *Protagoras.* In the first few lines (309a–310a), the Jowett and Ostwald translation uses "tell" four times and "listen" twice; the Lombardo and Bell translation uses "tell" four times and "listen" once; both the Taylor and the Guthrie translations use "tell" two times and "listen" twice; and the Hubbard and Karnofsky translation uses "tell" once and "listen" twice. It seems that

Plato, without stating the matter, is indicating what this dialogue is about, or how it works.

28. Euben observes that, in the *Protagoras,* Socrates makes the claim "that choosing a teacher is the most significant decision in [one's] life." Euben, *Corrupting Youth,* 41.

29. This leaves pending the Socratic question, "What counts as 'news' to us?" What Hippocrates takes to be news is, essentially, a piece of gossip: a stranger has arrived in town and it is the famous sophist, Protagoras. What Socrates takes to be news are matters such as these: that we often do not know what we are doing; and that we cannot define or explain as basic and central a concept in our lives and in our language as *areté,* or "virtue" or "excellence"; and that we do not have the slightest idea whether virtue is something that can be taught, or even whether it is simply a matter of luck or a gift from the gods. In this respect, Socrates asks that we reconsider what we count as important in our lives, and what we take to be interesting. In other words, he asks that we consider how we live.

30. My research assistant, Vasilios Spyridakis, informs me that the Greek here is simpler and more straightforward than Jowett's rendering. "It seems so, Socrates, from what you say," would be a more literal translation of this closing line.

31. As I stated in chapter 1, concerning the "aporetic" moment, the notion of *aporia* is helpfully presented in Robin Waterfield's "Introduction" to his recent translation of the *Meno.* As a reminder, here again is Waterfield: "Our basic and worst sin, [Socrates] thought, is believing that we know something when we really do not, and *aporia,* unlike plain ignorance, is a state where we are compelled to be aware of our ignorance and will hopefully be motivated to do something about it (though, oddly, few of the characters in the aporetic dialogues evince much interest in continuing their education)." Waterfield(2), viii. Further discussions of *aporia* by Waterfield as well as by Myles Burnyeat and Gareth Matthews can be found in chapter 1, note 24.

32. See Stanley Cavell, *The Claim of Reason: Wittgenstein, Skepticism, Morality, and Tragedy* (Oxford: Clarendon Press, 1979), 175–76: "[S]ince self-scrutiny, the full examination and defense of one's own position, has always been part of the impulse to philosophy, Wittgenstein's originality lies not in the creation of the impulse, but in finding ways to prevent it from defeating itself so easily, ways to make it methodical."

33. See also Stanley Cavell, "The Politics of Interpretation (Politics as Opposed to What?)," in *Themes Out of School: Effects and Causes* (San Francisco: North Point Press, 1984), 27, 51; and Stanley Fish, "The Aesthetic of the Good

Physician," in *Self-Consuming Artifacts: The Experience of Seventeenth-Century Literature* (Berkeley: University of California Press, 1972), 1–77.

34. See Gregory Vlastos, "The Socratic elenchus," in *Socratic Studies,* 7 (see also 136), regarding what Vlastos calls Socrates' "say what you believe" principle.

35. Cavell, "Existentialism and Analytical Philosophy," in *Themes Out of School,* 217.

36. While in this passage (313c–314b) the Jowett and Ostwald translation uses the term "knowledge" as identifying the food for the soul, the Greek term is *mathemata,* which might better be rendered as "learning." The Hubbard and Karnofsky translation speaks here in terms of "learning" and "instruction"; the Taylor translation speaks throughout this passage in terms of "learning"; and the Guthrie translation uses both "learn" and "knowledge." The Lombardo and Bell translation uses throughout this passage the term "teaching."

37. Vlastos, "The Socratic elenchus," in *Socratic Studies,* 9. Vlastos continues this passage by describing further his conception of Socrates' principle of elenchus:

> Thus elenchus has a double objective: to discover how every human being ought to live *and* to test that single human being who is doing the answering—to find out if *he* is living as one ought to live. This is a two-in-one operation. Socrates does not provide for two types of elenchus—a philosophical one, searching for truth about the good life, and a therapeutic one, searching out the answerer's own in the hope of bringing him to the truth. There is one elenchus and it must do both jobs, though one or the other will be to the fore in different phases of it. From this point of view, too, the "say what you believe" requirement makes sense. How could Socrates hope to get you to give, sooner or later, an account of your life, if he did not require you to state your personal opinion on the questions under debate?

Ibid., 10. Alexander Nehamas makes a similar point about the duality of Socrates' method of inquiry, but Nehamas does so in terms slightly different from Vlastos's description:

> Some people do, it is true, spend a reasonably large part of their lives examining Socrates' arguments and reading Plato's works again and again—I myself am one of them. But though a direct examination of the dialogues' doctrines and arguments is absolutely necessary to come to terms with Socrates, it is simply not enough. The Socratic dialogues de-

> mand of their audience what Socrates asks of his interlocutors: to examine their beliefs on any subject of importance to them, to determine to what other beliefs they are logically related, to accept only those that are compatible with one another, and to live their lives accordingly. That is a question we are as good at ignoring as any of Socrates' simple interlocutors.

Nehamas, *Art of Living,* 42. Thus, Nehamas concludes, "The logical examination of belief is a part—but only a part—of the examined life." Ibid.

38. The emphasis on the relative mismatch between Socrates' small concerns and Protagoras' grandiose expressions is more clear in the Lombardo and Bell translation of the *Protagoras* than it is in Jowett's somewhat dated version. In Lombardo and Bell, we find Socrates saying that he is persuaded by Protagoras, "except for one small obstacle which Protagoras will explain away, I am sure, since he has explained away so much already" [Lombardo & Bell at 23 (328e–329a)]. And, after referring to how orators respond with a long harangue to "one little question," Socrates allows that "I need one little thing, and then I'll have it all, [Protagoras,] if you'll just answer me this" [Lombardo & Bell at 23 (329b)].

39. Vlastos, "Paradox," in *Philosophy of Socrates,* 20; reprinted with slight changes, in Vlastos, *Studies in Greek Philosophy,* 2:17.

40. A similar scene is enacted, with a similar resolution to a debate about how to proceed with the discussion, in Book I of the *Republic.* There, Socrates suggests that the people gathered together to discuss the nature of justice should all participate in the conversation, sharing not only their views but also the burden of investigating and testing those views. "But if, on the other hand, we investigate the question, as we've been doing, by seeking agreement with each other, we ourselves can be both jury and advocates at once." Plato, *Republic,* trans. G. M. A. Grube, rev. trans. C. D. C. Reeve (Indianapolis: Hackett Publishing Co., 1992), 24 [348b], hereafter cited as Grube & Reeve.

41. Cavell, "Knowing and Acknowledging," in *Must We Mean What We Say?,* 239–40.

42. Nussbaum provides us with the following sketch of Socrates' concern with the defects of books:

> [Socrates] believed that the real value of philosophizing lay in the responsive interaction of teacher and pupil, as the teacher guides the pupil by questioning (sometimes gentle and sometimes harsh, depending on the pupil's character and degree of resistance) to become more aware of his own beliefs and their relationship to one another. Books (Socrates says in

> the *Phaedrus*) cannot perform this activity, for they are not "alive" (275D). They can, at best, remind you of what it is like. At worst, they lull the soul into forgetfulness both of the content and of the manner of real philosophizing, teaching it to be passively reliant on the written word (275A). Worse still, in some readers books can induce the false conceit of wisdom, since they may mistake information about many things for true understanding (275A–B). Books, furthermore, lack the attentiveness and responsiveness of true philosophical teaching. They "roll around" all over the place with a kind of inflexible inertness (275E), addressing very different people, always in the same way. . . . Real philosophy, by contrast, as Socrates saw it, is each person's committed search for wisdom, where what matters is not just the acceptance of certain conclusions, but also the following out of a certain path to them; not just correct content, but content achieved as the result of real understanding and self-understanding. Books are not this search and do not impart this self-understanding. . . . Dialogues, then, unlike all the books criticized by Socrates, might fairly claim that they awaken and enliven the soul, arousing it to rational activity rather than lulling it into drugged passivity. They owe this to their kinship to theater. . . . This aspect of the dialogue form urges us as readers to assess our own individual relationship to the dialogue's issues and arguments. In these ways, again, the dialogue seems to be both less "silent" and more responsive to individual differences than the books criticized by Socrates. They are books that each reader can read personally inside his pursuit of self-understanding, exploring the motivations and beliefs of the characters together with his own. There are conclusions here, and views of Plato; we are asked, however, not simply to memorize them, but to find them inside ourselves.

Nussbaum, *Fragility of Goodness,* 125–26, 127–28. In a similar vein, James Boyd White has commented that "Socrates says that writing is always worse than speaking, though thought by many to be better; the reason is that writing cannot respond when it is criticized or questioned, but simply repeats itself monotonously. The true life of the mind can be found only in living speech, which can be imagined as a kind of writing not on material things but on the soul of another." James Boyd White, "The *Phaedrus:* Philosophy, Rhetoric, and Love," in *The Edge of Meaning* (Chicago: University of Chicago Press, 2001), 139. (See also note 35 in chapter 4, where I quote John M. Cooper's similar commentary on the *Phaedrus* and the limitations of books.)

43. I have argued elsewhere that, in his speech to the jury at his trial, Socrates falls prey to this very problem. My claim is that Socrates' speech to the

Athenian jurors denies them the opportunity to participate in the inquiry that he sketches. Because of this failure, he denies his jurors the chance to get to know him. On the basis of his defense statement, his jurors are not able to learn whether or not Socrates is the kind of person—a searcher after truth, not a corrupter of Athenian youth—who he claims to be. But how can his jurors learn this when his defense statement fails to invite them to participate in the inquiry? See Eisele, "'Never Mind the Manner of My Speech,'" *Legal Studies Forum*, 253–88.

44. Myles Burnyeat has commented on the aspect of parody in Socrates' response to Protagoras' performance: "The action of the dialogue is a confrontation between Socrates and some of the most famous intellectual figures of his day. He argues with them; he reduces them to perplexity by his knotty, abstract reasoning; he parodies their own very different methods; he exposes their pretensions to have important knowledge to teach—all this in his most pugnacious style and with the savage irony which Plato, no doubt rightly, always made a prominent feature of his portrait of Socrates." Burnyeat, "Foreword," in Hubbard & Karnofsky, vii.

45. Plato provides us with an additional example of such interpretive glibness. Immediately upon Socrates' completion of his interpretation of Simonides' ode, a member of the audience, Hippias, jumps up and volunteers his own: "I think, Socrates, that you have given a very good explanation of the poem, but I have also an excellent interpretation of my own which I will propound to you, if you so desire" [Jowett & Ostwald at 50–51 (347a–b)]. Alcibiades stifles this interruption by citing the compact made between Protagoras and Socrates to let them finish their joint inquiry. When I ask myself why Plato would bother to insert this interjection at this point in the dialogue, I come to the conclusion that this interruption adds to the element of parody being directed toward Protagoras' supposed prowess at poetic interpretation.

This interjection also illustrates Socrates' point about the interpretation of poetry, namely, that anyone sufficiently glib can interpret poems. Mere verbal facility, however, does not assure correctness in a person's interpretations. In this regard, Plato's choice of Hippias is revealing. Even though Hippias is serious in extending his offer to participate, he is regarded as a superficial person. In the Hubbard and Karnofsky translation of the *Protagoras*, Hippias is described as follows: "A sophist of the mid-fifth century B.C. He had specialised in astronomy, but prided himself on being a polymath and rhetorician, and had a wide range of reputedly superficial knowledge and skill, and a talent for slick rhetoric laden with extravagant metaphor." Hubbard & Karnofsky, 162.

46. See Eisele, "'Never Mind the Manner of My Speech,'" *Legal Studies Forum*.

47. I think that the generally humorous tone in this passage is Plato's signal that Socrates' effort at interpreting Simonides' poem is not fully serious, nor is it to be taken as a serious attempt. The Socratic parody pokes fun at Protagoras, thus deflating him, or perhaps deflecting Protagoras' animus toward Socrates. It would be difficult to say, however, that Socrates' effort at parody refutes Protagoras, unless we care to say that an example of theater of the absurd operates as a form of refutation, perhaps as a kind of reductio ad absurdum.

48. Paul Woodruff, "Socratic Education," in *Philosophers on Education: Historical Perspectives*, ed. Amélie Oksenberg Rorty (London: Routledge, 1998), 15. Woodruff goes on to say: "He demands no prerequisites of the boys and men he draws into his conversations, and he claims no special qualifications for his own project in self-education. Education as Socrates conceives it is a lifelong pursuit." Ibid.

In her thought-provoking study of luck and ethics in Greek tragedy and philosophy, Martha Nussbaum notes in passing the centrality of Socrates in the *Protagoras:* "And in the light of these observations we can now see why, after all, the character Socrates is the real protagonist of the *Protagoras* and the real model for our activity as readers and interpreters, even of the speech of Protagoras. . . . Our understanding of the dialogue as a whole, too, required Socratic rather than Protagorean arts: for if the whole is a teaching of what rules out what, and what the cost is of what progress, seeing that will require the clarity, toughness, and flexibility of the Socratic examination, not the vanity of sophistical display." Nussbaum, *Fragility of Goodness*, 128.

In addition, consider the following remarks by Alexander Nehamas regarding the primacy to Socrates of the importance of self-education: "I claim . . . that, despite the overwhelming impression that Socrates devoted his life to the improvement of his contemporaries, his project was essentially more individualist than we have generally taken it to be. Socrates' primary concern was what he called 'the care of the self' . . . , where that self was, above all, his own. . . . Improving others, though a worthwhile and valuable end in its own right as well, was not a central part of the care he devoted to his own self." Nehamas, "Introduction," in *Virtues of Authenticity*, xxx–xxxi.

49. I should add, in this regard, that Socrates equally befriends himself. Socrates' ability to do so is an important part of the virtue that I see in his example. Gaining self-knowledge seems to require that we befriend ourselves. In this respect, if we are to learn who we are, then we need to treat ourselves as we treat others.

50. I discuss further the attribute of sharing as an element in teaching (and sharing as an element in a successful classroom) in another essay of mine. See Thomas D. Eisele, "What We Share," *University of Cincinnati Law Review* 71 (2002): 493–516.

51. Richard Poirier, *Robert Frost: The Work of Knowing* (New York: Oxford University Press, 1977), passim.

52. Cavell, "Politics of Interpretation," in *Themes Out of School,* 59.

THREE The Poverty of Socratic Questioning

1. Stanley Cavell, "The Thought of Movies," in *Themes Out of School: Effects and Causes* (San Francisco: North Point Press, 1984), 9.

2. Plato, *Meno,* in Jowett & Anderson. I also have consulted other translations of the *Meno,* all more modern than Jowett's: Waterfield(2), 97–143; *The Dialogues of Plato,* Volume 1: *Euthyphro, Apology, Crito, Meno, Gorgias, Menexenus,* trans. Reginald E. Allen (New Haven: Yale University Press, 1984), 131–86, hereafter cited as Allen; *Plato's Meno: With Essays,* ed. Malcolm Brown and trans. W. K. C. Guthrie (Indianapolis: Bobbs-Merrill Co., 1971), 17–61, hereafter cited as Brown & Guthrie; *Plato's Meno,* trans. G. M. A. Grube (Indianapolis: Hackett Publishing Co., 1976, 2d ed. 1980), 3–32, hereafter cited as Grube; and *Plato's Meno,* trans. George Anastaplo and Laurence Berns (Newburyport, Mass.: Focus Publishing Co., 2004).

3. Kierkegaard, too, felt the power of the *Meno.* In his tract on instruction, *Philosophical Fragments,* Kierkegaard's initial question ("How far does the Truth admit of being learned?") relates directly to the paradox of inquiry stated by Meno and complicated by Socrates. See Søren Kierkegaard, *Philosophical Fragments or A Fragment of Philosophy,* trans. and intro. David Swenson, rev. trans. Howard Hong, new intro. and commentary Niels Thulstrup (Princeton: Princeton University Press, 1936, 2d ed. 1962), 11–16.

4. Roslyn Weiss, in her fine study of this dialogue, makes a similar point: "The action of the *Meno* is driven by the character Meno, by his passions, his personal traits, his associations, his ambitions. Meno is Socrates' project, the current object of Socrates' ongoing efforts to reform anyone he meets—young or old, foreigner or citizen." Roslyn Weiss, *Virtue in the Cave: Moral Inquiry in Plato's* Meno (Oxford: Oxford University Press, 2001), 17.

5. These themes—of a student's being able to see things in what a teacher does, and of a teacher's being able to show a student how to make sense out of the teaching materials at hand—are explored further in the Epilogue, where I discuss them in the context of how I teach in a law school classroom.

6. In Stanley Cavell's study of the way in which Ludwig Wittgenstein's later philosophy depends upon eliciting authentic voices from various speakers, he makes the following characterization of certain dominant voices in Wittgenstein's writing: "Inaccessible to the dogmatics of philosophical criticism,

Wittgenstein chose confession and recast his dialogue. It contains what serious confessions must: the full acknowledgment of temptation . . . and a willingness to correct them and give them up . . . . (The voice of temptation and the voice of correctness are the antagonists in Wittgenstein's dialogues.)" Cavell, "The Availability of Wittgenstein's Later Philosophy," in *Must We Mean What We Say?*, 71. In responding to the voicing of our temptations, the voice of correctness (which also is a voice of correction) expresses a sense of propriety and a sense of responsibility.

7. For further details on Anytus' participation in Socrates' trial for impiety and corrupting the youth of Athens, see Plato, *Apology,* in Church & Cumming, 21, 22 n. 1, 23 n. 2, 28, 34, 35, 39 n. 8, 41.

8. This is the converse of the point made earlier regarding the requirement that the student be able to take what the teacher says as important or worthwhile. Here we are looking at the teacher, who needs to take the student's response as significant. Otherwise, the student will not learn. See, e.g., Cavell, *The Claim of Reason,* 28.

9. The traditional references to this interlocutor as a "slave-boy" may be misleading. Here the term "boy" does not connote youthfulness so much as it connotes the low social status and the relative lack of education of the slave, whatever his age. As a recent translator of the *Meno* states, "'Boy' (*pai*) is the term of address for a slave of any age, just as it was used in the U.S. . . . Its use here gave rise to the perception that the slave is a child. There is no indication of this anywhere in the text. Evidently Plato doesn't care how old we take the slave to be. His being a slave guarantees his lack of education in 'liberal arts' like mathematics." Adam Beresford, "Notes," in Plato, *Protagoras and Meno,* trans. Adam Beresford and intro. Lesley Brown (London: Penguin Books, 2005), 159 n. 32.

10. Plato, *Republic,* in Grube & Reeve, 25 [349a].

11. Cavell, *Cities of Words,* 174.

12. Ibid., 42. See also ibid., 50: "Moral standing is pushed to the center of the stage in [moral] perfectionism. . . . [Y]ou had better have some standing with me from which you confront my life, from which my life matters to you, and matters to me that it matters to you."

13. Ibid., 25.

14. E. R. Dodds makes the point several times that the tone of Socrates in the *Gorgias* differs from his tone in the other early and middle dialogues (as they have sometimes been termed in the secondary literature). See Plato, *Gorgias: A Revised Text with Introduction and Commentary,* ed. E. R. Dodds (Oxford: Clarendon Press, 1959, 1990), 16, 19–20. (I should mention that, after having settled on my title for this book, "Bitter Knowledge," I was heartened

when I happened across Dodds's remark concerning the "disillusioned bitterness" of the *Gorgias*. Ibid., 19.) Myles Burnyeat also mentions the contentious aspect of this dialogue: "The action of the *Gorgias* is the most stubbornly contested battle of argument in the Platonic corpus." Myles Burnyeat, "First Words: A Valedictory Lecture," *Proceedings of the Cambridge Philological Society* 43 (1997): 1, 11.

15. Cavell, "Foreword: An Audience for Philosophy," in *Must We Mean What We Say?*, xxviii.

16. Cavell, "Knowing and Acknowledging," in *Must We Mean What We Say?*, 239–40.

17. In chapter 1, I referred to Gregory Vlastos's characterization of the Socratic method as a shared enterprise based upon "common sense and common speech." I take Vlastos to be appealing in this regard to a phenomenon similar to Stanley Cavell's—namely, the equality of the positions as seekers that members of the joint conversational inquiry have.

18. Cavell, "Must We Mean What We Say?," in *Must We Mean What We Say?*, 40.

19. G. M. Young, "Maitland," in *Daylight and Champaign: Essays* (London: Jonathan Cape, 1937), 290: "Law, as [Maitland] understood it, is fundamentally a system of common thought about common things." See Frederic William Maitland, "The Hide," in *Domesday Book and Beyond: Three Essays in the Early History of England* (Cambridge: Cambridge University Press, 1897), 520: "Above all, by slow degrees the thoughts of our forefathers, their common thoughts about common things, will have become thinkable once more. There are discoveries to be made; but also there are habits to be formed."

20. Grube & Reeve, 24 [348b].

21. Wittgenstein put the point this way: "Concepts lead us to make investigations; are the expression of our interest, and direct our interest." Ludwig Wittgenstein, *Philosophical Investigations*, trans. G. E. M. Anscombe, ed. G. E. M. Anscombe and R. Rhees (Oxford: Basil Blackwell, 1953, 2d ed. 1958), §570.

22. Stanley Cavell, "The Avoidance of Love: A Reading of *King Lear*," in *Must We Mean What We Say?*, 270.

23. Some time ago, I said the following about this aspect of Socrates' method of inquiry: "A part of the virtue of Socrates that I see displayed in the *Protagoras* is his ability to call upon his capacity for inquiry in aid of anyone—this seems true friendship indeed. He is a stranger to no one deliberately—unless they estrange themselves from him or his methods." Eisele, "Must Virtue Be Taught?," *Journal of Legal Education*, 495, 498.

24. As I mentioned (and quoted) in my chapter on the *Protagoras*, Alexander Nehamas has drawn our attention to the fact that, more often than not,

Socrates' interlocutors choose him, not he them: "Contrary to what most people think, it is not Socrates who stops people in the street and, out of the blue, asks them to define virtue and to justify their lives but someone else who draws him into conversation." Nehamas, *Art of Living,* 36 (with citations to relevant sources).

25. Eventually, Socrates drops this demand because Meno refuses to heed it. But Socrates still manages to make the point that, by his lights, this is taking things backwards: "Had I the command of you as well as of myself, Meno, I would not have inquired whether virtue is given by instruction or not, until we had first ascertained 'what it is.' But as you think only of controlling me who am your slave, and never of controlling yourself—such being your notion of freedom—I must yield to you, for you are irresistible. And therefore I have now to inquire into the qualities of a thing of which I do not as yet know the nature. At any rate, will you condescend a little and allow the question, 'Whether virtue is given by instruction, or in any other way,' to be argued upon hypothesis?" [Jowett & Anderson at 45 (86d–e)]. His point (that, in their discussion, they have taken the respective topics in the wrong order) is reiterated by Socrates in the very last speech in the dialogue. [See Jowett & Anderson at 61 (100b).]

26. Socrates (or perhaps it is Plato) seems to assume that our knowledge of something—here, virtue—can always be expressed in the form of a definition. If we truly know what x is, then we should be able to define x. Consequently, Socrates' characteristic questions are requests for definitions (of virtue, of courage, of prudence, of piety, of wisdom, of justice, of knowledge, and so forth).

This is not how I proceed in law school, nor is it, I believe, how most of us teach in law school. It is true that my own teaching does sometimes rely upon a request for a definition: How, for example, are we to understand "possession," or "reasonable," or "reliance," and so forth here in this case or context? But, more often, I test the knowledge of my students either by asking them to describe a case, a legal rule, or a statute, or by asking them to explain one. (Asking for such descriptions and explanations is not tantamount to a request for a definition. And yet, I believe that such descriptions and explanations do sometimes adequately express the knowledge that we possess of these matters.) The entire topic (of the nature of Socrates' questions and what he meant to elicit by asking them) is pursued further in the following: Gerasimos Xenophon Santas, *Socrates: Philosophy in Plato's Early Dialogues* (London: Routledge & Kegan Paul, 1979), 59–135; and Gregory Vlastos, "What Did Socrates Understand by His 'What Is *F*?' Question?" in *Platonic Studies,* 410–17 (Ithaca: Cornell University Press, 1973, 2d ed. 1981).

27. It is reported that this saying was inscribed over the threshold of the temple at Delphi: "[A]t Delphi the educational power of Greek religion reached its maximum, and spread from there far beyond the frontiers of Hellas. The wise sayings of sages were dedicated to Apollo and inscribed in his temple, since their worldly wisdom was only a reflection of his divine wisdom. And at his door his worshippers saw the command *Know thyself*—the doctrine of sophrosyné, by which men learn to remember the limits of human power and ambition, expressed in the legislative form that was characteristic of the age." Werner Jaeger, *Paideia: The Ideals of Greek Culture,* 3 vols., trans. Gilbert Highet (New York: Oxford University Press, 1939, 2d ed. 1945), 1:167 (footnote omitted).

28. Perhaps it is more accurate to say that "torpification" is Jowett's word for translating Meno's experience. The other translators of the *Meno* whose versions I have consulted instead speak of Meno's "perplexity" and the fact that Socrates' questioning makes him "numb." (These translators do also speak, however, in terms of Meno's being "bewitched" and "beguiled," in terms of "magic," "witchcraft," and "enchantment.") See Allen, 162; Grube, 12–13; Brown & Guthrie, 30–31; and see generally Matthews, *Socratic Perplexity and the Nature of Philosophy.*

29. Meno's question (or paradox) has received considerable attention in the secondary literature. See, e.g., Bernard Phillips, "The Significance of Meno's Paradox," in *Plato's Meno: Text and Criticism,* ed. Alexander Sesonske and Noel Fleming (Belmont, Calif.: Wadsworth Publishing Co., 1965), 77–83; Jon Moline, "Meno's Paradox?," *Phronesis* 14 (1969): 153–61; and Nehamas, "Meno's Paradox and Socrates as a Teacher," in *Virtues of Authenticity,* 3–26. I also want to mention the treatment of Meno's paradox in Roslyn Weiss's book on the *Meno.* There, Weiss notices (as have some other commentators before her) that Meno's statement of his paradox differs significantly from Socrates' restatement. See Weiss, *Virtue in the Cave,* 58. Weiss says Meno's statement includes a "paradox of knowing," while Socrates' restatement only addresses a "paradox of inquiry"; and she draws a number of important lessons from these distinct formulations. See ibid., 52–63.

30. Wittgenstein, *Philosophical Investigations,* §89b.

31. Ibid., §90a.

32. This is only to say that we have all the data that we require in our own lives and experiences; nothing more exotic or esoteric need be sought (as Wittgenstein says). But this is not to say that philosophy as a discipline or tradition has always made use of these data. The fact that traditional philosophy has not, in fact, made use of the data available to it is one of the insights stated and

demonstrated in J. L. Austin's work. See, e.g., J. L. Austin, "A Plea for Excuses," in *Philosophical Papers,* ed. J. O. Urmson and G. J. Warnock (Oxford: Clarendon Press, 1961), 123, 128–37.

33. Weiss makes the point that Socrates' account is not to be accepted at face value. She contends, "Something comic and something serious occur simultaneously in the slave-boy demonstration." Weiss, *Virtue in the Cave,* 94. She goes on to enumerate the various ways in which Socrates' so-called demonstration is (in part) farcical. (In calling Plato's presentation of the discussion between Socrates and the slave a "farce," Weiss gives credit to an earlier recognition of this aspect of the dialogue, in an essay published by Amélie Oksenberg Rorty. See ibid., 14 n. 21.)

34. In his collection of essays on the *Meno,* Malcolm Brown says that there is "nearly universal doubt about . . . [whether] Socrates' interrogation [is] fair, or . . . [instead, whether] it resort[s] to questions 'blatantly leading.'" [Brown & Guthrie, at xv.] Brown goes on to ask: "[E]ven if it was fair, does the lesson support the momentous consequences (about the soul's ante-natal condition, about recollection) that Plato seems to be attaching to it?" [Ibid.] On the other side, Allen suggests that the charge of "asking leading questions" is unfairly made against Socrates: "It is often objected that Socrates' questions to the slave are leading questions, and thus his example in no way indicates that learning is recollection. But this objection is confused. A leading question is one which suggests its own answer, and so defined, many of Socrates' questions are clearly leading. But it is relevant to observe that, in matters mathematical, the mind of the boy is capable of being led. In the law of evidence, which deals with empirical fact, leading questions are open to objection on the ground that they may cause a witness to acquiesce in a false suggestion. But this is clearly irrelevant when questions deal with a complex geometrical proof. No false suggestions have been planted; the evidentiary problem does not arise." Allen, at 143. Allen may be right insofar as his answer goes, but does it go far enough?

The problem with using leading questions in this context is not that Socrates might mislead the slave into acquiescing to a false suggestion. That is, we are not trying to protect the slave here from having this threatened "acquiescence" held against him (as might occur in a court of law regarding an "admission against interest" that a party in the slave's position might make). Rather, we are trying to determine whether the answers that the slave gives in response to Socrates are produced because he possesses some inherent knowledge of these matters; or, instead, whether his answers are produced because he is merely facile enough to reproduce the answers suggested to him by Socrates' leading questions. As to this latter concern, I do not see that Allen's response is satisfactory.

How we are to understand Socrates' interrogation of the slave remains problematic, as does its relation to the more general theme of learning and recollection. See, e.g., Malcolm Brown, "Plato Disapproves of the Slave-Boy's Answer," in Brown & Guthrie, 198–242; Julius Moravcsik, "Learning as Recollection," in *Plato: A Collection of Critical Essays,* 2 vols., ed. Gregory Vlastos (Garden City, N.Y.: Anchor Books, 1971), 1:53–69; and Gregory Vlastos, "Anamnesis in the *Meno,*" *Dialogue* 4 (1965): 143–67.

35. Richard Kraut makes this point in a telling way: "[I]f we look at the *Meno,* we find Socrates insisting that he is not teaching the slave how to double the area of a square (82e4–5, 84c10–d2). He means, of course, that he is not *merely telling* the slave how to do so. But surely he is helping the slave to recollect, and Socrates must be aware of the important role his questions play in getting the slave to learn. . . . In the *Meno,* [Socrates] knows the solution to the mathematical problem he has given the slave, but he is not telling him the answer; that is why he says he is not teaching the slave." Kraut, *Socrates and the State,* 295, 297.

36. Again, Allen has a helpful comment: "[I]f learning and inquiry are recollection, then to inquire is to bring to explicit awareness what is already implicitly known. If this is true, the primary function of education and teaching is not to impart information, but to rid the soul of false beliefs which cloud vision and cause blindness; if the doctrine of Recollection is true, education in some primary sense is a process of refutation, and inherently Socratic." Allen, at 142. Allen's suggestion is that learning and inquiry, from Socrates' perspective, are inextricably connected to both the negative use of *elenchus* and the positive use of recollection. I agree.

The Socratic method of conversational inquiry consists of many activities: asking for definitions, hypothesizing cases, investigating examples, using arguments, imagining possible actions or events, telling stories, stating or inventing myths, and so on. But central to Socrates' way of inquiring into things are two strands: *elenchus* (the activity of trying to get someone to refute or to convict himself by way of his own words); and recollection (the activity of trying to get someone to recognize something by bringing it to consciousness). *Elenchus* has a negative aspect in that it aims at teaching us that we do not know what we think we know. But this lesson itself has a positive aspect, because learning that we do not know what we think we know is itself an addition to our store of knowledge. Similarly, recollection has a positive aspect in that it aims at teaching us that we know more (or other) than what we think we know. But, again, there also is a negative side, because what we eventually recollect may conflict with what we thought we knew. And, to the extent that we fail to recollect what is sought after, we learn that we do not know (or do not share these things in common). Or, we learn that something is still blocking our access to this purported knowledge. So the dual aspects of Socratic inquiry—negative and positive—run deep, and their relationship is complex.

On this dual aspect of Socratic inquiry, my undergraduate philosophy teacher, Jon Moline, says:

> It is important to distinguish between Socratic elenchus and recollection. Elenchus is a method of testing and refuting *false* opinions. Recollection is a process by which answerers are held to be able to supply *true* opinions on matters on which they have not been instructed. Recollection explains how the Socratic method or any other method is able to bring people into a condition of episteme. It is not itself a method, but rather a very tentative notion of the ontological and psychological basis on which philosophical methods can work. . . . A close examination of the arguments in the *Meno* will confirm that elenchus is finished at 84a, before recollection begins. Elenchus removes the false opinion that one already has episteme and thus has no need to inquire (to embark on the process of recollection that Plato identifies with inquiry). Elenchus culminates in aporia (perplexity) and in the realization that one does not understand what one thought one did. Inquiry with the slave boy begins at 84d. At 84c, Socrates points out to Meno that as a result of the perplexity the boy now feels, he "will discover something by inquiring with me." Only at 85c does the boy "recover true opinion out of himself," that is, recollect. Clearly elenchus by itself was no more sufficient for attaining episteme in Plato's view in the *Meno* than it was later in the *Sophist*.

Jon Moline, "Recollection, Dialectic, and Ontology: Kenneth M. Sayre on the Solution to a Platonic Riddle," in *Platonic Writings, Platonic Readings,* ed. Charles L. Griswold, Jr. (New York: Routledge, Chapman & Hall, 1988), 234–35 (footnote omitted).

37. Michael Oakeshott gives a careful account of the many activities involved in both teaching and learning:

> To teach is to bring it about that, somehow, something of worth intended by a teacher is learned, understood and remembered by a learner. Thus, teaching is a variegated activity which may include hinting, suggesting, urging, coaxing, encouraging, guiding, pointing out, conversing, instructing, informing, narrating, lecturing, demonstrating, exercising, testing, examining, criticizing, correcting, tutoring, drilling and so on—everything,

> indeed, which does not belie the engagement to impart an understanding. And learning may be looking, listening, overhearing, reading, receiving suggestions, submitting to guidance, committing to memory, asking questions, discussing, experimenting, practising, taking notes, recording, re-expressing and so on—anything which does not belie the engagement to think and to understand.

Michael Oakeshott, "Education: The Engagement and Its Frustration," in *Education and the Development of Reason,* ed. R. F. Dearden, P. H. Hirst, and R. S. Peters (London: Routledge & Kegan Paul, 1972), 25–26.

38. Taking what students have and showing them what they in fact possess, as well as testing what students can do with their capacities and the materials at hand, are matters more fully addressed in the Epilogue.

39. Peter Winch summarizes this Socratic lesson (in a way congenial to my reading of the *Meno*) when he says the following: "[W]hen, in Plato's dialogue *Meno,* Socrates introduced the slave boy to Pythagoras' Theorem not by *telling* him the answer to the problem but by *eliciting* the answer from him, that is not just a rhetorical device either. The suggestion . . . is that each of us has within him or herself the resources for answering the question: a point which Plato expressed picturesquely in terms of 'recollection.' The further suggestion is that . . . no one truly has the answer who has not arrived at it for him or herself." Peter Winch, "Who Is My Neighbour?" in *Trying to Make Sense* (Oxford: Basil Blackwell, 1987), 156–57.

40. Wittgenstein elicits and explicates our shared knowledge by means of language games, the criteria we possess, and the grammatical structure or schema that those criteria trace. In this way, he aims at making us conscious of the knowledge that we actually possess. See Wittgenstein, *Philosophical Investigations,* §§78, 90, 147–51, 371–74. I have attempted to work out some of the details of Wittgenstein's later philosophy, in regard to its reliance on our criteria and the grammatical structure of our language and of our experience, in two articles: see Thomas D. Eisele, "'Our Real Need': Not Explanation, But Education," *Canadian Journal of Law and Jurisprudence* 3, no. 2 (July 1990): 5–34; and Thomas D. Eisele, "Tom Morawetz's 'Robust Enterprise': Jurisprudence after Wittgenstein," *Philosophical Investigations* 29 (2006): 140–79.

41. Allen, 143–44.

42. See, again, Nehamas, "Meno's Paradox and Socrates as a Teacher," in *Virtues of Authenticity,* 7, 14, 17.

43. At his trial, Socrates relies upon his personal or economic poverty as an indicator that he speaks the truth. [See Church & Cumming at 28, 37 (23c,

31b–c).] He inquires philosophically into things without regard to his own personal profit or gain. Here I am trying to tie this claim of personal (economic) poverty to the sense in which his method can also be said to be (philosophically) impoverished; this too is a claim on behalf of its truthfulness. Also, the poverty of his conversational method of inquiry is another point of intimacy, or similarity, between Socrates' manner of working and Wittgenstein's later philosophical methods. For some thoughts on the "poverty" of Wittgenstein's methods, see Stanley Cavell, *This New Yet Unapproachable America: Lectures after Emerson after Wittgenstein* (Albuquerque, N.M.: Living Batch Press, 1989), 70–72.

44. In this regard, Weiss treats questions or problems relating to human virtue as sui generis:

> I propose that Socrates deletes the paradox of knowing from his restatement of Meno's paradox precisely because he [Socrates] recognizes that *with respect to the issue of virtue* he cannot answer it: it is in virtue inquiry that one will indeed not *know* that one has found the answer one seeks even if one does happen upon it; it is here that the need to go on testing and examining one's answers is never fully exhausted. Elenchus, Socrates knows, will not end the search. . . . It is virtue for which, as Socrates is well aware, there is in the Cave no objective test; it is in moral questions, questions of the best way for human beings to live, that there is in the Cave no clear-cut way of securing the answers one finds. In the Cave, therefore, the only thing one can do (and, from Socrates' point of view, the thing one consequently must do) is pit one opinion against another to see which coheres best with the deepest strivings and beliefs.

Weiss, *Virtue in the Cave,* 61, 62.

45. In her study of the *Meno,* Weiss relates Socrates' professed myth of "learning as recollection" to his faith or trust in the need for us to persevere in our inquiries. "[T]he conclusion that Socrates derives from his recollection myth is the moral lesson that belief in learning as recollection will have a salutary effect on human character (it will make men active and ready to search), whereas belief in the alternative, that is, in Meno's 'eristic' paradox, will have a deleterious one (it will make men lazy and is the sort of thing that men who are 'soft' . . . find pleasant to hear)." Weiss, *Virtue in the Cave,* 69. Weiss carefully distinguishes between Socrates claiming to know this, versus his trusting in its truth, when she then goes on to say, "Socrates 'puts trust' . . . in his thesis's truth but does not affirm its intrinsic merit." Ibid., 69 and n. 49.

FOUR The Labor of Socratic Inquiry

1. Plato, *Theaetetus,* trans. M. J. Levett, rev. trans. Myles Burnyeat and intro. Bernard Williams (Indianapolis: Hackett Publishing Co., 1992), 13 [151a], hereafter cited as Levett & Burnyeat. I also cite on occasion the following alternative translations: *Plato's Theaetetus,* in Sachs; *Plato's Theaetetus,* trans. Benjamin Jowett and intro. Irving Copi (Indianapolis: Bobbs-Merrill Co., 1949), hereafter cited as Jowett & Copi; Plato, *Theaetetus,* trans. John McDowell (Oxford: Clarendon Press, 1973), hereafter cited as McDowell; and Plato, *Theaetetus,* trans. and intro. Robin Waterfield (Harmondsworth: Penguin Books, 1987), hereafter cited as Waterfield(3).

2. Levett & Burnyeat, 59 [186b–c].

3. Socrates, in the cases with which he is concerned, seems to treat "wisdom" and "knowledge" as being interchangeable or synonymous. This point has been noticed and commented on by Vlastos. See Vlastos, *Socrates, Ironist and Moral Philosopher,* 237 n. 7; and Gregory Vlastos, "The *Protagoras* and the *Laches,*" in *Socratic Studies,* ed. Myles Burnyeat (Cambridge: Cambridge University Press, 1994), 110 n. 3.

4. Bernard Williams says the following in his "Introduction" to the Levett and Burnyeat translation of the *Theaetetus:* "Notwithstanding the achievements of his remarkable predecessors whose writings are lost to us (several are mentioned in this dialogue), [Plato] virtually invented the subject, philosophy. He was the first to express many distinctively philosophical questions and concerns; in the *Theaetetus,* he explores in an intense and closely argued way ideas which have shaped the ways in which people have subsequently discussed what knowledge might be, and whether we can have any" [Levett & Burnyeat at vii–viii]. Similarly, Irving Copi, in the Library of Liberal Arts edition of this dialogue, says that "[t]he historical importance of Plato's *Theaetetus* can hardly be overestimated. It records the first critical attempt to come to grips with certain intricate and vexing problems of human knowledge. . . . The *Theaetetus* not only posed the problems with which subsequent epistemologists have been forced to grapple, but also raised those objections to proposed solutions that have most severely limited the freedom of approach of later thinkers" [Jowett & Copi at vii].

Myles Burnyeat's testimony as to the lasting impact of the *Theaetetus* is this:

> No other dialogue of Plato's speaks so directly to the concerns of the working philosopher in modern times. This is the case even when, or especially

> when, the line of thought is one that would not occur to a modern philosopher. The *Theaetetus* is not only the first major treatment of the problem of knowledge, a problem which has remained central to philosophy ever since; it is a classic treatment in the full sense of a work to which the philosopher can return time and again to find a challenge or stimulus to reflection. It is also a literary masterpiece, but with this difference from many Platonic dialogues, that in the *Theaetetus* Plato's artistic imagination is excited less by the interplay of the three characters who conduct the discussion than by the philosophical ideas themselves and the to-and-fro of dialectical argument. . . . What lies before us, then, is a drama of ideas and argument.

Myles Burnyeat, *The Theaetetus of Plato* (Indianapolis: Hackett Publishing Co., 1990), 2.

5. Burnyeat, *Theaetetus of Plato,* 2. Burnyeat goes on to say, "As such it invites us not merely to witness but to participate ourselves in the philosophical activity of the speakers." Ibid., 2–3.

6. In discussing the choice that Plato made to write dialogues, and not treatises, Ruby Blondell makes a number of interesting points about the relative advantages and disadvantages of both forms or genres of philosophical writing (as she also recalls some of the elements mentioned in the *Protagoras* concerning the relative merits of speechmaking or oratory and dialectical discussion in philosophy):

> A treatise is the written equivalent of an extended, uninterrupted speech. Thus it is the implicit claim to intellectual authority in Protagoras' treatise that allows Sokrates to argue, in *Theaetetus,* that his [Protagoras'] relativism is self-defeating. By avoiding this mode of discourse in his own voice, Plato evades the charge of authoritarianism—though he may, at the same time, expose himself to the different charge of evading responsibility. Dialogue form also enables him to avoid the implicit claim that his—or anyone's—philosophical views can in fact be coherently conveyed through assertive discourse. The form thus has certain pedagogical implications, in contrast to a treatise. Some of these are spelled out in the Seventh Letter. But even without that evidence, we can infer from Plato's choice of form that he denies pedagogical value to the authoritative treatise as such. No matter what model of pedagogy Plato's characters enact, the choice of dialogue form saves Plato himself from instantiating the kind of pedagogy that would be implied by a continuous expository discourse in his own voice.

Blondell, *Play of Character in Plato's Dialogues,* 41.

7. The extent to which there is historical continuity in this desire for philosophical therapy, stretching from ancient to contemporary philosophical practice, is suggested in Stanley Cavell's characterization of an aspect of Ludwig Wittgenstein's later philosophy. Cavell reads Wittgenstein's later work as maintaining an inheritance from Plato's philosophical work:

> A word in conclusion about Wittgenstein's encouragement to think of his philosophical methods as like therapies, which some philosophers of my acquaintance have been discouraged by, taking Wittgenstein's proposal as signaling a wish to cure us of the impulse to philosophy. But why take it this way? "Like therapies" suggests that a philosophical question, or a question asked philosophically, is apt to have causes whose origins are not presented, to which a helpful response may be no more like a solution than like a cure, or say no more like finding an answer than like finding a further question. Is it sure that the invocation of therapy is meant to differentiate *Philosophical Investigations* from traditional philosophy, more than it is to assume its place in continuing philosophy, if in its discontinuous way? Has not philosophy itself, at least since Plato, claimed for itself the task of therapy, or say liberation from bonds of illusion, superstition, bewitchment, fanaticism, self-distortion? Wittgenstein's difference . . . lies in his sense that philosophical constructions are as apt to mask as to relieve philosophical perplexity, as if each of us has her or his own countless, diurnal ways of getting lost and recognizing help.

Stanley Cavell, "The Wittgensteinian Event," in *Philosophy the Day after Tomorrow* (Cambridge, Mass.: Belknap Press of Harvard University Press, 2005), 210–11.

8. Wittgenstein made some comments (published posthumously in *Zettel*) that speak to this thought: "In philosophizing, we may not *terminate* a disease of thought. It must run its natural course, and *slow* cure is all important. (That is why mathematicians are such bad philosophers.)" And, "In a certain sense one cannot take too much care in handling philosophical mistakes, they contain so much truth." Ludwig Wittgenstein, *Zettel,* trans. G. E. M. Anscombe, ed. G. E. M. Anscombe & G. H. von Wright (Oxford: Basil Blackwell, 1967), §§382, 460. While I am not well acquainted with Martin Heidegger's work, I also wonder whether this concern for allowing one's response to a philosophical problem or perplexity to unfold at its own pace, and on its own terms, is being addressed in Heidegger's phrase, "letting truth happen." See Cavell, *This New Yet Unapproachable America,* 3, 11.

9. Ludwig Wittgenstein, "Remarks on Frazer's *Golden Bough*," in *Philosophical Occasions, 1912–1951,* trans. John Beversluis, ed. James Klagge & Alfred Nordmann (Indianapolis: Hackett Publishing Co., 1993), 119.

10. This "negative" construal of the dialogue may or may not be the consensus reading of the *Theaetetus*. In the introduction to her book on this dialogue, Rosemary Desjardins says the following: "Perhaps the most conspicuous and well-known feature of the *Theaetetus* is its apparent failure to provide a satisfactory account of knowledge." Desjardins then goes on to state: "[I]t seems generally to be accepted without much question that the dialogue is indeed a failure as far as an account of knowledge is concerned." Rosemary Desjardins, *The Rational Enterprise: Logos in Plato's* Theaetetus (Albany: State University of New York Press, 1990), 2, 8 (with numerous citations). In her book, Desjardins very much contests this received view of the *Theaetetus.*

Bernard Williams, in his "Introduction" to the Levett and Burnyeat translation, offers the following thoughts on the supposed negativity of the *Theaetetus:*

> On its central question, "what is knowledge?", the dialogue's results are negative, but it is not supposed that we have learned nothing in disposing of the various answers which are proposed in the course of the argument. Moreover, the various answers themselves, as we shall see, are not merely suggestions randomly elicited by the question. They speak to various important preconceptions, and they help to identify theoretical problems which will have to be faced in any latter discussion of knowledge. . . . [T]he third Part [of the dialogue] is like the second, which more explicitly spells out its difficulties, and also like the first, which extensively deploys a complex argument, to the extent that they all belie the formally negative conclusion of the dialogue. We do not know at the end of it what knowledge is, but we understand better than we did at the beginning what might be involved in knowing what knowledge is. [Levett & Burnyeat at viii, xx]

Also, Irving Copi's preface to the Jowett translation offers the following account of the positive as well as the negative aspects of the *Theaetetus:* "Considered in isolation the conclusions of the *Theaetetus* might seem to be wholly negative. But properly understood those conclusions are seen to establish a positive position of the greatest importance. In destroying the empiricist relativism of the Sophist Protagoras, Plato showed that there must be a way of knowing in which the mind is not merely a passive spectator but performs an essentially synthetic function. The whole story is not told, of course, but it is shown that any theory which fails to include an account of this active judging function of the mind in knowing is an inadequate account of the knowledge process" [Jowett & Copi at x].

11. In speaking here about the "episodic" nature of Socratic conversational inquiry, I am aware that knowledge itself is not normally thought of as an episodic phenomenon. David Bostock has a useful passage on our normal characterization of knowledge and belief: "Belief, then, is essentially a dispositional notion, and this shows itself (in English) by the fact that we do not have an episodic present tense 'he is believing' to contrast with the habitual present tense 'he believes'. But we do have such a contrast between 'he is judging' (i.e. now) and 'he judges' (i.e. habitually). In this respect knowledge is similar to belief and not to judgement. Knowledge too is a dispositional rather than an episodic notion, and again we have no episodic present tense 'he is knowing' to contrast with 'he knows'. (Of course, this is not to deny that there are episodes of *coming* to know and *coming* to believe, but these are not episodes of knowing and believing.)" David Bostock, *Plato's* Theaetetus (Oxford: Clarendon Press, 1988), 156. In my comments on Socrates' method of conversational inquiry, I am emphasizing the side of his method that engages us in the process of coming to know, or the process of revisiting and revising what earlier we had taken to be our knowledge.

12. Cavell, *Cities of Words,* 326.

13. From Seth Benardete and, through him, ultimately from Leo Strauss, I adopt the notion that the action of any Platonic dialogue influences the argument that we find in that dialogue. In an essay in which Benardete discusses the teaching acumen of Strauss, he puts the point this way:

> Xenophon says that to converse (*dialegesthai*) meant for Socrates the coming together of men for the purpose of deliberation by dividing (*dialegein*) the things (*ta pragmata*) by kinds (*gené*). The middle voice *dialegesthai* contains within it the active, *dialegein*. The communication among men involves the articulation of things. This Heraclitean insight into the double nature of logos was the basis for Strauss' reading of Plato. He put this double nature into the title of one of his last books, *The Argument and the Action of Plato's Laws*. The "and" in the title is misleading; it does not mean that some sort of action is represented while the argument is being developed; it means that the action has an argument, and that that argument is the true argument of the *Laws*. That Strauss did not call his book, *The Argument in the Action* . . . underlines the initial separateness of argument and action in a Platonic dialogue and the latent community between them.

> Strauss was not the first to notice the dramatic setting of a Platonic dialogue; he was not even the first to suggest that the drama altered the apparent meaning of the argument; but what is peculiarly his discovery was that once argument and action are properly put together an entirely new argument emerges that could never have been expected from the argument on the written page.

Seth Benardete, "Strauss on Plato," in *Argument of the Action*, 408–9.

Everything that I do in this book is based on the thought that the educational activities that are portrayed between Socrates and his interlocutors influence the apparent arguments of the *Protagoras*, the *Meno*, and the *Theaetetus*. From my perspective, these activities comprise the overriding themes of these dialogues. Hence, in this respect, my book consists of an attempt to trace the arguments of the actions in these dialogues. Stanley Cavell avers that "those of us who share, or credit, Wittgenstein's and Austin's sense of their revolutionary tasks are responding (as part of the experience of their work in making problematic the relation of philosophy to its tradition) to the concern and implication of their work for correct instruction. (There is no revolutionary social vision which does not include a new vision of education; and contrariwise.)" Cavell, "Foreword: An Audience for Philosophy," in *Must We Mean What We Say?*, xxv.

14. This topic was one reason that I quoted Stanley Cavell in chapter 1 (see note 26), as to our knowledge of (and, simultaneously, our wilful ignorance of) what we mean by what we say. I want to reiterate Cavell's point: "[M]y motivating question . . . was the question of what it betokens about our relation to the world, and others, and myself, that I do in fact, to an unknown extent, inescapably know (barring physical or psychic trauma), and that I chronically do not know or cannot say what I mean, and that I can know further by bethinking myself of what I would rather or might or must or could say, or not say, or rather not." Cavell, "Preface to Updated Edition," in *Must We Mean What We Say?*, xviii.

15. In this regard, Stanley Cavell suggests the following thought: "Otherwise, where sincerity asserts itself, it calls for testing. I do not say that everyone has the passion or the knack or the agility to submit himself to philosophical test; I say merely that someone can *call* himself a philosopher, and his book philosophical, who has not subjected himself to it." Cavell, "Foreword: An Audience for Philosophy," in *Must We Mean What We Say?*, xxviii.

16. How to deal with the multiple meanings of *logos* is problematic. Myles Burnyeat comments as follows: "The Greek word *logos* has a wide spread of meanings. It is 'speech' or 'discourse' in general, and also particular kinds of

speech such as 'argument'; it is 'statement' in general, and also particular kinds of statement such as 'theory', 'explanation', 'definition'; it may even mean a 'tally' or 'list'. We have already begun to explore the possibilities allowed by this indeterminacy." Burnyeat, *Theaetetus of Plato,* 134.

Joe Sachs adds some pertinent thoughts in his recent translation of this dialogue: "The more important word is the one translated 'articulation,' which is *logos.* In its immediate context, it means something like 'rational account' (and it is translated elsewhere in the dialogue as 'statement,' 'argument,' or 'discussion'), but Socrates will open the word up to a much wider range of interpretations to explore what such an account might be. . . . Since this *logos* purports to be the thing that binds the perceptible and the intelligible, in the context of the dialogue as a whole, it amounts to some kind of return to the central question asked of Theaetetus at 187A." Sachs, at 112 n. 56 (citations omitted).

Robin Waterfield has an extended discussion in his essay on the *Theaetetus* concerning the difficulties in translating the term *logos.* [Waterfield(3) at 218–21.] After going through a number of possible preferred renderings, Waterfield settles for the term, "rational account."

17. As Joe Sachs points out in his translation of this dialogue, "what is remarkable is that Socrates has found a way to set Theodorus' various motives for resisting philosophy against one another to make him find that he has a stake in the outcome of a philosophic inquiry in spite of himself." Sachs, 80 n. 41.

18. A constant theme in this dialogue is the difficulty of making correct judgments of identity (as this topic relates to the nature of knowledge). There has developed in the secondary literature on the *Theaetetus* a debate over whether Socrates' (or Plato's) attention is directed solely toward false judgments of identity; or, instead, whether it includes any and all false judgments. This is not an issue into which I must delve, given my limited purposes in this book. Readers interested in further following this point might consult Burnyeat, *Theaetetus of Plato,* 70–73, 219–34; and Timothy Chappell, *Reading Plato's* Theaetetus (Indianapolis: Hackett Publishing Co., 2004, 2005), 154–57.

19. Theodorus' initial response toward Socrates' questioning is to avoid any discussion or debate. Early on, he always tries to escape Socrates' attempts to engage him in conversation, and his attitude changes only when Socrates "converts" him. "Conversion" amounts, in Theodorus' case, simply to getting him sufficiently interested in the questions being asked such that he becomes passionate in the pursuit of the truth about Heraclitus' and Parmenides' theories. [See generally Levett & Burnyeat at 50–52 (179b–181c).]

20. In giving us his account of *Walden,* Stanley Cavell says the following about Thoreau's figurative accounting in that book:

> This is what those lists of numbers, calibrated to the half cent, mean in *Walden*. They of course are parodies of America's methods of evaluation; and they are emblems of what the writer wants from writing, as he keeps insisting in calling his book an *account*. As everywhere else, he undertakes to make the word good. A true mathematical reckoning of the sort he shows requires that every line be a mark of honesty, that the lines be complete, omitting no expense or income, and that there be no mistake in the computation. Spoken words are calculated to deceive. How are written words different? The mathematical emblem embodies two ways. First, it is part of a language which exists *primarily* as notation; its point is not the fixing of a spoken language, which had preceded it, but the fixing of steps, which can thereby be remarked. Second, the notation works only when every mark within it means something, in its look and its sequence. Among written works of art, only of poetry had we expected a commitment to total and transparent meaning, every mark bearing its brunt. The literary ambition of *Walden* is to shoulder the commitment in prose.

Stanley Cavell, *The Senses of* Walden (New York: Viking Press, 1972), 30 (see also at 63).

21. These are secrets to strangers, but they are available to anyone who cares to pay attention and learn from Socrates. He withholds himself from no one.

22. David Sedley suggests, in his reading of the *Theaetetus,* that this kind of activity is central to (or even emblematic of) the action of this dialogue. Appealing to a number of historical considerations, Sedley argues that in this dialogue Socrates proves to be the midwife for Plato, in that his critical activities prepare the ground for the development or the derivation of Plato's mature doctrines. See David Sedley, *The Midwife of Platonism: Text and Subtext in Plato's* Theaetetus (Oxford: Clarendon Press, 2004). While the possibilities of Sedley's reading of the *Theaetetus* are intriguing, here I am attending only to the extent to which Socrates' activities elicit and elaborate the ties that bind between Theaetetus' view of knowledge and Protagoras' more extensive theory of knowledge.

23. James Boyd White conceives of the activity of translation as a way of recognizing and responding to others and their words. There is a sense in which "translation can be an image of thought, a model of social life, including in the law, for all of our life together requires the constant reading of one another's texts and the creation of texts in response to them. The activity of translation in fact offers an education in what is required for this interactive life."

James Boyd White, *Justice as Translation: An Essay in Cultural and Legal Criticism* (Chicago: University of Chicago Press, 1990), 257.

24. Theaetetus' capacity for philosophy is established not so much by means of his capacity for wonder, then, as it is by means of his ability to see what is "there" to be seen, regardless of its material status. Socrates cares about the reality of the issues and the puzzles that he pursues in his critical inquiries.

> *Socrates.* Then you have a look round, and see that none of the uninitiated are listening to us—I mean the people who think that nothing exists but what they can grasp with both hands; people who refuse to admit that actions and processes and the invisible world in general have any place in reality.
>
> *Theaetetus.* They must be tough, hard fellows, Socrates.
>
> *Socrates.* They are, my son—very crude people. But these others, whose mysteries I am going to tell you, are a much more subtle type. [Levett & Burnyeat at 19 (155e–156a)]

In addition to the hard-headed people and the sophists, "a much more subtle type," is a third kind of person, such as Socrates. This third type is willing to investigate and examine the world and its reality, wherever it may take us (as, say, in the *Republic,* either into a cave of shadows or out into the brightness of the sun).

25. One theme in the *Theaetetus,* consistently voiced by Socrates, is his contempt for the fact that sophists are merely argumentative. This is another sophistic trait on the basis of which Socrates tries to distance himself from them. For example: Socrates refers disparagingly to the "professional savants, who . . . [w]ould spend our superfluous time trying each other out; we [w]ould start a regular Sophists' set-to, with a great clashing of argument on argument." Later, he warns Theaetetus against "adopting the methods of professional controversialists." Socrates instead advises the two of them to practice dialectic, not rhetoric, as they have been doing: "[w]e profess to be philosophers, not champion controversialists; and we don't realise that we are doing just what those clever fellows do." Almost immediately thereafter, Socrates again warns Theaetetus, this time about the danger of being held hostage by "a million other questions with which one of the mercenary skirmishers of debate might ambush you." This mercenary (a sophist, who charges for his teaching) would keep refuting Theaetetus, so Socrates warns, until he "had got you thoroughly tied up by him . . . and he would set you free [only] for a ransom" [Levett & Burnyeat at 32, 33 (165d–e)]. And, later in the dialogue, Socrates alludes once

again to the mockery of the sophist directed at them and at their expense: "Our friend the expert in refutation will laugh" [Levett & Burnyeat at 78 (200a–b)]. From these excerpts, it is fair to infer that Socrates is at pains to separate himself from the rhetorical procedures as well as from the mantle of the sophists.

26. As mentioned earlier, I cited some pertinent thoughts of Stanley Cavell's on the connection between investigating what we say (or what we might say, or what we are tempted to say) and our ability to gain self-knowledge. Having already appealed to this stretch of Cavell's prose (see note 14 in this chapter), I simply mention once again that Cavell's remarks are relevant to the current discussion.

27. Consider, in this regard, Theodorus' early remarks on Theaetetus' honest and trustworthy character [see Levett & Burnyeat at 3–4 (144a–b)].

28. Robin Waterfield characterizes Theodorus (accurately, I think) as a "quasi-Protagorean, [who] is definitely not a Heraclitean" [Waterfield(3) at 79 n. 2]. The fact that Theodorus is relatively sympathetic to Protagoras' views, yet unsympathetic to Heraclitus' views, is established during the course of Socrates' extended accounts of both Protagoras and Heraclitus.

29. Stanley Cavell puts the task of criticism (and performing this task with a humble sense of fairness) as follows: "[T]he topics of criticism are not objects but works, things which are *already* spoken. And if arrogance is inherent in criticism (and therefore where not in the Humanities?), then humility is no less painful a task there than anywhere else. Nor is it surprising that the specific elements of arrogance afflict both criticism and philosophy: if philosophy can be thought of as the world of a particular culture brought to consciousness of itself, then one mode of criticism (call it philosophical criticism) can be thought of as the world of a particular work brought to consciousness of itself." Cavell, "Avoidance of Love," in *Must We Mean What We Say?*, 312–13. In this regard, Socrates' critical activities in eliciting the implications (and elaborating the possibilities) of Protagoras' theory, can be thought of as an effort to bring the world of Protagoras' theory (or of his work, entitled *Truth*) to a consciousness of itself.

30. Myles Burnyeat aptly captures this aspect of the *Theaetetus:* "As I see it, your task [as a reader] in Part I is to *find* the meaning of the text and follow the argument to a satisfactory conclusion. In Part II you are challenged to *respond* to the meaning in the text by overcoming the problems and paradoxes that it leaves unresolved. In Part III the task is nothing less than to *create* from the text a meaning which will solve the problem of knowledge. What matters, then, is not how much experience you have of philosophy or of Plato, but your readiness to engage in philosophical reflection for yourself." Burnyeat, *Theaetetus of Plato,* xii–xiii. (This passage from Burnyeat is also quoted with

approval by Bernard Williams in his Introduction to the Hackett edition of the *Theaetetus*. See Levett & Burnyeat, ix.)

31. Stanley Cavell suggests one philosophical moral that we should draw from such an impasse: "(This [moral or lesson] would not be a matter of keeping your mouth shut but of understanding when, and how, not to yield to the temptation to say what you do not or cannot exactly mean.)" Stanley Cavell, "An Emerson Mood," in *The Senses of* Walden*: An Expanded Edition* (San Francisco: North Point Press, 1981), 145.

32. Irving Copi, in his Introduction to the Library of Liberal Arts edition of Jowett's translation of the *Theaetetus,* characterizes Socrates' efforts in a manner congenial to my portrait here: "In this dialogue we find Plato's dialectic at a high and effective level. As he conceived it, dialectic was no mere bag of debater's tricks for silencing opposition. It was the art of asking and answering questions as a method of achieving truth. This is clearly seen early in the dialogue, when dialectic is used not to refute Theaetetus' first thesis, that knowledge is perception, but to explain it, to sound its implications, to compare and contrast it with related views, and to achieve a statement of the thesis that is most adequate and free from merely accidental or eristic objections. Once that statement is found, it is subjected to a merciless criticism" [Jowett & Copi at xi].

33. Gregory Vlastos, "Paradox," in *Philosophy of Socrates,* 11–12; reprinted with slight changes, in Vlastos, *Studies in Greek Philosophy,* 2:11–12. Cited earlier in chapter 1, n. 3.

34. Ludwig Wittgenstein, *Culture and Value,* trans. Peter Winch, ed. G. H. von Wright & Heikki Nyman (Chicago: University of Chicago Press, 1980), 56. I do not want to leave the impression that Wittgenstein thought that he had nothing more to learn about such a linguistic landscape. Later in his notebooks, he says: "The relations between these concepts form a landscape which language presents us with in countless fragments; piecing them together is *too hard* for me. I can make only a very imperfect job of it." Ibid., 78.

35. John M. Cooper makes a similar point:

> One might attend here to what Plato has Socrates say at the end of the *Phaedrus* about written discourses. Socrates is speaking in the first instance of speeches written for oral delivery, but he applies his remarks to all writing on political or other serious philosophical subjects. Actual knowledge of the truth on any of these matters requires a constant capacity to express and re-express it in relation to varying circumstances and needs and in response to new questions or challenges that may arise. Knowledge is a limitless ability to interpret and reinterpret itself—it cannot

> be set down exhaustively in any single set of formulas, for universal, once-for-all use. Accordingly, no book can actually embody the knowledge of anything of philosophical importance; only a mind can do that, since only a mind can have this capacity to interpret and reinterpret its own understandings.

Cooper, "Introduction," in Plato, *Complete Works,* xx.

36. It also has to be the appropriate time for such a comment or remark. In this respect, again, I find much similarity between Socrates' practice and that of certain ordinary language philosophers. Nothing can be said just anywhere or at just any time. What is said—in order to make sense, to have point—must fit the context or the case in which it is uttered. In this regard, Cavell makes the following observation: "Philosophy which proceeds from ordinary language is proceeding from the fact *that* a thing is said; that it is (or can be) said (in certain circumstances) is as significant as what it says; its being said then and there is as determinative of what it says as the meanings of its individual words are." Cavell, "Avoidance of Love," in *Must We Mean What We Say?,* 336.

37. Earlier in this chapter (see note 29), I quoted Cavell's remarks on the nature of philosophical criticism and characterized Socrates' activities as eliciting the implications and elaborating the possibilities of Protagoras' theory. These critical activities seem to me to be an effort to bring the world of Protagoras' theory (or of his book, *Truth*) to a consciousness of itself.

38. In the Focus Publishing Co. edition of *Theaetetus,* translated by Joe Sachs, the translator remarks about the variety of *logoi* offered us in this dialogue:

> This last subsection of the *Theaetetus* thus brings out most clearly what the dialogue itself is and is not. It is a treasure house of *logoi,* of arguments that give accounts for and against various claims about knowledge. It is not philosophy. It is an image that mimics conversation that might arise out of, or on the way to, philosophic activity. At best it may be an origin of such activity in a reader, but no one could predict what in it might spark in any particular reader an elevation to the philosophic level. The richness and variety of attempts, errors, new beginnings, and false turns that the dialogue presents strengthen its power to find and cross the philosophic boundary for a wide audience of people willing to respond actively to its promptings.

Sachs, 11.

39. Waterfield notes that this self-characterization of Socrates "is more true of the Socrates of the early dialogues than of [the Socrates] of *Theaetetus*" [Waterfield(3), 47 n. 3].

40. In a late note appended to his book on Socrates the ironist, Vlastos makes the point that Socrates' behavior in this dialogue is dissimilar to his behavior in earlier dialogues:

> Now consider what happens in the *Theaetetus*. The simple thesis which is put in Theaetetus' mouth and treated as the formal refutand is transformed by wonderfully inventive constructs which Socrates grafts on it. . . . What Socrates then proceeds to refute is a doctrine which by no stretch of the imagination could have been fished out of Theaetetus' own belief system. The naive identification of knowledge with perception allowed him [Theaetetus] at the start is changed past recognition into a mini-metaphysical system which is only too patently Socrates' own invention: what he refutes in the course of the long-winded argument that follows is his own imaginative construct, with which he chooses to saddle his docile interlocutor. . . . No one would wish to confuse these procedures with the peirastic arguments by which Socrates refutes interlocutors in the Elenctic Dialogues.

Gregory Vlastos, "Socratic Elenchus in the *Theaetetus*," in *Socrates, Ironist and Moral Philosopher* (Ithaca: Cornell University Press, 1991), 266.

41. Socrates acts as an advocate for Protagoras' theory, in which he does not believe and to which he does not adhere. This generous gesture serves further to heighten the contrast drawn between the philosopher and the lawyer (or the practical man). As is well known, these two figures are prominently featured and contrasted within the *Theaetetus* [see Levett & Burnyeat at 42–47 (172c–177b)]. Socrates, trying to be fair and just as a philosophical critic of Protagoras, does not shorten his defense of Protagoras to meet any artificial time limit (this is the basis of a complaint made against the lawyers). In defending and elaborating Protagoras's theory, Socrates pursues the digressions wherever they may lead. Hence, he takes whatever time is required by the nature of the theory he is expounding philosophically. The development of Protagoras' position, then, is determined by the time it takes to articulate and elaborate Protagoras' theory naturally (through Socratic conversational inquiry), what ever that time may prove to be. Also, in representing Protagoras, Socrates does not ask for any kind of payment in exchange for his able advocacy. So the contrasts between the two types are substantial.

42. Once again, I find pertinent a critical comment made by Stanley Cavell. In describing what he does in giving a reading of a particular film, or offering an interpretation of a text, Cavell says that, in regard to "what a complete interpretation could be, how it is one may end a reading," he finds it useful to consider the following: "Completeness is not a matter of providing *all* interpretations but a matter of seeing one of them *through*." Stanley Cavell, *Pursuits of Happiness: The Hollywood Comedy of Remarriage* (Cambridge, Mass.: Harvard University Press, 1981), 37.

43. This conclusion is foreshadowed by the following comment by Socrates in the dialogue: "And even so, Theaetetus, you have answered me in the way one ought—with a good will, and not reluctantly, as you did at first. If we continue like this, one of two things will happen. Either we shall find what we are going out after; or we shall be less inclined to think we know things which we don't know at all—and even that would be a reward we could not fairly be dissatisfied with" [Levett & Burnyeat at 60–61 (187b–c)].

44. William Shakespeare, *King Lear* V, ii, 9.

FIVE Learning to Find Ourselves at a Loss

1. Cavell, "Preface to Updated Edition," in *Must We Mean What We Say?*, xvii.

2. Stanley Cavell, "Philosophy the Day after Tomorrow," in *Philosophy the Day after Tomorrow* (Cambridge, Mass.: Belknap Press of Harvard University Press, 2005), 123.

3. Plato, *Apology*, in Church & Cumming, 21–49 [17a–42a].

4. John M. Cooper provides a brief description of the courtroom setting (in the king-archon court), which plays a role both in the *Euthyphro* and in the *Apology:* "The king-archon, one of the nine principal magistrates of Athens, had the responsibility to oversee religious rituals and purifications, and as such had oversight of legal cases involving alleged offenses against the Olympian gods, whose worship was a civic function—it was regarded as a serious offense to offend them." Plato, *Euthyphro*, in *Five Dialogues: Euthyphro, Apology, Crito, Meno, Phaedo*, trans. G. M. A. Grube, rev. trans. John M. Cooper (Indianapolis: Hackett Publishing Co., 1981, 2d ed. 2002), 2 n. 2.

5. More than a century ago, R. L. Nettleship spoke about this side of Socrates' life: "He passed his life in talking. It was the impulse given by his life that produced Plato's dialogues. Socrates is unique among philosophers because he lived his philosophy; he put out what he had to put out, not in books, but in his life, and he developed his ideas by constant contact with other men. . . . In his

case, then, it was apparent that philosophy is a living thing developed by the contact of living minds." Nettleship, *Lectures on the* Republic *of Plato,* 8.

6. The same point, or a very similar one, comes up earlier in the *Apology* in the following imagined exchange between Socrates and his jurors: "If you were therefore to say to me, 'Socrates, this time we will not listen to Anytus. We will let you go, but on the condition that you give up this investigation of yours, and philosophy. If you are found following these pursuits again, you shall die.' I say, if you offered to let me go on these terms, I should reply: 'Athenians, I hold you in the highest regard and affection, but I will be persuaded by the god rather than you. As long as I have breath and strength I will not give up philosophy and exhorting you and declaring the truth to every one of you whom I meet'" [Church & Cumming at 35–36 (29c–d)]. Socrates obeys the god, not the people or popular opinion. He holds to what is important, not to what is ephemeral. Moreover, as Socrates makes clear throughout his defense statement, he is not sure (i.e., he is not persuaded) that to die is a bad thing. Is death an evil thing, to be avoided; or a good thing, to be embraced?

7. In a slightly different context, once again Socrates makes this point. When he acknowledges that his defense speech does not include, on his behalf, any special entreaties to his jurors, Socrates avers that were he to engage in such pleas, he would be corrupting the jurors and thereby subverting the city's judicial process. Thus, he would be showing contempt for the law and for the sanctity of the jurors' souls. This Socrates refuses to do, both on principle and on the basis that he would be proving his own impiety, thereby confirming one of the charges lodged against him by his enemies: "Therefore, Athenians, do not require me to do these things, for I believe them to be neither good nor just nor pious; especially, do not ask me to do them today when Meletus is prosecuting me for impiety. For were I to be successful and persuade you by my entreaties to break your oaths, I should be clearly teaching you to believe that there are no gods, and I should be simply accusing myself by my defense of not believing in them. But, Athenians, that is very far from the truth. I do believe in the gods as no one of my accusers believes in them" [Church & Cumming at 42 (35c–d)].

8. Plato, *Gorgias,* trans. and intro. W. C. Helmbold (Indianapolis: Bobbs-Merrill Co., 1952), 11 [453a–b], hereafter cited as Helmbold.

9. Plato, *Republic,* trans. and intro. Robin Waterfield (Oxford: Oxford University Press, 1993, 1994), hereafter cited as Waterfield(1). The specific passage is as follows:

> "Next," I said, "here's a situation which you can use as an analogy for the human condition—for our education or lack of education. Imagine people living in a cavernous cell down under the ground; at the far end of the

cave, a long way off, there's an entrance open to the outside world. They've been there since childhood, with their legs and necks tied up in a way which keeps them in one place and allows them to look only straight ahead, but not to turn their heads. There's firelight burning a long way further up the cave behind them, and up the slope between the fire and the prisoners there's a road, beside which you should imagine a low wall has been built—like the partition which conjurors place between themselves and their audience and above which they show their tricks. . . . Imagine also that there are people on the other side of this wall who are carrying all sorts of artefacts. These artefacts, human statuettes, and animal models carved in stone and wood and all kinds of materials stick out over the wall; and as you'd expect, some of the people talk as they carry these objects along, while others are silent." [Waterfield(1) at 240–41 (514a–515a)]

10. See Plato, *Protagoras,* in Jowett & Ostwald, 8–9 [313a–e].

11. One recent master of analytical philosophy (Bernard Williams) suggests that this question remains fundamental for anyone wishing to think about ethics and moral philosophy. In one of Williams's books, he says: "Socrates' question is the best place for moral philosophy to start." Bernard Williams, *Ethics and the Limits of Philosophy* (Cambridge, Mass.: Harvard University Press, 1985), 4.

12. "[I]n our view, Socrates, as Plato depicts him, is not a teacher at all; he is a seeker after moral wisdom who encourages others to engage in the same search. Socrates' interlocutors are invited to join him in the pursuit of wisdom, rather than to be passively 'instructed' in whatever Socrates has already learned himself." Brickhouse and Smith, *Plato's Socrates,* 4.

13. Alexander Sesonske, "To Make the Weaker Argument Defeat the Stronger," *Journal of the History of Philosophy* 6 (1968): 217–31.

14. I believe that certain aspects of his defense statement treat his jurors unfairly. See Eisele, "'Never Mind the Manner of My Speech,'" *Legal Studies Forum,* 253–88.

15. Sesonske, "To Make the Weaker Argument," *Journal of the History of Philosophy,* 217–31.

16. Socrates offers the image of himself as a pesky "gadfly" that torments his fellow citizens and attaches itself to the lethargic Athenian *polis.* While this image purports to characterize Socrates' social role, he himself calls the image "ludicrous" or "ridiculous." Given the importance of his social role and the gravity of the situation (he is on trial for his life), the image seems laughable. Nevertheless, Socrates does offer this as one way of conceiving of his relationship to others in Athenian society. How seriously are we to take Socrates liken-

ing himself to a gadfly stinging a lethargic horse? Here it is possible that Socrates is engaging in irony (or perhaps it is sarcasm); it even may be that the image is intended to be self-deflating. We should consider the possibility, however, that this image represents Socrates' understanding of how his fellow citizens think of him: he is a pest. And, for his efforts on their behalf, they will make him drink hemlock.

17. Nettleship, *Lectures on the* Republic, 25.

18. Ibid., 24.

19. Ibid., 25.

20. The mistake of taking Socrates for a sophist is actually made in the *Protagoras.* There, as Socrates and Hippocrates attempt to visit Protagoras in order to ask him some pointed questions, initially they are turned away at the door to Callias' house, where Protagoras is staying during his visit to Athens. The porter rudely slams the door on Socrates and Hippocrates, muttering something like, "Ah, more sophists; he's busy, go away!" [see Jowett & Ostwald at 10–11 (314d–e)]. Thus, the danger is real that his fellow Athenians might mistake Socrates for a sophist. This misidentification is what I believe Socrates is attempting to avoid in the *Apology* by means of his denial of being a teacher, or, at least, by his denial of being a sophistic teacher.

21. Nehamas nicely expresses a similar point about Socrates: "[T]his [issue] . . . goes to the heart of Socrates' personality as well as of his method. It is that Socrates, unlike all other teachers of *areté,* does not constitute a danger to his students precisely because he refuses to tell anyone what *areté* is, especially since he denies having that knowledge in the first place. Whatever claim Socrates has to the teaching of *areté* lies exactly in his disclaiming any such ability." Nehamas, "Meno's Paradox and Socrates as a Teacher," in *Virtues of Authenticity,* 13.

22. In a later essay, Nehamas puts the point very well: "In fact, no mode of teaching is more dogmatic than what goes by the name of 'the Socratic method' today. In this we are completely untrue to the Socrates who appears in Plato's early dialogues, for reasons I will mention later on. Socrates is light and tentative all the way down. Though he insists on following his own dialectical method, he is constantly expressing the willingness to reexamine his views and to review his arguments." And Nehamas also says, later in the same essay, "Taking Socrates' attitude toward his teaching as ironical robs him of much of his strangeness. Taking it as sincere supplies him, paradoxically, with a much more profound ironical mask—a mask that is very difficult, perhaps impossible, to remove. . . . Far from having anything to teach, Socrates is engaged in a search in the most literal sense of the term." Alexander Nehamas, "What Did Socrates Teach and To Whom Did He Teach It?," in *Virtues of Authenticity: Essays on*

Plato and Socrates (Princeton: Princeton University Press, 1999), 65, 71, 77. (See also my note 12 in this chapter.)

23. *The Republic of Plato,* trans. and intro. A. D. Lindsay (New York: E. P. Dutton & Co., 1957), xiii, hereafter cited as Lindsay.

24. Waterfield(2), 112 [80b].

25. Martha Nussbaum makes the point that Socratic dialogues are, in part, built upon the premise that we can learn from examples or exemplars. As she says, "through its depiction of the dialectical process the dialogue can show us moral development and change taking place. Like a dramatic poem (like the *Antigone*), it can show us the forces that lead to change or increased self-knowledge, and the fruits of change in practical life. Seeing examples of learning is surely an important part of *our* learning from a written text. It is, however, a part of learning that the inertness and the one-voiced structure of non-dramatic didactic moral texts denies us." Nussbaum, *Fragility of Goodness,* 128.

26. Myles Burnyeat reinforces this idea, specifically with reference to the opening scene of the *Meno*. Burnyeat says:

> The *Meno* . . . begins with a question, this time a question which amounts to a demand that Socrates should tell Meno the answer to the main philosophical question of the dialogue. . . . The *Meno* is . . . the dialogue that introduces Plato's Theory of Recollection, the great point of which is that, where philosophical questions are concerned, no one can be taught or told the answer. In some sense that remains true of philosophy today, you have to work it out for yourself, under the stimulus of tough dialectical questioning. Hence, even if Socrates knows the answer to Meno's question, it would do no good to tell him. The very fact that Meno demands to be told shows his ignorance of the nature of philosophical inquiry. Yet we as readers will not appreciate this fully until we have done some work ourselves on the long discussion in the central portion of the dialogue on, precisely, the nature of philosophical inquiry.

Burnyeat, "First Words," *Proceedings of the Cambridge Philological Society,* 1, 12–13.

27. See, e.g., Vlastos, "Paradox," in *Philosophy of Socrates,* 1–21; reprinted with slight changes, in Vlastos, *Studies in Greek Philosophy,* 2:3–18. One of the most important aspects of Vlastos's later work, I believe, is that he begins his studies of Socrates by stating his conviction that Socrates' paradoxes (some of which constitute what Vlastos calls "the strangeness of Socrates") are central to who Socrates is. What we can learn from the figure of Socrates and his method of search is, Vlastos argues, a function of his strangeness (i.e., his fondness for

paradoxes and paradoxical statements). "[H]is paradoxes, pushed to the margins in that [earlier, unpublished] book, had to be brought into dead center." Gregory Vlastos, *Socrates, Ironist and Moral Philosopher,* 2.

28. In addition to the later work of Vlastos (cited in the preceding note), there is, for example, the work of George Grube, who makes the following catalogue of "Socrates' own paradoxical views": "These views included the belief that 'the unexamined life is not worth living for a man;' that goodness is a matter of knowledge; that no man does wrong deliberately, but only because he does not *know* any better, and that the essence of wisdom is to realize one's own ignorance. . . . The greatest Socratic paradox, however, is Socrates himself." G. M. A. Grube, "Introduction," in *Plato's Republic,* trans. G. M. A. Grube (Indianapolis: Hackett Publishing Co., 1974), vii–viii.

29. Vlastos, "Socrates' Disavowal of Knowledge," *Philosophical Quarterly,* 1–31; reprinted with changes in *Socratic Studies,* 39–66.

30. More completely, Emerson's statement (originally delivered in 1838) is this: "It is an intuition. It cannot be received at second hand. Truly speaking, it is not instruction, but provocation, that I can receive from another soul. What he announces, I must find true in me, or wholly reject; and on his word, as his second, be he who he may, I can accept nothing." Ralph Waldo Emerson, "The Divinity School Address," in *Nature, Addresses, and Lectures,* ed. Robert E. Spiller and Alfred R. Ferguson (Cambridge, Mass.: Belknap Press of Harvard University Press, 1971, 1979), 80.

31. Nehamas, "Meno's Paradox and Socrates as a Teacher," in *Virtues of Authenticity,* 21. In anticipation of this remark (and preparing the scene for its appearance), Nehamas earlier in this essay states the following: "What is crucial to knowledge is that the information in which it consists has been acquired in the proper way, no less and no more." Ibid., 19.

32. Education founded upon conversational inquiry is directed toward the goal of gaining self-knowledge. Indeed, Socratic conversational inquiry proceeds on the basis of repeated moments of self-revelation, or self-denial. Michael Oakeshott reinforces this idea when, at one point in an essay, he quotes from a master at Eton, William Cory, who "understood education as a preparation for participation in conversation." Oakeshott then goes on to quote Cory approvingly as follows:

> At school "you are not engaged so much in acquiring knowledge as in making mental efforts under criticism. . . . A certain amount of knowledge you can indeed with average faculties acquire so as to retain; nor need you regret the hours you spend on much that is forgotten, for the shadow of lost knowledge at least protects you from many illusions. But you go to a

> great school not so much for knowledge as for arts and habits; for the habit of attention, for the art of expression, for the art of assuming at a moment's notice a new intellectual position, for the art of entering quickly into another person's thoughts, for the habit of submitting to censure and refutation, for the art of indicating assent or dissent in graduated terms, for the habit of regarding minute points of accuracy, for the art of working out what is possible in a given time, for taste, discrimination, for mental courage and mental soberness. And above all you go to a great school for self-knowledge."

Michael Oakeshott, *The Voice of Poetry in the Conversation of Mankind: An Essay* (London: Bowes & Bowes, 1959), 12–13 n. 1; reprinted as Michael Oakeshott, "The Voice of Poetry in the Conversation of Mankind," in *Rationalism in Politics and Other Essays* (New York: Basic Books, 1962), 200 n. 1.

33. Here my reading of Socrates' disavowal of knowledge diverges from Vlastos's reading of that disavowal. At the beginning of his book on Socrates as ironist and moral philosopher, Vlastos takes Socrates' profession of ignorance to be his "central paradox," and Vlastos goes on to say that "the traditional view" of various commentators on Socrates "emasculates Socrates' profession of ignorance by reducing it to a pedagogical feint." Vlastos, *Socrates, Ironist and Moral Philosopher,* 3, 5. Vlastos's claim merits some scrutiny.

Does the recognition that Socrates' disavowal has a pedagogical point, implicitly reduce the function of that disavowal to one of being merely a "feint"? Vlastos suggests that the pedagogical reading construes Socrates as engaging in trickery, as though he were using a teaching ploy to enforce some didactic lesson, and acting disingenuously in order to do so. But to see the pedagogical point in what Socrates is saying and doing, need not take him to be acting disingenuously merely for the sake of teaching us a lesson. It is possible, I believe, to take Socrates at his word, and to read his behavior rather as instancing one way in which a teacher might make the meaning of the teacher's hesitancy or disavowal clear to his or her student-auditors. Why take such a recognition of Socrates' practice as though it must thereby reduce his philosophical activity to the level of a ploy or "feint"?

In my view, Socrates' disavowal of knowledge has both an epistemological and a pedagogical side. As to the first, his disavowal serves as a limit to what he is willing to say or claim—he wants to say no more than he knows. As to the second, Socrates' profession of ignorance serves as a goad to action. It exhorts us to inquire further into the matter at hand, the matter causing us pain or trouble or confusion. As Vlastos elaborates in his interpretation, Socrates' disavowal is seen as being "intelligible only if understood to disclaim one sort of knowledge, while claiming another in the same breath." Vlastos, *Socrates, Ironist and Moral Philosopher,* 13. To the extent that I attribute to Socrates the twin lessons of disillusion and of renewal, I share with Vlastos this sense of the duality of Socrates' philosophical practice.

Still, I cannot find myself agreeing with Vlastos's remark that "the disavowal is a 'complex irony,' a figure of speech in which what is said both is and isn't what is meant." Ibid., 13–14. On my reading, Socrates' profession of ignorance is meant, epistemologically, to remind us of how little we know; and it is meant, pedagogically, to encourage us to find ourselves at a loss, so that (out of a sincere acknowledgment of our own ignorance) we may renew our search. In this regard, contra Vlastos, I believe that for Socrates the pedagogical point is as important, and as fully meant, as is the epistemological moral of his disavowal.

34. In her preface to her translation of the *Laches,* Rosamond Kent Sprague points out that it is the self-assurance of the speaker, the person who claims to know, that forces Socrates to engage in refutation. Given the speaker's prideful claim to know, what else can Socrates do, except to seek the speaker's refutation? "Socrates considered false conceit of knowledge to be the greatest barrier to human wisdom. A man like Laches, for instance, who is quite confident of knowing what courage is . . . , will not prove receptive to a fresh definition until he is first made to see the contradictory nature of the old one. Hence the necessity for the destructive tactics of the Socratic *elenchus.*" Plato, *Laches and Charmides,* trans. and intro. with notes Rosamond Kent Sprague (Indianapolis: Bobbs-Merrill Co., 1973), viii.

Sprague's remarks suggest that the Socratic *elenchus* is used as a way of converting error into truth, or as a way of making room for the truth, by removing error. Socrates makes his conversational partner readier to search for the truth by first showing that partner that he is living in error. Or, in the terms of the *Republic,* refutation shows a person that he or she "lacks" something. To make a person receptive to the truth, one first has to awaken that person to the possibility that he or she does not yet possess the truth. This situation calls for someone to be refuted.

35. Wittgenstein expresses in slightly different terms the temptation to speak beyond the limits of what we actually know: "In philosophy one is constantly tempted to invent a mythology of symbolism or of psychology, instead of simply saying what we know." Ludwig Wittgenstein, *Philosophical Grammar,* trans. Anthony Kenny, ed. Rush Rhees (Berkeley: University of California Press, 1974), 56. Regarding claims to know, both Wittgenstein and Socrates speak from a position of relative poverty or impoverishment. They urge us to claim the least (not the most) that we may know, and then to see where that takes us on our journey of inquiry.

36. As J. Peter Euben says, "the sheer fact of our mortality dictates the limits of our understanding and power, which is one reason why Socrates emphasizes that the kind of wisdom he has is human in contrast to the kind of wisdom claimed by his accusers and the sophists. . . . For Socrates there could always be something he had missed and someone, no matter how seemingly ignorant, socially unconnected, or poor, from whom he could learn and whom he could 'teach.'" Euben, *Corrupting Youth,* 43.

37. In a different context, Stanley Cavell makes the point that divine knowledge is not a possibility for human beings: "Put it this way: to know the world as a whole, or the world as it is in itself, would require us to have God's knowledge, to know the world the way we more or less picture God to know the world, with every event and all its possibilities directly present. And this simultaneous, immediate intuition of the world is not merely beyond us in fact or in extent; it is not a matter of having more of something we now have a little of. It is beyond us in principle; human knowledge is not like that." Cavell, *Pursuits of Happiness,* 76.

38. Cavell, *This New Yet Unapproachable America,* 19.

39. In Socratic conversational inquiry, we seek to learn something about ourselves. If this is true, then employing the Socratic method seems to be a matter of asking ourselves who we are, and how we live, and what we find worth doing in our lives. These are matters that, seen from one perspective, are apt to strike us as moral notions or moral concerns. This may be one reason for Gregory Vlastos characterizing Socrates' method as a "method of moral inquiry." From this perspective, his characterization seems correct.

But, from another perspective, we might emphasize that what Socrates puts us in a position to access and assess is personal knowledge, our knowledge of persons. The task in this respect becomes a matter of surveying people as they are in the process of acting and thinking and speaking. If so, then this may be why we find ourselves, during the course of Socratic conversational inquiry, investigating and discussing questions of justice and virtue and excellence and self-control and temperance and courage. These are moral concepts, to be sure, but they are moral concepts *because* they concern human beings and how they act. Since we are seeking knowledge of the self, a knowledge of persons, we find ourselves investigating the kinds of concepts and cases (or contexts) where we best can observe human behavior. Cases and contexts involving questions of virtue or excellence or knowledge or justice or courage are apt to be the places where human beings find themselves (and their forms of life) displayed and revealed. These are the situations, the fixes, in which we human beings may become conscious of ourselves, conscious of what we are thinking and saying and doing. These are, then, the kinds of cases in which we can study who we are and what we do in (or with) our lives.

40. Vlastos asserts, late in his study of Socrates, that "[k]nowledge in the moral domain is the sole object of Socrates' epistemic concern," and that "the correct conclusion is that he was an exclusively *moral* philosopher." Vlastos, *Socrates, Ironist and Moral Philosopher,* 237 n. 5. Similarly, in his paper on Socrates' disavowal of knowledge, Vlastos contends: "But the Socrates of this paper is no epistemologist. He is a moralist pure and simple who practices moral inquiry but never inquires into the theory of moral inquiry." Vlastos, "Socrates' Disavowal of Knowledge," *Philosophical Quarterly,* reprinted in *Socratic Studies,* 63.

41. Here I want to refer again to my earlier notation of Myles Burnyeat's remarks about Socrates' method being a way of achieving self-knowledge (see chapter 1, note 10). Along similar lines, there are some pertinent remarks made by Alexander Nehamas: "Separated from Plato's own systematic educational interests, Socrates constitutes a peculiar figure, concerned primarily if not exclusively with the improvement of his own soul. . . . Or should we return to Socrates' superficially more modest approach, knowing, however, that once we engage in the care of the self we will never know when we can stop, that the limits of the self are also the limits of the world?" Nehamas, "What Did Socrates Teach and To Whom Did He Teach It?," in *Virtues of Authenticity,* 78.

Self-knowledge seems to me to be the aim of Socratic conversational inquiry. And Socrates is not the only one interested in this topic. Anyone with a commitment to therapeutic philosophical activity is likely to fasten on the topic of how we can gain self-knowledge. Here I am thinking in particular of the following claim made by Stanley Cavell with respect to the methods used by Wittgenstein in his philosophical investigations: "If it is accepted that 'a language' (a natural language) is what the native speakers of a language speak, and that speaking a language is a matter of practical mastery, then such questions as 'What should we say if . . .?' or 'In what circumstances would we call . . . ?' asked of someone who has mastered the language (for example, oneself) is a request for the person to say something about himself, describe what he does. So the different methods [used by Wittgenstein] are methods for acquiring self-knowledge." Cavell, "The Availability of Wittgenstein's Later Philosophy," in *Must We Mean What We Say?,* 66–67.

42. In Plato's dialogues, there are, as we know, three groups of people who squander the opportunity of the philosophical moment that Socrates makes available to them. First, there are the sophists, such as Protagoras and Gorgias, who are so confident that they despise any suggestion that there might be

something for them to learn. They prefer their rhetorical devices to Socrates' proffer of dialectical examination. Second, there are the various politicians and poets and artisans in Athens. These people cannot be troubled to think themselves less knowledgeable than they smugly believe themselves to be. Their response to their own ignorance is not to stop and inquire; rather, it is to feel anger and indignation toward Socrates. Third, there are the gentlemen and aristocrats, men such as Hippocrates and Anytus and Theodorus, whom we met in the dialogues we have been examining in this book. All of them seem unable or unwilling to begin a philosophical search.

43. Woodruff, "Socratic Education," in *Philosophers on Education,* 14.

44. Sachs, *Plato's Theaetetus,* 2.

45. Woodruff, "Socratic Education," in *Philosophers on Education,* 14.

46. Lesley Brown, "Introduction," in Plato, *Protagoras and Meno,* trans. Adam Beresford and intro. Lesley Brown (London: Penguin Books, 2005), xxiv.

47. Socrates was perhaps the first of such teachers as companions, but certainly he was not the only such figure. We have, from a much later period, testimony as to Michael Oakeshott's similar attitude toward his students: "Those who know Michael Oakeshott will insist first and foremost he is a great teacher. He, on the other hand, has always thought of himself, first, as a learner. His schooldays, he will tell you, were the happiest time of his life. And it was his never forgotten experience as a schoolboy that led him to become a teacher and the kind of teacher he was: unavoidably a lecturer and a critic of his pupils' work, but more at home in the conversational give-and-take of a class or a seminar; a guide rather than an instructor, a fellow-traveler rather than a leader." Timothy Fuller, "Introduction: A Philosophical Understanding of Education," in Michael Oakeshott, *The Voice of Liberal Learning,* foreword and intro. Timothy Fuller (Indianapolis: Liberty Fund, 2001), xv.

48. Euben, *Corrupting Youth,* 42. And earlier in his book, Euben attributes to Socrates the idea that "we teach our character as much as a subject matter." Ibid., 11 n. 25. "Teaching by example" is instructively considered by Oakeshott (but at a length that I cannot reproduce here) as a genuine instance of teaching. See Michael Oakeshott, "Learning and Teaching," in *The Voice of Liberal Learning,* 59–60.

49. I take Socrates' being a seeker or a searcher engaged in a joint inquiry *not* to exclude or to negate the possibility that he also is, simultaneously, thereby being a teacher. Others look at the same Socratic activities and see something different. (See, e.g., the comments of Brickhouse and Smith in note 12, and the comments of Nehamas in note 22.) I understand Brickhouse, Smith, and

Nehamas to be arguing that Socrates' status as a seeker shows him *not* to be teaching but rather, to be searching for answers or knowledge that he does not have. I grant to Brickhouse, Smith, and Nehamas that Socrates is truly seeking for knowledge he does not yet possess. I also agree that Socrates is being sincere in this regard, not ironic. He genuinely searches without knowing. Still, Socrates *leads* the search. If he does not yet know the substance of the answer or knowledge for which he is (and we are) seeking, he still knows *how* to seek what he and we need to learn. Socrates teaches us his method of conversational inquiry, and he remains confident that his method will teach us what we need to know. (This may be another way of saying that Socrates rejects Meno's paradox of inquiry.)

J. Peter Euben makes a similar point, I think, in an exemplary manner:

> But whatever our response, Socrates' disclaimer [of being a teacher], together with the fact that he remains one of the great moral teachers in the West, raises a series of questions about what it means to teach—more particularly, what it means to teach actual or future fellow citizens in a democracy.
>
> In part Socrates denies being a teacher because of the way most people think about teaching and about themselves as teachers (and students). Many suppose that teaching is a matter of transmitting specific doctrines or attitudes so that students come to know what their teachers know and act as their teachers intend them to act. But as any teacher knows, there is a radically contingent relationship between intentions and consequences, between what is taught and what is learned. . . .
>
> Part of the contingency between what teachers teach and what students learn . . . derives from the fact that we teach who we are as fully as we teach any idea or text. For Socrates, knowing who we are in the sense of the kind of character we present as we teach is only possible if we are able to be students of our students so we can be teachers of them. Even then there is an instability to our identity as teachers because for Socrates (or Plato), the question "Who are we?" is not simply a self-critical one as it is for Kant, but a self-transformative one as it is for Nietzsche. Only if teaching is dialogic and the risks of revelation and discovery are shared, only when what and how we think are tied to something in our life that does *not* have some final form or the order of narrative, but emerges from intense encounters with real and/or fictive interlocutors, only then might Socrates have allowed himself to agree that he was indeed a teacher.

Euben, *Corrupting Youth,* 41, 42.

50. Cavell, "Foreword: An Audience for Philosophy," in *Must We Mean What We Say?*, xxviii.

51. Roslyn Weiss makes an interesting point regarding how we should understand the statement by the oracle at Delphi that "No one is wiser than Socrates": "As Socrates recounts at *Ap.* 23a5–b4, he comes to understand the oracle to be saying that the height of human wisdom is Socratic wisdom, namely, the knowledge that one lacks wisdom concerning the most important thing (*ta megista*): human virtue. The oracle, Socrates says, in proclaiming him wisest, uses the name 'Socrates' as a mere place-holder; the oracle's intention is to designate as wisest that man, any man, who knows that he does not know virtue. The oracle maintains, then, not that, as a matter of fact, no one is wiser than the man Socrates, but rather that the wisest of men, the man who is as wise as a man can be, knows, *like* Socrates, no more with respect to *ta megista* than that he does not know." Weiss, *Virtue in the Cave*, 23–24 n. 19.

52. Plato, *Laches and Charmides*, 77 [165b–c].

Epilogue

1. Cavell, *Pursuits of Happiness*, 270.

2. Let us recall Roslyn Weiss, who says that "the oracle's intention is to designate as wisest that man, any man, who knows that he does not know virtue." Weiss, *Virtue in the Cave*, 23–24 n. 19.

3. Thomas D. Eisele, "Must Virtue Be Taught?," *Journal of Legal Education*, 495–508.

4. Eisele, "The Activity of Being a Lawyer: The Imaginative Pursuit of Implications and Possibilities," *Tennessee Law Review* 54 (1987): 345–89.

5. Thomas D. Eisele, "From 'Moral Stupidity' to Professional Responsibility," *Legal Studies Forum* 21 (1997): 193–219.

6. W. B. Gallie, *Philosophy and the Historical Understanding* (New York: Schocken Books, 1964), 157–91.

7. Some law teachers may find my description inapplicable to their own preparatory process. In particular, I suspect that many may say that they go into class with a much less rigid or explicit scheme of presentation in mind, and that they are happy just to provoke discussion, which then may take unexpected yet productive turns. I do not deny that this kind of teaching can be done successfully by a teacher using a Socratic method, but I do wish to add two thoughts. First, the process of preparation that I have just described helps me to understand students' questions better, to make better sense of them, than I otherwise seem able to do (when, for example, I go to class less prepared or

organized than I like to be). So, for me, the structure helps; and I think it helps the students too. Second, while I do not want to underestimate the possibility of innovation or improvisation occurring in my law classes, I believe that even innovation and improvisation proceed on the basis of a script. Or, perhaps better, they take off from a script. In other words, a structure can itself be a necessary condition for making innovation or improvisation possible. See David Sudnow, *Ways of the Hand: The Organization of Improvised Conduct* (Cambridge, Mass.: Harvard University Press, 1978).

8. It is old news to say that teaching is in part a performance. Here, especially with regard to legal education, it should not be surprising to find a significant theatrical element in the teaching of a profession, when that profession itself has important theatrical dimensions. See, e.g., Milner S. Ball, "The Play's the Thing: An Unscientific Reflection on Courts under the Rubric of Theater," *Stanford Law Review* 28 (1975): 81.

9. 3 Caines 175 (N.Y. Sup. Ct. 1805). This is the famous fox case, with which many Property teachers still begin their classes.

10. Here it might be appropriate to discuss some of the thoughts on law school teaching expressed by Paul Hayden in his article on right and wrong answers. See Paul Hayden, "On 'Wrong' Answers in the Law School Classroom," *Journal of Legal Education* 40 (1990): 251–55. I take his basic point to be that even purportedly "wrong" answers can be educationally useful. I grant him this. But I would want to continue the argument by saying that while a wrong answer may teach us any number of useful lessons, it still remains to be learned how and why the answer is demonstrably wrong.

11. One way of stating the difference between these two scenes of instruction is to focus upon a useful ambiguity in the sentence, "I am looking for an answer." In the first scene (where I think I know the answer), I am "looking for" an answer in the sense that I am expecting it; I look to my students to provide it to me in response to my question. In the second scene (where I do not know the answer), I am "looking for" an answer in the sense that I am searching for one; I am seeking it along with my students. As Roslyn Weiss puts a similar point, "Inquiry . . . is, for Socrates, the attempt to solve a problem—virtually any sort of problem—to which the answer is *not* already known. It is the looking into a matter rather than the narrower looking for a thing." Weiss, *Virtue in the Cave*, 54 n. 18.

I have been helped to think in terms of "scenes of instruction" by the attention that Stanley Cavell has paid this aspect of teaching and learning in the later writings of Wittgenstein. Here I refer the reader to Cavell's discussion of the opening section of Wittgenstein's *Philosophical Investigations*, which he characterizes as both a "scene of inheritance" and a "scene of instruction": see Cavell,

This New Yet Unapproachable America, 60–61, 64–65. See also Stanley Cavell, *Conditions Handsome and Unhandsome: The Constitution of Emersonian Perfectionism* (La Salle, Ill.: Open Court, 1990), 64–100 (the second chapter of which is entitled "The Argument of the Ordinary: Scenes of Instruction in Wittgenstein and in Kripke").

12. This is another reason why I said earlier that, in order for my teaching to be most effective, I find that I need an awareness of the structure of the lesson plan for each class, and that even innovation and improvisation begin with a script. See note 7.

13. This is one reason why I wish to dissent from some of the remarks made by Paul Hayden about right and wrong answers in law school. See note 10.

14. On several occasions, I have received comments on students' evaluation forms that my continual interruptions are an irritating habit of mine as well as distracting and impolite. This may be an inevitable cost of what I see as the benefits of such a teaching technique, but I do not deny that this reaction means that I must continually rethink both its efficacy and ethics.

15. I have suggested elsewhere that this insight into the student's responsibility for finding a solution to the problems that plague him or her in the law, can be one goal of a course in Jurisprudence. See Eisele, "Activity of Being a Lawyer," *Tennessee Law Review*, 346–49.

16. In the secondary literature on Socrates and his teaching, I have not found anyone who formulates the dual lessons of the early and middle dialogues this way, and I believe that my formulation is original. But, when subsequently I came across Gregory Vlastos's book on Socrates the ironist and moral philosopher, containing certain cryptic comments, I found some support for my formulation: "Socrates' central paradox . . . [is] his profession of ignorance. He *asserts* that he has no knowledge, none whatever, not a smidgin of it, 'no wisdom, great or small' (*Ap.* 21b–d). But he speaks and lives, serenely confident that he has a goodly stock of it—sufficient for the quotidian pursuit of virtue. And he *implies* as much in what he says. To keep faith with Socrates' strangeness some way has to be found to save both the assertion of his ignorance and the implied negation." And, "irony served as the vehicle of his profession of ignorance, [which is] intelligible only if [it is] understood to disclaim one sort of knowledge, while claiming another in the same breath." Vlastos, *Socrates, Ironist and Moral Philosopher*, 3, 13.

17. I am led to this label in part by the following remarks of Stanley Cavell on the nature of self-knowledge: "Both [Freud and Wittgenstein] thought of their negative soundings as revolutionary extensions of our knowledge, and both were obsessed by the idea, or fact, that they would be misunderstood—

partly, doubtless, because they knew the taste of self-knowledge, that it is bitter. It will be time to blame them for taking misunderstanding by their disciples as personal betrayal when we know that the ignorance of oneself is a refusal to know." Cavell, "The Availability of Wittgenstein's Later Philosophy," in *Must We Mean What We Say?*, 72.

18. If the lack of self-knowledge is mine and not the student's, then the revelation of one's ignorance will once again have been achieved by means of Socratic questioning. Sometimes it is the Socratic questioner who refutes himself.

19. About the nature of *elenchus* in Socrates' dialectical method, James Boyd White says:

> The one who claims to know knows nothing after all. This is the *elenchus*, or refutation, of which Socrates repeatedly speaks, and it is the heart of dialectic. It results in a mortification or humiliation of a special kind, for one is mortified by the invocation not of new facts or ideas but of what one already knows or claims to know. One part of the self is appealed to against another part, and in the process a previously unknown self-contradiction is revealed. . . . [A] dialectical refutation (*elenchos*) requires that one make the other agree with what one says . . . . What matters between us is not the other witnesses who can be brought forward to support your view or mine but whether you can make me your witness or I can make you mine. For dialectic to exert its full force upon the individual mind, complete frankness is essential, a kind of shamelessness in saying what one really thinks.

James Boyd White, *When Words Lose Their Meaning: Constitutions and Reconstitutions of Language, Character, and Community* (Chicago: University of Chicago Press, 1984), 95, 102.

20. In response to my claim that it is important to have law students volunteer to answer in class, I have been told that to characterize them as "volunteers" is false. In most law schools, this critic says, students speak not voluntarily but from a sense of implicit coercion. And, it is further said, even purported volunteers feel coerced into speaking: they understand that they are expected to participate in class, and that their final grade can be lowered if they fail to do so (this is true in my classes).

This criticism identifies an important limitation to my description of law school teaching. But this critical comment may itself go too far. On this alternative understanding, it may become impossible ever to characterize anyone as "volunteering." Such an alternative means that we have lost, or are at risk of losing, our concept of voluntary action in law school teaching. But, in addition, this alternative understanding shows at most that volunteering is a rare phenomenon in law school; it does not show that my claims about the logic or the dynamics of volunteering are wrong. (A more complete response to this objection would explore how comfortable or uncomfortable, how threatened or intimidated, students feel in any given law school class. But I find it difficult to assess the extent to which student participation is truly voluntary, without also looking at the nature and quality of the teaching going on in a given class. Do we invite students to participate? Does our teaching encourage them to volunteer?)

21. The way in which I am formulating these doubts is directly indebted to Stanley Cavell's analysis of the opening moments in traditional philosophical skepticism. While I do not use this material in any concerted way here, I want to draw attention to the possibilities of pursuing these lines of inquiry elsewhere. Cavell's generating question in his inquiry of skepticism is, specifically, "How does the failure of a particular claim seem to cast doubt on the validity of knowledge as a whole?" Cavell, *Claim of Reason*, 135–40.

22. This saying, as we know, was inscribed over the threshold of the temple at Delphi. "And at [Apollo's] door his worshippers saw the command *Know thyself*—the doctrine of sophrosyne, by which men learn to remember the limits of human power and ambition." Jaeger, *Paideia*, 1:167. The Delphic saying, "Know thyself," also comes under Socratic scrutiny in the *Charmides* [see 165a, 167a] and in the *Protagoras* [see 343b].

23. I have thought about the ways in which this knowledge can be said to be bitter. First, it is bitter because it is unwanted. It comes to us or to our students unbidden, unasked for, unsought. Second, it is bitter because it is unacceptable. It tells us something about ourselves and our world that we do not like to hear or do not want to know, and it also stings our pride or our vanity. Thus, it requires an acknowledgment from us before it can truly become an operative part of our understanding of ourselves and the world. And third, it is bitter because it is undeniable. The proof is there, right in front of us, and this makes it a hard truth. It confronts us, even haunts us, until we relent, yet we reject it because it is so bitter.

24. If I delude myself about something, I am being foolish; but if I am the victim of (or fall prey to) an illusion, then I am being fooled.

25. The philosophical "argument from illusion" is thoroughly and helpfully analyzed in ways pertinent to the present discussion in J. L. Austin's set of lecture notes discussing issues related to knowledge and perception. See J. L. Austin, *Sense and Sensibilia*, ed. G. J. Warnock (Oxford: Clarendon Press, 1962). For Austin's careful distinction between illusions and delusions, see ibid., 22–26.

26. Cavell, "Politics of Interpretation," in *Themes Out of School*, 54.

27. Emerson, if I read him correctly, believed that illusions are a necessary part of human life and experience:

> Dream delivers us to dream, and there is no end to illusion. Life is a train of moods like a string of beads, and, as we pass through them, they prove to be many-colored lenses which paint the world their own hue, and each shows only what lies in its focus. . . .
>
> The secret of the illusoriness is in the necessity of a succession of moods or objects. Gladly we would anchor, but the anchorage is quicksand. This onward trick of nature is too strong for us: *Pero si muove*. When, at night, I look at the moon and stars, I seem stationary, and they to hurry. Our love of the real draws us to permanence, but health of body consists in circulation, and sanity of mind in variety or facility of association. We need change of objects. Dedication to one thought is quickly odious. We house with the insane, and must humor them; then conversation dies out.

Ralph Waldo Emerson, "Experience," in *Essays and Lectures*, ed. Joel Porte (New York: The Library of America, 1983), 473, 476 (originally published in 1844).

28. See, e.g., *The Republic of Plato*, trans. Allan Bloom (New York: Basic Books, 1968), 193–96 [514a–517a].

29. See T. S. Eliot, "Burnt Norton," in *The Complete Poems and Plays, 1909–1950* (New York: Harcourt, Brace & World, 1971), 118.

30. This phenomenon is explored carefully and perceptively by James Boyd White in his book, *The Legal Imagination: Studies in the Nature of Legal Thought and Expression* (Boston: Little, Brown & Co., 1973), 10–13, 689–94.

31. I am not happy with calling "skepticism" an "inference" that we draw from our disillusioning experience. Rather than an inference, skepticism is more truly speaking a mood or a settled attitude (a conviction). This change in characterization has implications for how we should respond to skepticism (the threat or the allure of it); for whether we think that skepticism is capable of refutation; and even for whether we find it to be a natural human reaction to certain situations and experiences. I can point the reader to the best book available that discusses this matter, namely, Stanley Cavell's *Claim of Reason*.

32. James Boyd White, "The Judicial Opinion and the Poem: Ways of Reading, Ways of Life," in *Heracles' Bow: Essays on the Rhetoric and Poetics of the Law* (Madison: University of Wisconsin Press, 1985), 127.

33. See Wittgenstein, *Philosophical Investigations*, §§143–51, 179, 323.

34. I have said something about this aspect of Socrates' teaching in two earlier essays that discuss his teaching in Plato's dialogues. See Eisele, "Must Virtue Be Taught?," *Journal of Legal Education*; and Eisele, "'Never Mind the Manner of My Speech,'" *Legal Studies Forum*, 253, 267–68.

35. Cavell, *Claim of Reason*, 28.

36. Showing this side of legal education and practice has been a constant theme of James Boyd White's work. See, e.g., White, *The Legal Imagination*; *When Words Lose Their Meaning*; and *Heracles' Bow*.

37. G. M. Young, "Maitland," in *Daylight and Champaign: Essays* (London: Jonathan Cape, 1937), 291.

38. I would claim, if I knew how to make it intelligible, that this insight is expressed with a Wittgensteinian twist, given his own kind of translation, in the following maxim: "Knowledge is in the end based on acknowledgement." Ludwig Wittgenstein, *On Certainty*, trans. Denis Paul and G. E. M. Anscombe, ed. G. E. M. Anscombe and G. H. von Wright (Oxford: Basil Blackwell, 1969), §378.

BIBLIOGRAPHY

Aristotle. *Nicomachean Ethics*. Translated and with an introduction and notes by Martin Ostwald. Indianapolis: Bobbs-Merrill Co., 1962.

Austin, J. L. "A Plea for Excuses." In *Philosophical Papers*. Edited by J. O. Urmson and G. J. Warnock. Oxford: Clarendon Press, 1961.

———. *Sense and Sensibilia*. Edited by G. J. Warnock. Oxford: Clarendon Press, 1962.

Ball, Milner S. *Called by Stories: Biblical Sagas and Their Challenge for Law*. Durham, N.C.: Duke University Press, 2000.

———. "The Play's the Thing: An Unscientific Reflection on Courts under the Rubric of Theater." *Stanford Law Review* 28 (1975): 81.

Benardete, Seth. "Strauss on Plato." In *The Argument of the Action: Essays on Greek Poetry and Philosophy*. Edited and with an introduction by Ronna Burger and Michael Davis. Chicago: University of Chicago Press, 2000.

Beresford, Adam. "Notes." In *Protagoras and Meno*. Translated by Adam Beresford and with an introduction by Lesley Brown. London: Penguin Books, 2005.

Blondell, Ruby. *The Play of Character in Plato's Dialogues*. Cambridge: Cambridge University Press, 2002.

Bostock, David. *Plato's* Theaetetus. Oxford: Clarendon Press, 1988.

Brann, Eva. *The Past-Present: Selected Writings of Eva Brann*. Edited by Pamela Kraus. Annapolis, Md.: St. John's College Press, 1997.

———. "Plato's Theory of Ideas." In *The Past-Present*.

———. "Statement on Educational Policy." In *The Past-Present*.

Brickhouse, Thomas C., and Nicholas D. Smith. *Plato's Socrates*. New York: Oxford University Press, 1994.

Brown, Lesley. "Introduction." In *Protagoras and Meno*. Translated by Adam Beresford and with an introduction by Lesley Brown. London: Penguin Books, 2005.

Brown, Malcolm. "Plato Disapproves of the Slave-Boy's Answer." In *Plato's Meno: With Essays*. Edited by Malcolm Brown and translated by W. K. C. Guthrie. Indianapolis: Bobbs-Merrill Co., 1971.

Burnyeat, Myles. "First Words: A Valedictory Lecture." *Proceedings of the Cambridge Philological Society* 43 (1997): 1–20.

———. "Foreword." In *Plato's Protagoras: A Socratic Commentary*. Translated with notes and commentary by B. A. F. Hubbard and E. S. Karnofsky. Chicago: University of Chicago Press, 1982.

———. "Plato." *Proceedings of the British Academy* 111 (2001): 1–22.

———. "Socratic Midwifery, Platonic Inspiration." In *Essays on the Philosophy of Socrates*. Edited by Hugh H. Benson. Oxford: Oxford University Press, 1992.

———. *The Theaetetus of Plato*. Indianapolis: Hackett Publishing Co., 1990.

Cavell, Stanley. "The Availability of Wittgenstein's Later Philosophy." In *Must We Mean What We Say?*

———. "The Avoidance of Love: A Reading of *King Lear*." In *Must We Mean What We Say?*

———. *Cities of Words: Pedagogical Letters on a Register of the Moral Life*. Cambridge, Mass.: Belknap Press of Harvard University Press, 2004.

———. *The Claim of Reason: Wittgenstein, Skepticism, Morality, and Tragedy*. Oxford: Clarendon Press, 1979.

———. *Conditions Handsome and Unhandsome: The Constitution of Emersonian Perfectionism*. La Salle, Ill.: Open Court, 1990.

———. "An Emerson Mood." In *The Senses of* Walden*: An Expanded Edition*. San Francisco: North Point Press, 1981.

———. "Existentialism and Analytical Philosophy." In *Themes Out of School*.

———. "Foreword: An Audience for Philosophy." In *Must We Mean What We Say?*

———. *In Quest of the Ordinary: Lines of Skepticism and Romanticism*. Chicago: University of Chicago Press, 1988.

———. "Knowing and Acknowledging." In *Must We Mean What We Say?*

———. "Must We Mean What We Say?" In *Must We Mean What We Say?*

———. *Must We Mean What We Say? A Book of Essays*. New York: Charles Scribner's Sons, 1969.

———. "Notes after Austin." In *Encounters*. Edited by Kai Erikson. New Haven: Yale University Press, 1989.

———. "Notes and Afterthoughts on the Opening of Wittgenstein's *Investigations*." In *Philosophical Passages: Wittgenstein, Emerson, Austin, Derrida*. Cambridge, Mass.: Blackwell Publishers, 1995.

———. *Philosophy the Day after Tomorrow*. Cambridge, Mass.: Belknap Press of Harvard University Press, 2005.
———. "Philosophy the Day after Tomorrow." In *Philosophy the Day after Tomorrow*.
———. "The Politics of Interpretation (Politics as Opposed to What?)." In *Themes Out of School*.
———. "Preface to Updated Edition of *Must We Mean What We Say?*" In *Must We Mean What We Say? A Book of Essays*. Cambridge: Cambridge University Press, 1976. Updated ed. 2002.
———. *Pursuits of Happiness: The Hollywood Comedy of Remarriage*. Cambridge, Mass.: Harvard University Press, 1981.
———. *The Senses of* Walden. New York: Viking Press, 1972.
———. *Themes Out of School: Effects and Causes*. San Francisco: North Point Press, 1984.
———. *This New Yet Unapproachable America: Lectures after Emerson after Wittgenstein*. Albuquerque, N.M.: Living Batch Press, 1989.
———. "The Thought of Movies." In *Themes Out of School*.
———. "The Wittgensteinian Event." In *Philosophy the Day after Tomorrow*.
Chappell, Timothy. *Reading Plato's* Theaetetus. Indianapolis: Hackett Publishing Co., 2004, 2005.
Cooper, John M. In Plato, *Complete Works*. Edited with an introduction and notes by John M. Cooper. Indianapolis: Hackett Publishing Co., 1997.
———. "Editorial Note to *Protagoras*." In Plato, *Complete Works*.
———. "Introduction." In Plato, *Complete Works*.
Copi, Irving. "Introduction." In *Plato's Theaetetus*. Translated by Benjamin Jowett and with an introduction by Irving Copi. Indianapolis: Bobbs-Merrill Co., 1949.
Desjardins, Rosemary. *The Rational Enterprise: Logos in Plato's* Theaetetus. Albany: State University of New York Press, 1990.
Eisele, Thomas D. "'The Activity of Being a Lawyer: The Imaginative Pursuit of Implications and Possibilities." *Tennessee Law Review* 54 (1987): 345–89.
———. "From 'Moral Stupidity' to Professional Responsibility." *Legal Studies Forum* 21 (1997): 193–219.
———. "Must Virtue Be Taught?" *Journal of Legal Education* 37 (1987): 495–508.
———. "'Never Mind the Manner of My Speech': The Dilemma of Socrates' Defense in the *Apology*." *Legal Studies Forum* 14 (1990): 253–88.
———. "'Our Real Need': Not Explanation, But Education." *Canadian Journal of Law and Jurisprudence* 3, No. 2 (July 1990): 5–34.

———. "Tom Morawetz's 'Robust Enterprise': Jurisprudence after Wittgenstein." *Philosophical Investigations* 29 (2006): 140–79.

———. "What We Share." *University of Cincinnati Law Review* 71 (2002): 493–516.

Eliot, T. S. "Burnt Norton." In *The Complete Poems and Plays, 1909–1950*. New York: Harcourt, Brace & World, 1971.

Emerson, Ralph Waldo. "The Divinity School Address." In *Nature, Addresses, and Lectures*. Edited by Robert E. Spiller and Alfred R. Ferguson. Cambridge, Mass.: Belknap Press of Harvard University Press, 1971, 1979 (originally published in 1838).

———. "Experience." In *Essays and Lectures*. Edited by Joel Porte. New York: The Library of America, 1983 (originally published in 1844).

Euben, J. Peter. *Corrupting Youth: Political Education, Democratic Culture, and Political Theory*. Princeton: Princeton University Press, 1997.

Finley, John. *Thucydides*. Cambridge, Mass.: Harvard University Press, 1942.

Fish, Stanley. "The Aesthetic of the Good Physician." In *Self-Consuming Artifacts: The Experience of Seventeenth-Century Literature*. Berkeley: University of California Press, 1972.

Frede, Michael. "Introduction." In Plato, *Protagoras*. Translated by Stanley Lombardo and Karen Bell. Indianapolis: Hackett Publishing Co., 1992.

Frost, Robert. "The Figure a Poem Makes." In *Selected Prose of Robert Frost*. Edited by Hyde Cox and Edward Connery Lathem. New York: Collier Books, 1966, 1968.

Fuller, Timothy. "Introduction: A Philosophical Understanding of Education." In Michael Oakeshott, *The Voice of Liberal Learning*. Foreword and introduction by Timothy Fuller. Indianapolis: Liberty Fund, 2001.

Gallie, W. B. *Philosophy and the Historical Understanding*. New York: Schocken Books, 1964.

Grube, G. M. A. "Introduction." In *Plato's Republic*. Translated by G. M. A. Grube. Indianapolis: Hackett Publishing Co., 1974.

Hayden, Paul. "On 'Wrong' Answers in the Law School Classroom." *Journal of Legal Education* 40 (1990): 251–55.

Heffernan, William. "Not Socrates, But Protagoras: The Sophistic Basis of Legal Education." *Buffalo Law Review* 29 (1980): 399–423.

Hubbard, B. A. F., and E. S. Karnofsky. "Preface." In *Plato's Protagoras: A Socratic Commentary*. Translated with notes and commentary by B. A. F. Hubbard and E. S. Karnofsky. Chicago: University of Chicago Press, 1982.

Jaeger, Werner. *Paideia: The Ideals of Greek Culture*. 2d ed. 3 vols. Translated by Gilbert Highet. New York: Oxford University Press, 1939, 1945.

Kierkegaard, Søren. *Philosophical Fragments or A Fragment of Philosophy*. 2d ed. Translated and with an introduction by David Swenson, revised translation by Howard Hong, new introduction with commentary by Niels Thulstrup. Princeton: Princeton University Press, 1936, 1962.

Klein, Jacob. *A Commentary on Plato's* Meno. Chapel Hill: University of North Carolina Press, 1965.

Kraut, Richard. "Introduction to the Study of Plato." In *The Cambridge Companion to Plato*. Edited by Richard Kraut. Cambridge: Cambridge University Press, 1992.

———. *Socrates and the State*. Princeton: Princeton University Press, 1984.

Luban, David. "Epistemology and Moral Education." *Journal of Legal Education* 33 (1983): 636–61.

Maitland, Frederic William. "The Hide." In *Domesday Book and Beyond: Three Essays in the Early History of England*. Cambridge: Cambridge University Press, 1897.

Matthews, Gareth. *Socratic Perplexity and the Nature of Philosophy*. Oxford: Oxford University Press, 1999.

Moline, Jon. "Meno's Paradox?" *Phronesis* 14 (1969): 153–61.

———. "Recollection, Dialectic, and Ontology: Kenneth M. Sayre on the Solution to a Platonic Riddle." In *Platonic Writings, Platonic Readings*. Edited by Charles L. Griswold, Jr. New York: Routledge, Chapman & Hall, 1988.

Moravcsik, Julius. "Learning as Recollection." In *Plato: A Collection of Critical Essays*. Vol. 1: Metaphysics and Epistemology. Edited by Gregory Vlastos. Garden City, N.Y.: Anchor Books, 1971.

Nehamas, Alexander. *The Art of Living*. Berkeley: University of California Press, 1998.

———. "Introduction." In *Virtues of Authenticity*.

———. "Meno's Paradox and Socrates as a Teacher." In *Virtues of Authenticity*.

———. "Socratic Intellectualism." In *Virtues of Authenticity*.

———. "What Did Socrates Teach and To Whom Did He Teach It?" In *Virtues of Authenticity*.

———. *Virtues of Authenticity: Essays on Plato and Socrates*. Princeton: Princeton University Press, 1999.

Nettleship, Richard Lewis. *Lectures on the* Republic *of Plato*. 2d ed. Edited by Godfrey R. Benson. London: Macmillan & Co., 1897, 1901, 1961.

Nussbaum, Martha. *The Fragility of Goodness: Luck and Ethics in Greek Tragedy and Philosophy*. Cambridge: Cambridge University Press, 1986.

Oakeshott, Michael. "Education: The Engagement and Its Frustration." In *Education and the Development of Reason*. Edited by R. F. Dearden, P. H. Hirst, and R. S. Peters. London: Routledge & Kegan Paul, 1972. Reprinted in *The Voice of Liberal Learning.*

———. "Learning and Teaching." In *The Voice of Liberal Learning.*

———. *The Voice of Liberal Learning.* Foreword and introduction by Timothy Fuller. Indianapolis: Liberty Fund, 2001.

———. *The Voice of Poetry in the Conversation of Mankind: An Essay.* London: Bowes & Bowes, 1959. Reprinted in *Rationalism in Politics and Other Essays.* New York: Basic Books, 1962.

Phillips, Bernard. "The Significance of Meno's Paradox." In *Plato's Meno: Text and Criticism.* Edited by Alexander Sesonske and Noel Fleming. Belmont, Calif.: Wadsworth Publishing Co., 1965.

Plato. *Apology.* In *Euthyphro, Apology, Crito.* 2d ed. Translated by F. J. Church, revised translation and with an introduction by Robert D. Cumming. Indianapolis: Bobbs-Merrill Co., 1948, 1956.

———. *The Dialogues of Plato,* Volume 1: *Euthyphro, Apology, Crito, Meno, Gorgias, Menexenus.* Translated by Reginald E. Allen. New Haven: Yale University Press, 1984.

———. *Euthyphro.* In *Euthyphro, Apology, Crito.* 2d ed. Translated by F. J. Church, revised translation and with an introduction by Robert D. Cumming. Indianapolis: Bobbs-Merrill Co., 1948, 1956.

———. *Euthyphro.* In *Five Dialogues: Euthyphro, Apology, Crito, Meno, Phaedo.* 2d ed. Translated by G. M. A. Grube, revised translation by John M. Cooper. Indianapolis: Hackett Publishing Co., 1981, 2002.

———. *Gorgias.* Translated and with an introduction by W. C. Helmbold. Indianapolis: Bobbs-Merrill Co., 1952.

———. *Gorgias: A Revised Text with Introduction and Commentary.* Edited by E. R. Dodds. Oxford: Clarendon Press, 1959, 1990.

———. *Laches and Charmides.* Translated and with an introduction and notes by Rosamond Kent Sprague. Indianapolis: Bobbs-Merrill Co., 1973.

———. *Meno.* Translated by Benjamin Jowett and with an introduction by Fulton H. Anderson. Indianapolis: Bobbs-Merrill Co., 1949.

———. *Meno and Other Dialogues: Charmides, Laches, Lysis, Meno.* Translated and with an introduction and notes by Robin Waterfield. Oxford: Oxford University Press, 2005.

———. *Plato's Meno.* Translated by George Anastaplo and Laurence Berns. Newburyport, Mass.: Focus Publishing Co., 2004.

———. *Plato's Meno.* 2d ed. Translated by G. M. A. Grube. Indianapolis: Hackett Publishing Co., 1976, 1980.

———. *Plato's Meno: With Essays.* Edited by Malcolm Brown and translated by W. K. C. Guthrie. Indianapolis: Bobbs-Merrill Co., 1971.

———. *Protagoras and Meno*. Translated by Adam Beresford and with an introduction by Lesley Brown. London: Penguin Books, 2005.

———. *Protagoras and Meno*. Translated and with an introduction by W. K. C. Guthrie. Harmondsworth: Penguin Books, 1956.

———. *Plato's Protagoras: A Socratic Commentary*. Translated with notes and commentary by B. A. F. Hubbard and E. S. Karnofsky. Chicago: University of Chicago Press, 1982.

———. *Protagoras*. Edited with an introduction by Gregory Vlastos, and translated by Benjamin Jowett, revised translation by Martin Ostwald. Indianapolis: Bobbs-Merrill Co., 1956.

———. *Protagoras*. Translated by Stanley Lombardo and Karen Bell. Indianapolis: Hackett Publishing Co., 1992.

———. *Protagoras*. Translated with notes and commentary by C. C. W. Taylor. Oxford: Clarendon Press, 1976.

———. *Protagoras*. Translated and with an introduction by C. C. W. Taylor. Oxford: Oxford University Press, 1996.

———. *Plato's Republic*. Translated by G. M. A. Grube. Indianapolis: Hackett Publishing Co., 1974.

———. *Republic*. Translated by G. M. A. Grube, revised translation by C. D. C. Reeve. Indianapolis: Hackett Publishing Co., 1992.

———. *Republic*. Translated with an introduction by Robin Waterfield. Oxford: Oxford University Press, 1993, 1994.

———. *The Republic of Plato*. Translated with notes and an interpretive essay by Allan Bloom. New York: Basic Books, 1968.

———. *The Republic of Plato*. Translated with an introduction by A. D. Lindsay. New York: E. P. Dutton & Co., 1957.

———. *Plato's Theaetetus*. Translated by Benjamin Jowett with an introduction by Irving Copi. Indianapolis: Bobbs-Merrill Co., 1949.

———. *Plato's Theaetetus*. Translated and with an introduction by Joe Sachs. Newburyport, Mass.: Focus Publishing Co., 2004.

———. *Theaetetus*. Edited with an introduction by Bernard Williams and translated by M. J. Levett, revised translation by Myles Burnyeat. Indianapolis: Hackett Publishing Co., 1992.

———. *Theaetetus*. Translated and with notes and commentary by John McDowell. Oxford: Clarendon Press, 1973.

———. *Theaetetus*. Translated and with an introduction by Robin Waterfield. Harmondsworth: Penguin Books, 1987.

Poirier, Richard. *Robert Frost: The Work of Knowing*. New York: Oxford University Press, 1977.

Sachs, Joe. "Introduction," *Plato's Theaetetus,* translated and with an introduction by Joe Sachs. Newburyport, Mass.: Focus Publishing Co., 2004.

Santas, Gerasimos Xenophon. *Socrates: Philosophy in Plato's Early Dialogues.* London: Routledge & Kegan Paul, 1979.

Scott, Gary Alan, ed. *Does Socrates Have a Method? Rethinking the Elenchus in Plato's Dialogues and Beyond.* University Park: Pennsylvania State University Press, 2002.

———. *Plato's Socrates as Educator.* Albany: State University of New York Press, 2000.

Sedley, David. *The Midwife of Platonism: Text and Subtext in Plato's* Theaetetus. Oxford: Clarendon Press, 2004.

Sesonske, Alexander. "To Make the Weaker Argument Defeat the Stronger." *Journal of the History of Philosophy* 6 (1968): 217–31.

Shakespeare, William. *King Lear.* Edited by Russell Fraser. New York: New American Library, 1963.

Snell, Bruno. *The Discovery of the Mind: The Greek Origins of European Thought.* Translated by T. G. Rosenmeyer. Cambridge, Mass.: Harvard University Press, 1953.

Sudnow, David. *Ways of the Hand: The Organization of Improvised Conduct.* Cambridge, Mass.: Harvard University Press, 1978.

Teloh, Henry. *Socratic Education in Plato's Early Dialogues.* Notre Dame, Ind.: University of Notre Dame Press, 1986.

Versényi, Laszlo. *Socratic Humanism.* New Haven: Yale University Press, 1963.

Vlastos, Gregory. "Anamnesis in the *Meno.*" *Dialogue* 4 (1965): 143–67.

———. "Introduction: The Paradox of Socrates." In *The Philosophy of Socrates: A Collection of Critical Essays.* Edited by Gregory Vlastos. Garden City, N.Y.: Anchor Books, 1971. Reprinted with slight changes as "The Paradox of Socrates." In *Studies in Greek Philosophy,* Volume 2: *Socrates, Plato, and Their Tradition.* Edited by Daniel W. Graham. Princeton: Princeton University Press, 1995.

———. "Postscript to 'The Socratic elenchus.'" In *Socratic Studies.*

———. "The *Protagoras* and the *Laches.*" In *Socratic Studies.*

———. "Socrates' Disavowal of Knowledge." *Philosophical Quarterly* 35 (1985): 1–31. Reprinted with changes in *Socratic Studies.*

———. *Socrates, Ironist and Moral Philosopher.* Ithaca: Cornell University Press, 1991.

———. "The Socratic elenchus." In *Socratic Studies.*

———. "Socratic Elenchus in the *Theaetetus.*" In *Socrates, Ironist and Moral Philosopher.*

———. *Socratic Studies*. Edited by Myles Burnyeat. Cambridge: Cambridge University Press, 1994.

———. "What Did Socrates Understand by His 'What Is *F*?' Question?" In *Platonic Studies*. 2d ed. Ithaca: Cornell University Press, 1973, 1981.

Weiss, Roslyn. *Virtue in the Cave: Moral Inquiry in Plato's* Meno. Oxford: Oxford University Press, 2001.

White, James Boyd. "The Judicial Opinion and the Poem: Ways of Reading, Ways of Life." In *Heracles' Bow: Essays on the Rhetoric and Poetics of the Law*. Madison: University of Wisconsin Press, 1985.

———. *Justice as Translation: An Essay in Cultural and Legal Criticism*. Chicago: University of Chicago Press, 1990.

———. *The Legal Imagination: Studies in the Nature of Legal Thought and Expression*. Boston: Little, Brown & Co., 1973.

———. "The *Phaedrus:* Philosophy, Rhetoric, and Love." In *The Edge of Meaning*. Chicago: University of Chicago Press, 2001.

———. *When Words Lose Their Meaning: Constitutions and Reconstitutions of Language, Character, and Community*. Chicago: University of Chicago Press, 1984.

Whitehead, Alfred North. *Process and Reality*. New York: Free Press, 1979.

Williams, Bernard. *Ethics and the Limits of Philosophy*. Cambridge, Mass.: Harvard University Press, 1985.

———. "Introduction." In Plato, *Theaetetus*. Edited with an introduction by Bernard Williams and translated by M. J. Levett, revised translation by Myles Burnyeat. Indianapolis: Hackett Publishing Co., 1992.

———. *Plato: The Invention of Philosophy*. New York: Routledge, 1997, 1999.

Winch, Peter. "Who Is My Neighbour?" In *Trying to Make Sense*. Oxford: Basil Blackwell, 1987.

Wittgenstein, Ludwig. *Culture and Value*. Edited by G. H. von Wright and Heikki Nyman, and translated by Peter Winch. Chicago: University of Chicago Press, 1980.

———. *On Certainty*. Edited by G. E. M. Anscombe and G. H. von Wright, and translated by Denis Paul and G. E. M. Anscombe. Oxford: Basil Blackwell, 1969.

———. *Philosophical Grammar*. Edited by Rush Rhees and translated by Anthony Kenny. Berkeley. University of California Press, 1974.

———. *Philosophical Investigations*. 2d ed. Edited by G. E. M. Anscombe and Rush Rhees, and translated by G. E. M. Anscombe. Oxford: Basil Blackwell, 1953, 1958.

———. "Remarks on Frazer's *Golden Bough.*" In *Philosophical Occasions, 1912–1951*. Edited by James Klagge and Alfred Nordmann, and translated by John Beversluis. Indianapolis: Hackett Publishing Co., 1993.

———. *Zettel.* Edited by G. E. M. Anscombe and G. H. von Wright, and translated by G. E. M. Anscombe. Oxford: Basil Blackwell, 1967.

Woodruff, Paul. "Socratic Education." In *Philosophers on Education: Historical Perspectives*. Edited by Amélie Oksenberg Rorty. London: Routledge, 1998.

Young, G. M. "Maitland." In *Daylight and Champaign: Essays*. London: Jonathan Cape, 1937.

INDEX

THOMAS D. EISELE

is professor of law at the University of Cincinnati, College of Law.

www.ingramcontent.com/pod-product-compliance
Ingram Content Group UK Ltd.
Pitfield, Milton Keynes, MK11 3LW, UK
UKHW041131071026
15587UKWH00009B/420

9 780268 027742